£35-00

Oxford Socio-Legal Studies

A VIEW FROM THE SHADOWS

OXFORD SOCIO-LEGAL STUDIES

GENERAL EDITORS Max Atkinson John C. Boal
Donald R. Harris Keith Hawkins

Oxford Socio-Legal Studies is a series of books published for the Centre for Socio-Legal Studies, Wolfson College, Oxford. The series is concerned generally with the relationship between law and society, and is designed to reflect the increasing interest of lawyers, social scientists and historians in this field.

Already Published (by Oxford University Press)

Genevra Richardson, with Anthony Ogus and Paul Burrows
POLICING POLLUTION: A Study of Regulation and Enforcement
P. W. J. Bartrip and S. B. Burman
THE WOUNDED SOLDIERS OF INDUSTRY Industrial Compensation Policy 1833–1897
Donald Harris *et al*
COMPENSATION AND SUPPORT FOR ILLNESS AND INJURY
Keith Hawkins
ENVIRONMENT AND ENFORCEMENT Regulation and the Social Definition of Pollution
Robert Baldwin
REGULATING THE AIRLINES Administrative Justice and Agency Discretion
John Eekelaar and Mavis Maclean
MAINTENANCE AFTER DIVORCE

Already Published (by Macmillan)

J. Maxwell Atkinson and Paul Drew
ORDER IN COURT: The Organization of Verbal Interaction in Judicial Settings
Ross Cranston
REGULATING BUSINESS: Law and Consumer Agencies
Robert Dingwall and Philip Lewis (*editors*)
THE SOCIOLOGY OF THE PROFESSIONS: Lawyers, Doctors and Others
David P. Farrington, Keith Hawkins and Sally M. Lloyd-Bostock (*editors*)
PSYCHOLOGY, LAW AND LEGAL PROCESSES
Sally M. Lloyd-Bostock (*editor*)
PSYCHOLOGY IN LEGAL CONTEXTS: Applications and Limitations
Mavis Maclean and Hazel Genn
METHODOLOGICAL ISSUES IN SOCIAL SURVEYS
Doreen J. McBarnet
CONVICTION: Law, the State and the Construction of Justice
Alan Paterson
THE LAW LORDS

A VIEW FROM THE SHADOWS

The Ministry of the Solicitor General of Canada and the Making of the Justice for Victims of Crime Initiative

PAUL ROCK

CLARENDON PRESS · OXFORD
1986

Oxford University Press, Walton Street, Oxford OX2 6DP
Oxford New York Toronto Melbourne Auckland
Delhi Bombay Calcutta Madras Karachi
Petaling Jaya Singapore Hong Kong Tokyo
Nairobi Dar es Salaam Cape Town
Associated companies in Beirut Berlin Ibadan Nicosia

Oxford is a trade mark of Oxford University Press

Published in the United States
by Oxford University Press, New York

British Library Cataloguing in Publication Data
Rock, Paul
A view from the shadows: the ministry of the Solicitor General of Canada and the making of the justice for victims of crime initiative.—
(Oxford socio-legal studies)
1. Victims of crimes—Government policy—Canada
I. Title
362'8'8'0971 HV6250.3.C2
ISBN 0–19–825523–3

Library of Congress Cataloging-in-Publication Data
Rock, Paul Elliott,
A view from the shadows.
(Oxford socio-legal studies)
1. Reparation—Canada. 2. Victims of crimes—Legal status, laws, etc.—Canada. 3. Reparation—Government policy—Canada. 5. Canada. Ministry of the Solicitor General. I. Title. II. Series.
KF1312.R63 1986 344.71'03288 86–16143
ISBN 0–19–825523–3 347.1043288

Printed in Great Britain by
Butler & Tanner Ltd, Frome and London

‘VICTIMS
A View From the Shadows

Each year in Canada there are over
one million crimes involving
violence or loss of property.

Over one million crimes.
Over one million victims.

As victims, these people
have one thing in common . . .

They have just entered the
Criminal Justice System.

A Labyrinth of rules and regulations.
People to talk to. Places to go.
Most of them unknown.
Most of them unadvertised.

A confusing muddle of organizations
that do one thing, but not another . . .
of bureaucracies that
refer you to other bureaucracies.

During the course of their exposure
to the System, the victim or witness
can expect to be moved around,
inconvenienced, asked questions of
and dictated to . . .

All in the name of Justice.

The System.
The machinery of justice
Somehow overlooking the very people
it was built to serve.

But not everyone has forgotten the VICTIM . . .

In pockets across the country
there are organizations helping
victims and witnesses of crime.

Most are voluntary, many existing
on charitable donations . . .

or on funds provided by the
federal and provincial governments.

Some programs are affiliated
with police departments . . .

others work from within
the court system.

But few of these services can
be called truly nation-wide.

A group operating in one part
of the country might have no
counterpart in another.

And often the services that exist
in the city are rarely found
in the countryside.

Advocating rights for victims
and witnesses does not mean
lessening rights for the offender.

It's a question of balance.
It's a question of justice.

The offender. The police.
The legal fraternity. The witness.
The victim.

Some are bathed in the limelight
of public attention . . .

Some stand unnoticed in the shadows.'

From the script of a slide-show, 'Victims: A View from the Shadows', prepared by the Communications Division, Solicitor General of Canada, Ottawa, 1981.

Contents

I	The Ministry of the Solicitor General of Canada	1
II	On the Diffuseness of Origins and Other Problems	33
III	A Science and a Social Movement	71
IV	The Moral Entrepreneur	100
V	Victimization Surveys and Peace and Security	121
VI	The Police	143
VII	The Province and the United Nations	168
VIII	Women	210
IX	The Interdepartmental Committee on Family Violence and the Speech from the Throne	241
X	Priorizing the Options	280
XI	The Cabinet Submission	313
XII	Out of the Shadows	341
XIII	A Short Summary and Some Conclusions	379
	Index	389

Tables

page

1. Organization of the Secretariat 1983–1984 25
2. Workshop on Services to Crime Victims, 24–25 March 1980: Canadian Participants 196
3. Resolutions and Recommendations Adopted at General Meetings, Annual Meetings, and Conferences of the National Action Committee on the Status of Women 231
4. Canadian Participants in the 1981 NOVA Conference 356

Preface

I harboured an ambition for some time to explore the social world of the policy-making process. It had seemed to me that criminologists and sociologists have had to work with rather meagre conjectures about the character of power, the phrasing of decisions, the interplay between research and politics, and the nature of causality in the criminal justice system. There have been very few sociological descriptions of how policies are constructed, presented, and applied.[1] And most available description has had little to do with the practical logic-in-use of the policy process. In effect, surmise and inputation have supplanted observation. Policy-making has been reduced to the analytic status of a small Black Box which is allowed to be neither very puzzling nor particularly threatening to other models and ideas.

Some analyses seem to hold that policies are coerced by struggle; some that they are the result of a conspiracy to suppress and deflect popular anger; and others that they are the achievements of professional reformers who stand outside the clamour of politics altogether. Almost all appear to be the lightly disguised appendages of existing theories of the State and society. They fill a void with arguments supplied by their parent systems of thought. It is not easy to judge between them. They are all plausible enough if their paternal theories are accepted. What they do lack is the independent ethnographic and empirical detail which would enable the outsider to appraise them intelligently. A map of the inner workings of one Black Box might provide just enough illumination to reveal some of the contours of the criminal justice policy process.

What follows is one incision into one Black Box. It is the result of an attempt to reconstruct the career of a single episode of policy-making in Canada. I am aware that other sociologists might have made that incision differently, asking their own questions about the political economy of the State, the functions of social control, the effectiveness and rationality of decision-taking, or the qualities of official discourse. I could take but one route into the process and I borrowed from the interactionist arguments that have always interested me. Assembling one orderly

[1] See J. Ekstedt, foreword to P. Solomon, *Criminal Justice Policy: From Research to Reform*, Butterworths, Toronto, 1983, p. ix.

natural history was taxing enough and it yielded a reasonably contained piece of analysis. It is not the only description that could have emerged, enquiry being inexhaustible, but it is what one focus and one method of questioning disclosed.

The book began without elaborate preparation. In 1981 I was fortunate enough to become Visiting Scholar at the Programs Branch of the Ministry of the Solicitor General of Canada. Visiting Scholars are invited from time to time and they are supposed to act as something of a bridge between universities and the research staff of the Ministry. Their role is allowed to remain quite fluid. There had been no precise specification of my duties before I went to Canada. Neither had there been any exact statement of what I could expect from the Ministry. The part which I played was open to negotiation. When the time came to decide on what I should do, the head of the Programs Branch and I rediscovered our common interest in understanding the forms of the policy process. It was a matter which we had discussed before. In turn, it was agreed in consultation with policy officials that I could write a case history of any instance of policy work that the Ministry had undertaken. No barriers were to be placed in my way. I was to be free to read files, speak to staff, and attend meetings. The sole check on what I wrote was that I could not quote from statements that were expressly described as confidential.

I hit upon the Justice for Victims of Crime Initiative for two principal reasons. One was that it was current, preoccupying staff, filling their talk, and organizing their activity. Such an initiative bulked large in the lives of staff and it gave me the chance to observe and interview people as they busied themselves with a particular problem. Secondly, I was a little fond in imagining that victims had a short pedigree, that they would form a simpler and more manageable subject than other social problems that had attracted sustained attention over a number of years. I was deceived: as I shall show, victims were at the centre of abundant activity and they were not simple.

Having fixed upon victims, I could not but move tentatively and one step at a time. Deposited in the midst of a strange part of a strange Ministry in a strange country, it was difficult to recognize pattern and meaning in the world about me. I was not familiar with the staff, their work, their problems, and their universe of assumptions. I was not sure how information was stored and how it could be retrieved. My role and local identity were unclear. People were manifestly busy and I had no wish to plague them with silly questions. As a Visiting Scholar, imported from abroad, I presumed that I was supposed to know how to do research without undue fuss: there might be only a modest stock of curiosity and tolerance which would be depleted by an incompetent who asked the wrong questions of the wrong people. Accordingly, I sought to be unobtrusive, pretending to be invisible, secluded in an office, reading the first of a great succession of files about victims.

The first few files could not but be a little meaningless. I was unable to make much of the meetings, institutions, procedures, and people that were listed. Yet, as time passed, I moved out into the corridors and rooms that adjoined my own; I listened to gossip and ventured some questions; I inspected more files; I started to appreciate a little of the social ecology of the Department; and I began to acquire the rudiments of a sense of structure. The structure that took shape before me appeared to be animated by three intertwined logics: a logic of the files, a logic of the social relations of the officials who had produced the files and been reported in them, and a logic of my method of enquiry. The files furnished an organized record of the events and etiquette of the policy-maker's world, enabling me to ask people about the things they had done. The officials' replies, in their turn, offered an interpretation of the files and the manner in which such paper histories are constructed. Each logic seemed to constitute the other, supplying a context and a framework. Each encouraged the phrasing of new questions and a dialectical movement that took analysis backwards and forwards between the reports, the reported, and the reporters.

On one level, that early sample of files could be read as an incomplete chronicle of the social problem of victims in Canada. On another level, it was also a catalogue of institutions, meetings, and occasions that had to be investigated. Every file was the centre and impression of a distinct cluster of events; every file threw neighbouring events out of focus; and every file refracted the world in a peculiar manner. It became useful to move purposefully from one report to the next, collecting a linked array of different perspectives on phenomena. Multiple images of organizations and relations were there produced, each contributing to a kind of web-like history. The history's segments were given their place and significance by the initiative's own documents and talk. They were joined by an internal grammar that had grown out of materials known, supplied, and deployed by officials themselves. They formed something of a working facsimile of the initiative.

Not only did I read documents, I also proceeded methodically to interview the people who had written reports and had become prominent in them. The central papers of the initiative, its happenings, its heroes, its heroines, and its constitutive logic then began to meet again in my own description. To be sure, the elements thus assembled were not much more than caricatures and fragments. But they did compose a story with considerable detail and intricacy.

At the end of a year, in the summer of 1982, I returned to Ottawa with a draft of what I had written, a list of questions that had welled up in the process of drafting, and several more months of history to chart. My arguments were subjected to criticism from a number of those whose work I had described. Much was questioned. For example, there was a rejection of my initial characterization of officials as the dispassionate and disinterested agents of the State. It became evident that I had misunderstood some of what I had seen, discussion having borrowed from my experience of British thought and practice. My answer was a reconstructed analysis.

I returned to Canada in 1983, 1984, and 1985 and, at each stage, I prepared a new description intended to be more readily recognizable to its subjects. After all, the world I was attempting to reproduce was not mine but that of the staff of the Ministry of the Solicitor General. Its phenomenological standing would have been a little suspect if officials failed to acknowledge much of it as their own.

What emerged was a particular story possessing some very special properties. My history could never have been a straightforward chronicle of events. It has its emphases and foci, and it would be well for the reader to be alert to the manner in which I reconstructed events rather than reported what took place. At a very general level, *A View from the Shadows* is based on records and memories of the Ministry of the Solicitor General in the 1970s and early 1980s. It is an account that captures a limited period in the Ministry's life, a period that was dominated by a Liberal Government and by one Solicitor General, Bob Kaplan. That period has now passed and with it has gone a distinct organizational and political environment. For instance, policies for victims were much affected by the planning system that revolved around the Ministry of State for Social Development. That Ministry was later to be abolished. Much of what I have written is not timeless but time-bound. Indeed, on a more minute level, my analysis consists of what an official has described as a series of 'snapshots'. It bears the mark of my concentration on the genesis of the Justice for Victims of Crime Initiative, and references to the Ministry and its work should usually be read in that context. When the staff, processes, and assumptions of the Ministry are discussed, it is as they were revealed by the study of the appearance of a single initiative. Moreover, those phenomena were illuminated only when they touched on critical phases of the initiative's development. It would have been foolish and tedious even to attempt an exposition of all the possible connections that could have been unearthed. The snapshots are of particular facets of particular structures. It follows that they cannot be examined as if they disclose very broad truths.

A View from the Shadows is supposed to marry some of the officials' working visions of the world with some of the disciplines of a sociological argument. It is obvious that I remained the story-teller and the story is probably not one that any single official could or would have narrated. I never knew any local part of the initiative as well as those who had been its immediate authors. I never lost my role as outsider in certain groups. And I had my own specific purposes and problems. I spoke to people, puzzled about matters, and used examples in a way that would have been foreign to the busy policy-maker. My interests were necessarily somewhat alien to the staff. Moreover, it was proper and ethical not to report information that was given to me in express or implicit confidence. Inevitably, I came to learn about people and their lives and it would not have been right to describe everything I learned without restraint. I tried to refrain from inflicting unnecessary embarrassment on those I met. I was witness to no great scandal, but even the lesser gossip of a social world can hurt. Parts of this analysis are inevitably a little misshapen in consequence. It is a price that I considered well worth paying.

A Short Calendar of Events

1966

First meeting of the group that would become the National Action Committee on the Status of Women

Founding of the Ministry of the Solicitor General

1967

Appointment of the Royal Commission on the Status of Women

1970

December: Publication of the Report of the Royal Commission on the Status of Women

1972

Founding of the Secretariat of the Ministry of the Solicitor General

27 November: Warren Allmand becomes Solicitor General

1973

January: Unsuccessful attempt by the Solicitor General, Warren Allmand, to abolish capital punishment

February: Vaillancourt murders Constable Maitland in Toronto

Founding of London Family Consultant Services

1974

LEAA Crime Victim Initiative

Founding of Victim–Offender Reconciliation Program in Ontario

May: Irvin Waller enters the Ministry of the Solicitor General

1975

International Year of Women and start of the Decade for Women

May: Founding of Joint Justice Committee

5 May: Execution date set for René Vaillancourt

June: Drafting of Peace and Security Legislation by the Ministry of the Solicitor General

1–12 July: International Study Institute on Victimology, Bellagio

November: Liberal Party Convention approves resolution foreshadowing Peace and Security Measures

December: Draft legislation ready for Peace and Security

1976

February: Status of Women Canada becomes an independent agency

February: Peace and Security proposals laid before Parliament

February: Victim surveys approved as crime prevention measures.

May: Inauguration of National Organization for Victim Assistance in the USA

August: Appointment of official to work on the development of victim surveys

September: Proposal to test victim survey methodology approved by the Ministry Research Projects Committee

1977

June: Gordon Walker elected MPP for London South

1978

2 February: Jean-Jacques Blais becomes Solicitor General

May: Bill C-52 presented before Parliament

October: Gordon Walker becomes Minister of Correctional Services

December: *Burglary: The Victim and the Public* published

December: Government approval of report *Towards Equality for Women*

1979

LEAA Victim Assistance Initiative

March: First meeting of the Federal Interdepartmental Committee on Family Violence

May: Restigouche Family Crisis Intervention Project proposed

May: First draft of recommendations by the Interdepartmental Committee on Family Violence

22 May: General Election

4 June: Conservative Government takes office

6 June: Allan Lawrence becomes Solicitor General

September: Founding of Brampton Victim–Witness Assistance Program

14 October: Gordon Walker speaks about victims at the Federal–Provincial Conference of Ministers Responsible for Criminal Justice

18 October: Prime Minister affirms support for the Interdepartmental Committee on Family Violence

November: Founding of City of Edmonton Police Victim Services Unit

November: Regional consultation preparatory to the 1980 Congress on Crime Prevention and the Treatment of Offenders

1980

January: Publication of Linda MacLeod's *Wife-Battering in Canada*

January: Decision made by Ministry to initiate Workshop on Services to Crime Victims

2 February: General Election

3 March: Bob Kaplan becomes Solicitor General

24–5 March: National Workshop on Services to Crime Victims

28 March: Effective withdrawal of Ministry of the Solicitor General from the Interdepartmental Committee on Family Violence

14 April: Speech from the Throne refers to violence against women

24 April: Completion of first Strategic Overview

June: Founding of Ministry of State for Social Development

August: Resignation of Irvin Waller from the Ministry of the Solicitor General

August: Sixth United Nations Congress on the Prevention of Crime and Treatment of Offenders

October: Follow-up meeting of the Canadian delegation to the Sixth United Nations Congress on the Prevention of Crime and the Treatment of Offenders

October: Secretariat Workshop discusses potential of developing policies for victims

December: Announcement of Ministry of the Solicitor General's contribution to Calgary Victim Services Unit

December: Issuing of Report of the Canadian Delegation to the Sixth United Congress on the Prevention of Crime and the Treatment of Offenders

December: Programs Branch Workship gives priority to work on victims

1981

Publication of the Report of the Proceedings of the National Workshop on Services to Crime Victims

February: First drafts of the Departmental planning document omit references to policies for victims

13 February: Ministry of State for Social Developments suggests that the Departmental planning document should make provision for measures to alleviate violence against women

10 March: Official asked to draft proposals on victim assistance for inclusion in the Departmental planning document

13 March: Solicitor General approves Strategic Overview

17 March: Deputy Solicitor General proposes that victims be placed on the agenda of the Joint Justice Committee

1 April: Linda MacLeod appointed to the Ministry of the Solicitor General

10 April: First draft of discussion paper on victim justice

16 April: Meeting of the Joint Justice Committee approves the drafting of proposals for a victims initiative

7 May: Federal–Provincial Conference of Deputy Ministers Responsible for Criminal Justice

14 May: Letter from Deputy Minister of State for Social Development encouraging proposals for a victims initiative

6 June: Government considers social policy Strategic Overviews

11 June: Joint Justice Committee considers draft Cabinet discussion paper

23 June: Conference of Deputy Ministers Responsible for Criminal Justice reveals provincial anxieties about federal plans for victims

9 July: Ministry of State for Social Development considers Victims Initiative

July: Government approval given to Justice for Victims of Crime Initiative

23 September: First Meeting of Interdepartmental Committee on Justice for Victims of Crime

2 October: Conference of the Provincial Council of Attorneys General and Ministers of Justice discusses victims

14–17 October: Conference of the National Organization for Victim Assistance in Toronto

7–9 December: Federal–Provincial Conference of Ministers responsible for Criminal Justice

December: Announcement of victim survey

1982

January: Beginning of briefing sessions on the Justice for Victims of Crime Initiative

February: Founding of Victims of Violence in Ajax, Ontario

May: Report on Violence in the Family, Standing Committee of Health, Welfare and Social Affairs

August: Passing of Bill C-127

Acknowledgements

I am deeply grateful to the staff of the Ministry of the Solicitor General for allowing me to undertake work in such a liberal and congenial setting. I cannot imagine a more frank, helpful, and forbearing group of people. I am also grateful to the library of the Centre of Criminology, University of Toronto; the National Library of Canada; the Toronto *Globe and Mail*; Status of Women Canada; and the Ontario Provincial Justice Secretariat. The British Economic and Social Research Council awarded me a Personal Research Grant to complete the final phase of my work. Without that aid, this project might well have failed to come to a satisfactory end. I would like, too, to give personal thanks to Susan Lee, Colleen Wetmore, Gerry Leger, Karen Cannings, Peter Manning, Tony Dittenhoffer, and Susan Tanner. Above all, I am grateful to Sheila Arthurs, Sol Shuster, Linda MacLeod, Francine Bertrand, Irvin Waller, the Nuttalls, and my own family.

The views expressed in this report are my own and do not necessarily reflect the views of the Solicitor General of Canada.

I. The Ministry of the Solicitor General of Canada

Introduction

I intend to describe some of the principal phases of the birth of the Justice for Victims of Crime Initiative that was to be christened in Ottawa at the Federal–Provincial Conference of Ministers Responsible for Criminal Justice on 9 December 1981. The Conference resolved that victims of crime suffer from the problems that are inflicted both by the criminal act itself and by subsequent encounters with the criminal justice system, that immediate measures should be taken 'to stimulate and improve information and support services', and that officials should return inside a year with 'specific proposals for further action . . . to more effectively assist victims'.[1] That resolution was the result of protracted effort and was itself part of a major enterprise. The initiative was to be diffuse and ramifying, directed at battered and raped women, abused children, those who had been burgled, robbed, and assaulted, and those who appeared as witnesses in court. It was to implicate many of the agencies of the Canadian criminal justice system, shaping them in return. Its earlier history was straddled over a long stretch of time, growing fitfully and awkwardly. It was, indeed, the outcome of a process whose evolution had been slow, uncertain, emergent, and largely obscure. Much of the time it had not even been entirely clear that an initiative *was* in the making. Like a number of other 'major new ventures' in Canada, it had tended to 'bubble through the system for years before bursting on the scene'.[2]

I shall attempt to reconstruct a number of the larger features of the initiative stage by stage and in chronological order, trying to retrieve something of the logic by which they were first put together. Not only will this procedure enable me to examine each layer in turn before it became clouded by its successors, it should also reveal a little of the important temporal organization of the initiative, an organization which served as an evolving context for the different parts, merged them, and

[1] Federal–Provincial Conference of Ministers Responsible for Corrections, Crininal Justice, Law Enforcement, and of Attorneys General; *Communiqué*, Ottawa, Ontario, 9 Dec. 1981, p. 3.

[2] M. Prince and J. Chenier, 'The Rise and Fall of Policy Planning and Research Units', *Canadian Public Administration*, Winter 1980, Vol. 23, No. 4, p. 540.

made them loosely one. The formal and rhetorical structure of the initiative was much affected by its passage through a sequence of planned and unplanned events. The order, relationships, and emergent properties of that passage left their own distinct impress upon policy. They gave character.

I shall dwell particularly on the manner in which victims came to acquire an organized political presence in the lives of the officials who came to tend them. The practices by which victims were summoned and attained form conferred an identity upon them and, once summoned, they altered those practices and the structure of the world in which they appeared. My focus will be upon all that complicated interplay between the initiative, its authors, and the social arenas in which it was produced. In a sense, it will investigate the growth of a portion of social reality and I shall employ the methodology most appropriate to that task, seeking, as Van Maanen describes it, 'to report on what it is that members of worlds know and how it is that such knowledge can be said to guide and constrain their behavior'.[3]

The Secretariat of the Ministry of the Solicitor General of Canada is at the centre of the 'system' which fashioned the federal initiative and it supplies both a subject and a framework for analysis. Its workings have been so densely entangled with those of the initiative that it is difficult or even absurd to prise them apart: in large measure, the logic of the initiative is the practical methodology of the Secretariat. One explains the other. To be sure, the initiative did extend well beyond the Ministry of the Solicitor General and its origins were very diverse. Yet, as I shall show, the Ministry did give a special organization and distinct limits to policy. It does represent a discrete world with recognized frontiers, inhabitants, and corporate responsibility. It has its own style. Its work composes an identifiable entity whose coherence can be drawn on in description. As a Visiting Scholar at the Ministry, I was awarded extraordinarily generous access to people, events, papers, and meetings inside the Secretariat. My knowledge of other happenings outside the Ministry's walls is more haphazard and unsure. Accordingly, this book will offer a history of the victims initiative as it was shaped by the Secretariat. To do otherwise would be to embark on an indefinitely vast project. I shall adopt the emerging perspectives of the Ministry to describe the initiative, just as I shall treat the initiative as a lens with which to gaze upon the Ministry. The one will define the other as the analysis unfolds.

[3] J. Van Maanen, introduction to *Varieties of Qualitative Research*, Sage Publications, Beverly Hills, 1982, pp. 17–18.

So important is the Ministry that I shall devote the rest of this and the whole of the next chapter to a discussion of its external and internal relations, delaying my description of the initiative itself until an organizational frame has been first set in place.

The Ministry of the Solicitor General of Canada

It is useful to begin by examining something of the legal and constitutional history of the Ministry. It is a history that gave the Secretariat its place, purpose, and character and it is of immediate practical concern to officials. Above all, it is implicated in problems of resolving a sphere for bureaucratic action. It provides a licence and a mandate. Hughes has defined a licence as 'a successful claim ... to carry out certain activities which others may not' and a mandate as the right to insist upon the 'proper conduct of others towards the matters concerned with ... work'.[4] History supports assertions about territorial claims. It is needed. Anxiety about what some officials call 'turf' and 'turf wars' can arise from time to time because the jurisdictional complexity of the Canadian criminal justice system prepares obstacles for all but the most carefully contrived projects. Crime, the police, the courts, the prison and probation services of Canada are regulated by two federal ministries, the ministries of ten provincial governments, and an array of municipal, territorial, and voluntary bodies. That division of labour is a little unstable, being subject to occasional review, discovery, and discussion. A great web of formal and informal agreements and contracts has added intricacy to an already confusing scheme, and there is not always general accord about the legitimacy of what has been done.

Since most federal projects in criminal justice invade or jostle the proprietorial interests of others, delicacy is required of their authors. Intervention must be based upon negotiation, supplication, and consent. It is not politic merely to announce a federal resolve. As a policy analyst of the Ministry of Justice observed at a meeting, 'we are the Government of Canada. We cannot tell people how to do things.'[5] And what is done must be well supported by arguments and documents. There is a perennial problem of authority.

Authority to act flows from a number of founding documents, the most important in the history of the victims initiative being the British North

[4] E. Hughes, *Men and Their Work*, Free Press, Illinois, 1958, p. 78.
[5] Notes. From henceforth, it should be assumed that unattributed quotations are based on my notes of meetings or interviews.

America Act of 1867.[6] It was that Act which provided Canada with a constitution, assigning responsibilities to federal and provincial governments, and mapping a division of labour in the administration of criminal justice. Amongst the twenty-nine legislative powers allotted to the federal Parliament were 'the criminal law, excepting the constitution of courts of criminal jurisdiction, but including the procedure in criminal matters', and the 'establishment, maintenance and management of penitentiaries', penitentiaries being institutions built to house those sentenced to two or more years imprisonment. Provincial legislatures, in their turn, were given exclusive powers of establishing, maintaining, and managing public and reformatory prisons, asylums, and hospitals; the 'administration of justice . . . including the constitution, maintenance and organization of provincial courts'; and the 'imposition of punishment by fine, penalty or imprisonment for any law of the province'.

In short, the federal government supervised penitentiaries and the framing of the criminal law. The actual execution of the law and the workings of the lower courts were chiefly entrusted to the provinces. There was, however, a major federal presence introduced into policing by the Dominion Police which, when amalgamated with the Royal North-West Mounted Police in 1920, became the Royal Canadian Mounted Police. And further complexity was brought about by the practice of permitting the Royal Canadian Mounted Police to exchange service contracts with municipal and provincial authorities. The first such policing contracts were made between the Royal North-West Mounted Police and Alberta and Saskatchewan in 1905.[7] The first municipal contract was exchanged between the Royal Canadian Mounted Police and Flin Flon, Manitoba, in 1935. At present, all the provinces but Ontario and Quebec have contractual arrangements with the RCMP.

In 1868 the Department of Justice was formed to assume federal responsibility for matters relating to the criminal law. Within it, in 1886, a separate Office of the Solicitor General was established to administer penitentiaries and the federal police. Eighty years later, that Office was itself detached altogether to become the Department of the Solicitor General of Canada.[8] It was maintained that the administrative complexity of the criminal justice system had increased appreciably, that there was a special and urgent problem of organized crime which

[6] 30 and 31 Victoria, c. 3. Since repealed, it was nevertheless in force throughout the 1970s and in 1981 when the initiative came to life.

[7] Much of this section is based on J. Woods and H. Sim, *Highlights of Federal Initiatives in Criminal Justice: 1966–1980*, Ministry of the Solicitor General of Canada, Ottawa, 1981.

[8] *The Government Organization Act, 1966*, 14–15 Elizabeth II, Chap. 25.

demanded a focused response, and that the Department of Justice was expected to perform an excessive number of important yet disparate tasks. The Prime Minister announced in debate that 'we have tended to overload our legal advisers'[9] and that the Minister of Justice had been 'obliged to expend his energies in endeavouring to discharge his primary duty as the principal law officer of the Crown, while maintaining control of a number of associated agencies, each of vital importance in its own sphere of operation'.[10] It was proposed that the Department of Justice be returned to 'the full discharge of their traditional functions: the drafting of legislation and documents; the conduct of litigation and prosecutions'.[11] Complementing it in a new and more rational system would be an independent department to manage the RCMP, criminal investigations, federal institutions, paroles, and pardons. It was recognised that the connection between the two departments was one of the pivotal relationships of the Criminal Justice System, but it was a connection with quite endemic ambiguities. According to a paper prepared in support of the establishment of the Ministry Secretariat in 1972, 'it is not possible nor feasible to develop specific, hard and fast rules as to which department . . . should have a primary role in the development of specific policies or programs. These questions should be decided as the issues arise and such decisions should be based on the impact that the proposals are likely to have on each department's programs or areas of concern and the politics of the situation at any given time.' The division of 'turf' was thus allowed to become a matter of contingency and circumstance, shifting from occasion to occasion. It has given rise to what one policy analyst at the Department of Justice somewhat dramatically described as 'appalling jurisdictional jealousies and misunderstandings with respect to almost any justice issue you can imagine'. Less forcibly, the Department of the Solicitor General itself declared that 'the division of responsibility for the "administration of justice" is complex and sometimes ill-defined'.[12] Many officials are relatively little exercised by the problem of the institutional marches, but there are persistent, often petty, and probably inevitable uncertainties about spheres of interest.

In May 1975 relations between the two departments underwent a special strain during the protracted and intricate preparations for what

[9] Debate in the House of Commons, 9 May 1966.

[10] Debate in the House of Commons, 23 Feb. 1966.

[11] Debate in the House of Commons, 9 May 1966.

[12] *1982–83 Estimates: Part III Secretariat Expenditure Plan*, Solicitor General Canada, Ottawa, 1982, p. 4.

was to become the 'Peace and Security Package'. I shall describe in a later chapter how the departments jointly assembled a bundle of deterrent and regulatory measures with the principal but not sole intention of compensating for the abolition of capital punishment. The package was grounded in two omnibus Acts which were focused on a great sweep of issues, issues which included the suppression of organized crime, telephone tapping, gun control, the granting of parole, the minimum length of sentence for convicted murderers, the incarceration of dangerous offenders, and, presciently, the compensation of victims of violent crime. So central and numerous were the matters addressed by the proposed legislation that they were generously covered by the mandates of both sponsoring departments. There was some consequent disagreement about which Ministry should assume principal responsibility for the measures. The Ministry of Justice asserted its interest because the legislation would have a major effect on the Criminal Code. The Ministry of the Solicitor General claimed sovereignty because its client agencies were critically affected: it was argued that dangerous prisoners, parole, police work, and the protection of police officers properly fell under its aegis. The two departments could not resolve their jurisdictional dispute without some further negotiations. It was agreed that they establish a co-ordinating committee, the Joint Justice Committee, which was to provide advice on policies, programs and legislation affecting the Criminal Justice System. The new committee was to be used as a means of consultation on all measures affecting the criminal justice system which might be brought to Cabinet for decision. A rough division of labour was negotiated: the Department of Justice was held to be ultimately responsible for advice on proposed amendments to the criminal code and would remain responsible for the content of the criminal law; and the Ministry of the Solicitor General would have a special interest in dealing with all measures dealing with the protection of society from the effects of crime. But it was thought that the fundamental role problem remained.

It is a fundamental problem that flows from the difficulty attending any effort to dissect crime and criminal justice into discrete, insulated components. The effects of action tend to swamp over any boundaries that departments may fix. They cannot be neatly contained. Research, for instance, defies enclosure. Thus the Acting Assistant Deputy Minister of the Programs Branch stated, 'a research organization is naturally expansionist. It becomes very difficult, say, to be able to do corrections research without knowing about what's going on in the courts'. And the result is that talk about the relations between the departments returns insistently to the problem of patrolling the frontiers, to mandates, and to conflict.

It is imperative to consider the character of that talk. It must be treated with great caution. On one level, it should be regarded with seriousness: it informs and shapes policy-making. It is the end of much policy-making. It clearly affects action. On another level, it must be recognized that the drafting of policy is a reflexive process, talk and speech fold back on themselves as positions are planned and developed. Things are not said artlessly. Nothing in the criminal justice system is allowed to remain quite as simple or as complex as it may first have seemed. Policy analysts and politicians are required to scan the phenomena around them for possibilities of argument and action. They use those phenomena rhetorically to build a persuasive portrait of the world. As one official observed, 'remember ... re-creation and mystery are part of the game'. In this sense, the significance of events will tend to become a little detached, removed to do work in a number of causes. It follows that, like much else in Ottawa, it is not necessarily possible to make straightforward judgements about the meanings of processes and utterances. On the contrary, officials themselves cannot always make a firm distinction between what is 'objective' and what has been argued with all the appearance of objectivity. One official jokingly remarked at a meeting, for example, 'don't believe the rhetoric we put into our submissions. It's not going to help the initiative!' (None the less, it should not be imagined that officials are indifferent to what they do, that their work is just a game.)

It would be most unhelpful to diminish interdepartmental relations to any single, simple state. On the contrary, much discussion seemed amiable enough. What is at work is the rhetorical construction of an environment which gives order to activity. In the main, disagreements have been translated into a kind of symbolic presence which does occasional service in reminding officials of the limits and possibilities of action. It is a symbolic presence that lends interest and character to the bureaucratic round. It has been built into a set of ritualized exchanges that confer organization on the sometimes diffident dealings of the departments. Disagreement may be discovered in what has happened and in what may yet happen rather than in what daily occurs. In part, therefore, it appears to be a means of stabilizing and crystallizing relations, defining the outer boundaries of possible activity, and remaining available for invocation when a speculative venture is contemplated or the politics of Ottawa seem to warrant it. Thus the sometime Director General of Research at the Ministry of the Solicitor General, Irvin Waller, recalled that he had been advised in 1977 that a victims initiative was not then feasible because victims belonged properly to the Department of Justice. Justice had already developed a stake in victims, being involved in the administration of criminal injuries compensation schemes.

In this sense, present procedures and relations are an amicable 'acting out of the underlying conflict and legitimation of the terms on which it is currently resolved'.[13] And I would repeat that considerable caution should be applied in the decoding of words like 'disagreement'. Disagreements may not be so much imposed or coerced as willed and embraced, reflecting the official propensity to transform the world into a bank of opportunities for argument. Thus the threat of discord stopped Irvin Waller in 1977 but it did not bar action when the idea of a victims initiative was raised again by others in 1981. Threatened discord is not therefore unequivocal in meaning. Its significance waxes and wanes in sympathy with political need and context.

In that setting, it becomes rather difficult to know what disagreements *are* and how they may be recognized. A world which is substantially anchored in documents and talk is precisely itself, a written and spoken artifact. It is unclear whether the disagreements which people discuss reside principally in their talk and documents, whether they have an 'independent' existence, and what mening should be attached to differences reported in documents, to the idea of 'independence', and to a difference 'outside' documents and talk that can be discovered only in those sources. Such interpretative problems cluster most obviously around the issue of exaggeration: there are not many indices which would permit one to assess the scale of disagreement or describe its character. My answer has been to fall back on to a conception of the social world that is grounded in the speech and writing of its inhabitants, arguing with Berger that 'it is in conversation, in the broadest sense of the word, that we build up and keep going our world'[14] and with Strauss that 'the nature or essence of an object does not reside mysteriously within the object itself but is dependent on how it is defined by the namer'.[15] If people talk about disagreements from time to time, it may be presumed that their world is tinged with discord for some practical and descriptive purposes. The debates between the Departments of Justice and the Solicitor General did seem to influence their relations.

Yet if conversation supplies a social world, its character must be appreciated. The talk of Ottawa's officials is not always sober, literal,

[13] M. Edelman, *Politics as Symbolic Action*, Markham Publishing Company, Chicago, 1971, p. 22.

[14] P. Berger, *A Rumor of Angels*, Doubleday Anchor, Garden City, 1969, p. 34.

[15] A. Strauss, *Mirrors and Masks*, Free Press, Illinois, 1959, p. 20.

and plain. It is refracted and amplified in the busy organizations in which it occurs. Bureaucracies devoted to the manufacture of words and papers inevitably feed detail into anything that passes through them, adorning arguments and elaborating their possibilities. As Manning has observed, 'the [operation] of an organization as a communication-processing system is such that it adds complexity to events reported or existing in the external environment'.[16] Moreover, much bureaucratic talk is playful and gossipy, replete with little scandals and excitements. Gossip must be taken seriously. It is an important medium of control[17] and knowledge.[18] But it is also fun. Gossipy talk about other people and agencies can multiply and exaggerate their features, leading to the fabrication of detail and nuance.

Matters of disagreement and co-operation between the departments have been resolved by resort to an intricately organized sequence of meetings and consultations. It is as if the two Ministries participate in a dance with elaborate steps and a complicated choreography scripted by the Joint Justice Committee procedure and the Policy and Expenditure Management System that was instated in 1981. Much of this book will actually follow the serpentine path of a single initiative through all the moves and stages that bind the departments together, and the dance will be revealed a little at a time. In practice, there are abundant informal consultations between the departments. A working agreement must be obtained in the Joint Justice Committee before major new initiatives are broached to the provinces or presented to Cabinet. Decisions have been channelled into a long, almost ceremonial sequence of different meetings between officials.

The Ministry and the Provinces

Criminal justice in Canada ... is jurisdictionally complex. This is a characteristic it shares with many other areas of social and economic concern. Political jurisdiction is, in fact, a national pastime. I was once told that there was a class of four people, an American, a Frenchman, a Japanese and a Canadian who were asked to write an essay on elephants. The American entitled his essay, 'Elephants: How to Make them Bigger and Better'. The title of the Frenchman's essay was, 'The Love Life of the Elephant'. The Japanese entitled his essay, 'Elephants: How to Make Them Smaller, More Efficient and Easier to Sell than American

[16] P. Manning, 'Semiotics and Loosely-Coupled Organizations', paper presented to the Southern Sociological Society, Atlanta, Georgia, April 1979, p. 4.

[17] See R. Coser, 'Laughter among colleagues', *Psychiatry*, 1960, Vol. 23.

[18] T. Shibutani, *Improvised News*, Bobbs-Merrill, Indianapolis, 1966.

Elephants'. And the Canadian entitled his essay: 'Elephants: Are they Federal or are they Provincial?'[19]

Criminal justice in Canada has been portioned out between the federal government in Ottawa and the ten provincial legislatures. It is massively decentralized, some 70 per cent of all expenditures being made by the provinces in 1979.[20] Provincial governments were awarded very broad powers under the British North America Act to administer justice in their territories, to establish and maintain criminal and civil courts, and to regulate the procedure of civil matters in those courts. The connections between federal and provincial courts are occasionally a little complicated, and there is some uncertainty about the manner in which authority can and should be shared.

So important are the courts and matters of justice in the work of the provinces that all ten governments maintain a department concerned with justice issues. They do not, however, invariably support a ministry which could be regarded as the proper counterpart of the federal Ministry of the Solicitor General. Federal–provincial relations have accordingly become somewhat contorted, the staff of the Ministry of the Solicitor General having to liaise with officials from those provincial Ministries of Justice or Departments of the Attorney General with which federal Ministry of Justice also has dealings.

Policing is also distributed among federal, provincial, and municipal agencies. In 1972 there were 23,969 municipal police, 3,862 Ontario Provincial Police, 3,861 Quebec Police, and 10,960 members of the RCMP.[21] By 1979–80 the number of members of the RCMP had grown to 16,389 and the force's budget was $534,397,000.[22] In 1981–2 there were 20,547 officers serving in the RCMP. The RCMP has responsibility for the North-West Territories and the Yukon, for some 200 municipalities, and for eight provinces under the jurisdiction of the provincial Attorney General. It has also been entrusted with the enforcement of federal laws involving security, narcotics, customs and excise, immigration, and the protection of federal property. For instance, it patrols the lands of the National Capital Commission in and about Ottawa, intersecting with the beats of provincial forces in Quebec and Ontario.

[19] *Notes for a Speech by the Hon. Bob Kaplan, P.C., M.P., Solicitor General of Canada, on the Occasion of 'Semaine du Detenu'*, Sherbrooke, Quebec, 13 Mar. 1982.

[20] See J. Woods and H. Sim, *Highlights of Federal Initiatives in Criminal Justice*, p. 10.

[21] Figures based on A. Parizeau and D. Szabo, *The Canadian Criminal-Justice System*, Lexington Books, Massachusetts, 1977, p. 95.

[22] *Estimates for the Fiscal Year Ending March 31, 1981*, Minister of Supply and Services, Hull, 1980, pp. 28–2, 28–36.

The RCMP provides specialist services to the Ministry of Transport, the Department of Agriculture, and a number of provincial agencies. It may thus be discovered working in the same geographical area as local police, executing different laws or the same laws in federal or other enclaves. It represents the most prominent participation of federal government in the administration of criminal justice, constituting one of the Ministry of the Solicitor General's principal points of entry into the world of practical policy-making, and an opportunity for other federal agencies to gain access to otherwise sealed areas of social control and service.

Federal–provincial relations sometimes convey an appearance of fragility. It will be recalled that there has been a recent history of political argument and turbulence. Secessionist movements and parties have threatened to dismantle the federation. In the late 1970s and early 1980s, in particular, the constituution itself was to become the centre of considerable agitation. At the very time that federal officials were considering how best they could give birth to the victims initiative, the Premiers of a number of provinces were entering into critical opposition to Ottawa and the Premier of New Brunswick pronounced that 'Ottawa's concept of operating unilaterally is dead wrong. And it is, in my opinion, the greatest threat to national unity that I have seen for a long time.'[23]

Criminal justice itself tends to play a modest part in all that disturbance. It is not generally taken by provincial and federal officials to be overtly or theatrically 'political'. Rather, the politics of justice tend to revolve quite quietly around problems of nuance, priority, and proprietorship. In many provinces there are no gross differences of ideology with Ottawa. More especially, the victims initiative was largely held to be free of obvious partisanship. As one Regional Consultant stated, 'victims is a no-lose political issue for everyone, Conservative and Liberal'.[24] Yet sensitivities do persist and not all provinces were to join in the initiative or accede to the Ministry's right to busy itself with victims.

There is a delicacy of language and approach which has been introduced to mirror the sensibilities of the participants in federal–provincial negotiations about criminal justice matters. Thus the Ministry attempts to avoid seeming to be *dirigiste*. Its role is to stimulate and counsel but not to command. After all, it has no jurisdiction over the major part of the administration of justice. The Secretariat is accordingly fastidious in its use of words, emphasizing in a memorandum, that:

> It should be noted that the terms 'policy initiatives' or 'areas of policy development' are employed here rather than 'programs'. This is because the nature

[23] *Globe and Mail*, 14 Sept. 1981.

[24] The role and functions of Regional Consultants will be described below.

of the Secretariat's work is almost exclusively policy development or policy support, as distinct from the delivery of 'programs' as commonly understood. To be sure, those policy initiatives undertaken by the Secretariat are likely to have program impact—but the programs are delivered by others.

Again, it has been noted that the federal government plays a 'subtle role in program development', attending to 'the establishment of national standards through cost-sharing and the use of federal funds in demonstration and research projects, rather than direct intervention in program delivery'.[25] The deployment of funds and the shaping of a role are matters for the exercise of a special caution. A federal partner or sponsor can offer a provincial ministry access to the revenues of the central government. It can bring about an enlargement of the scale and ambition of criminal justice projects. It can lead to national, interprovincial and sometimes to international co-operation. It can also implicate Ottawa in schemes which represent parts of jealously tended provincial preserves. It requires the cultivation of much symbolic and practical detail to enable some forms of collaboration to thrive. Symbolically, the province is often awarded prominence or, indeed, pre-eminence in an enterprise. The chairman or responsible authority will frequently be provincial. The authorship of documents and statements will appear as provincial. Announcements about co-operative work will usually be made in the province by a local person. There will be conspicuous consultation in advance of any work. Requests may be made for the latterday Canadian equivalent of a safe conduct to allow federal agents into provincial terrain.

There is thus something of a ceremonious respect for the sovereignty of provincial jurisdiction and for 'the multitude of sensitive interpersonal relationships' which have to be 'established and maintained'.

Practically, there are financial and temporal limits to participation by the federal Ministry. The Ministerial budget for 1980–1 was estimated to be $1,052,835,000.[26] Much of it was to be devoted to paying the costs of very major institutions: thus, $602,632,000 was appropriated for the RCMP, $426,400,000 for the Correctional Services of Canada, and $9,122,000 for the Parole Board. Yet only $1,549,000, a mere 0·147 per cent of the estimates, was allotted to 'the provinces, territories, public and private bodies in support of activities complementary to those of the Solicitor General'. That sum was kept quite deliberately small in order to ward off private and provincial criticism and to restrain the Ministry

[25] G. Norquay and R. Weiler, *Services to Victims and Witnesses of Crime in Canada*, Ministry of the Solicitor General, Ottawa, 1981, p. 81.

[26] *Estimates for the Fiscal Year Ending March 31, 1981*, p. 28–2.

of the Solicitor General from intervening too liberally in the debated zone of criminal justice. It was the outward sign of an act of self-discipline, an appreciable curb on the Ministry's power to initiate and shape policy. Indeed, the acquisition of large sums of money can embarrass the Secretariat staff. In July 1981, for example, there was evident diffidence displayed at a meeting to deliberate on the spending of money which had just been approved to fund victim assistance projects. The Director of Policy declared, 'there's a lot of money ... we don't want to do the obtrusive things that would upset the provinces.'

Financial discipline has been reinforced by the refusal of the Ministry to fund projects for longer than three years. Old projects may give birth to new schemes, but three years is the life of a single venture. After that period, the Ministry is supposed to retreat, leaving a demonstration project to die or become wholly provincial, municipal, or private. That strategy of judicious withdrawal is not unusual in federal states, being customary in America for instance, and it seems to have become acceptable enough. In Ontario, the Regional Consultant asserted, 'I don't have any problem with that. I see our role as an initiator. I'm very clear to anyone that comes to see us that that is what we're going to do and we will be *out*. And if there's a true need you will find the money. And the province, if there's a need, then they'll pay for it.' In corroboration, an official of the Ontario Justice Secretariat stated, 'I think if you're realistic, you know that when you get into a project, you have to look to the future, and it's not helpful to set up expectations which you can't meet. So, if you get into a project, you know you may have to continue because the expectations are there.' But it is also the case that some opprobrium has been attached to the practice of retreat. Federal self-control is vulnerable to redefinition as faddishness and irresponsibility by clients, outsiders, and, indeed, some insiders: faddishness because support for individual projects is necessarily brief, and irresponsibility because federal projects can impose difficult burdens on the provinces, municipalities, and private organizations. As the Director of Programs of a major private policy institute argued:

> The federal government in this country has a history, a recent history, of dabbling in useful but somewhat faddish policy and programme initiatives ...

The appearance of faddishness can be very real. It can lend an impression of federal inconstancy as different ideas are funded one after another in a long stream. Each new episode seems to follow on the heels of its predecessor, only to be displaced in its turn. Those involved in promoting and developing work may then become a little wary of committing too much enthusiasm to what will fade in a short while. Thus an Associate Regional Consultant reflected, 'I've seen so many fads go through the system. There's the whole medical model and they were going to fix up all the offenders, and then they went into this hard-nosed model, and victims are another one of that sort of fashion.' And the co-ordinator of a major demonstration project devoted to victims observed rather wistfully, 'the current concern with victims is likely to be just another fad that will pass'. Such a funding strategy has laid the basis for one of the perspectives on time which I shall discuss in the next chapter: different groups of officials tend to describe the natural histories of policies in quite distinct ways, their sense of time being a mirror of their experience of work.

However diligent officials may be in presenting themselves and their activites as modest and unobtrusive they encounter numerous hazards in their forays into the provinces. After all, policy initiatives do frequently touch on alien territory. Except when policy affects the RCMP, the penitentiaries, and a few other areas, the Ministry of the Solicitor General is manifestly open to the charge of interference. Approaches consequently tend to be rather tentative, conducted gingerly and slowly: one Regional Consultant remarked, for instance, 'we do stretch the boundaries. That's what we do. We're constantly pushing them a wee little bit and testing the water. But my style is to do that gradually in a nonconfrontative manner. That happens to suit me and it also happens to suit [the province]'. But problems cannot be wholly dispelled by a diplomatic style. Affairs can go awry sometimes. Not only does Ministry action impinge on the preserve of Attorneys General and others who are eager to defend their own. It also lends itself to symbolic transcription as a federal attack on provincial independence, threatening the very basis of the constitution and provincial rights. The effects of federal innovations are thereby capable of undergoing a boundless amplification, becoming an issue in the larger politics of the Canadian state. In the late 1970s and early 1980s, especially, the Ministry Secretariat was prone to define itself as rather embattled. A policy paper of the time reflected:

> With most of the provinces we have now moved to confrontation federalism on many issues. We can expect even more challenges to federal authority and out of this we are faced with a more difficult task in doing our share to improve the state of criminal justice and the criminal justice system. On most issues of federal–provincial interest we can expect more difficult negotiations and more formal mechanisms of collaboration.

Some provincial authorities maintained that victims were the natural dependents of the courts, and the courts, in their turn, were provincial terrain. An official of the Ministry of the Solicitor General remembered one province's reply to an invitation to participate in a workshop: '[the province] said "but this is a provincial area. What the hell are you guys doing without consultation with us?"'

It thus becomes apparent why federal–provincial co-operation is mentioned repeatedly as a goal in Ministry documents, papers, and talk. It also becomes apparent why the accomplishment of that co-operation is treated as a major event in its own right. Manifest provincial support for a federal position can thereby attain the greatest importance in the construction of argument in Ottawa. If rhetoric is taken to be the 'art of using language so as to persuade or influence others',[27] provincial interest can become rhetorically potent. It can propel an initiative quite far through the linked stages and committees which constitute the business of decision-making in the federal government. It gives evidence of the objective worth of a project which might otherwise be represented as the limited, parochial concern of one agency or government alone. It indicates that others esteem what is proposed and that esteem is itself desirable in the politics of a fragile federal state.

Some provinces were to have little to do with the victims initiative. Quebec refrained from any participation. Such ostracism is unusual and it developed in the excitable context of debate about the return of the constitution to Canada. In the main, there is a substratum of uneventful working relations between the officials of the federal and provincial governments. After all, their work is very different from that of politicians proper. Much parliamentary politics is about public arguments which are dramatically presented to wide, external audiences. It is correspondingly implicated in the oratorical requirements of the staged performance. It has theatrical or dramaturgical properties which are independent of content. This kind of politics is directed at anonymous others and it celebrates a routine form of conflict: adversaries are almost always criticized and colleagues are almost always praised. Bureaucratic action, by contrast, is pointed at small, informed groups who know one another well. It may be little more than yet another phase in a long sequence of acts which demands no elaborate explanation or prologue. Of course, it must be dressed properly, but it should not be phrased as if it were a major speech. It would seem absurd to address a few familiar colleagues as if they were a mass rally. Moreover, those colleagues are likely to be insiders, the knowing and enduring members of a relatively stable social world that is to be contrasted with the evanescent world of politics.

[27] *Shorter Oxford English Dictionary.*

Ministers change office with some frequency. Indeed, the Solicitor General who supervised much of the federal initiative on victims announced in 1981 that 'I am the first [Solicitor General] in ten years who has lasted more than one year'.[28]

Officials stay. They establish connections with one another that can last the bulk of their working lives. An early involvement in conflict would not only inject strain into an already complicated role. It would also pre-empt possibilities of liaison that might arise in the years to come. A present enemy may always present himself or herself as a future ally. As Heclo and Wildavsky observe of Whitehall, 'mutual trust is considered paramount by officials who know they will have to continue doing business with each other year after year on issue after issue'.[29] So exposed to one another, officials cannot be considered a naïve audience for one another. They are conversant with the arts of performance, with the history of policy-making, and with the gossip of the world in which policy is made. There is little scope for theatre when so much is known about the artifice and content of argument.

Federal–provincial relations appear to be accompanied by some stagecraft. They combine public protestations of wariness with private co-operation. They convey an impression of resistance to co-optation which wittingly or unwittingly sustains the very possibility of collaboration. It is an impression that interests many because Canada is not only fissured by a gulf between tiers of government but also by a roughly defined divide between East and West. Western provinces are held to be suspicious of an alleged Ottawa–Toronto–Montreal axis. Formal protestations thus become important in emphasizing the independence of the provinces, and of the Eastern provinces in particular. They allow federal and provincial strategies to retain precautionary themes, anticipating what might happen if plans break down. After all, accountable agents require a story to tell if events go awry. They cannot present themselves as gullible or unguarded. What Edelman had to say about labour–management negotiations in the United States of America applies with some force to federal–provincial relations in Canada: 'in this policy area the salient elements are: a high measure of agreement among ... leaders about their relative vulnerability and bargaining resources; a set of stylized procedures that both signal aggression and reassure both sides that it will be held within acceptable limits, while at the same time they marshal

[28] *Notes for Remarks by the Honourable Bob Kaplan, P.C, M.P., Solicitor General of Canada, to Abbotsford, B.C., Public Forum*, 10 Dec. 1981.

[29] H. Heclo and A. Wildavsky, *The Private Government of Public Money*, Macmillan, London, 1974, p. 15.

the support of . . . members and of the mass public for the leadership and for the outcomes of the bargaining'.[30]

Federal–provincial relations have become increasingly formalized in the last decade. At Ministerial level, there have been meetings between Ministers of Justice and Attorneys General and between Ministers responsible for Corrections. In 1977 the different groups of Ministers met separately and then together to discuss matters of common interest. There has been joint participation in a number of task forces, steering committees, *ad hoc* committees, and permanent committees of officials. Each is intended not only to achieve a co-ordination of effort but also to make a symbolic statement about the federal process. But the most significant body has been the Federal–Provincial Conferences of Ministers Responsible for Criminal Justice which met for the very first time in October 1979. It has become a forum in which all major national initiatives are submitted for discussion. It has also become the chief federal–provincial ceremony within the Canadian criminal justice system, a convening of the powers and an affirmation of federation. It is thus apparent why, when the Minister of Corrections for Ontario made a speech advocating victims rights at that inaugural Conference in October 1979, victims should become politically salient to federal officials and politicians. It was so salient that it deserves separate attention in its own chapter.

The Ministry and the Private Sector

There is at least one other major corporate presence in the environment of significant events and phenomena that surrounds the Ministry of the Solicitor General. It is identified as the 'private sector' and it consists of those nongovernmental organizations and people who 'have important roles to play in the treatment of offenders'.[31] It is a most intricate entity which enjoys a complicated dialectical and symbiotic relationship with the Ministry. It is imperative to understand some features of that relationship so that one of its offspring, the victims initiative, may itself be better appreciated.

It must first be reported that the landscape about the Ministry is rather thinly populated. In the history of the victims initiative, that landscape was almost entirely empty. For quite a while, staff developing policies for victims claimed that they worked in what was virtually a

[30] M. Edelman, *Politics as Symbolic Action*, p. 142.

[31] *Notes for Opening Remarks by the Deputy Solicitor General of Canada*, André Bissonnette, to the Workshop in Services to Crime Victims, Ottawa, 24 Mar. 1980.

political void.[32] After all, bodies concerned with victims were no part of the conventional furniture of the Department in the beginning: that had to come with the success of the initiative. Of course, staff were required to accommodate other Ottawa departments and agencies and the Department of Justice above all. They had dealings with provincial ministries. But they also experienced some of the sensations and problems of the solipsist: 'one who accepts [the] theory that self is the ... only thing really existent'.[33] They claimed that they heard few pleas and criticisms from the wider world and few answering voices when they acted. The Ministry is not particularly visible or audible in the political arena. Its work does not play a large part in the Federal Government. For example, the concerns of the Ministry did not directly enter the Speech from the Throne throughout the earlier history of the Department and all the formative years of the victims initiative. Much of the time, indeed, the entire field of criminal justice appears to be beyond or beneath politics. As the Director of Policy argued, 'it doesn't belong to government. It isn't something you'd expect them to change quickly or even want them to. And it doesn't belong to them or the provinces or the private sector. It's a kind of overall historical thing that grows and you add to'. And Peter Solomon has stated, 'except in times of political crisis ... law enforcement occupies the attention of politicians only intermittently'.[34] The epithet applied to the visible work of the Ministry is 'fire-fighting',[35] indicating that it is only during brief and unpredictable crises that the Solicitor General is to be seen, that his role is to quell a disturbance or repair some flaw, and then retreat into invisibility again. The Minister's experience of the political world appears to be built around periods of quiescence punctuated by abrupt and dangerous episodes of action. Allan Lawrence, a former Solicitor General, remarked, 'by its jurisdiction [the post] has some great yawning pits for any politician'.[36] The Solicitor General attains prominence when there are penitentiary riots, prisoners dramatically awaiting execution as once they did, security scandals implicating the RCMP, or tales of strippers performing before inmates. He tends to be conspicuous when things have gone amiss.

[32] Interestingly, an embryonic political lobby that began to form around the victims issue in the early 1980s complained about Ministry indifference just at the same time. See J. Amernic, *Victims: The Orphans of Justice*, Seal Books, Toronto, 1984.

[33] *Shorter Oxford English Dictionary*.

[34] P. Solomon, 'The Policy Process in Canadian Criminal Justice: A Perspective and Research Agenda', unpublished paper, undated, p. 9.

[35] See I. Waller, 'Organizing Research to Improve Criminal Justice Policy: A Perspective from Canada', unpublished paper, p. 12.

[36] The Kingston, Ontario, *Whig-Standard*, 19 Aug. 1982.

As an official who had once worked in the Prime Minister's Office reflected, 'let's be honest. One of the Solicitor General's main functions is to keep the world ticking over so that there are no catastrophes. If you don't hear from him, he's doing a good job.' And the Solicitor General himself observed that political demands 'relate to incidents a lot. It's an incident that triggers public interest in something. In the economy, it's a condition rather than an incident which calls public or government attention to something. Whereas with us it's an incident: you'll have an escape or a parolee committing a crime or a particularly horrible murder.'

In the absence of sustained and substantial parliamentary political interest in the Ministry's work on policy development, it becomes necessary to turn elsewhere for an external voice and a larger audience. In a process which I shall explore later and at some length, much can be done autonomously and within the Ministry. There is enough activity in the world of criminal justice, criminology, and penology to supply a long train of policy initiatives. but the successful production and promotion of policy is a pre-eminently political matter. It requires a political style. Policy analysts argue that academic research and general argument play a somewhat peripheral part in the construction of successful proposals. One asserted rather astringently, 'researchers insist on empirical purity and detail but you don't need all that because Cabinet Ministers aren't interested'. And another said, 'policy is a very political thing and the research becomes important only in a hidden way. When it finally gets to the purely political level where the final decision is made, it comes down to the kind of political sense of the politicians, if they feel it's going to be publicly saleable or not.'

What *can* be compelling is the contention that someone, somewhere, is vociferously demanding the service or programme that is contemplated and that, further, there may well be appreciable public criticism if it is not forthcoming. That is, policy becomes attractive when it promises to satisfy a pronounced demand or defuse a damaging attack. It will then cease to be merely another bright idea of a department or politician and become an instrument that is politically useful to government. Accordingly, in 1976, a working group on Ministry objectives and priorities developed five general criteria for defining an issue as Ministry-wide in importance. The final criterion was whether 'the issue is politically significant (the Minister will have to deal with it in public)'.[37] Clearly, that last criterion points to the responsibility which the Minister

[37] *Plans for June 1976 Ministry Workshop*, p. 2.

must assume for his Department as a whole. He is accountable. It also describes political significance as an importance bestowed in public by outsiders who must be taken seriously. The possible reactions and the character of outsiders are manifestly politically consequential.

Similarly, the critical long-term planning document deployed by the federal government in the early 1980s, the *Strategic Overview*, was required to make very precise reference to the important groups and populations that might be affected by any policy proposal. Under the heading of 'objectives', the Ministry was to specify 'target beneficiary groups and benefits to be conferred', including 'who will benefit from realization of the priority initiative (i.e. elderly, handicapped, natives, women, young people, etc.)'. Under 'background', the Ministry had to describe 'what social pressures will either be alleviated or eliminated ... and through what organization(s) have the social pressures been brought to the attention of the government?'[38] Rephrased, it is apparent that an eligible policy proposal had to be properly drafted, defended, and presented. If it were to succeed, it had to bear on the interests of particular groups favoured by government; offer gains which could be listed precisely; and be open to a special form of historical explanation that could demonstrate how the initiative might be construed as a response to the demands of those selfsame groups. In this sense, policy was made to occupy a distinct place in a landscape of involved figures: its fate would hinge on the topography of that landscape, the composition of those figures, and its power to reach them. A draft which could not refer to selected groups and organizations in an approved fashion was unlikely to prosper. As Wildavsky argued of Washington, the first budgetary strategy is to 'find a clientele'.[39] Part of the skill of the policy analyst is the identification of significant outsiders and legitimate clients. Indeed, a senior official from a central agency remarked:

> We often tend to neglect the importance of building constituencies in the public for our proposals and, since political process responds to that kind of pressure, more emphasis should be given to making sure that there are constituencies out there who support particular initiatives and will speak up in favour ... Quite often, I've heard Ministers say, 'well look, nobody's pressing for this. Let's not do it.'

Of course, not all outsiders are authoritative or significant. Some are discredited and some are unheard. And the process of heeding outsiders

[38] *Policy Initiatives: Strategic Overview Information Requirements*, pp. 1–2.

[39] A. Wildavsky, *The Politics of the Budgetary Process*, Little Brown, Boston, 1974, p. 65. See also C. Wiener, *The Politics of Alcoholism: Building an Arena Around a Social Problem*, Transaction Books, New Jersey, 1981, esp. Part II.

is complicated by the manner in which changing objectives and plans alter contexts. Constituencies tend to beome important only when they demand the right things. Even the most eminent person or group can be devalued when statements jar with the interpretative frameworks established by a particular purpose. In some measure, legitimacy and sagacity reflect utility. Thus research may be discounted by politicians when it disagrees with their ideas. Let me provide an example from the debates on capital punishment that took place in 1976. The Member of Parliament for Villeneuve asserted:

What is important is not what a sociologist believes or thinks, but what the majority of Canadians think and what they desire and ask.... There is an old maxim, Mr. Speaker: Tell me who pays you and I'll tell you who you are. The Solicitor General is the milk cow that feeds those criminologists who do not know what to do with their ten fingers. Do you think guys like that would take the chance of making the Solicitor General of Canada angry? In my view, Mr. Speaker, these criminologists are not stupid. He is the one who feeds them, who enables them to live and consequently they prepare the reports he wants.[40]

Disagreeable research may them be displaced by the pressing demands of the Canadian people. However, when it is those demands that are disagreeable, they too may be displaced. The Solicitor General himself remarked in an earlier debate on capital punishment: 'we have a duty [to listen to our constituents] and we should take it seriously. But this means we listen openly and honestly to their arguments, the reasons for their opinions—and if they are convincing we adopt them. It does not mean that we should be swayed by protests, volume, shrillness or mere numbers'.[41] It is thus evident that the persuasiveness and authority of others are situated qualities, pragmatic constructions as it were, which change systematically with task and history. They certainly are not 'given' but are part of an exchange between the politician or policy-maker, the world, and an audience. Research, criminologists, and the public are socially manufactured in a changing process of political enterprise.

The chief complaint made by Ministry staff working in and about the victims initiative was not about the character of outsiders but that there were so very few vocal outsiders to be heard at all. Policy documents drafted for committees and Cabinet must refer to organized groups, the

[40] Mr Caouette, Member of Parliament for Villeneuve, *House of Commons Debates*, 14 May 1976.

[41] Remarks made by Warren Allmand, PC, MP, Solicitor General of Canada, on introducing Bill C-2 in the House of Commons on 25 Jan. 1973.

public, and public opinion. Yet the outer world actually refused to burst in on the Ministry with any noise.

A small number of lobbies and pressure groups *do* exist. The John Howard Society was born in its first incarnation as the Prisoners' Aid Society in 1882, becoming involved progressively with visiting and helping inmates, supervising men on parole, administering community programmes, and advocating prison reform. The Elizabeth Fry Societies, founded in 1939, are engaged in counselling, court assistance, prison visiting, and rehabilitation work for women.[42] There are organizations committed to the advancement of women. But, generally, there was something of a silence around those regions of the Ministry in which work on victims began to grow. External pressure tends to be applied selectively to specific, established issues. It was about those issues that groups first began to form and they have continued to define their functions, politics, and audiences. There is consequently some reticence about a broadening of interests to embrace wider or novel ventures. Thus, when an evangelist of the Canadian victims movement, Irvin Waller, tried to turn the minds of the members of the John Howard Society of Ontario towards victims at a meeting held in 1981, he was told that there was but one principal group of victims that concerned the John Howard Society: prisoners were the victims of an oppressive social order and they chiefly merited the Society's attention. Any other focus would muddle the Society's work. It was a stance that was to change, but the initial response was to place the victims of crime outside the Society's boundaries. It is in this fashion that reticence discourages new undertakings that are unconnected with the approved and the old. And the result is that it is often difficult to point precisely to those external pressures and public demands which might give legitimacy, objectivity, and solidity to plans which affect new territory and unconventional problems. In the Ministry of the Solicitor General, and in federal and provincial government as a whole, there is a very real strain to cultivate and educate what few lobbies there are. Policy-makers nurture their public environment, attempting to make it as lively and versatile as possible. As Pross observes, 'government assistance and encouragement of pressure groups have increased in recent years . . . at both provincial and federal levels government subsidy has created or sustained a large number of voluntary organizations, which in turn use part of their funds to influence public policy'.[43] Sandra Gwyn has written of Departments

[42] See 'Private Sector in Corrections', *Let's Talk*, 15 Aug. 1982, Vol. 7, No. 14.

[43] A. Pross, 'Canadian Pressure Groups in the 1970s: their Role and their Relations with the Public Service', *Canadian Public Administration*, Spring 1975, Vol. 18, No. 1, pp. 128–9.

creating 'their own constituency, and, it has to be added, their own dependents'.[44]

The Ministry attends to its environment in three interlaced ways. Financially, the Solicitor General awards grants to private sector bodies. In 1980–1 $50,000 was given to the Canadian Association of Chiefs of Police, $125,000 to the Canadian Association for the Prevention of Crime, and $50,000 to the John Howard Society.[45] Other money was given in an *ad hoc* manner to subsidize projects, programmes, and conferences. All that funding did not produce mere complaisant clients of the State. There is a display of independence.

Private bodies cherish their privacy. A paradoxical consequence has been that the private sector periodically petitions federal departments for money to support its independence. Thus, in 1980, the co-ordinating body used by federal government to convene with the private sector, the National Associations Active in Criminal Justice, urged the Ministries of the Solicitor General and Justice:

> To develop and publicize their own Ministry Policy Statements to use existing private sector resources, or, if adequate resources do not exist, to provide the finances and specialist services to develop such private sector resources, i) before expanding any of their own services or establishing new services, and ii) whenever possible, as alternatives to their existing services.
>
> To establish a consultation process with the private sector to monitor and evaluate the implementation and operationalization of this policy on privatization, and,
>
> To finance the activities created by this policy and the consultation process . . .[46]

Practically, the Ministry advises, encourages, and funds projects initiated by private sector organizations. It was to that end that $1,549,000 was devoted in 1980–1. The Ministry has much to gain from coaxing local schemes into life. In the charged area of criminal justice, it has only the most limited access to applied work. Whilst the RCMP, penitentiaries, and a number of miscellaneous duties plot out some territory for the Ministry, much is under the sway of provincial Attorneys General and Solicitors General. A succession of direct attempts to found projects and programmes would be construed as somewhat invasive. Requests from local community, religious, and police groups have a

[44] S. Gwyn, 'The Great Ottawa Grant Boom (And How it Grew)', *Saturday Night*, October 1972.

[45] *Estimates for the Fiscal Year Ending March 31, 1981*, p. 28–8.

[46] *CAEFS Newsletter*, Canadian Association of Elizabeth Fry Societies, May 1980, Newsletter No. 5, p. 5.

legitimacy and political innocence that threaten less disturbance. Moreover, the Ministry manifestly lacks the people and money to do all that work itself. Partly as a result of the self-denying ordinance, partly as a result of the quite massive sums that would be involved, it is impossible for the Ministry to do other than acquire a host of voluntary organizations as partners, and talk about partnership has become routine in the official speeches and releases of the Department. One quite typical instance was offered in the Solicitor General's speech to the St Leonard's Society in 1980. He claimed that his presence gave him 'the opportunity to acknowledge and re-affirm the integral *partnership* we have developed within the corrections community'.[47]

The activities and advocacy work of the private sector can be translated into a field of opportunities for symbolic use. As I shall argue, the Ministry attends to its surroundings in a most diligent fashion, creatively examining and interpreting them as a repository of aids in argument. The private sector then becomes a bank of material for the production of a certain kind of social reality to which the Ministry can respond. It is nursed. As Pitt and Smith argued about government departments in Britain: 'departments do not merely respond to pressure. They are capable of orchestrating it. They can select the groups that they will listen to. Access can be made easier for some than others. Groups may be helped in their campaigns with vital information'.[48]

The Internal Organization of the Ministry of the Solicitor General

The Ministry is a major employer, being responsible for 30,964 people in 1981–2. The RCMP accounts for 30 per cent of national policing strength and the Correctional Service of Canada for 45 per cent of total prison staff. The Ministry itself controls 29 per cent of spending on criminal justice at all levels of government and for 95 per cent of federal expenditure. The mainspring of policy-making is, however, within the relatively small Secretariat which employed only some 256 people in 1981–2 and spent only 1·54 per cent of the Department's budget.[49] It is with the Secretariat that I shall remain.

The Ministry of the Solicitor General of Canada is young, having been

[47] *Notes for a Speech by the Honourable Bob Kaplan, P.C., M.P., Solicitor General of Canada, to the St. Leonard's Society Annual Conference and Meeting at Windsor*, Ontario, 19 Sept. 1980.

[48] D. Pitt and B. Smith, *Government Departments: An Organizational Perspective*, Routledge and Kegan Paul, London, 1981, p. 37.

[49] Based on *Statement of the Hon. Robert Kaplan, P.C., M.P., Solicitor General of Canada, to the Justice and Legal Affairs Committee Re: Main Estimates 1982/83*, 13 May 1982.

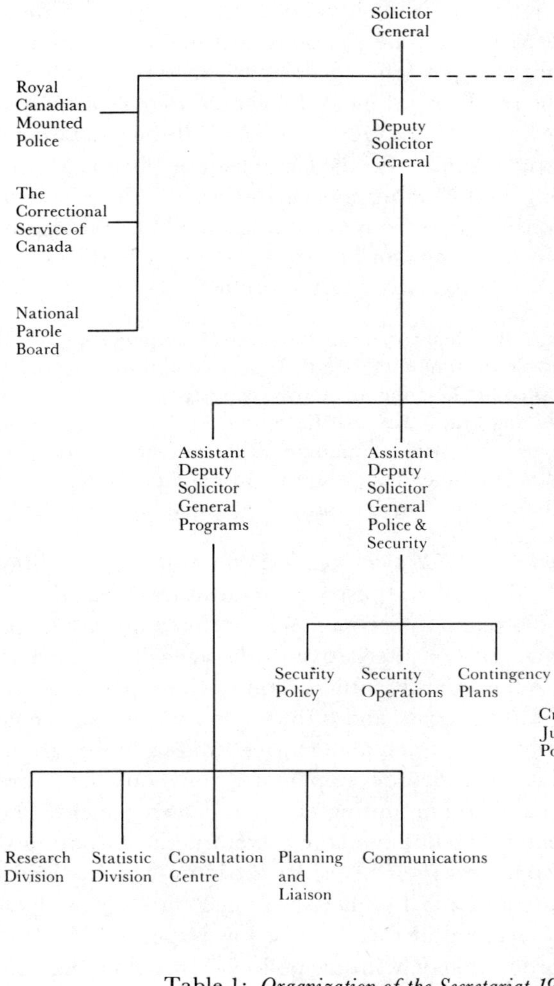

Table 1: *Organization of the Secretariat 1983–1984*

founded in 1966, and its Secretariat is even younger. It had originally been thought that the Ministry would play the role of a Headquarters for the different agencies which it superintends, but the agencies successfully countered that it had not been the intention of Parliament to have them report to the Deputy Minister. The relations between a government department and the heads of powerful agencies are often uneasy: in the United States, it will be recalled, J. Edgar Hoover enjoyed a substantial independence, and the British Home Office has passed through a parallel history of negotiation and dispute with the Commissioner for the Metropolitan Police and the Prison Commissioners. In Canada, the problems attending those relations led to some initial confusion about the appropriate naming, organization, and working of the Ministry and its component departments. As a fairly early analysis argued:

> Ever since the formation of the Department in 1966, the Headquarters has had difficulty in defining its role. Ultimately, it settled for a compromise role. On the one hand, it attempted to function in a way consistent with a unitary department, in which the final authority for the control of resources rested at Departmental Headquarters, but with a minimum of interference in the operations of the agencies. On the other hand, it tried to maintain some sort of consultative and research role. The two roles proved incompatible.

It was not until November 1972 that some of those incompatibilities were structurally resolved and the Ministry Secretariat was created with diffuse and somewhat discrepant objectives. Some defined the role of the Secretariat as complementary or alternative to the agencies, providing discrete policy advice to the Minister; others claimed that their responsibility should include setting goals and strategic plans for the whole Ministry, including the departmental agencies; and a third group described their mandate as policy development throughout the entire criminal justice system and compromising all levels of government. The tasks, character, and external relations of the Secretariat have continued to be rather vague, vagueness itself being an attribute which permits negotiation and change. Periodically, there have been attempts to fix a definition. In 1975 the Secretariat was described as responsible for 'the development and co-ordination of Ministry policy'.[50] In 1980 a meeting of the Programs Branch Management Committee offered a 'semi-official statement on the overall responsibility of the Secretariat':

> The Secretariat of the Ministry of the Solicitor General is responsible for the analysis, evaluation and provision of advice to the Solicitor General in matters

[50] *Guide Research Program, 1975–75*, Solicitor General, Canada, Ottawa, 1975, p. 4.

relating to Canadian corrections, police and law enforcement, and national security. In this context, the Secretariat develops the strategic policy framework for the Ministry, formulates policies and programs, coordinates Ministry involvement, conducts research, monitors and evaluates new and existing legislation, policies, and programs related to the criminal justice system.[51]

The Solicitor General himself later described his 'policy Secretariat' as 'a few hundred experts and analysts [who] develop policies, research and programs in such areas as crime prevention, victims of crime, family violence, and natives in the criminal justice system'.[52]

The Secretariat was itself to evolve, its departments moving through a series of phases, constitutions, and titles. Its growth mirrored and fed a more substantial expansion of the wider federal bureaucracy in Ottawa. During the late 1960s and early 1970s, especially, there was an efflorescence of policy units and planning departments which housed a conception of administration as a special skill requiring special qualifications and training.[53] They were newly manned by young staff with an expertise in sociology, economics, and policy analysis. Those staff were, as I have remarked, young, liberal, reformist, and often confident, having their counterparts in the expanding bureaucracies of London[54] and Washington[55] and coming to compose substantial sources of innovation in their own right. After all, their task had been defined as policy development. The work which they accomplished, particularly in the central agencies, so transformed processes within Ottawa that department after department was constrained to establish its own policy units to contend with the novel complexity that had been created: 'without their own experts, departmental deputy ministers were unable to navigate through the central decision-making process and to negotiate with the central agency gate-keepers who had achieved pivotal positions within the process. Thus, in the early seventies, each department created its own policy analysis unit, planning branch and/or program evaluation group ...'[56]

[51] Acting Assistant Deputy Minister, *Draft Memo Re Role of Programs Branch*, 17 Nov. 1980, p. 1. For a very similar statement, see *1982–83 Estimates Part III Secretariat Plan*, Solicitor General Canada, Ottawa, 1982, p. 5.

[52] *Notes for a Speech by the Honourable Bob Kaplan, P.C., M.P., Solicitor General of Canada, to the 112th. Annual Congress of the American Correctional Association*, Toronto, Canada, 19 Aug. 1982.

[53] See M. Prince and J. Chenier, 'The Rise and Fall of Policy Planning and Research Units', *Canadian Public Administration*, Winter 1980, Vol. 23, No. 4, p. 540.

[54] See K. Banting, *Poverty, Politics and Policy*, Macmillan, London, 1979.

[55] See N. Glazer, 'A New Look in Social Welfare', *New Society*, 7 Nov. 1963. M. Prince, *Policy Advice and Organizational Survival*, p. 1.

[56] R. French, *How Ottawa Decides: Planning and Industrial Policy-Making 1968–1980*, John Lorimer and Company, Toronto, 1980, p. 26.

The Secretariat forms just such an accumulation of competence, being organized into distinct components intended to foster and steer policy through what an outsider, working in a private policy institute, described as 'the craziest . . . Chinese Box of committee meetings'.

The Secretariat has been in flux throughout its life. It has been made up of a changing number of branches with different names and shifting functions. In 1978, for instance, there were four branches which bore on the production and development of policy: Policy Planning and Program Evaluation; Research and Systems Development; Communications and Consultation; and Police and Security. In 1981 there were three such branches: Policy; Programs; and Police and Security. In the main, the Police and Security Branch tends to be somewhat apart from the rest, dealing with its client agency, the police, and playing an inconspicuous part in the development of wider policy. An official from the Programs Branch, a person of some experience, commented 'it's hard to know what they're doing'. The Police and Security Branch certainly did not make a mark on the generation of the victims initiative despite the close links that tie the police to the politics of the victim. Its model would seem to have been that or replying to a client demand for policy guidance, a model which embodied a major preoccupation with provincial relations and susceptibilities. Thus a senior official in that branch stated that his task should be a responsive one because most policing is not federally controlled and an overly active federal concern with police work could upset provincial and municipal forces. By extension, he said that he was wary of the interest in victims that his colleagues elsewhere were developing. It was his contention that such an interest exceeded the limits of the Ministry's mandate.

At the very core of the Secretariat, and as the chief setting for the formation of a victims policy, were two branches, Programs and Policy. The Programs Branch is itself a composite, in 1981 being made up of divisions concentrating on research, statistics, planning and liaison, library services, documentation, communication, and consultation. At the divisional level, units may actually be rather small, containing only a few officials and their supporting clerks and secretaries. Yet the Research Division had some thirty-five staff in 1981 and a research budget of about $3 million a year. The job of the Programs Branch is defined liberally enough. It encompasses a range of ambitions: the identification of problems and areas within the criminal justice system that require examination and attention; the improvement of the effectiveness of that system by exploring methods of increasing police productivity and the like; 'policy development'; 'policy support'; 'fostering improved federal–

provincial relations in the justice field'; and 'fostering improved international relations in the justice field'.[57] Much of that development of connections inside and outside Canada is done by the Communication and Planning and Liaison Divisions, bodies that are concerned with the 'dissemination of knowledge' strategy of the Programs Branch, maintaining a library, publishing books, journals, and papers, running workshops and conferences, preparing courses and seminars, and distributing speeches and statements.

Research is intended to accomplish a number of ends. Its principal objective is supposed to be 'practical [and] applied ... looking for ways of reducing the total social and economic cost of criminal activity in Canada by helping to further understanding of the phenomenon of crime'.[58] Accordingly, work is undertaken and commissioned which seems best able to contribute to the Ministry's programme of practical activities in the realm of criminal justice. The Department has a moving agenda which refracts a succession of political and criminological interests. In 1974–5 there was a concentration upon 'Community Attitudes to the Criminal Justice System', diversion, correctional services, and rehabilitation; in 1975–6 there was a catalogue of concerns established by the Peace and Security Package, a catalogue that included violent crime and the dangerous offender; and, in 1976–7 stress was placed on victimization and crime prevention.[59] For a while, that agenda was signalled to a wider population of criminologists in research organizations and universities, the intention being to 'involve the research community in this most important endeavor'.[60] And the external funding of research has deliberately eclipsed 'in-house' work. From the start, research contracts have been used to stimulate and foster criminological competence in Canada, representing another instance of the Ministry trying to cultivate a network of constituents, critics, and dependents. Again, quite typically, that network has acquired considerable autonomy and the business of sponsoring client organizations has not been entirely pacific. University and research staff have complained about delays in the publication of their reports, close control of their work, and a strong departmental conception of what constitutes adequacy.

'Policy development' and 'policy support' are catholic terms which refer in large measure to the work that is performed in and through the Consultation Centre. Confronted with the colossal geography and the

[57] Acting Assistant Deputy Solicitor General, *Draft Memo.*

[58] *Guide Research Program 1975–76*, Solicitor General, Ottawa, 1975, p. 7.

[59] Based on successive *Guide Research Programs* issued by the Solicitor General.

[60] *Guide Research Program, 1974–75*, Solicitor General, Ottawa, 1974, p. 5.

fragile politics of Canada, the Ministry has established a chain of regional offices in Moncton, Vancouver, Montreal, Toronto, and Saskatoon. Each is devised to symbolize the interest of the Solicitor General, particularly in those regions which are very remote from Ottawa. Each is an attempt to diminish the political and social distance between an often distant capital and local activity. Each is manned by a Regional Consultant who plays a kind of consular role in relating Ministry concerns to private, municipal, and provincial bodies, and reporting back local diplomatic intelligence in turn. Indeed, the maintenance of amicable federal–provincial relations is, as an official put it, 'a big hunk of the job'. It is the Regional Consultant who acts as one of the people who solicit and receive requests for the funding of seminars, workshops, conferences, and research. Further, he or she will support what are carefully called 'demonstration projects', exemplary schemes which illuminate 'the validity of new or alternative approaches to persistent problems, . . . develop resources to fill gaps in the existing system, and . . . encourage joint efforts in diminishing duplication and redundancy of services'.[61] Fifty-nine such projects were financed in 1979–80, sixty-three in 1980–1, contributing to the proselytization and dissemination of central policy.[62] Collectively, the work of the projects and the Consultants is intended to inject some coherence and cohesion into the Canadian criminal justice system.[63]

The Policy Branch is required to formulate 'strategic policies', provide policy advice to the Minister and Deputy Minister on those problems of criminal justice which need 'public policy determination', and tend the 'strategic policy framework for the Secretariat and [guide] the development of the strategic policy of the Ministry as a whole, within the context of over-all government direction and policies'.[64] All that activity is itself to be conducted in collaboration with the other departments and agencies of government in Ottawa and the provinces.[65] A most particular meaning seems to have been attached to policy in all these settings. It is largely construed as the artful exercise of statecraft. In this sense, it is rather specially defined as the expert business of shepherding ideas and papers through the maze of committees and stages which await any innovatory proposal. It is concerned with the craft of constructing formal arguments so that they assume the proper appearance in the proper

[61] *Annual Report, 1979–1980*, Solicitor General, Ottawa, 1980, p. 10.

[62] *Consultation Centre Operational Plan FY 1980–1981*, Solicitor General, Ottawa, 1980, p. 2.

[63] See 'Working Together', *Correctional Options*, Fall 1982, Vol. 2, No. 1.

[64] *Annual Report 1979–80*, p. 3.

[65] See *1982–83 Estimates Part III Expenditure Plan*, p. 5.

situation. The substance of policy is a little secondary, entrusted to research staff and politicians, and of interest principally as a guide to organizations that must be cited and consulted and to rhetoric that may be deployed. What *is* important to Policy Branch officials are the forms, manners, and ceremony of presenting argument. Indeed, their work is very substantially taken up with the transformation and manipulation of raw materials furnished by others. As a senior Policy official put it, 'if anything has to do with moving a programme and shifting a priority, in developing it, priorising it and moving it forward, that's the responsibility of the policy centres of the Ministry.' And one of his staff described her work as 'meaning basically that you are more responsible for process than content. To put it academically, it means that you have to facilitate the production of the types of paper that make [policy] go through the system, as opposed to actually investigating the topic for its meat.' She, in her turn, was described by the Director of Policy Planning as 'a terrific process person'. The recurrent emphasis is on form, the structuring of ideas, arguments, and occasions in the most propitious fashion. In this sense, policy becomes the management of the words and documents which are convoyed through Ottawa. It is the job of the policy official to chart the terrain which must be covered, appreciate who might present himself or herself as an ally, opponent, or obstacle, what is likely to be considered rhetorically persuasive or unpersuasive, and so propel a proposal forwards. The Policy Branch official thus takes on the trappings of a scout, pilot, or guard of otherwise ill-protected ideas.

I do not propose to linger with the analysis of how policy arguments are amassed and escorted because most of the rest of this book will pursue that theme. Processes do not always move uneventfully from one sector to another. On the contrary, there are disputed zones where it is unclear or undecided which Branch should assume overall direction. As the Director of Policy Planning observed, 'now that's a border that you're going to fudge frequently.' Uncertainty stems from definitional problems about the ripeness of ideas for development: there is a strain in the Programs Branch to retain schemes for proper assessment and scrutiny, whilst the Policy Branch would advance them when it is politically advantageous to do so. The evolutionary timetables of processes move at different rates and with different phases in the two Branches. And there is a structured difference between the Branches' judgements about the significance of episodes in the life of policy development. The staff of the Programs Branch tend to attach importance to knowledge accumulated in research and experience gained from demonstration projects.

The staff of the Policy Branch believe that ideas begin to move with a real purpose only when they become exposed to an audience of the politically powerful. Political animation flows from political settings.

II. On the Diffuseness of Origins and Other Problems

I must enlarge the framework which I began to prepare in the first chapter. This rather extended and elaborate introduction is necessary because no appreciation of the victims initiative can begin to emerge until some critical features of the Ministry and its work have first been described. By dwelling on those features, I can illuminate a number of the larger themes which infused the initiative. In particular, I shall dwell upon the working personalities of the staff, the processes which they orchestrate, and the habitat in which they spend much of their life.

The Staff of the Secretariat of the Solicitor General

Doctrine holds that officials are the dispassionate executors of the political will of Parliament and Government: 'in constitutional theory, all is well as long as Cabinet makes policy, Parliament passes laws, and the bureaucracy faithfully implements programs.'[1] It is a doctrine that does exercise a most pronounced constraint on the organization of policy-making, framing all that is done, and I shall allude to its influence repeatedly. Indeed, the manufacture of the victims initiative would be quite unintelligible in its absence. Yet a large number of bureaucrats are quite other than the utterly neutral instruments and vessels of alien ideas. Many would choose to distance themselves from an injunction to be neutral, although not all would do so, and the adoption of an occupational style is itself embedded in position and experience. Officials are enmeshed in a complicated net of shifting positions and stances which define their careers, their identities, and their achievements. I shall describe that net in other places, but it would be helpful to discuss some of its qualities here.

It will be remembered that the Ministry of the Solicitor General is a young institution, having been founded in 1966, and its Secretariat is some six years younger. Posts had been filled in a short space of time by quite substantial recruiting. At the beginning of the 1980s, then, the Secretariat was staffed, in the main, by a group of graduates in their

[1] C. Campbell and G. Szablowski, *The Superbureaucrats: Structure and Behaviour in Central Agencies,* Macmillan Company of Canada, Toronto, 1979, p. 18.

thirties and forties.[2] It was stocked by the members of an intellectual generation who had moved through time together. Mannheim once argued that 'the problems of generations is important enough to merit serious consideration. It is one of the indispensable guides to an understanding of the structure of social and intellectual movements.[3] He defined a generation, in turn, as 'a particular kind of identity of location, embracing related "age groups" embedded in a historical–social process'.[4] It would be a little ambitious of me to dilate on the historical–social process of the generation that worked in the Secretariat of the Ministry. But the staff of the Solicitor General had typically passed through the burgeoning universities of the late 1950s and early 1960s, saw the flowering of the social sciences, observed and shared the radicalism of students, and knew a particular kind of politics.[5] The head of the Programs Branch, indeed, had left England to study politics at Berkeley because of the excitement generated by the Free Speech Movement. Staff diverged from one another but they also participated in a rough community of experience and could point to common existential benchmarks. They subscribed, as Prince put it, to the idea of 'a new age of reason in governing, a period of tremendous faith and optimism in rationality and reform in governmental policies, structures and processes'.[6] One of their senior officials talked of the way in which they were under the sway of a 'simple, liberal (small "l"), do-gooding, social reforming drive . . . the fundamental characteristic of the Solicitor General's Secretariat is just that. If you look at the people who are there: I mean the Consultative Centre is *dedicated* to criminal justice improvement; Programs Branch's number one priority is criminal justice improvement, it's a reforming, reformist group; and Policy Branch is largely the same.' Many members of the Secretariat would spurn any other designation. One stated simply of his colleagues that they 'do care deeply about others', and another remarked, 'I think that with professionals working within the Ministry etcetera working on something like victims or crime

[2] See M. Prince, 'Policy Advisory Groups in Government Departments', in G. Doern *et al.* (eds.), *Public Policy in Canada,* Macmillan, Toronto, 1979.

[3] K. Mannheim, 'The Problem of Generations', in *Essays on the Sociology of Knowledge,* Routledge and Kegan Paul, London, 1952, pp. 286–7.

[4] Ibid., p. 292.

[5] Even their least sympathetic critics have endowed Canadian criminology and criminal justice policy with a central strand of liberalism. See R. Ratner and J. McMullan, 'Ideological Foundations of Criminology in Canada', paper presented to the American Society of Criminology, Toronto, 4–6 Nov. 1982. I. Taylor, *Crime, Capitalism and Community,* Butterworths, Toronto, 1983. M. Brake, *Comparative Youth Culture,* Routledge and Kegan Paul, London, 1985, Ch. 6.

[6] M. Prince, *Policy Advice and Organizational Survival,* Gower, Aldershot, 1983, p. viii.

prevention or policing whatever, it's much more than a job to them. It's very much related to a cause.' And yet another official commented, 'one of my insights about bureaucracy which I was just so shocked by when I first came, and it's continued to be true, it that I find bureaucrats strangely enough among the most caring people I've ever dealt with and, I mean, among the most emotionally committed to issues.'

Not only were many officials expressly given to a kind of humane, compassionate pragmatism, they had never been exposed to the unpalatable demands that might have revealed the extent of their willingness to act as dispassionate agents of the State. After all, the Secretariat was youthful, having been born and matured in a period demonstrated by Liberal Governments and liberal thinking. No official I spoke to claimed ever to have been asked to work on any project that was deeply distasteful to him or her. No official seemed to have speculated about the organization of possible responses to such a request.

An official asserted that the train of projects, initiatives, and plans in progress possessed such a momentum and engendered so many commitments that it could not easily be redirected towards uncongenial ends:

> I don't have a long history so I've never seen [anything really disagreeable] happen. I mean, I've seen changes of perspective and I've seen disappointment, but the usual reaction is to try to redefine, not to sort of totally drop everything you're doing. You can't just sort of totally drop things. First of all, you can't just totally drop things because you've got other commitments. I mean, almost everything we do also has a kind of provincial input or you've got responsibilities to other people.

It should also be appreciated that the reforming drive of officials is not merely a matter of contemplation. It is profoundly implicated in the evolving structures which they themselves create. Policies are not simply exuded by Ministries: they are actively promoted, tended, and planned. As I shall argue at length, they come out of copious social organization and they fold back on that organization to change it. In this sense, the passionate and the dispassionate are contingent features of an emerging order. The bulk of this book will be devoted to an examination of how policy-making came to supply motives and passions for those who were engaged in it.

Those who were at the very centre of the victims initiative, in particular, tended to undergo a transformation of experience and motivation. At the very least, people who have devoted considerable effort to an enterprise will discover that it has become significant, possibly a central passage in their biographies. It will become intertwined with their lives and there may be a great reluctance to disclaim it. Facts can thereby define the self, and it is difficult to disown those facts and be neutral towards them. There is a propensity to become proprietorial to the work that one has done. As an official who was structurally marginal to the victims initiative reflected, 'there are very few people who like to be seen as not doing good, as not having a mission'.

It follows that it would be analytically and descriptively unhelpful to represent federal officials as dispassionate and neutral in their dealings with the world. They have very real passions. But their passion is also carefully modulated and regulated. It does not do to disclose emotion at all times and in all places. There are occasions when it is held to be appropriate and there are ways of displaying it. Emotionality should not be allowed to impair performance. It should not simply be vented but purposeful: it is regarded, as an official observed, '[as improper] if it interferes with productivity ... If you're evangelical without purpose or focus, you know. Sure, if you're just spewing forth, who wants to listen to someone proselytise? You know, proselytising is not appropriate. Proselytising with a plan of action *is* appropriate.' Further, those who proselytize should be in the appropriate position: not all posts are legitimate platforms for the making of emotional displays. Passion must be controlled by a sense of the limitation of one's office: 'you respect the bounds of your position and you respect the definition of your mandate.' And passion must be revealed pleasingly. As another official stated, 'all people I've ever met, and I have yet to find an exception, run away from people who bore the hell out of them, and anybody who hammers on one issue bores the hell out of them, and that's a human phenomenon.' In a world given to the clever use of words and gestures, much attention is devoted to the careful cultivation of that which is graceful and decorous. There is a propensity to regard ideas and phrases with some fascination, officials toying with their forms and discovering their possibilities. Like much else, work can sometimes attain the features of a game,[7] speech becoming banter and reflection becoming mildly self-mocking. The style of some officials may tend to verge on the self-deprecatingly mannered. Conversation may tend to consist of little performances designed to amuse oneself and others. It is intensely reflexive and disciplined. In all that stylized speech, there is some disapproval of the maladroit and the clumsy. There is a censorship of those who barge around the bureaucratic world emitting an unrefined emotionality. As one official put it, 'emotionality is situational. The trick is to switch it off when necessary.' The

[7] See J. Huizinga, *Homo Ludens*, Routledge and Kegan Paul, London, 1949.

Ministry itself abounded in salutary stories about officials who lacked the capacity to present themselves and their projects with style. The Homeric epithet of 'Chinese water torturer' was applied to one who had pressed too unremittingly and inflexibly for a victims policy. And those who are under the sway of driving passions can experience frustration. Thus Irvin Waller, a man critical to the emergence of the victims initiative, called himself 'obsessed' by victims. He felt obliged to resign his position as Director General of Research. '"In criminal justice, we take up the symbolic issues and avoid the major ones", Irvin Waller said in an interview on the last day of his job. "If we ran the economy like that ..." He is leaving government to take up a teaching post ... saying he feels he might have more influence on government from there.'[8]

Performances in the Ministry and in Ottawa at large must then be recognized as a series of controlled displays which defer to the settings in which they are exhibited. There is no prohibition on sentiment or attachment. To the contrary. But there is an overarching sense of order, an injunction to be civil, sensitive to occasion, and graceful in conduct. The unremitting, the impolite, and the inelegant are censured. After all, some reasonably formal conception of manners must be evolved to regulate the busy conduct of numerous people who continually jostle one another in their work. It is in this sense that Bittner's discussion of organizations as a mode of stylistic unity becomes apposite. Bittner holds that an organization is much more than a device to couple sets of means and ends together. Rather, structure emanates from the 'sensibility of esthetic appreciation [which] is summoned for direction, information and control in various concrete situations. The dominant consideration underlying this construction ... is an all-pervading sense of piety. ... [which may be investigated by examining the] ties and performances that appeal to bureaucrats as incongruous or in bad taste.'[9]

Amongst the qualities condemned by officials of the Solicitor General were too fulsome a presentation of self, inflexibility, a lack of wit, laziness, incompetence, and ponderousness. Possessiveness was deplored: it would not do to tend one's own little projects and expertise without a willingness to co-operate with others. It was important to respect the limits and proprieties of a role: it was wrong to 'push too hard by stepping on other people's turf'. It was wrong to be emotional without useful effect: 'there's not very much tolerance for sloppy thinking.' And it was wrong to be ungainly. All those are qualities which are disliked in the wider world,

[8] *Globe and Mail*, 5 July 1980.

[9] E. Bittner, 'The Concept of Organization', *Social Research*, September 1965, Vol. 32, pp. 252–3.

but they receive an added emphasis in official settings. Social and conversational form becomes significant in an organization devoted to the preparation of argument and bureaucratic action. As one official remarked, 'I think ultimately it's a question of style. You know, at the most cynical, you can get away with anything if you do it right. Content doesn't matter or it matters as much as process. I'm inclined to think that's everyday life. You know: what you say to your wife doesn't matter as much as how you say it. Why should it be different here?' Another official paid great heed to charm. What seemed to give unity to their aesthetics was a pleasingly presented deference to the disciplines of time, place, and purpose. Theirs was not an unbounded or loosely structured world, and they had organized a cosmology and an etiquette to complement it. And that was not very remarkable in a bureaucracy.

That etiquette gave order to many of the dealings which the Solicitor General's officials had with other Ministries and the provinces. It permitted the emergence of working links across the boundaries of formally autonomous or antagonistic institutions. In the instance of Ontario, one federal official stated that between 'the Justice Secretariat ... and the Minister or Deputy Minister [in Ottawa] there's an official sort of posturing that goes on but unofficially our day-to-day working relationships don't change'. And another remarked, 'there's a lot of people who work in both systems. Here,

. . .

worked with the Justice Secretariat.

. . .

came from the [Ontario] Ministry of Correctional Services. And we *know* each other as people. It's a very small group. It's almost incestuous.' Relationships in the 'criminal justice community' centre on a few common sites and a few projects. The numbers of people engaged are small and they exchange roles with one another. The apparent chasms and divisions of federal–provincial relations actually mask the structure of a little society with much of the character of the village life described by Heclo and Wildavsky. The criminal justice village is marked by 'coherent patterns of praxis [and] the shared experiences that facilitate learning'.[10] It rests on gossip, friendship, enmity, and informal reputation. It has its own private successes and scandals, its meeting places in Toronto, Edmonton, Vancouver, Winnipeg, St Johns, and elsewhere. It is built on an interchange between private conduct and public performance.

[10] H. Heclo and A. Wildavsky, *The Private Government of Public Money*, p. 2.

The Work of the Staff as a Sequence of Processes

I have observed that staff are prone to distinguish between form and content, process and substance, declaring that their work is made up of recurrent acts which may be performed on any of the diverse materials that pass through the Ministry and beyond. On one level, therefore, 'process' is intended to refer to those standard practices which transform unique problems into neat, manageable tasks organized for purposes of policy: it is practical, political, and abstracting. As a senior Policy official argued, a policy issue comes into being when:

they say, 'Okay, let's do something about this'. At this point, it becomes a question of taking the circumstances, the issues, developing what the alternatives are and suggesting what the new policy ought to be and how one would implement it. ... Research is providing decision-making information. They're providing insights which will be useful for the policy decision-makers. ... [They're also] actually delivering the product. That's not actually our role. That's policy support. That's their role. But in terms of deciding what the policy ought to look like with some specificity, I think that's very much our role.

Thus, the production, development, and application of substantive ideas are held to lie within the province of the Programs Branch. The construction and arrangement of appearances are policy matters. It is clear that these two styles of activity can never be kept apart with any ease because there can be no substance without form, no programme without organization. Yet some would claim that the two are separate enough to demand the cultivation of their own peculiar arts and skills. Indeed, one policy analyst maintained, 'there's nobody in Research Programs who knows about policy stuff.'

Redefined and on another level, process becomes an attribute of the unfolding timetable of routine bureaucratic events which gives pattern and life to the work of the Ministry staff. The larger history of the Department and the smaller developments that compose it are punctuated by a flow of more or less known and orderly happenings. It is a flow which describes, limits, animates, and lends context to the evolution of work. It enables officials to understand, predict, relate, and pace the making of policy so that it can undergo a successful passage through a planned sequence of phases and changes. More particularly, it imposes meaning on problems so that they emerge as objects requiring a simple and standard manipulation, as 'normal cases'[11] which may be organized

[11] See D. Sudnow, 'Normal Crimes: Sociological Features of the Penal Code in a Public Defender's Office', *Social Problems,* 1965, Vol. 12.

practically. Process then becomes the structure of stages and connections that comprises the work of Ottawa. The Department itself is but an aspect of that structure and, as an aspect, it dictates performance, timing, and objectives within its own sphere. It is a phase of temporal organization, taking some of its character from the succession of events. In turn, the policy-maker must comprehend, master, and enact a series of linked operations which tend to confer increasing authority and solidity on their objects. Policies come to life in those operations, being constituted by them in several distinct ways. Without them, policies would be void, lacking legitimacy, form, substance, and order.

Process of this sort establishes a calendar for action. Failure to comply with that calendar can lead to a postponement or abandonment of an initiative, and demands for appropriately timed and orchestrated action are accordingly quite coercive. There are larger and lesser as well as general and individual calendars, and they significantly intermesh to create a densely figured projection of events into the future. In the early 1980s the chief timetable was the Government's five-year cycle, called a 'rolling horizon', which was altered from year to year. Within that, there was the minor planning cycle based on the Policy and Expenditure Management System, an annual preparation and refurbishing of plans that propelled departments through a great succession of controlled moves. The five-year cycle was itself regulated by the Government Fiscal Plan, a plan which was revised each September and was intended to provide for the current year and the four years which follow it. The Plan embodied a continually altered statement of Government priorities, conceptions of fiscal opportunities and constraints, and the estimated costs of policies and programmes. It specified how funds should be allocated to each of the Cabinet Policy Committees, groupings of departments which were taken to represent natural sectors of policy and administration. The Ministry of the Solicitor General itself was part of the Cabinet Committee on Social Development, chaired by the Minister of State for Social Development, and composed of a considerable aggregation of departments: Communications, Employment and Immigration, Environment, Indian Affairs and Northern Development, Labour, National Health and Welfare, Public Works, Secretary of State, Social Development, Treasury Board Canada, Veterans Affairs, Justice, and the Solicitor General's own department. The common theme which was held to unite the interests of those Ministries was 'the development of approaches to improve and integrate the delivery of social benefits. [The Committee] leads and coordinates the government's efforts to establish and clarify cooperative relations with provinces, the public, and organizations to foster conditions that allow and assist the development of the individual, the family and the community.'[12]

The administration of expenditure was controlled by departments coexisting within different 'envelopes', the Ministry of the Solicitor General sharing the Justice and Legal Envelope with the Department of Justice. Every envelope was allotted a general sum which was to be further divided and awarded to member departments after a period of negotiation between them about the proper size of each share. The business of bargaining, centring on what are called 'trade-offs', was given structure by three principal documents which each department had to draft each year: the Budget Year Operational Plan, the Multi-Year Operational Plan, and the Strategic Overview. The first was a list and justification of short-term expenditures, setting out the 'key operational goals or targets to be realized in the year for which the Estimates are being prepared and the associated resource requirements'.[13] The second included:

> The long-range objectives and strategies which the department is pursuing, the manner in which the department is pursuing [them] through its programs, activities and projects defined in a manner which makes it possible to identify clearly: how each program and activity contributes to the objectives of the department, the benefits and results . . . anticipated for each program and activity for each year over the planning period, [and] the manner in which the efficiency and effectiveness of programs and activities can and will be evaluated as part of the department's program evaluation plan; and historical and projected future trends of the level of demand of program benefits or services and the associated costs.[14]

The Multi-Year Operational Plan was repeatedly revised as the years passed, incorporating shifts in Cabinet social and economic policy, and being subjected to monitoring by the Treasury Board. It was thus itself injected into the annual planning cycle although its timetable was lengthier than a year.

The third document, the Strategic Overview, was an annual prospectus of a department's 'long term objectives and the departmental strategies, policies and programs which meet these objectives'.[15] It was

[12] *The Policy and Expenditure Management System,* Privy Council Office, Ottawa, 1981, p. 23.

[13] *Guide to the Policy and Expenditure Management System,* Ministry of Supply and Services, Canada, Ottawa, 1980, p. 21.

[14] Ibid., p. 21.

[15] Ibid., p. 19.

supposed to contain all the major innovations that a department might contemplate making. Since it is formally maintained that it is Government which formulates policy and departments which execute it, every such innovation had to be related explicitly to stated Government intentions. The Strategic Overview was thus phrased as a response to the signals that were put out by the Priorities and Planning Committee of Cabinet, the annual Speech from the Throne, Ministerial statements, and the like. So defined, it was required to furnish a general review of departmental plans, a discussion of alternative methods of realizing them, and a summary of the findings of evaluation programmes and suggestions for their implementation. In sum, the Strategic Overview was a proposed marriage between departmental plans and expressed Government ambitions, a proposal which other departments had to co-ordinate with their own. It came to represent the major warrant or mandate for future policy development in a department, and its production became one of the chief preoccupations of officials.

I am concerned with the development of the Justice for Victims of Crime Initiative whose midwife was the 1981 Strategic Overview of the Ministry of the Solicitor General. In consequence, I shall remain with the Strategic Overview as an illustration of the bureaucratic process. If my description is dense and detailed, that is in itself evidence of the character of policy-making in Ottawa.

Ministry officials spent much of their time in shepherding papers through the thirteen-part annual cycle which generates the Strategic Overview. By the end of September, the very first phase should have been completed, an anticipatory phase which entailed briefing and confirming with officials the work that was to come. The internal processes of the Ministry were tied in with those of other agencies from the beginning, policy officials reviewing their timetable with colleagues from the Privy Council Office and their superintending central agency, the Ministry of State for Social Development. By the end of October the products of the previous year's Strategic Overview were supposed to have been transferred to the new Budget Year and Multi-Year Operational Plans. During the next month, the foundations of the next Strategic Overview should have been laid, consisting of a synthesis of the local interests of the department and the wider interests of Government and the co-ordinating departments elsewhere in Ottawa. Incorporated into that foundation was expected to be a report on social and economic trends, broad government policy trends, 'specific social policy trends, criminal justice trends, workload trends, status of broad organization, planning procedures, public opinion trends, provincial and private sector conditions and views'.[16] Policy officials were supposed to scan the environment of signs and cues that seemed to reveal Government policy; liaise with other departments, Regional Consultants, Agency and Secretariat Branches; and 'review and incorporate findings and results of recent program evaluations, special research studies, commissions, etc., including results and findings of special conferences, national and international workshops, etc.'.[17]

Another month was then to pass, and in that time the Agencies and Secretariat Branches were to report on what they had accomplished and what they proposed to accomplish in the year to come. After yet another month a draft Strategic Overview was to be distributed to the Agencies and the Secretariat, submitted to the Department of Justice and the Joint Justice Committee, the principal medium for discussion being a series of workshops. By the end of February that draft Strategic Overview was then to be perused by the Minister and his senior officials, ready for presentation to other agencies. The final document was to be in a state of readiness by the end of March, the Ministry of State for Social Development having been consulted, and presented to central agencies in April. And there was much else that attended and stemmed from the central column of work on the Strategic Overview. Indeed, one of the principal functions of the Overview was to provide a licence to proceed with the further labour of developing proposals for submission to Cabinet and the Treasury Board.

The orderly procession of stages that comprises the bureaucratic year achieves a number of distinct and important effects. First, and most obviously, it imposes a rudimentary structure, direction, and composition on any argument that is prepared. Different committees and phases offer an order and sequence of statements. Cabinet documents, for instance, 'have a rigid format. You don't just sort of write one. You have to follow a format. And the only place where you really get into concepts at all is in definition of the problem.' Those committees are intended to achieve particular ends and satisfy particular constituencies: their membership and mandate will also affect the drift of argument. The Joint Justice Committee will demand a proper deference to the interests and projects of the Department of Justice. Joint federal–provincial committees must respect provincial concerns. Interdepartmental committees inject other sensitivities and definitions of problems. In this manner, the future path of a policy development will guide it through a succession of events and interrogations that will elicit a responsive organization of rhetoric, focus,

[16] *1982–83 Strategic Overview Process*, Ministry of the Solicitor General, p. 23.

[17] Ibid.

and substance. When it does finally emerge, that development is likely to bear a relatively standardized impression that records the claims which have been made upon it. Its arguments will bear a set of recognizable signatures, and they will be piled one on the other in a predictable fashion.

Secondly, the introduction of clearly marked stages tends to stagger the flow of events so that work is periodically interrupted. Certain breaks have been transformed into opportunities for officials to 'stop and think' about what they are doing. Even the relatively reflexive work of policy formation is pursued usually without continuous attention to the remoter origins and more distant goals of activity. Instead, staff become absorbed in the immediate detail of their tasks. As a move is made from one stage to another, so a real discontinuity may be introduced that invites reflection. Officials may be called upon to ascertain what they have been doing and what it is that they may yet achieve. In its most generous guise, such a survey of the past and future can be conducted in a workshop or conference, and the bureaucratic year of the Department is peppered with those meetings. They represent an act of withdrawal from the stream of events in which staff are immersed, an interruption in what Bergson called *durée*. As the then Deputy Solicitor General wrote about a proposed Secretariat Workshop, 'I think it very important that organizations such as ours pause every once in a while to take stock of our activities and direction.'[18] It was to be just such a review that prompted officials of the Programs Branch to recognize their involvement with aid to the victims of crime. I shall discuss it below.

Thirdly, the bureaucratic year gives definition and form to the objects of work. It establishes a series of benchmarks stretching back into the past, available in the present, and extending into a set of possible futures. It therefore maps out histories with a discernible shape and intelligible motion. Structured by significant markers and taking shape in time, events come to attain a form that can be grasped and inspected. They begin to acquire a beginning, a middle, and an end. In this sense, the year is read as a source and foundation of the careers of initiatives,[19] and careers are themselves expressions of meaning. As McHugh has argued:

> Actors assume before the fact that a pattern of meaning will be discovered in the events they observe. They are *future oriented*, in that they take it for granted they will be able to make something of what is yet to occur. They are also past oriented, in that they take it for granted that what has already occurred will

[18] Memo to Assistant Deputy Ministers, undated.
[19] See J. Roth, *Timetables*, Bobbs-Merrill, Indianapolis, 1963.

inform the future. Each of these orientations folds back as an actor's description of the present.'[20]

It is the regular train of meetings that allows processes to attain a pattern in time. Officials can proceed to define what is before them, timing what they do and anticipating problems that are to come. Indeed, 'timely' is a word that is employed frequently in Ottawa. It connotes a sense of the unfolding of things. It conveys the idea that the frame of a career and its alignment with other movements will reveal particular moments as opportune and others as inopportune. And policy work will become adjusted to the temporal character of processes. As a policy analyst at Status of Women Canada remarked, political effectiveness depends in part on an intelligent appreciation of what meetings are in the offing, which meetings are critical, and how they combine to form a coherent progression which must be mastered.

An organic metaphor has been introduced into working descriptions of policy: it is as if phenomena are born, mature, and die. Policies themselves begin to acquire a personality and a logic of motion. Policy-makers in their turn believe that they must recognize and move with that rhythm of events. In August 1981, for instance, a senior Programs Branch official announced to a meeting that 'the notion of victims came out of an idea whose time has come'. Not only was the policy developed enough to deserve cultivation, but its environment was equally propitious.

The lives of policy initiatives have more than a structure. They also display different rates and styles of growth which demand their own management. Initiatives will come to assume something of an autonomous and coercive character which can constrain the actions of their authors. Instead of remaining plastic and passive, they will seem to regulate their sponsors.

Interpreted in a special way, timetables may be conceived as a trail of causality, a number of steps logically following upon one another and culminating in a particular effect. They are lists of what must be done, when it must be done, and in what order, mapping out what are tantamount to the bureaucratically potent causes of action. They are teleology at work, future causes feeding back into the present and summoning a response.

It should not be assumed that policy-makers are in full command of bureaucratic processes. On the contrary, timetables are liable to interference, collapse, and collision. As I shall argue, a number of critical turning-points in the history of the victims initiative arose out of unex-

[20] P. McHugh, *Defining the Situation*, Bobbs-Merrill, Indianapolis, 1968, p. 37.

pected incursions from other agencies, departments, and governments. During the course of its evolution, hitherto hidden plans and courses of action revealed themselves, forcing changes on the work of the Solicitor General's officials.

Policies rarely form in isolation. Every stage of an initiative can coincide with some development elsewhere. When timetables and campaigns meet, events are brought together and patterns of causality are introduced to one another. An initiative may then be open to new causes and acquire a new past and a new future which are only dimly understood by its authors. It will be at the play of influences that are alien and unplanned. It may become translated into a kind of communal property, the shared concern of an extended range of people and organizations. Others will come to grasp it as their own, treating it as a convenient vehicle for the promotion of their own ends. Moreover, an initiative, often slow and leisurely in its development, may be expected to pass through a number of political and bureaucratic regimes. It will move from policy environment to policy environment. In its association with diverse contexts and priorities, it can achieve a surprising variety of meanings. A new juxtaposition may always give it sudden importance or rob it of importance altogether.

Policy-making may thus be described as a tangle of timetables and intentions which overlap, strain against one another, and support one another in the different sections of its length. One stage may be a phase of more than one timetable, attaining very different significance in the histories of which it is a part. Indeed, the growth of a major policy is an agglomerate of many little histories which are raggedly distributed within and about it. Some of those little histories will touch on it but fleetingly. Others will become enveloped in it or even fused with it. Their interplay forms another, more complicated layer of causality upon the primary teleological thread of the policy planners.

For example, what appeared as the beginnings of a federal initiative on assistance to the victims of crime was construed by the staff of Status of Women Canada as the faltering of their attempt to develop an initiative on battered women. The politics of family violence may have spurred the Ottawa victims initiative, but the initiative was not to be solely about women. Similarly, all the various projects and programmes supported by the Ministry of the Solicitor General could later come to be clustered together and redefined as the emerging phases of an interest in victims. The Ministry's work on family violence, crime prevention, police training, and victimization surveys could be reappropriated as the necessary precursor of a policy on victims.

Policies moving through bureaucracies in time can produce social structures of some complexity. They are the developing outcomes of processes of organizing which shape and are shaped by their own attendant webs of social relations. When a particular initiative is in motion, it will tend to become the subject of a special division of labour. People will concentrate on its production. It will become an object of interest to outsiders, drawing them in and preparing a geography of relations and activities. As it unwinds, so it will resolve itself into a succession of tasks, each task leading to a possible revisiting of the initiative, its reformulation, and the redeployment of the people who work on it. Every stage will then regroup and repopulate the social circles which animate it. Moreover, as it unwinds, involved officials will discover themselves being propelled through new experiences which transform their knowledge of policy and their reasons for working on it. As one recalled of his induction into work on victims in Ontario, 'I got involved with victims by working on a community alternatives project in 74. The more I dealt with victims, the more I knew that nothing was done and so the community alternatives area expanded and we developed more victims programmes. And the more VORP [Victim–Offender Reconciliation Projects] I developed, the more I got to know about victims.' There is a dialectical form to such experiences, an initiative constituting knowledge and knowledge constituting an initiative. Importantly, it is a dialectic that can change selves. It is an embedded career, and careers have been described by Van Maanen as 'lives in progress'.[21] In this sense, policies place people, build social worlds, and generate pools of knowledge and motives which return to alter the direction and significance of work. They will produce co-ordinated changes of context, structure, action, and actors, a series of wave functions that ripple through Ministries and affect their environment.

As I describe the unfolding of the initiative, so I shall point to the way in which people were assigned to work for differing lengths of time on various facets of the project. As the initiative entered their careers, so it was to be modulated by their experience, aspirations, social relations, and special duties. Parts of that initiative were to be incorporated into the biographies of officials in an uneven manner. For some, the initiative was to be of fleeting interest although, as one observed, 'if you put a lot of work into something you don't want to see it fall dead. Not that I'm particularly committed to that area [of victims].' For others, it was to be a matter of passionate engagement and lasting involvement. Indeed,

[21] J. Van Maanen, preface to *Organizational Careers: Some New Perspectives*, John Wiley and Sons, London, 1977, p. i.

some had gathered about the initiative in order to pursue policies that were of grave concern to them. Outsiders began to associate the initiative with the lives and doings of named individuals, giving the policy a personality that was to be merged with that of its authors. It was to become a form of bureaucratic property, the recognized complement of particular people, bearing their mark and becoming an extension of their selves. And there were to be different ways in which that ownership could be exhibited. There were those identified as 'stars', 'and you need stars because they get visibility and that's important ... they're the stars, the publicisers'. There were also the 'quiet people' who worked unobtrusively to attain their ends. 'Stars' tend to attract some opprobrium, it being suspected that initiatives are employed in some measure as vehicles of self-aggrandizement. One official talked of the style of one star as 'overly flamboyant and assertive, it was "me, me, me!!" you know'.

It is evident that officials create initiatives that create something of themselves. After all, there would be no activity at all without human agency. At different times and in different ways, people would attain a strategic role which allowed them to impel the initiative onwards. And officials would try to place themselves in just such a role, creating it if necessary, in the effort to give prominence to issues that concerned them. Their activities were grounded in the flow of bureaucratic processes, being symbiotic with them. I shall describe them as 'animating', although animation captures only part of what they do. In the emerging social structure of an initiative, animators arise to shape what is happening, nursing events to ensure that streams of approved ideas and proposals move before the appropriate audiences at the correct speed and in proper sequence. They will sometimes proselytize, trying to modify or deflect the thinking of others. They are much more than the passive recipients of structures and schemes established elsewhere and by other people. They energetically work to transform organizations. One who played a strategic role in the victims initiative reflected:

I've played, I think, a pushing role or whatever in terms of getting other people on board, you know. And the way I did that, for example, was I've written memos and gone to Directors in the Branch to say victims would be a good area for a model project for the Branch to show close relationships between the Consultation Centre and Research and Communications and Statistics etcetera. You know. But many of those things just end and we really don't know what happens to them. But combine that with memos that I've written for the ADM's signature to the ADM in Policy saying 'we think victims should be something that we do more on', and things like that, you know. Letters that I've prepared for the Minister's signature in response to letters that the Minister had received that touched on victims. ... I mean, where the people preparing the drafts etcetera came to see me and I gave them material to read and I talk to them for an afternoon or whatever and go over various issues.

Animation and attachment are in some measure the situated properties of evolving initiatives. Every stage and part of a piece of policy-making can prepare special experiences for those who encounter them. There is an inevitable strain towards the differentiation and compartmentalization of knowledge and sentiment, events being immediate to some officials and not to others, and that strain can transform an initiative into a topography of different regions, some well known and the subject of emotion, others distant and relatively devoid of interest. Such mapping tends to have repercussions on the way in which animating roles are negotiated, assumed, maintained, and relinquished. A policy proposal may be a matter that is easily relinquished. It may become the intimate property of an official. As areas get marked off, so responses and motives develop. Those officials who work in an area for any length of time, form an expertise and perhaps a reputation, will probably acquire an existential stake and pride in what they do. Their fondness for the area will lead to an enhancement of expertise, and so a dialectic is carried onwards. Those officials who have only tangential contacts with an initiative may form a somewhat more appraising and cool stance, a structural marginality being mirrored by a marginality of sentiment. One such official had not worked continuously on the victims' initiative. He commented about the formation of attachments to the victims' initiative:

There are very few people who like to be seen as not doing good, and as not having a mission. Maybe I'm not as different as I'd like to think I am. I happen to think I don't have any illusions. ... I've almost made it one of my stocks in trade not to have any illusions. I'm often seen as cynical but I really think I am without illusions. And I think there are a lot of people in this world who have illusions and need to have them. And they're very nice to have. Like they're generally very comforting. So I don't think people like to say that they are good manipulators of the system (and I'm not using the word manipulate in a pejorative sense). I don't think people like to say that that's what their stock in trade is. ... It's not considered an attractive notion that you deal with an issue like victims just because ... like today you're selling soap and yesterday you sold nails.

By contrast, it will be recalled, there were many officials who described themselves and their colleagues as moved by compassion. And there was some uncertainty about how those different postures evolved and whether they should be ascribed to social position, to personality, or to some interweaving of the two. It is none the less interesting that the most committed seemed to be discovered at the core of the division of labour that centred on the victims' initiative, the least committed on the periphery. In part, their location stemmed from election, in part from the vagaries of chance.

Opportunities for animation, sentiment, and detachment were never settled. They pulsated in sympathy with the movement of the initiative from bureaucratic setting to bureaucratic setting, with the traffickings of staff, and with the emergence and demise of crises. Every official seemed to regard the initiative as an amalgamation of little personal histories that were sometimes quite disjointed. Indeed, the lives of projects and individuals were not still, and they intersected in odd ways. Ottawa is a small world and its population is busy and mobile. Officials tend not to remain with one task for very long. Their work will take them from place to place and duty to duty, allowing them to develop their ideas and experience as they go. The history of the victims' initiative itself has been peopled with only a modest cast of actors who seem to have changed roles with each new scene. Thus the Solicitor General who fostered the initiative had been a Member of Parliament without Cabinet rank in 1975. As a Member of Parliament, he had sat on the Standing Committee on Health, Welfare, and Social Affairs which had studied 'appropriate measures for the prevention, identification and treatment of child abuse and neglect'.[22] It had been he who had questioned the then Solicitor General, Warren Allmand, about Ministerial policy towards a group of victims. He also questioned Bruce Rawson, at that time Deputy Minister of Health and Welfare, who was later to become Deputy Minister of State for Social Development, a major sponsor of the victims' initiative and a significant collaborator with the Deputy Solicitor General. Similarly, an official of the Department of Justice had served on the Interdepartmental Committee on Family Violence which examined wife battering. In 1981 she had become a policy analyst at the Ministry of State for Social Development, perusing the Strategic Overviews of the Ministry of the Solicitor General and of her own former Department, making recommendations based on her experience of the Interdepartmental Committee. Again, an official of the Ministry of the Solicitor General had advised the Canadian Delegation to the Sixth United Nations Congress on the Prevention of Crime. He had also convened a

[22] *Minutes of Proceedings and Evidence of the Standing Committee on Health, Welfare and Social Affairs,* House of Commons, 1975–6.

Secretariat Workshop in October 1980. Both the Delegation and the Workshop were to make significant contributions to the formation of a victims' initiative. But when the time came for the Departments of the Solicitor General and Justice to prepare a joint Memorandum to Cabinet, the official had removed to the Department of Justice and it was he who liaised with his former Ministry. It is in this fashion that a few names are repeated incessantly in the documents and talk which bear on the initiative. It is as if there were an elaborate masked ball in which the steps, costumes, and partners changed continually in a great patterned movement. As the ball proceeds, and as officials pass from department to department and committee to committee, they bear with them evolving and fragmented stocks of knowledge and conceptions of the process.

Not only do officials move through committees in serial manner, they may also be members of a number of committees at any one time, representing a personal synthesis of different little histories and experiences. For instance, some policy analysts are members of feminist organizations and they have injected ideas from those associations into the proceedings of government bodies. Others are police officers, or affiliated with private sector groups like the John Howard Society or academic groups involved with criminology and victimology. Collectively, they weld together a great mass of different pieces of Canadian and international history, forming conduits along which pass very diverse influences. It is in their persons that causality is realized, allowing organizations to work on one another.

The interplay between people, organizations, and committees is even more complex because of the curiously dense and intertwined quality of relations in Ottawa. Official Ottawa is a small world made up of those who know each other well, form attachments and enmities, have families and contract marriages. A site of work is also a site of sociability. In a felicitous phrase, Heclo and Wildavsky have chosen to describe Ottawa's British counterpart as a society organized by kinship and the life of the village.[23] A social anthropological map of the Ottawa departments would also reveal elaborate patterns of consanguinity, affinity, and friendship, patterns which also serve as the basis of flows of communication and practical activity. Businesses, organized crime networks,[24] and civil services seem to display common features. They are mediated by the gossip and activity of the little society. They are structured by kinship. Cousin

[23] See H. Heclo and A. Wildavsky, *The Private Government of Public Money*.

[24] See F. Ianni, *A Family Business: Kinship and Social Control in Organized Crime*, Russell Sage-Basic Books, New York, 1972.

may face cousin or brother face brother in meetings. Thus, the Minister responsible for the Status of Women was the brother of the Parliamentary draftsman who composed the Throne Speech of 1980. Policy documents prepared by an official of the Ministry of the Solicitor General were inspected by his cousin at another department. Formal flows of authority were thereby shaped and complemented by informal flows.

A palpable result of all this complexity, turbulence, and uncertainty is that it is never quite clear what will become of present action. After all, no official can know what is taking place in all the other agencies and departments of Ottawa, in ten provincial governments, in the United States, and beyond. Neither can he or she predict changes of governments, the rise and fall of Ministers, the fortunes of the economy, or the crises that beset the criminal justice system. And those events tend to play themselves out in surprising ways. There is an organized preparedness for the unexpected. Apparently promising events might lead nowhere or take odd directions. Old and seemingly extinct initiatives may sometimes be revived and brought to a new conclusion. When so much is tentative, officials are sometimes forced to content themselves with the erection of skeleton structures that can always be more fully exploited in time to come. They place token markers which can be revived when it is timely to do so. Those markers are necessarily ambiguous, designed to be used later in strange contexts and for purposes as yet unknown. Ottawa officials do as their colleagues in Washington do, prepare for an undisclosed future. As Feldman remarks of the writing of policy papers in the American federal government:

> People writing reports do not know if the reports will be used or how. They do not know which aspects of which issues will become controversial and which ones will cease to be questioned. . . . I suggest that it may make sense to think of policy papers not as responses to specific problems but as an inventory of responses to possible future problems.[25]

Ambiguity and tentativeness are features that inevitably flow out of the convention that policy statements must be produced as replies to Government decisions. Constitutionally, as I have argued, government departments are required to execute the priorities established by Cabinet and Parliament. They are not independent and they have little authority to move as if they are. There can be no substantial and costly work undertaken unless it furthers goals already confirmed by the Govern-

[25] M. Feldman, 'Producing Policy Papers', paper prepared for a symposium on information processing in organizations, Carnegie-Mellon University, 14–16 Oct. 1982, pp. 30, 33.

ment. Neither is it possible to undertake such work in the hope that it may sway Government. It must be justified by what has been expressly approved. It is for this reason that a number of the documents bearing on victims had to be grounded in a minute exegesis of Cabinet and Government statements.

A curious distortion emerges. Since present activity has to be lodged in an environment of stated Government priorities, all work tends to be defined by what has been chronicled of the past. Proposals must be rhetorically draped around the particular concerns of Government. They take on an occasionally alien disguise. For instance, I shall show how victims first entered the Ministry of the Solicitor General as part of the Peace and Security Package of 1976. The Package contained a collection of measures which were intended to bring an end to capital punishment. Plans for a victimization survey were offered as an instrument of crime prevention, aimed at easing the effects of abolition. Arguments were marshalled to explain the survey's relevance to crime prevention and the survey did bear the mark of those arguments. But it should be noted that those who had first contemplated surveying victims had not considered linking their work with the ending of the death penalty. Neither was the survey to remain in the framework set by the abolition debate. At the moment of its adoption, however, not only was there no other available initiative to bear a survey but the Package offered a plausible enough anchorage for survey work.

It is in this manner that policies in train give special significance to their elements. Work is always stamped by a special kind of political genetics. Yet it is known that what has been done can be rearranged, grasped and put to different use later in a different context and with a new meaning. Settings and their constituents are not fixed. They move together or apart as historical events evolve in Ottawa. Policy-makers must be correspondingly alert to the presence of multivocality, recognizing the ambiguity of processes, and allowing a continuous work of reconstruction to occur. There is no stability about the political past. As Mead argued, 'a past never was in the form in which it appears a past. Its reality is in its interpretation of the present.'[26] The Canadian past changes to provide causality for the present. What might not have been causal can become so if it is needed and, curiously, the influence which it will then exert will be as 'real' as any other. It can constrain the present, altering conduct and supplying motives. It is as if officials haul a shifting past after them, its changes reflecting present necessities. That

[26] G. Mead, *The Philosophy of the Act*, University of Chicago Press, Chicago, 1938, p. 616.

past is convincing enough, acting as an increasingly solid backcloth to action. One official recalled, for instance:

It's so difficult to know what one thought at the time because what happened is that one developed all sorts of arguments to persuade other people and then you started believing them. I mean, one of the things that I've used in arguments to advance the notion of the victims issue is the notion that it's cost effective for the system. Well, I think there's lots of good reasons for doing things that have nothing to do with being cost effective but, if that's an argument that holds sway, then use it. And I've used the argument that if victims are not treated in a reasonably dignified manner, if their passage through the criminal justice system isn't expedited in some way, they become unco-operative witnesses and less likely to turn to the system in the future. And that does have cost elements because it has something to do with the quality of justice in the system. I can't remember whether those are arguments that I developed after the interest or whether they were there and prompted the interest.

The ambiguity and indeterminacy of policy processes are reinforced in other ways that demand some preliminary sketch. First, as initiatives move out into the world, they are likely to implicate an increasingly wide circle of people and organizations who acquire a stake in their future. Policies recede from the immediate control of their original authors, becoming exposed to the influence of those whose intentions and interests can never be completely transparent at the outset. Indeed, those intentions are emergent, themselves framed by new initiatives and dependent on the course taken by policies.

When the victims initiative attained a rudimentary form, it was presented to an array of departments and agencies by its creators, the Ministries of the Solicitor General and Justice. Those consultations, in their turn, prepared the way for further talks with other organizations. The initiative was revealed to an evolving group which progressively redefined its character and the populations which it might affect. As a policy analyst remarked at the time, 'to get something recognised as an initiative, as opposed to just doing it piecemeal, you have to go through this procedure. It's got a number of reasons for being. It pulls departments together. It forces people to talk to each other. It's a kind of catalytic tool.' She was also to remark, 'there's so many departments and interest groups that have some kind of a connection with a service, or have an intellectual pursuit that has some kind of connection with victims. And everybody defines it differently. It's a problem. The definition is one of the enormous problems and, in a way, it's being defined simply by which departments and agencies are taking some interest in it.' It was in this sense that the victims initiative generated a social structure that transformed it. No policy official can predict with certainty how that dialectical process will resolve itself.

All that officials can have is a set of vague and stereotyped expectations about probable conduct, expectations which he or she realizes might well be confounded. It was not evident at the very beginning that National Defence Canada would take an interest in the initiative because of its concern with the battering of wives on military bases. Nor was it evident that National Health and Welfare, responsible for transition houses and rape crisis centres, would take rather little interest in the initiative. The staff of the Ministry of the Solicitor General were puzzled:

> It was mentioned to Health and Welfare that if they wanted to sort of attach themselves to it, that would be just fine. And that strengthens any submission, you see. The more departments you get submitting it, the more likely it is it's going through. . . . And it was quite surprising in a way that Health and Welfare didn't become more involved because they're launching a Clearing House on Family Violence and it would have been a lovely opportunity for them to get some extra funds. And I still don't know why they decided not to. They're deciding just to find the funding for this Clearing House from within, and I know they don't have a whole ton of money. So it's quite puzzling why they would do that. I mean they were given a golden opportunity. It was so easy for them to just add on.

It is the business of policy analysts to make intelligent forecasts of the replies which others will make to their work. But there is evident unpredictability and a changeability of structure. Moreover, work and its answering replies fold back on themselves in an endless regression of causes and effects. And predictions must accommodate their own consequences. There is no real confidence that can be sensed in officials' visions of the future. Not only does the object of description change, but frameworks of interpretation shift in sympathy with it and with other, as yet unknown events. None of the officials I met felt certain about the eventual fate of the victims initiative. One stated, 'I don't know, it feels funny, doesn't it? In a way, it's interesting to talk about because it points out how very uncertain it is and how very ill-defined. . . .' And another stated, 'I have no conception of what it's going to look like in four or five years. Whether it's going to be another kind of diversion-like exercise or child abuse-like exercise which sounds like a good idea but doesn't go anywhere, or whether it really will become something of importance.' And the Director of Policy Planning himself asserted that he had no long-term conception of the future of the initiative: 'no, oh no. My own planning horizon's about twenty four months.' Of course, certainties shift along the length of an initiative's history, but there was a continual openness to the prospect of untoward things happening.

Perhaps the most interesting source of indeterminacy is the deliberate policy of political self-restraint which must be practised by the officials of a federal government. Vagueness and flexibility are actually nurtured as necessary components of much Canadian criminal justice policy. It will be remembered that the federal government must play a somewhat restricted role in the administration of the criminal justice system. At the very least, it is politic to approach provincial and private sector organizations in a conciliatory and co-operative fashion. It would be especially imprudent to present them with proposals that appear so coherent and well argued that no further work needs to be done. Raggedness and incompleteness are deliberately fed into many of the documents which come out of Ottawa. Like Persian carpets, they are deliberately flawed to ward off anger. It is as if proposals were designed to advertise the indispensability of consultation. Indeed, provincial and private bodies are well placed to tender useful advice. They are the potential executors of much policy, receiving and creating the local knowledge that will affect its reception. Thus one of the authors of a critical memorandum observed, 'it was very awkward because it was very difficult to sort of second guess what was going to happen with the federal–provincial thing, to write it in such a way that we would leave ourselves open enough that if something happened with the federal–provincial thing that wasn't what we'd predicted, we'd still be covered for it, and yet make it look convincing enough that in fact we'd get money for it.' And an Acting Assistant Deputy Minister stated a little later and before some crucial meetings, 'you don't want the plans so cut and dry by, say, October or November or whenever it is that there's no flexibility in them, so that you can't take account of what's going on at the NOVA Conference.' Indeterminacy and looseness are thus introduced for political reasons. Policy cannot be given a rigid form in Ottawa until it has been sanctioned by others. As Marsland has observed of the process at large, 'in many organizations policies are left inexplicit for good organizational reasons and their explication would be resisted'.[27]

The Ministry as a Site: the Workplace of the Staff

As a site, the Ministry may be identified principally with a large building in Laurier Avenue West, Ottawa. It is a place where a considerable

[27] D. Marsland, 'Sociologists and Social Policy', *Social Policy and Administration,* Spring 1983, Vol. 17, No. 1, p. 7.

number of people gather and work every day. Some 225 Secretariat staff congregate, talk, gossip, and view one another in the relatively unobstructed arena formed by a series of open plan offices. In this sense, the Ministry may be regarded as a concentration and acceleration of social life which is both physically and formally separated from a wider environment. In the daytime, officials are obliged to have rather more to do with one another than with people outside the building. They must resolve ways of accommodating themselves to continuous, running relationships and surveillance. They must publicly present themselves, their projects, and their plans, forming assessments of the character of others and being assessed in their turn. Of course, the little worlds that are so formed do not merge into one another without boundaries. The Policy and Programs Branches are housed on separate floors of the building: Programs Branch staff see and know more of each other than they do of their colleagues in policy work, and the work and characters of the Progams Branch attain greater familiarity as a result. Moreover, not all are equally exposed. The most senior officials are shielded by being located in somewhat inaccessible parts of the building, protected by their secretaries and staff. The Minister himself has been provided with an office with locked doors and controlled entrance. Other officials have been given solid walls which guard them from the gaze of others. Indeed, as a rough principle, social standing can be gauged by the extent to which one is exposed to monitoring.

Most officials *are* required to conduct their affairs in the sight of their colleagues. Mutual surveillance was to become especially pronounced when, in the summer of 1981, a reorganization of the offices introduced only the most token divisions between the spaces occupied by junior staff. Slender portable barriers were placed around different areas, ostensibly marking out private and public territory. Those barriers did not obstruct vision entirely and they certainly did little to suppress sound. Further, there seemed to be a very real uncertainty about the significance and boundaries of privacy: staff were constrained to engage in private talk in public space. Intentional or unintentional eavesdropping became commonplace. Telephone conversations were to become widely audible.

Much work within the Ministry has thereby taken on an inescapably public complexion: it is set within a context of collective concerns and judgement, generalized rather than individualized. It is the subject of chatter and talk as officials wend their way along the paths traced by the positioning of barriers. There are meeting places near coffee machines and photocopiers. A social geography of relationships has developed, a kind of village life, based on thoroughfares, public spaces, and the physical arrangement of offices. People in adjoining rooms or areas share an enforced or willed neighbourliness, and there is much of what Young and Willmott's East Enders would have called 'popping in'.[28] In their encounters, in their casual talk before and after committee meetings, in the little asides made during the meetings themselves, in the conversations at conferences and in airport departure lounges, a social world is created and reproduced. It is a world constituted by gossip and, as Heclo and Wildavsky observe of the British Treasury, 'one could commit no greater error than to think that this village gossip, because it is sometimes frivolous and haphazard, is therefore unimportant. . . . Co-ordination . . . is based, above all, on a never ending round of personal contacts among people who know each other and have a strong professional interest in talking about their work.'[29] The social world of the Ministry of the Solicitor General has come to acquire something of a corporate identity, a special way of doing things that sets it apart. Thus a frequent visitor to the Ministry and a contributor to the victims initiative remarked, 'I guess over the years, most of us now working in victims services have met one another many, many times over many meetings, cups of coffee, social and professional meetings, that we have really begun to accept one another's points of view and integrated with a common purpose.'

To be sure, the victims initiative also developed in other meetings held inside and outside Ottawa, in telephone conversations and in letters. But a major catalyst was the housing together of a group of people over a long period of time. For them, the Ministry has come to represent an environment in which people can be met, business conducted and projects formulated. It has come to acquire a large range of meanings. Small areas have been carved out and set aside as personal territories. Offices have been domesticated, decorated with prints, tapestries, and ornaments, displaying bits of their occupants' biographies. They have become homely. It is revealing, for instance, that distress was voiced when the 1981 programme of office reorganization proposed that officials' house-plants should be replaced by specimens supplied and tended by a contractor. There was resentment that a symbolic assertion of territory and ownership should be dismissed. Thus transformed, the Ministry has become significant as a place in which people spend a great portion of their lives, acquire the makings of an identity, form attachments and antipathies, and build perspectives on themselves and their work. It is

[28] See M. Young and P. Willmott, *Family and Kinship in East London,* Routledge and Kegan Paul, London, 1957.

[29] H. Heclo and A. Wildavsky, *The Private Government of Public Money,* p. 71.

much more than an instrument of government: it is a social world with all the interest, intrigue, and intricacy of any other sizeable social setting.

The Problems of Origins

It would be misleading to imagine that the Ministry is homogeneous. It is differentiated internally by role, rank, and function. Its staff tend to be grouped by the tasks which they are set. They are sometimes separated physically. Over time, the Ministry has come to resemble a shifting and unstable collection of parallel social universes which do not necessarily duplicate or complement one another. Working inside those universes, officials tended to understand the history of the victims initiative rather differently. Instead of attending to the same project with a common purpose, they seemed for a long while to be participating in a number of distinct enterprises with different priorities, pasts, and conceptions of the future. Indeed, there was no agreement until quite late that there was a joint task at hand. In time, documents and official accounts began to supply something of a master history of the initiative, a history which assumed authority and supplanted the lesser and more tentative accounts. But it could well have been otherwise: the work that was done might have been classified and arranged in any number of ways, being covered by very different histories.

The segmentation of experience into separate streams is almost certainly typical of any complex social process. After all, who but the historian with his or her vision of a closed and determinate world could ever see everything that took place?[30] Those embedded in processes witness only a little, can ask few questions and cannot always foresee the ends of their activity. And the historian's everything is an analytic abstraction based on a surmise about what was important. Unless a common response is coaxed or forced into being by some event, objective, or group, it is likely that people will continue to inhabit their own small and somewhat secluded strips of existence. Institutions do not require their members to share an identical experience of the world. Such an identity is impossible and it is not clear how it could ever be recognized by an observer. It is only after the event that there may be a limited agreement about what was significant. In any practical situation, a working complementarity of perspectives will usually do. There is little alternative: common understandings are not necessary, they are not feasible, and they are not ascertainable. Indeed, when tasks and cir-

[30] See A. Schutz, 'The World of Predecessors and the Problem of History', in *Collected Papers*, Vol. II, Martinus Nijhoff, The Hague, 1964.

cumstances do not demand the fitting-together of thought and action, even complementarity may be unnecessary. At most times, experience and knowledge are parochial enough matters with their own pace and structure of development. All that is required is the assumption that common understanding could arise at need.

It is only when a comprehensive history is produced that people may begin to grasp some of the wider meanings of what they have done. What can later be reconstructed as the orderly and ineluctable movement of groups and processes is usually experienced as a mass of fleeting episodes that are both ambiguous and confusing. Events are often negotiated pragmatically and from second to second. Those who fight in battle, for instance, rarely undergo a process which is even remotely similar to the story told in military dispatches or conventional histories. Thus Keegan argued:

> The soldier is vouchsafed no . . . well-ordered and clear-cut vision. Battle, for him, takes place in a wildly unstable physical and emotional environment; he may spend much of his time in combat as a mildly apprehensive spectator, granted, by some freak of events, a comparatively danger-free grandstand view of others fighting; then he may suddenly be able to see nothing but the clods on which he has flung himself for safety, there to crouch—he cannot anticipate—for minutes or for hours; he may feel in turn boredom, exultation, panic, anger, sorrow, bewilderment, even that sublime emotion we call courage. And his perception of community with his fellow-soldiers will fluctuate in equal measure.[31]

Very similarly, Punch argued that the Dutch police force is not known to its members as 'a cohesive bastion of the repressive state apparatus' but as an organization based on 'fluidity, bargaining for power and status, coalitions, conflicts, the keeping up of appearances, disharmony, accounts, various interpretations of reality, and the ubiquity of rule-breaking'.[32] It seems that, even in the best regulated worlds, everyday life is rarely grasped as a comprehensively planned, orderly, and unambiguous part of a larger entity called social structure or social history.

For most of its evolution, the victims initiative should be described as little more than an agglomerate of discrete experiences. Indeed, the very discussion of its earliest phases as part of an initiative is somewhat illegitimate. No one really conceived of the initiative as an initiative at that time and the word 'victim' was not generally applied for quite a while. Events lacked the coherence which they were to attain later. They had a different coherence. A number of people laid claim to them.

[31] J. Keegan, *The Face of Battle,* Penguin Books, Harmondsworth, 1978, p. 46.

[32] M. Punch, *Management and Control of Organizations,* H. E. Stenfert Kroese B.V., Leiden, 1981, pp. 19, 5.

Instead of one consistent history, there were several unrelated stories which reflect the initially dispersed distribution of knowledge and experience. There were many pools of knowledge within the Ministry itself, each one offering a distinct account of the origins and causal texture of the process and each one consequently guiding it in a different direction.

As people moved in and out of the stream of events, so their movements left an imprint on the interpretations which they made of what took place. Most vivid in their memory were recollections of the pieces of action in which they had actually participated. Around that central core was a somewhat murkier zone which housed memories of reports read and talk heard. Yet still further out was another zone composed only of generalized expectations and surmises about the probable course of events. Every official who had worked on the initiative was an authority on some aspect of it, but that authority did not necessarily extend very far and it was lodged in its own very personal context of significance.

One particularly vital boundary to knowledge was drawn by the timing and duration of an official's immediate exposure to the policy process. The dates and length of personal involvement shaped what fragments of the history would have been seen, how they were surveyed, in what company, and what sense would have been attached to them. Some people joined the flow after a major turning point had passed. Others left before important events became fully visible. Thus Irvin Waller had been the principal champion of victims assistance within the Ministry. In August 1980 he said that he resigned in protest at the failure of the Ministry to develop an effective commitment to the victims of crime. But it was only eleven months later that Cabinet agreed to the mounting of a federal initiative on the problem.

Most of the staff who advanced the initiative had been employed in the Department for rather a short while. Of the nine who were most strategically placed, three had been engaged in 1974, one in 1975, two in 1976, one in 1977, one in 1978, and one in 1981. In a young Ministry, it was only three officials who had witnessed most of the evolving span of the initiative. The others had come to it when events were already in train, being able to piece together no more than a second-hand account of what had gone before. Moreover, they did not work incessantly on one problem but experienced a number of contacts of varying lengths, at different times, and with more or less abrupt beginnings and endings. For instance, one official was to play a critical role in convening and organizing a National Workshop on Services to Victims in 1980 but she had no part in the preparation of the Strategic Overview the next year. Similarly, much of the early work on victims was undertaken by a policy analyst who was to become involved in other matters, being replaced by another official in the critical month of April 1981. The Solicitor General himself had known little of the initiative before his appointment in March 1980. It is this mobility of staff that has produced a patchwork made up of little areas of intense competence that are often unrelated to one another and to their surroundings.

The second major boundary to knowledge was drawn by the functional and physical location of officials. Staff are scattered throughout the Ministry, working on various tasks and collaborating with a range of people from inside and outside the building. The initiative was to enter their domains in a number of special forms, acquiring its personality from their practical interests and their place in the division of labour. Their work offered officials a series of windows on the world, allowing them to view facets of the initiative and give them an organization. For instance, policy analysts working in the Police and Security Branch and in the Royal Canadian Mounted Police tended to endow the initiative with a past that was fused with the concerns and activities of the police. A major animator of the initiative, a Staff Sergeant based at the Royal Canadian Mounted Police Crime Prevention Centre, remarked, 'the police officer sees the victims when they've just been beaten up. They've seen them when they're bloody and they're torn and they're afraid. . . . And when our whole criminal justice system, for many years, has been paying attention to the offender . . . the police have constantly been crying almost alone within the criminal justice system, "what about the victim?"'

By contrast, a senior official, then in the Community Programs Division of the Ontario Ministry of Correctional Services attributed the rise of the victims initiative largely to community work pioneered in the United States and Canada. He pointed to the contribution of a former colleague who was to join the Ministry of the Solicitor General in Ottawa. That colleague himself argued that the initiative might be traced back to the early community programmes that had been launched in Ontario and elsewhere. It had been stipulated that regard must be paid to the protection of the victim when offenders were released from prison to join community projects. From that initial concern had grown all the policy development which was to mature into the federal proposals for victims assistance.

Again, feminists searched the history of their own world and explained the appearance of an interest in victims by the opposition that had been mustered to confront proposed changes in the law on rape. One feminist lawyer asserted:

I think one of the big reasons that those problems became issues may have been the increase in the number of professional women, women who were able to articulate those issues. Prior to that, we didn't have a lot of women in the legal profession much before the early '70s. Now I think the motivation . . . came from women in the legal profession. Those were women who were most aware of it.

Each social circle thereby affords its own focused vision of what had happened. And each provides an accompanying blurring of vision. Officials and participants did not know, and normally knew that they did not know, all that had passed. Theirs was an inevitably circumscribed understanding. Thus a senior official could not explain how it was that the suppression of violence to women had been asserted as a Government priority in the Speech from the Throne of 1980. A policy analyst could not give an account of the part played by provincial officials who had significantly publicized the needs of victims. The man who organized a most important conference on victims assistance knew little about its intended political links with a forthcoming conference of Federal and Provincial Ministers Responsible for Criminal Justice. And so it went on. Each person tended to have a more or less sophisticated comprehension of a portion of activity. Each in turn had a different story to tell, a story with its own plot, chapters and heroes. Each person modelled that plot on identified causes whose development explained the present.

The very conception of the structure and passing of time seemed to be affected by the social organization of the initiative. Seniority and function conspired to provide very different ideas about the character of policies as objects and the manner in which they came to life over time. Consider research. Very often the bureaucratic sensibility defined research as relatively slow, continuous, and incremental. It translated its materials into a gradually expanding and diffusely interconnected programme of action. Segments of that activity might have paraded under different official names as the legitimating mantle of policy and budgets changed, but research staff regarded it as one coherent and largely uninterrupted enterprise. Since the Ministry was first established in 1966, it had concentrated on crime prevention, diversion, police–community relations, assistance to victims, and a host of other measures. It was really all one to the Research Division of the Programs Branch.

By extension, proprietorship was itself diffuse and incremental. There were no abrupt fissures or faults that announced the abandoning or supercession of the Research Division's concerns. Projects and programmes did not begin and end suddenly. Instead, they blurred into one another. Thus I was reproached a number of times by an official who thought that I was endowing the victims initiative with an excess of individuality and isolation. He maintained that the initiative could not be distinguished from its environment of research and projects:

A lot of the things we do are related to crime prevention. Now we may sometimes, for financial reasons for example, put it under the victims initiative but it is intertwined with the Ministry's longstanding interest in policing, for example, crime prevention. ... These things are longstanding and will continue to be longstanding issues of the Ministry, and the Cabinet decision on victims may add some additional emphasis to the victims perspective, it certainly has, but it's still part and parcel, it's artificial to say this is a victims initiative or a crime prevention initiative or a policing initiative. It's all three. It relates to all three. It tries to impose a simplicity to ask, 'oh, which one is it?' You know, many of the things we do relate to many different activities, and one mustn't be confused because, for financial purposes, we have to assign a particular project to one of our codes—victim, crime prevention, policing. ... We shouldn't confuse that oversimplification with the fundamental reason why we're doing it. You know we're doing it for a lot of things, you know, victims certainly, but there's also the Ministry's ongoing mandate which is in terms of policing and crime prevention. And those have long been priorities of the Ministry and will continue to be priorities of the Ministry. ... So I'm saying that simply to keep things in focus because, as an outsider, it's fairly easy to say, 'oh, this is victims and that's this'. For a lot of projects it's a simplification for administrative and budgetary purposes. You shouldn't confuse that with why we're doing it. Why we're doing it is part of a much larger and much more complex interrelated kind of activity.

Research concerns also tended to be slowly paced by the local standards of bureaucratic time, consisting of activities that might last three years in isolation but stretch over much longer periods when yoked together. The life of a piece of research could then be quite protracted, undertaken by staff or contracted to outsiders, planned, discussed, organized, piloted, executed, assessed, and reported. It might take years before an answer of any moment might appear.

Policy work is characteristically designed to grasp the propitious moment. It is dominated by a sense of the timeliness of things, an apprehension that political opportunities will appear and disappear. There is a presumption that an occasion lost can condemn a policy, and it may lead policy officials to seize their chances even when research staff would protest that they are not ready. There is rarely a perfect coincidence of research and policy timetables because the opportune moment is often independent of official planning. A project could become timely when a Government or a Minister or an economy changes, and policy officials must respond. To be sure, the Policy Branch can modulate its environment and create openings for itself. It can also reconstruct events and projects so that they complement one another. But there is always the

projects so that they complement one another. But there is always the problem of the adventitious happening, the colliding timetable and the sudden accessibility of funds. When the moment occurs, other timetables must be distorted or aborted. Activities may then tend to arrive in relatively short spurts which are intense. Their objects are rather more precisely bounded and discrete than those of the Research Division. Of course, there is a recognition of the continuing interests of the Ministry and of the manner in which they form a whole, but policy work focuses on well-defined and restricted jobs. Unless some permanent institutional arrangements are established to monitor and maintain a policy, as they were in the instance of firearms control, work tends to take the guise of distinct parcels of activity. Speaking in the summer of 1982, the Director of Policy Planning stated that the matter of victims would be 'past history by the Fall of 83. ... For us it will be. It should be. You've got to let it go at some point. ... It'll be all over the system and then, having done that, you're going to go away and maybe come back to it in ten years.'

For those who attend to specific aspects of policy development, the timing and character of initiatives will also take on rather local forms. Officials in the Planning and Liaison Division, for example, concentrate on the dissemination of knowledge about policies, organizing meetings, setting-up resource centres and the like. Their competence is exploited at particular periods only. Indeed, as I shall argue, there are occasions when they feel excluded from the larger work of the Ministry. Touching on initiatives when policies require publicization, assessment, and discussion, they attain an imagery of fitful eruptions of business separated by periods of inactivity. One official observed, 'I would look at it as blips, okay? So it's a constant, almost, and then it's profile. It has an orgasm every so often. I mean now it has an incredibly high profile at this point and then it will diminish.'

Again, and as I have argued, those who feed initiatives into the world, and those who receive and witness that process of feeding, tend to describe federal work as a long succession of little, disconnected projects. The word commonly employed to make sense of what occurs is 'fad'. Federal sensibilities about provincial and private sector responses set limits on what can be done and how it is presented. Budgetary restrictions and the three-year deadline make policies seem segmented, modest, and short-lived. Thus an outsider wrote about the victims initiative:

> Some observers fear that concern for victims is just another fad. Partly because the issues are so emotionally volatile and partly because answers that make sense are so frustratingly elusive, the criminal justice system is easy prey to fads. The issues that hold the platform are mercurial; they come and go in quick succession.

Each new palliative shunts aside its predecessor as the cure-all for society's ills. And it, in turn, is soon replaced.[33]

The social structure that engulfs and is created by a policy initiative thereby engenders an array of visions. The very tempo, scale, and environment of policy development refract the position and purposes of the observer. They are contingent, and those implicated in the process are often quite aware of such contingency. For instance, an official in the Planning and Liaison Division reflected that a Regional Consultant would see the material of policy as cyclical: 'and the Regional Consultant's perspective is quite right from where she sits in terms of her tasks and what she has to do with it. For [one working in the Causes and Prevention Division] it's a constant. . . . So for a while it was going along just as there are many streams or strands that are going along. Then all of a sudden he was plucked, you know, it's like your star was born. . . . And then eventually victims will go into its rightful place. He'll never have to switch because victims will still be a concern. It's always been a concern, but the profile, the texture, the effort, the quality changed.' Constancy, fitfulness, and faddishness are grounded definitions.

It is in this sense that the origins, personality, and explanation of the victims initiative are almost as diffuse as the number of people who are prepared to discuss them. Further, accounts tend to merge and fold into one another as they cross the frontiers of the worlds in which they first appeared. As the initiative emerged, so there was much talk about what was in the making. That talk, in its turn, typically revolved around what was known and familiar, events being woven into coherence. Those who were seen to act became identified as causal agents. Importance was attached to the known representatives of the social circles in which some significant event had occurred. They were to become the visible face of policy-making, recognizable figures standing for a portion of history. And even if their influence could not be fixed with precision, courtesy recommended that they be awarded some responsibility for the praiseworthy events that had happened in their vicinity. Not only did that process of organization allow particular people to stand symbolically for events, it was their stories that filtered and mediated the knowledge that their intimates acquired. Thus it will be remembered that some Ontario officials bestowed special importance on the doings of one of their former colleagues who had moved to the Ministry of the Solicitor General. In another instance, a senior official in a provincial ministry gave great weight to the work of a close acquaintance in the Department. That

[33] L. Krotz, 'What About the Victims?', *Quest,* June/July 1982, p. 70.

acquaintance had channelled much of his information and he was granted a commensurate eminence. The official transformed his friend into an embodiment of the federal response to victims. And the friend observed, 'as far as [the official] is concerned, I tend to be the person he 'phones up in Ottawa. He doesn't always do it that way but whenever he wants anything *informal* he does do it. He always 'phones me and says "what do you think?"' The manner in which different circles are aligned will then shape the flow of knowledge, moulding the extent, character and movement of ideas and accounts.

The search for causes becomes acutely baffling in such a social universe. It must be conducted in what is tantamount to a wilderness of mirrors. Indeed, bafflement is a vital part of the causal texture of policy-making. Lines of action do not progress smoothly from event to event in a fashion that can be demonstrated by any competent observer. They are supplied by officials who deploy them in argument. Causes shift from setting to setting and within settings over time. It would be foolish and uninstructive to try to rank those causes by some general criterion of historical importance. It is not clear what purpose that ranking would achieve and policy-making does not submit easily to such evaluation. Rather, different causes waxed and waned in significance, being given varying degrees of influence within the limits which they imposed upon one another. Instead of *forcing* officials to take particular courses of action, they were frameworks, objects, and resources for the making of choices. Matza argued that 'man participates in *meaningful* activity. He creates his reality and that of the world around him, actively and strenuously. Man *naturally*—not supernaturally—transcends the existential realms in which the conceptions of cause, force, and reactivity are easily applicable.'[34] That argument would seem to be extraordinarily appropriate to the history of the victims initiative. In Ottawa's paper world there was little obstruction to the development of a reasonably credible policy initiative based on talk and writing. The limits of structure were set initially by the formal constraints of the bureaucratic process, problems of mandate and authority, and the properties of official discourse. As a senior Policy Branch official reflected at an early stage, an edifice had been built out of symbols, paper, speech, and argument:

> I think we've got a real good start to this one. We've got a real solid basis from which to develop a good policy. We've covered our bases well, we have a sense of direction, we've taken care of our jurisdictional concerns, both internal and external. Although, as I was saying earlier [to a colleague] 'you know, you think

[34] D. Matza, *Becoming Deviant*, Prentice-Hall, New Jersey, 1969, p. 8.

of the hours and hours we've put in on this and we haven't yet helped one victim'.

Any quest for the origins of the victims initiative would unearth a variety of eligible explanations which lend themselves to different layers of analytic abstraction and emphasis. It is a quest made particularly complicated by the propensity of officials to furnish ther own history and causality as they explore and justify what they do. As a matter of course, officials read about what others have done, excavating deeper and deeper into the past of a policy. Thus, when an outside contractor was engaged to undertake research for the Department, he spoke with officials and devoted himself 'to a rapid familiarization with the literature on victim needs. For the most part, the reports and papers examined have been provided by Dr. Gerry Leger from his files'.[35] Dr Leger is an official of the Causes and Prevention Division, and his own stored documentation thereby served as a plinth upon which new work could rest, becoming the recorded prehistory of the contractor's own project. In like manner, it is customary for the Department to compile or commission a bibliography when any new area of interest is charted. Indeed, the Ministry announced that 'formal state of the art reviews are considered to be essential in those areas where knowledge is in existence but has never been assembled and analysed within the context of Canadian legislation, policy and particular operational programs.'[36] The Department has accordingly sponsored bibliographies on a list of problems that include child abuse, rape, family violence, services to victims, and Canadian criminology. Its reach has been immeasurably extended of late by its connection with an electronic information retrieval service that pours out great masses of references and abstracts at the pushing of a few buttons. Those exposed to such information will find themselves pushed back to ever earlier stages of writing, revisiting epoch after epoch. There has even arisen the apparent convention that discussions of services to victims should allude first to the code of Hammurabi and then move into a disquisition about early Anglo-Saxon law. It was Schafer who seems to have provided the standard account of the history of the victim, beginning with a Golden Age before kings and barons usurped the victim's place.[37] In that process of searching and reading, those earlier stages can become available as the precursor of a current pursuit, a piece of its history, and an influence upon its development. In the process, history may be tacked together

[35] C. Meredith, *Needs of Crime Victims: First Progress Report,* 31 Mar. 1982, p. 1.
[36] *Guide Research Program, 1975–76,* p. 11.
[37] S. Schafer, *The Victim and His Criminal,* Random House, New York, 1968.

and extended, ramifying influences and connecting events. The result is that the past is never still and never settled. Causes and origins are as diverse as officials choose to make them. Indeed, as initiatives progress and move out into the world, so their authors will encounter other examples of enterprise which may be absorbed and assimilated. For instance, it was not until quite late in the development of the initiative that reference was made by federal officials to the work of the John Howard Society of Saskatchewan. The Society had been quite busy in the area of victims services, having been active since 1976 but unknown in Ottawa until 1982. It was in 1982 that that earlier phase could be used as part of the story of Canadian services to victims. The past unfolds as present activity expands to meet it.

That movement through time has been reinforced in the Ministry and elsewhere by the tendency to support officials' applications to attend conferences and meetings. Every attendance plunges a person into the middle of a string of developments which possess their own history, problems, and concerns. Thus, when federal and provincial officials participated in the meetings of the National Organization for Victim Assistance they became the instant heirs of all that passed in the American politics of victims.

In everyday life, the origins of the initiative are something of a mirror of those who describe them, reflecting needs and knowledge, and disclosing what has been remembered. For narrative purposes, the beginning becomes the earliest moment which an official can identify amongst a mass of events that have been lumped together and identified with a policy on victims. Officials in the Department of Justice, for example, tend to refer to the Criminal Injuries Compensation Schemes that were introduced to Canada in the 1960s. Their colleagues in the Ministry of the Solicitor General have no dealings with compensation and they do not mention it as a cause or a beginning. Research staff tend to attach importance to the work they accomplished, acknowledging the political significance of the activities of the Policy Branch, but claiming that they prepared the ground for a sound policy. Policy analysts prefer to look back to the time when victims became politically salient, a time that might be associated with the first expression of provincial interest in October 1979 or when the Minister approved the preparation of proposals.

It is difficult to decide which of those many strands should receive attention in this book. All deserve attention, if only because a number of participants defined them as important and appear to have been influenced by them. As Mills once argued, 'the vocalized expectations of an act, its "reason", is not only a mediating condition of the act but it is a proximate and controlling condition for which the term "cause" is not inappropriate.'[38] If a cause is described as real, it is real enough in its consequences. People were manifestly influenced by the accounts which they offered and it is not my business to neglect them.

My solution to the dilemma of choice will be resolved by the working interpretations of the staff of the Ministry of the Solicitor General who had had dealings with the victims initiative. I shall adopt the Ministry as a topic and resource, dwelling on the events which officials created or declared significant. I shall give special attention to the police, women, the victimization survey, and the politics of the provinces, ignoring the contribution of what might otherwise have been defined as important events. The Criminal Injuries Compensation Boards and the Law Reform Commission of Canada simply failed to make an appreciable impact on the Department of the Solicitor General. However busy they may have been in the area of victims services, I shall neglect them. What follows in the next few chapters is a succession of the little histories that were patently important in forming the Department's contribution to the federal initiative. Moreover, my version of those little histories will mirror my purposes. It will be a reconstruction intended to illuminate the focused work of the Ministry. Each history will be incomplete, lacking a proper beginning and end, and devised to serve the problem at hand. Each is therefore descriptively inadequate but my task would become quite impossible if I did not resort to such a strategy. After all, each of the little histories could become as taxing as my principal project, and each sets its own massive problems of analysis. Many have not been reported before, and they are opaque or tacit even to those who know them well. There are very real difficulties of description, ideas having to be teased cautiously out of their contexts instead of being recorded in a photographic manner. Consider, for instance, the report of a provincial committee charged with examining its Ministry's involvement with victims. It is evident that that committee confronted no clear structure or history. It stated, 'little formal policy exists and ... what policy does exist is primarily implied in its victim assistance activity or lack thereof, rather than stated explicitly.'[39] My problems are doubled because some of the little histories are based on inferences about inferences, on knowledge that has been filtered a number of times.

[38] C. Wright Mills, 'Situated Actions and Vocabularies of Motive', *American Sociological Review,* 1940, Vol. 5, No. 4, p. 906.

[39] *Interim Report of the Executive Committee,* Victim Assistance Policy Assessment Committee, Ministry of the Attorney General, British Columbia, 20 Apr. 1982, p. 2.

III. A Science and a Social Movement

Introduction

The subjects of my first little history touched the federal victims initiative directly and indirectly and with rather contradictory results. They were an enduring and important environment for the politics of victims and their effects are substantial. Those subjects are victimology and the victims movement, two intertwining social and intellectual groups which seemed to follow a great elliptical orbit around the Ministry of the Solicitor General. On occasion, their orbit appeared to be both geographically and socially distant; geographically because much of the early work on the problems of crime victims was organized south of the border in the United States of America, and socially because many Ministry staff were quite evidently uneasy about features of its development. Yet the orbit came very close sometimes. On one occasion, the victims movement was actually imported into Canada by the Ministry when the National Organization for Victim Assistance met in Toronto. Together, and they were often inseparable, victimology and the victims movement supplied ideas and activities which affected the making of federal policy at a number of critical points. They served as a pattern for projects and ventures across Canada. They were to be fed into the very core of the Secretariat by one man, and then by his colleagues, becoming a clear catalyst for the emergence of an official interest in the victims of crime.

Victimology

Victimology is one of the small hybrid disciplines that have grown in and around the more conventional version of criminology. It has only recently emerged as a discernible enterprise with its own supporting structure of journals, writings, learned societies, meetings, adherents, academic courses, and a name. In truth, there has been little organized discussion of crime victims anywhere until quite recently. As the United States Department of Justice asserted, 'traditionally, both public attention and the criminal justice system have focused on criminal offenders. Criminal justice resources have been used to pursue, judge, and imprison offenders and have paid little attention to their victims.'[1] Victimology itself appeared at about the time of the Second World War. The standard history traces its genealogy back to the work of Von Hentig[2] and Mendelsohn in the 1940s, and it was Mendelsohn who actually bestowed a title on the discipline.[3] Victimology is as yet a little marginal and unestablished, an agonistic discipline striving to gain full academic recognition. One of its chief patrons observed, 'any new field ... initially struggles to develop its terminology, define its boundaries, justify its existence, gain respectability and eventually claim its place among the already established disciplines. ... Victimology is no exception.'[4]

A number of the social sciences are lent a tenuous unity by their concentration upon a particular fragment of the empirical world. They are not to be distinguished primarily by their dependence on an intellectual tradition, a special set of analytic methods, or a common universe of discourse. Instead, they share a substantive problem which has been probed and produced by a miscellany of techniques emanating from a variety of parent disciplines. David Downes once called them 'rendezvous' subjects, and they have tended to evolve around such social problems as race relations, education, prisons, crime, and, latterly, victims. It is the substance of victimization which tends to define victimology, and the discipline is correspondingly somewhat catholic. After all, there are few criteria for rejecting ideas and people, the frontiers are not strongly policed or marked, and the outcome is a diverse collection of scholars and thoughts. Indeed, one rather unfriendly critic has written of 'the alarming number of eccentrics who have invested themselves as victimologists' and he has also claimed 'it is difficult to restrain the urge to dismiss victimology as the lunatic fringe of criminology'.[5]

Victimologists would probably agree that victims have been wrongly neglected in the past and that they require some form of rescue. They would agree that their interest is in the scientific study of victims, the process, etiology, and consequences of victimization'.[6] There is not much other accord. The perspectives which have been brought to bear on the

[1] *Victims of Crime,* Bureau of Justice Statistics, US Department of Justice, Washington, 1981, p. 1.

[2] See, for example, H. Von Hentig, *The Criminal and his Victim,* Yale University Press, New Haven, 1948.

[3] See B. Mendelsohn, 'The Origins of the Doctrine of Victimology', reprinted in I. Drapkin and E. Viano (eds.) *Victimology,* D. C. Heath and Company, Lexington, 1974.

[4] E. Viano, introduction to *Victims and Society,* Visage Press, Washington, 1976, p. 3.

[5] C. Becker, Criminal Theories of Causation and Victims' Contributions to the Etiology of Crime, Ph.D. dissertation, University of Cambridge, 1981, p. 4.

[6] M. Wolfgang, 'Concluding Remarks at the Second International Symposium on Victimology', Boston, 11 Sept. 1976, Mimeograph, p. 1.

victim are so diffuse that they seem sometimes to compose an unpatterned kaleidoscope of nuances, definitions, and problems. There is probably no compelling reason why intellectual coherence should ever arise out of that mass of ideas. In 1975 it was declared of the conclusions of the International Study Institute on Victimology that 'so far it can only be stated that the universe of events that have some probability of being defined as victimizing, conceptually define the parameters of victimology. Beyond this admittedly circular definition, little consensus has emerged.'[7] In 1977 it was reported of the Second International Symposium on Victimology, 'there were more data offered ... than were theories and hypotheses. There are few victimological theories available to scholars.'[8] And Becker has written, 'victimologists cannot at present be said to share much more than a common interest in victims of crime, and even that assertion is sometimes in doubt ...'[9] Very often, it is a practical concern with the lot of victims, not some theoretical unison, that holds victimology together. Discord should not be deplored. There is no social science which is dominated by a single theory and the prospect of such domination is a little alarming. The reproach that victimology lacks one voice is not then very wounding. But the victimologists do seem to be troubled by it and the drift towards a form of empiricism does have consequences which I shall discuss below.

Definition having flowed out of a process of induction, the agenda of victimology cannot but take the form of a long list of problems whose common denominator is the word 'victim'.[10] For instance, the prospectus for the World Society of Victimology announced:

> From its beginning, victimology has been an international and an interdisciplinary subject. The need for information about the victim's contribution to the commission of crime, the offender–victim relationship, the victim's vulnerability and recidivism, the victim's role in the criminal justice system, the potential victim's fear of crime and attitudes towards legislation and law enforcement stimulated victimological research throughout the world. Victim service centers, victim–witness assistance programs, rape crisis centers, victim advocates offering comprehensive integrated responses to the legal, financial, social and emotional needs of the innocent crime victim and his family have been established in many countries.

[7] 'Conclusions and Recommendations. International Study Institute on Victimology. Bellagio, Italy, July 1–12, 1975', in E. Viano (ed.) *Victims and Society*, p. 604.

[8] E. Flynn, 'Report of the Discussion Sections of the Second International Symposium on Victimology', *Victimology*, Spring 1977, Vol. 2, No. 1, p. 34.

[9] C. Becker, *Criminal Theories of Causation*, p. 6.

[10] See K. Levine, 'Empiricism in Victimological Research', *Victimology*, 1978, Vol. 3, Nos. 1–2.

The fragmented and dispersed quality of things studied would be of little consequence if it did not seem to worry the victimologists. Many victimologists do appear to be concerned about their theoretical and collective disunity. They make frequent pleas for greater cohesion and, as I shall argue, those pleas give special urgency to the occasions when they all meet together. Quite significant effects flow from the tendency to lament the absence of coherence and unanimity. When a prominent victimologist, Edith Flynn, concluded after one Symposium that 'the need is for an integrated approach to the study of the victim',[11] and when she reiterated her complaint in 1982,[12] she gave voice to an important and enduring strain that was to have repercussions on the politics of victims in Canada. I shall touch upon it in the next chapter.

Victimology and Politics

Victimology is a minor social science and it is beset by the problems of all the social sciences. Those disciplines are without agreed principles, strategies, or organization. Not only are there unsettled debates about the nature of social life, the utility of competing methodologies, and the limits of enquiry, but central questions of mandate and justification remain unresolved. From the first, there have been disputes about the scope of the disciplines' moral and political purpose.

Victimology is little more than an extension of criminology, designed to correct imbalances and omissions within its parent discipline. It has taken into itself many of the sources of contention and strain which are to be discovered in social science at large. There is much that is scholarly and dispassionate. There is much that was never intended to be dispassionate. What impelled many people to sponsor the discipline and mould its development was the conviction that the victim has been seriously abused, oppressed, and forgotten. Politics and scholarship were woven into victimology from the first. Thus John Dussich described the discipline's two major concerns as victim-centred research and victim assistance.[13] Similarly, Mendelsohn himself stated that the essential goal of victimology is to achieve fewer victims in all sectors of society.[14]

[11] E. Flynn, 'Report of the Discussion Sections of the Second International Symposium on Victimology', p. 34.

[12] E. Flynn, 'Theory Development in Victimology', in H. Schneider (ed.), *The Victim in International Perspective,* Walter de Gruyter, Berlin, 1982, p. 97.

[13] J. Dussich, 'Overview of Victimology', in W. Taylor and M. Braswell (eds.), *Issues in Police and Criminal Psychology,* University Press of America, Washington, 1978.

[14] B. Mendelsohn, 'Victimology and Contemporary Society's Trends', *Victimology,* 1976, Vol. 1, No. 1.

Again, the advertisement for the Third International Symposium on Victimology declared that with the criminological 'emphasis on the legal rights of the accused and convicted and the increased acceptance of the goal of rehabilitating the offender, the victim has been overlooked as having as much right to be fairly treated by society'.[15] And at the Symposium itself, victimology was defined by a rapporteur as a 'movement' whose 'original and continuing aim was and is to reduce as much as possible the suffering of victims'.[16] These are not analytic objectives. Victimology is in large measure a campaign or crusade to alleviate pain, redress injustice, and protect the weak. It has been given over to the study of victims because they are an appealing and important object of sympathy. It has cultivated professional links with those working in the area of assistance to victims. It has made awards to those who have contributed significantly to the succour of victims.[17] The conclusions and recommendations of its meetings are as much occupied with policy as with research and exposition.[18] In short, there have undoubtedly been many justifications for restoring the victim to a salient position in explanation, but compassion is prominent, and those whose interest in the victim is chiefly analytic might hesitate to call themselves victimologists at all. Those who discuss victimology as a science tend often to gravitate towards describing it as a form of morality or politics, drifting back and forth between description and prescription.[19]

Indeed, an orthodox history seems to have emerged. At the beginning, victimology was preoccupied with the study of crime and its victims, sometimes locating the responsibility for suffering in the activities of the victim. In time, that focus was to be displaced by 'affirmative action for the victim of crime. The theoretical advances in victimology resulting from efforts of pioneer victimologists have recently been overshadowed by major developments in the applied field intended to alleviate the plight of the victim ...'[20]

[15] Advertisement for Third International Symposium on Victimology, Münster, Westphalia, 2–8 Sept. 1979.

[16] J. Dussich and G. Kirchhoff, 'A Summary of the Rapporteurs' Report from the Third International Symposium on Victimology', *World Society of Victimology Newsletter*, 1981, Vol. 1, No. 1, p. 20.

[17] See *Concern for Victims and Witnesses of Crime*, Sept. 1979, Vol. 1, No. 3, p. 1.

[18] See, for instance, *Conclusions and Recommendations Adopted by the First International Symposium on Victimology Held in Jerusalem*, 2–6 Sept. 1973.

[19] G. Mueller, 'Towards a Whole Victimology Within a Whole Criminology', in H. Schneider (ed.), *The Victim in International Perspective*, p. 2.

[20] E. Fattah, 'Some Recent Theoretical Developments in Victimology', *Victimology*, 1979, Vol. 4, No. 2, pp. 198–9. Waller has made very similar observations: 'in its first stages, victimology was focused on what victims to study and why persons became victims. The last decade has seen many practitioners and researchers develop a new focus which

It is evident that there are irreconcilable themes in victimology which threaten continually to worry at one another. Most marked is the problem created by the tendency of particular arguments to defy the wider political intentions of the movement. There are several distinctly disagreeable and mutinous ideas which upset the social construction of the victim as one who is suffering, innocent, and worthy of political support. It is an unambiguous description that promotes social and political action,[21] and victimology continually clouds what might otherwise be simple, effective argument. The subject is politically contradictory. As a policy adviser to National Health and Welfare reflected, 'victimology is a relatively new field of systematic human enquiry, with double-edged consequences for women'.[22]

Victimology and victim surveys do seem to unearth disconcerting associations between the events and people that centre on crime. For example, one sizeable survey of Londoners reported 'to a considerable extent the police deal with a limited clientele of people who tend to be in trouble both as victims and as offenders ... people who tend to be repeatedly victims, also have a much higher average chance of being arrested'.[23] Again, some have pointed to the seductive role played by the child in cases of paedophilia.[24] Others have described how murder victims can cause their own deaths: 'many so-called murders are really suicide. The victim wants to die yet is incapable of taking his own life, so he incites someone else to kill him.'[25] Others have focused on the compromising relations that may bind the rapist and the victim of rape.[26] In all this work on precipitation,[27] the vital moral and political contrasts between victims and criminals can waver and falter. There are the beginnings of a very real erosion of the distinction between the guilty offender and the innocent sufferer. As Antilla argued:

emphasizes both the impact of crime and harm on victims and ways to assist their recovery.' I. Waller, 'Crime Victims: Needs, Services and Reforms', Paper delivered at Fourth International Symposium on Victimology, Tokyo/Kyoto, 29 Aug–2 Sept. 1982, p. 1.

21 See R. Turner and S. Surace, 'Zootsuiters and Mexicans', *American Journal of Sociology,* July 1956, Vol. 62, No. 1.

22 F. Paltiel, 'Female Circumcision', *Atlantis,* Vol. 6, No. 1, p. 92.

23 D. Smith, *Police and People in London,* Policy Studies Institute, London, 1983, Vol. 1, p. 124.

24 See C. McCaghy, 'Drinking and Deviance Disavowal', *Social Problems,* 1968, Vol. 16, No. 1.

25 Interview with M. Wolfgang in the *Toronto Star,* 4 Feb. 1972. See his *Patterns in Criminal Homicide,* University of Pennsylvania Press, Philadelphia, 1958.

26 See M. Amir, *Patterns of Forcible Rape,* University of Chicago Press, Chicago, 1971.

27 For a more detailed discussion, see L. Curtiss, 'Victim Precipitation', in S. Halleck *et al.* (eds.), *The Aldine Crime and Justice Annual 1974,* Aldine, Chicago, 1975.

New scapegoats are available for explaining criminality ... Generally, one can say that the earlier stereotypes of 'black and white' have been exchanged for 'grey versus grey'. ... Once the stereotype of the innocent and unsuspecting victim has proved to be false, it has seemed natural to plan measures that are suppose to change the behaviour of the victim.[28]

The imagery of the culpable victim is most subversive to the politics of victims. It tends to present the victim as morally undeserving, inhibit condemnation of the criminal, and silence demands for remedial politics. Especially disturbing is the argument which denies any fundamental ontological difference between certain categories of victim and offender. Thus it has been asserted that there is much that is accidental in the casting of particular roles. For example, some victims of serious violence and homicide could just as well have been offenders. They share many of the same qualities, come from the same milieux, and resort to the same strategies of attack and defence in their relations.[29] It is not a moral divide that shapes destiny, but 'the superiority of the weapon, physical strength and/or skill in the use of weapons that have been the decisive factor in the choice of the victim from the two participants'.[30] And Wolfgang remarked, 'it is probably only chance which results in one becoming victim and the other an offender'.[31] It is difficult to mobilize the politics of moral indignation around such a theme. On the contrary, victimology can enfeeble those who would defend the victim.

One pronounced consequence has been the ambivalence of members of the victims movement towards victimology. Fattah, indeed, has written of 'the paranoid attitude generated by the concepts of victim–precipitation and victim–participation'.[32] Feminists have been markedly hostile, redefining 'victim precipitation' as 'victim blaming' and portraying victimology as a weapon of ideological oppression. Erin Pizzey has been ostracized by the women's movement in Britain as a response to her claim that women sometimes seek out those who will hurt them. And, in Canada, two women have had a cardinal significance in turning politics against victimology and the idea of precipitation. Clark and Lewis have declared that 'victim blaming has become institutionalized

[28] I. Antilla, 'Victimology—A New Territory in Criminology', *Scandinavian Studies in Criminology*, Vol. 5, Martin Robertson, London, 1974, p. 8.

[29] See S. Singer, 'Homogeneous Victim–Offender Populations—A Review and Some Research Implications', in J. Dahmann and J. Sasfy (eds.), *Victimology Research Agenda Development*, 1980, Vol. 1.

[30] A. Porterfield and R. Talbert, *Midcentury Crime in Our Culture*, Leo Potishman Foundation, Fort Worth, 1954, p. 48.

[31] M. Wolfgang, *Patterns in Criminal Homicide*, p. 265.

[32] E. Fattah, 'Becoming a Victim: The Victimization Experience and its Aftermath', unpublished paper, undated, p. 14.

within the academic world under the guise of victimology', that the discipline is practised by men, that 'the typical victim blamer is a male person who is doing reasonably well in a sexual way', and that the function of victimology is to serve 'a structural need in justifying the *status quo*, and in providing a diversionary option to reform'.[33] Further, some have claimed that men have no business studying victims at all. Men are unable to understand female experience, the experience of female victims least of all. Thus the head of a woman's organization wrote to officials complaining about my having undertaken this research: 'it is incomprehensible to me that a white, middle-class male has been hired to prepare such a paper.'

The outcome has been major schism between segments of academic victimology and a number of Canadian institutions organized around the politics of violence against women. The discipline which provided a piece of the spur for a victims initiative was not well regarded by those who were to be defined as an important lobby.[34] Moreover, and even more importantly, there has been a tendency for some principal Canadian feminists to refuse to extend the very label of 'victim' to women. Part of their refusal may be ascribed to a reluctance to allow women to become lost in the larger mass of victims: the raped and battered woman is of special concern whilst the general title of 'victim' is somewhat more neutral. They argue that it would be misleading and improper to lump such a woman with male victims when violence against women is committed by males: rape is 'the outcome of a conflict situation which reflects the sexual politics that are part of the collective exploitation and oppression of women'.[35] The word 'victim' connotes a loss of political meaning and personal innocence which some women find deeply offensive. Many of the projects established by women thus eschew the name 'victim'. Lorenne Clark stated[36] 'no rape crisis centre even saw itself as a fundamentally victim-oriented service centre'. Initiatives on battering and rape were not an outcrop of a campaign for victims at large, they were about the lot of women, referring to women and not to victims. It is in this sense that many women did not claim an affinity with the victims movement, did not allude to victims, displayed a distaste for victimology, and preferred to discuss 'violence against women' as a

[33] L. Clark and D. Lewis, *Rape: The Price of Coercive Sexuality*, The Women's Press, Toronto, 1977, pp. 147–8, 150, 180.

[34] See J. Ridington, 'Women in a Violent Society', *Kinesis*, June 1978, Vol. 7, No. 6, p. 12.

[35] R. Kasinsky, 'The Rise and Institutionalization of the Anti-Rape Movement in Canada', in M. Gammon (ed.), *Violence in Canada*, Methuen, Toronto, 1978, p. 158.

[36] Quoted in M. Amir and D. Amir, 'Rape Crisis Centres in Ontario: An Appraisal', A Report to the Solicitor General of Canada, Ottawa, 1977, p. 6.

theme.[37] Their preoccupation stemmed from a distinct politics with its own history and separate discourse, a politics that touched the victims movement at different points and with curious consequences.

The Victims Movement

In the first chapter, I observed that the Ministry staff occupied with victims believed that they had affinities with the solipsist, being subjected to no major pressure or criticism from without. The woman's movement was something of an exception and it was cited frequently and eagerly as a goad and justification for action when the victims initiative began to emerge. But no other substantial and persistent organization could be heard to voice demands. In their experience of what was a virtual political insulation, Ministry officials were not at all unusual. A political silence has been detected elsewhere in the environment of the government of Canada. It exists around the governments of other states. Indeed, many of the important reforming policies of the last few decades have been accomplished without struggle or clamour. Thus Moynihan has described how social reform was professionalized in the United States, becoming the pursuit of experts and officials who worked alone and without any obvious external political catalyst. The War on Poverty, for instance, was declared by federal officials who lacked significant allies in the world outside Washington.[38] Similarly, in Britain, it has been claimed 'the rediscovery of poverty and the policy response to it were the products of the internal dynamics of the social policy process'.[39] So it was with the victims of crime and the Canadian federal victims initiative of 1981.

Gusfield has defined a social movement as 'socially shared activities and beliefs directed towards the demand for social change in some aspect of the social order'.[40] There was no significant social movement revolving around the politics of crime victims in Canada. In time, a working co-operation *did* begin to develop between a number of social groups, but its conception must be attributed largely to the work of federal and provincial officials and it occurred when an initiative was starting to take shape. Victims of Violence was to emerge very much later when the initiative was in full spate. Throughout much of the formative history of

[37] See F. Paltiel, 'Shaping Futures for Women', *Women's Studies International Quarterly,* 1981, Vol. 4, No. 1, p. 22.

[38] See D. Moynihan, 'The Professionalization of Reform', *The Public Interest,* Fall 1965, 1.

[39] K. Banting, *Poverty, Politics and Policy,* p. 139.

[40] J. Gusfield, introduction to *Protest, Reform, and Revolt,* John Wiley, New York, 1970, p. 2.

the initiative, and in the uncertain years at the beginning, there were no socially shared activities and beliefs about victims in Canadian society. Neither was there any marked tendency to capture the social response to crime victims and form a private institution around it. Becker once argued that concern 'must be embodied in an organization or institution if a problem is to achieve lasting success as a defined social problem',[41] but no such act of private embodiment ever took place. Instead, the lay social reaction to victims was mute and unorganized, being regulated by government alone. There was no reaction and the word 'victims' was not in political use. Thus Geoffrey Norquay of the Canadian Council on Social Development stated:

> I've been involved in social development policy programmes for eleven years now in two provinces, one year in a federal–provincial task force and, when this study [preparing *Services to Victims and Witnesses of Crime in Canada*] started, two years in a national voluntary agency. And I had never once heard the term 'crime victim' in the sense of it being a policy issue, an unmet social need, etcetera. It just wasn't in the currency. It wasn't being talked about. What we found when we went to do the study was that very few people in Canada, even though they might actively be involved in the business of providing services to a certain type of crime victim, thought of themselves as part of a broader policy area, thought of themselves as part of the victims services' field or movement or whatever.

It is never easy to understand how some process or phenomenon did not come to pass. I cannot pretend to offer a firm explanation of the absence of a Canadian victims movement in the early phases of the initiative, but it *is* possible to trace three blocks to its development. The first and most evident barrier resides in definition. The victim of crime is a comparatively isolated figure. Indeed, that was to be one of the complaints made about the experience of victimization. Unless they have been exposed to a visibly collective attack, victims share no necessary communal identity *as* victims. Very often, the victim will not claim such a significant existential bond with other victims that he or she will seek them out in order to further a common purpose. As a relative of a victim of murder argued, 'crime victims are ... unlike other minorities. They are not a cohesive group ... Crime victims are usually randomly chosen targets, united only by fate.'[42] Moreover, being a victim may not always bring about that symbolic reorganization of the self which could prepare the foundations for enduring membership in a new group. Thus a bur-

[41] H. Becker, introduction to *Social Problems*, John Wiley, New York, 1966, p. 12.
[42] J. Barkas, *Victims*, Charles Scribner's Sons, New York, 1978, p. 5.

glary victim might cease to define himself or herself as a victim after a while. Being a victim might be less important than membership of a political party, a religious group, a community organization, or a bridge club. It is only the particularly critical or repetitive crime that is likely to alter one's standing for a long period. It must jolt one or present one with a problem demanding solution within a framework prepared by the criminal justice system.

And a victim need not define his or her experience as primarily a consequence of *criminal* activity at all. Loss, change, and injury may not be associated with crime but with some other mediate process or condition. For instance, a speaker at the 1981 Conference of the National Organization for Victim Assistance disclosed that he had lost the sight of an eye during a criminal assault. At first, he had identified himself and his state with people who were visually impaired because they were a conspicuous and socially organized group. His initial categorization of himself had not been as a crime victim but as one who had suffered from a loss of vision. Similarly, a John Howard Society observed in a grant proposal to the Ministry of the Solicitor General:

> people involved in assaults and the like are very often involved in continuing personal relationships; not uncommonly the problem they identify is not 'victimization' but drug/alcohol treatment, family counselling, legal advice, shelter following a separation, etc. In many instances, given their definition of the problem ... referral to other services seems more appropriate than attempting to provide them under the label victimization.

Crime victims actually form several possible groupings that can be put to quite different intellectual and political ends. It is not always their involvement in crime that is most salient within a particular field of ideas. Victims can illuminate many facets of the world. I have already touched on the special meanings which women's organizations attach to battering and rape, and it would be useful to return to them here. Many do not take the most notable features of violence against women to be embedded in a context provided by crime and criminal justice. They are, instead, regarded as problems associated with relationships between men and women living in an unjust society. Thus a collection of essays on 'the victimization of women' was clearly intended to document the pathologies of a sexist social order rather than some analytic points about crime, criminology, and criminal justice: 'this is a book about violence, sex, and power. It tells of helpless women and female children who are beaten and sexually abused. And it is the story of a society that appears unable or unwilling to stop this victimization. ... The editors agree with the point of view which argues that this state of affairs is the natural result of a sexist social order.'[43] Similarly, a senior official working in Status of Women Canada reflected that there was a major difference between commonplace victims of crime and women who had been subject to violence:

The reasons why women are attacked and the reasons why women are battered within the family are quite different from the reason why someone is assaulted on the street. I mean, it's different. It's qualitatively different. It's embedded ... in our society. It has to do with a sexist, patriarchal society. It has to do with lack of economic power. Different from break and entry victims, victims of assault in bars, and what not. It's qualitatively different.

In this sense, the criminal context of assault is of only minor importance compared with the framework of definitions prepared by the politics of patriarchal society. It is not even very interesting. If Status of Women Canada and other feminist organizations were to band victimized women together, it would not be as the victims of crime. And those who work with assaulted and raped women do not regard them as those who have suffered primarily from crime. As the Amirs remarked, 'rape crisis centres are one segment of the Feminist Movement.'[44] There is thus a very real strain to deny the appropriateness of the classification of 'crime victim' in cases involving sexual assault and male attacks on women. *Crime* is not taken to be a key word. Neither is it regarded as the most remarkable aspect of the problem. Some women were organized in Canada, and they were organized around the provision of aid to the victims of violence, but their mobilization had arisen in a setting alien to a victims movement and they did not associate themselves with any such body.

What *was* paraded before federal and provincial officials was composed of three principal parts: a loose coalition of Canadian feminist organizations, a coterie of Canadian victims assistance programmes and projects, and the American victims movement. The Canadian feminists were only hesitatingly approving of a victims initiative but they were politically influential and I shall discuss them in a chapter of their own. They certainly would not have embraced the title of a victims movement. Other Canadian institutions did expressly serve the victims of crime: Mennonites, the United Way, the Salvation Army, church and other bodies initiated a range of assistance schemes. Yet they were never part of a coherent political association and they did not attempt to introduce

[43] M. Gates, introduction to J. Chapman and M. Gates (eds.), *The Victimization of Women*, Sage Publications, Beverly Hills, 1978, p. 9.

[44] M. Amir and D. Amir, 'Rape Crisis Centres in Ontario', unpublished paper, p. 9.

profound changes into the politics of victims. What did provide a visible demonstration and display of a victims politics was the work of Americans, and Canadian policy was obliquely affected by what happened in the United States.

The American Victims Movement

This is not a book about the origins and structure of the American victims movement and I do not pretend to know why a social movement should have formed around victims in the United States in the 1970s and not in Canada. To be sure, there are some gross differences in the apparent frequency and quality of crime that may explain why the population of one society should have given an early political complexion to victimization. Those crimes which are most wounding and distressing occur with a much greater frequency in America. For instance, the admittedly misleading figures of reported crime suggest that there were some 80 victims of violent crime for every 100,000 Canadians in 1973 but 400 for every 100,000 Americans. Between 1964 and 1973 the American rate of recorded crime increased by 120 per cent and, in Canada, the rate grew by 102 per cent. The Canadian homicide rate was less than one quarter that of the United States.[45] And so it goes on. Yet those differences must be treated with great caution. People do not necessarily monitor changes and comparisons of the crime rate. General contrasts may not explain local variations or local reactions. It may be presumed that so minute and special an entity as a victims movement cannot be described as the effect of gross differences in reported crime. And Canadians seem unaware of those differences anyway. Much of their understanding of criminality appears to flow from their scrutiny of American news, talk, and drama. Doob remarked that Canadians exaggerate the volume of violence in their society: 'they think that we are closer in levels of violence to the United States than in fact we are; they see the number of murders are increasing over the past six years when in fact they have decreased.'[46]

In part. the prominence of the American victims movement may be explained plausibly by the early, substantial intervention of the federal government of the United States. There was a dawning of the fear of crime as a political entity at the end of the 1960s and the beginning of

[45] Figures taken from A. Michalos, *North American Social Report,* D. Reidel Publishing Company, Dordrecht, 1980, Vol. 1, pp. 15, 17.

[46] A. Doob and J. Roberts, 'Crime: Some Views of the Canadian Public', unpublished paper, August 1982, p. 2.

the 1970s;[47] a special politics was mobilized around the 'war against crime';[48] the Law Enforcement Assistance Administration was established as part of that war; and the Administration devoted some of its resources to supporting schemes devised to assist the victims and witnesses of crime. The American federal government was there first, anticipating some of the work of the Canadian federal government by a decade, and encouraging a victims movement which staged political displays before a Canadian audience. Indeed, as I shall show, Canadian officials witnessed the decline of portions of the American initiative at the very time they were planning their own.

The American victims movement is itself rather small, recent and tentative. Marlene Young, the Chairperson of its umbrella organization in 1980–1, asserted that no large popular American movement had yet emerged to represent and aid the victims of crime.[49] What does exist is a modest collection of agencies and voluntary organizations with very diverse histories and political postures. One prominent phalanx can trace its history back to that time in the 1960s when American radical groups attempted to redefine the world, an ideological project which critically revolved around the discovery and magnification of the role of particular victims.[50] Richard Quinney, for instance, announced that the definition of a victim is a political and existential accomplishment: 'our own character is indicated by the kinds of persons that we single out as being the victims of crime. ... When any person imagines a victim—and what should be done for or to him—he is displaying his own self.'[51] In the late 1960s, that documented self was largely female. Certain victims were awarded significance in order to elucidate the mechanics of an inequitable society. Rape, especially, revealed essential facts about the character and processes of 'sexism'. Blackmore has observed, 'the victims movement was spearheaded by the scores of rape crisis centers that sprang up around the country in the late sixties and early seventies.'[52]

[47] See, for example, M. Hindelang, 'Public Opinion Regarding Crime, Criminal Justice, and Related Topics', *Journal of Research in Crime and Delinquency,* July 1974; W. Skogan, 'Public Policy and the Fear of Crime', paper presented at the Annual Meetings of the Midwest Political Science Association, Chicago, May 1976; S. Riger and R. Lebailly, 'Women's Fear of Crime', *Victimology,* 1978, Vol. 3; M. Rifai, *Justice and Older Americans,* D. C. Heath and Co., Massachusetts, 1977; R. Sundeen and J. Mathieu, 'Fear of Crime and its Consequences Among Elderly in Three Urban Communities', *Gerontologist,* June 1976, Vol. 16, No. 3.

[48] See J. Epstein, *Agency of Fear,* Putnam, New York, 1977.

[49] Seminar delivered at Carleton University, Ottawa, 8 Oct., 1981.

[50] See D. Miers, *Responses to Victimisation,* Professional Books, Abingdon, 1978, p. 2.

[51] R. Quinney, 'Who is the Victim?', in I. Drapkin and E. Viano (eds.), *Victimology,* pp. 103, 107.

[52] J. Blackmore, 'Focusing on the Victim', *Police Magazine,* March 1979, p. 24.

Attentiveness to rape and its political meaning was interlaced with the wider politics of feminism, the one feeding the other as political organization and belief swelled. American women's groups 'raised their consciousness' by discussing a succession of problems which were identified as specifically feminist in import. Abortion, employment practices, and rape came to stand as indices or metonyms of the general condition of women.[53] In turn, rape was to be politically dramatized at a series of 'speak-outs' in which victims recounted their experiences in public.[54] One incident was singularly charged with the central symbolism of the American radical politics of that time: the case of the raped Inez Garcia who, having shot one of the prison guards who had ravished her, was tried by a Californian court in 1974. That case tended to condense perfectly matters concerning sexual violence to women, the position of ethnic minorities, and the exercise of coercion by the state. It gave rise to a moral crusade of major proportions.

Rape crisis centres began to be established in the early 1970s, the claim being made that the Washington centre was the very first in 1972.[55] By 1981 some 750 centres were in operation.[56] And American women have agitated about the general treatment of rape victims by the police, hospitals, and courts, helping to bring about change in about forty states. Battering, too, has been at the heart of a radical politics, illustrating patriarchy and the exploitation which is at the core of the family. The management of battering, in its turn, was also taken to document patriarchal attitudes in the law, medicine, and social services.[57] Approximately 500 shelters had been founded by 1981.[58] Not all rape crisis centres and shelters came out of feminism and feminism is neither a simple nor an undivided ideology. Moreover, all those different projects and schemes failed to coalesce into one united association.[59] Yet the prospect of women helping women who had been hurt by men was an impressive staging of moral lessons about the relations between the sexes.

[53] See J. Freeman, 'The Origins of the Women's Liberation Movement', *American Journal of Sociology,* January 1973, Vol. 78, No. 4.

[54] See N. Connell and C. Wilson, *Rape: The First Sourcebook for Women,* New American Library, New York, 1974.

[55] See M. Wasserman, 'Rape: Breaking the Silence', *The Progressive,* November 1973.

[56] See V. Jaycox, *Creating a Senior Victim/Witness Volunteer Corps,* National Council of Senior Citizens, Washington, 1981.

[57] See E. Stark *et al.,* 'Medicine and Patriarchal Violence', *International Journal of Health Services,* 1979, Vol. 9, No. 3.

[58] Center for Women Policy Studies, *Programs Providing Services to Battered Women,* Washington, 1981.

[59] See E. O'Sullivan, 'What Has Happened to Rape Crisis Centers?' *Victimology,* 1978, Vol. 3, Nos. 1–2.

Most importantly, unlike many other classes of victim, many women were already the subject and members of political organizations. Young males and Blacks may have been more frequently victimized, but significant sections of those classes were either unprepared to define themselves by their experience of victimization, were unorganized as a class, or were compromised politically by their definitional entanglements with crime. It must be recalled that some Blacks were radicals at the time, as were some women, but their radicalism tended to celebrate violence. Eldridge Cleaver had praised the raping of white women as an act of racial justice and none had conspicuously reproved him.[60] Cleaver, too, had written of 'the most beautiful sight I had ever seen: four black men wearing black berets, powder blue shirts, black leather jackets, black trousers, shiny black shoes—and each with a gun!'[61] And Bobby Seale had talked ecstatically of 'niggers with guns!'[62] Such enthusiasm does not lend itself to the makings of a victims movement. On the contrary.[63] If victimization is raised at all, it is held to be a condition of an entire race which demands a revolutionary response. Of course, many black militants were not disposed to romanticize crime, yet the divisions were enough to prevent the emergence of the Black as crime victim coming to the fore. It was radical women, already mobilized, who championed their own victims. As Marchand observed, 'some of the early leaders of the victims' movement in the United States were women associated with the women's movement—members of a "minority group" now well versed in expressing grievances.'[64]

A second phalanx had grown out of organized efforts to improve the efficiency and legitimacy of the police and courts. It had become a standard argument that victims were doubly victimized, once by the crime itself and once by the negligent response which they were likely to receive from law enforcement agencies. Indeed, so often repeated was that argument that it seemed to have become a taken-for-granted ingredient of official discourse about the social reality of crime.[65] By extension, the idea of the negligent response was to give birth to its own Homeric epithet. In much of the formal talk about victims may be discovered the phrase, 'the forgotten person [or party] in the criminal

[60] See E. Cleaver, 'The Primeval Mitosis', in *Soul on Ice,* Jonathan Cape, London, 1969.

[61] E. Cleaver, 'The Courage to Kill: Meeting the Panthers', in *Eldridge Cleaver,* Random House, New York, 1969, p. 29.

[62] B. Seale, *Seize the Time,* Hutchinson, London, 1970.

[63] See, for example, C. Howard, *The Zebra Killings,* New English Library, London, 1980.

[64] P. Marchand, 'Crime Victims: A Forgotten Minority Speaks Up', *Chatelaine,* February 1982, p. 78.

[65] See, for instance, E. Viano, *Victims and Society,* p. xv.

justice system'.[66] It is a commonly used epithet that conveys the belief that the state has displaced and thereby estranged the victim in law, adjudication, and punishment. Estrangement can be felt painfully. For instance, one manifesto opened by quoting Harold Rosenberg: 'without the victims' hatred of their oppressors the quest for justice lacks substance.' It then moved on: '*once you become a victim of a violent crime you are launched on a career of social injustices, of callous post-crime victimization by the police, the courts, the legal profession, and the human service systems of the nation.*'[67] That alienation led those who man the criminal justice system of the United States to win back what were thought to be innumerable lost victims and witnesses. Without those lost people, it was argued, there would be little reporting of crime, little willing attendance in court, and little co-operation with the police.[68] One such scheme addressed the victim thus: 'as a victim or a witness of a crime, your assistance is vital to our system of criminal justice ... you have a job to do which is important not only to us and to yourself, but most important to the American system of justice.'[69]

The chief sponsor of remedial programmes was the Law Enforcement Assistance Administration and it was the director of that organization who said:

'Remember me? I'm the victim'. That plea, voiced by a New York woman to the judge hearing her case, is increasingly echoed in station houses, prosecutors' offices and courtrooms throughout the country. In the past, it often fell on deaf ears as busy criminal justice professionals went about their jobs insensitive to the feelings and needs of the crime victim. Unwittingly, a system designed to aid innocent people instead added to their burden. And justice suffered: cases were dropped and suspects released because victims—or witnesses—were turned off by an impersonal bureaucracy, or worn out by lengthy legal maneuvering that took time out of their lives and money out of their pockets.[70]

The Law Enforcement Assistance Administration was to spend several tens of millions of dollars repairing the damage that was thought to be

[66] See E. Viano; 'Victims, Offenders, and the Criminal Justice System', in B. Galaway and J. Hudson (eds.), *Offender Restitution in Theory and Action,* Lexington Books, Massachusetts, 1978, p. 91. A. Meade *et al,* 'Discovery of a Forgotten Party', *Victimology,* Fall 1976, Vol. 1, No. 3. *Remembering Forgotten Victims,* Office of the Attorney General, Sacramento, 1980.

[67] R. Reiff, *The Invisible Victim: The Criminal Justice System's Forgotten Responsibility,* Basic Books, New York, 1979, pp. x, xi (Italics in original).

[68] See M. Knudten *et al.,* 'Will Anyone be Left to Testify?', in E. Flynn and J. Conrad (eds.), *New and Old Criminology,* LEAA, Washington, 1978.

[69] *The Witness Guide to Court Proceedings,* Office of the District Attorney, County of Sacramento, Sacramento, undated, pp. 1, 2.

[70] H. Dogin, foreword to R. Rosenblum and C. Blew, *Victim/Witness Assistance,* LEAA, Washington, 1979, p. i.

done by the estrangement of their victim. In 1974 it launched a 'crime victim initiative' in response to reports about the high failure rates of prosecutions and the reluctance of witnesses to work with the courts.[71] The initiative was to concentrate on such practical matters as notifying victims and witnesses about their court appearances, providing transport, offering child care facilities, segregating waiting-rooms for defendants and witnesses, and organizing social services. The original eight demonstration projects of 1974 mushroomed to some seventy-one identified by Stein in 1977[72] and 220 named by Cronin and Bourque in 1979.[73] Almost all were sited in prosecutors' offices and were at first unambiguously associated with the promotion of a rapid and effective system of prosecution.[74] Examples of such projects included the Brooklyn Victim/Witness Assistance Project which began in July 1975 and was centrally concerned with the 'non-cooperative witness issue':[75] cases were 'tracked' by computer, witnesses' appearance dates negotiated, and people called to testify only when it was certain that they would be needed. Similarly, the Witness Information Service of Anne Arundel Country, Maryland, provided information about court schedules, a glossary of courtroom language, and Witness Advocates who would meet witnesses and brief them.[76] A scheme in Elmira, New York, offered aid in replacing stolen documents, personal papers, and cards; help in arranging for the repair of damaged property; information on police and court procedures; help in applying for New York State Victim Compensation; crime prevention information; and contacts with other agencies.[77] The Sacramento Victim-Witness Program printed a list of twenty-six suggestions about how victims and witnesses should deport themselves in court: recommendations included telling the truth, answering questions succinctly, refraining from chewing gum, and avoiding loss of temper.[78] Again, the Pima County Victim/Witness Program of Arizona furnished a crisis intervention service, social service referrals, trial notification, crime pre-

[71] See K. Williams, *The Role of the Victim in the Prosecution of Violent Crime,* Institute for Law and Social Research, Washington, 1973. For later work, see F. Cannavale and W. Falcon (eds.), *Improving Witness Cooperation,* LEAA, Washington, 1976, and R. Knudten, *Victims and Witnesses,* LEAA, Washington, 1977.

[72] J. Stein, *Better Services for Crime Victims,* Blackstone Institute, Washington, 1977.

[73] R. Cronin and B. Bourque, *National Evaluation Program Phase I Assessment of Victim/Witness Assistance Projects,* American Institutes for Research, Washington, 1980.

[74] See *The Victim Advocate,* National District Attorneys' Association, Chicago, 1977.

[75] M. Favuzzi, director, quoted in J. Blackmore, 'Focusing on the Victim', *Police Magazine,* p. 26.

[76] *Witness Information Service,* Office of the State's Attorney, Annapolis, 1981.

[77] *Offender Aid and Restoration Neighborhoood Justice Project,* Elmira, New York, undated.

[78] *The Witness Guide to Court Proceedings,* pp. 7–8.

vention information, and the like.[79] Inevitably, functions and connections were to multiply so that victim–witness programmes ceased to work solely for one end. They became progressively implicated in an increasing variety of tasks that touched the utilitarian goals of law enforcement in ever more oblique fashion. As their range expanded, so their staff began to have dealings with people working in other projects. And their search for support and co-operation was impelled further by the Law Enforcement Assistance Administration's practice of providing funds for three years only. Just as in Canada, it was incumbent on the organizers of projects to secure money from elsewhere after a while. Their anxiety about the insecurity of their revenues and their eagerness to exchange advice propelled them into the politics of victims and the victims movement.

The Law Enforcement Assistance Administration was to have one last explosive impact on the field of assistance to victims. In 1979 its director stated that 'victim–witness assistance is a growing, but still fledgling, trend in criminal justice ... LEAA is seeking to encourage ... cooperation by developing a comprehensive national strategy for victim–witness assistance that will seek to involve all levels of government. ... In this role, we will act as a catalyst ...'[80] Within a few months the Administration had announced a major concentration of effect upon witnesses and victims 'to restore public confidence in the criminal justice system'. It was argued that 'the "real clients" or the "forgotten clients", victims and witnesses may get less than optimum treatment in a system geared to identifying and prosecuting the offender.'[81] $50 million were awarded in block and discretionary grants to nearly 200 projects, a National Victim/Witness Resource Center was established, and it was planned to publish a manual, newsletters, and directories. Within only a few more months, the Law Enforcement Assistance Administration had itself been dissolved although, as an American state politician declared at the 1981 NOVA Conference, it was 'focusing on victims with its dying breath'. A new austerity was introduced with uncertain consequences for the victims movement in the United States. The LEAA Victim Assistance Initiative had been set up as a sunset programme to be reviewed in 1981 and, in 1981, it was disbanded. Yet the President had clearly announced that 'the jungle is always there ... ready to take over'

[79] See D. Lowenberg, 'Integrated Victim Services Model', in B. Galaway and J. Hudson (eds.), *Perspectives on Crime Victims*, C. V. Mosby Company, St Louis, 1980.

[80] H. Dogin, foreword to R. Rosenblum and C. Blew, *Victim/Witness Assistance*, p. i.

[81] 'Who Are the "Real Clients" of the Justice System?, *National Criminal Justice Reference Service*, SNI 153, February 1980.

and that, in order to 'hold back that jungle and restrain the darker impulses of human nature', he planned to create a bundle of measures which included a task force to study the problems of victims of crime.[82] He proclaimed 20–6 April as National Victims Week. But it was also evident that funding had become insecure, voluntary organizations being thrown back on their own devices. The American victims movement was told in October 1981, 'the truth is, the people and their volunteer organizations have obligations for the welfare of their communities at least as great as those of official bodies of government. You all know that the Federal criminal justice block grant program has ended. Hence the need for your contributions has increased.'[83]

A third lesser phalanx is made up of a miscellany of organizations devoted to specific problems and specific victims. One instance is provided by a network of groups that originated in Cincinnati, Ohio, in 1978 and has since spread to some twenty other states. Parents of Murdered Children is a self-help organization which encourages mourning parents to meet one another for support and consolation: 'the parents discovered that by listening to each other, by crying together if they felt like doing so, by understanding how each felt, their grief was lessened.' Members will visit and write to those whose children had been killed, guiding them to others and helping them to 'work through their grief and use it constructively'.[84]

Another cluster of organizations developed around the Feminist Karate Union of Seattle, Washington. Instructors from that Union have produced an 'Acquaintance Rape Packet' of exercises which 'encourage women to maintain control of their physical space and to be assertive in protecting their integrity. They do not deal with physical self defense, concentrating instead on promoting changes in life style that will signal—"I am not a good victim".' The Union has sponsored an Alternatives to Fear Program which centres on Parent/Child Self Protection. Intended to help children to stave off sexual attacks and molestation, it shows how the signs of abuse may be recognized, offers suggestions about how children can resist adults, promotes discussion about sexuality between members of a family, and organizes 'karate classes for boys and girls ... Children study the traditional Japanese art in an atmosphere of equality between the sexes and with women as strong role models.' The Union

[82] *Globe and Mail,* 29 Sept. 1981.

[83] Address by the Honorable Robert F. Diegelman, Acting Director, Office of Justice Assistance, Research, and Statistics, before the seventh Annual Conference of the National Organization for Victim Assistance, 15 Oct. 1981.

[84] Charlotte Hullinger, co-founder of Parents of Murdered Children, quoted in D. Magee, 'Bereaved Parents', *Us,* 7 July 1981, p. 65.

has also initiated a Senior Citizen Self-Protection Program to counter the effects of the attitude which 'tends to regard older people as weak and helpless'. Instructors from the Feminist Karate Union offered a set of four seminars on coping with the fear of crime, crime prevention techniques, negotiating the hazards of the streets, and the maintenance of independence and dignity. In addition, 'participants will learn how to keep their balance and prevent falling during a struggle. They will practice getting out of choke holds and other grabs, as well as learning how and where to punch.'

Collectively, the American victims movement appears to have become large enough to compose a significant audience and market. There are the beginnings of a superstructure of commercial and ancilliary institutions growing up around it, a superstructure that provides services, ideas, and imagery to victims assistance organizations themselves. In a sense, that secondary grouping is shaping something of a visual and symbolic identity for the member organizations of the victims movement. Centred chiefly on firms making and supplying educational films, there is an appreciable industry devoted to the pictorial reconstruction of the character of victims, victimization, and victim relief. Aims Media Inc., for instance, distributes Osanka's *Sexual Abuse of Children*. It describes Osanka as a 'leading authority on child abuse and neglect' and as a 'one-man crusade against child abuse'. His film is designed to 'open your eyes to the secret that one million abused and neglected children want you to see. ... Perhaps for the first time communities will see what child molestation does to our society.' MTI Teleprograms Inc., another firm, offers a catalogue in which 'at every turn there's something exciting to discover'. MTI was formed in 1978 and has a stock of 250 titles on cults, hitchhiking, rape, juvenile justice, women's studies, vandalism and violence, runaways, suicide and drugs, child abuse and family violence, teenage pregnancy and the like. Its Acquaintance Rape Prevention Series includes *The Party Game*, which 'illustrates the damage that can result from ineffective communication'; *Just One of the Boys* 'shows how peer pressure can motive an attack'; *The Date* 'pinpoints sex role stereotypes as a cause of acquaintance rape'; and *End of the Road* 'demonstrates how assertive behavior can sometimes prevent an assault'. Amongst the 1981 New Releases and An MTI Bestseller is *A Place to Go: Battered Women and their Perilous Flights to Freedom*. Another New Release and Bestseller in 1981 was *Burnout*, a study of 'all hard-working professionals in the helping services' accompanied by a 48-page manual written by Dr Ayala Pines, 'pioneer in burnout research'. And there are other catalogues published by other firms.

In reply the staff of some of the victims assistance institutions have taken to publishing their judgements on the products of the movement's secondary industry. The Ontario Provincial Secretariat for Justice, for example, issued *Helping the Victims of Sexual Assault,* one section of which was devoted to film reviews. Twenty-eight films were assessed, fifteen being recommended and the others criticized or rejected as poor, out of date, or unsuitable for Canadians. Thus the report endorsed *Rape Alert:* 'this film gives sound advice, portrays victims sensibly, and shows the attitude of a rapist (violence-oriented). It destroys the myths surrounding rape.' But it condemns *Rape*: 'of poor technical quality, this American film is very negative to men in general and police and courts in particular. Legal aspects not applicable to Canada.'[85] Out of these processes of creation and exchange, the artefacts and insignia of a separate culture are about to emerge, a culture with its own language of terms like 'burnout', its own concerns, heroes, personalities, events, calendar, and symbolic representations of the world.

It is apparent that the American victims movement is, in Becker's phrase, something of 'an uneasy coalition of victim-related interest groups'.[86] Presiding over it and lending it a frail coherence is the National Organization for Victim Assistance. NOVA was born in 1975 and emerged publicly at the Second National Conference on Victims Services which was held at Fresno, California, in May 1976. A principal endeavour of that conference had been the attempt to pool information and practical advice in a novel area of work, to take stock of what was being done in the United States, and to prepare an organizational foundation for further activity. A large number of those who attended the conference decided to approve 'an organization aimed at the unification of professional and lay people who are committed to the humanization of the criminal justice system through victim assistance'.[87] NOVA itself is a most heterogeneous organization, held together only by the deliberate effort of its board to subdue quite manifest ideological and intellectual rifts. As I have reported, the professional and lay people who compose the American victims movement include potentially warring groups of radical feminists, district attorneys, police officers, and social workers. There are dormant schisms about the political and symbolic significance of gender, the family, state, class, race, and victims themselves. There are profound differences about the political import of organizational

[85] *Helping the Victims of Sexual Assault,* Provincial Secretariat for Justice, Toronto, 1979, p. 65.
[86] C. Becker, *Criminal Theories of Causation,* p. 14.
[87] A. Lassiter and J. Rowland, 'The Second National Conference on Victim Services', *Victimology,* Summer 1976, Vol. 1, No. 2, p. 331.

style: radical feminists veering towards a profession of collectivism and anarchism, others working with a more conventionally structured bureaucratic allocation of power and authority. The NOVA board encompasses and contains all these diverse strains and ideologies, being made up in 1981 of a President, two Vice-Presidents, a Secretary, and four Directors who were lawyers; four Directors drawn from Victim–Witness programmes; two Directors from rape crisis centres; two police officers; a member of a Crime Commission; a judge; a councilman; a probation officer; a district attorney; and two university teachers. The larger support for NOVA is a mirror of its board, and the composition of those who attended the 1981 conference in Toronto is instructive. The Americans present who could be identified were ten district attorneys, twenty-two representatives of victim–witness programmes, eight people from rape crisis centres and transition homes, two university teachers, a probation officer, three people attached to Criminal Injuries Compensation Schemes, four police officers, a member of a Crime Commission, a representative of a hospital, one who worked with the victims of burns, and a member of a church group.[88]

NOVA's own statement of objectives declares that its 'paramount purpose is victim advocacy—to express forcefully the victim's claims, too long ignored, for decency, compassion, and justice; to press those claims for the victims of crime . . .; and to insure that victim rights are honored by government officials and all others who can aid in the victim's relief and recovery'. NOVA organizes an annual conference, publishes a *Newsletter*, the *Victim Assistance Program Directory*, and the *NOVA Fund-raising Manual*. It maintains a clearing-house of information about techniques of assisting victims. It sponsored the first of a number of Victims Rights Weeks in 1981, a venture which received Presidential endorsement. But all this work is very recent. Like so much else in the history of the politics of victims, NOVA itself has only just begun to attain prominence. As Irvin Waller, himself a NOVA director, remarked, it was the substantial funding from a dying Law Enforcement Assistance Administration that transformed the organization and enabled it to acquire a presence: 'NOVA only really got going when they had money. [In 1981] it's seven or eight years old but it's only in the last couple of years that they've been able to start doing something actively. I think the general movement to try and do more for victims is really, in terms of concrete steps, a couple of years old.' The history of a victims policy is emergent and new, uncertain in shape and direction.

[88] Based on list of registrants for the NOVA Conference on Victim Assistance in Canada and the United States, Toronto, October 1981. List prepared 8 Oct. 1981.

The Science, the Movement, and the Ministry

At the beginning, then, and in the words of the Federal–Provincial Task Force on Justice for Victims of Crime, 'there [was] a vital and growing victims' movement in the U.S.A., whereas in Canada such a development [was] in the embryonic stage'.[89] The politics of victims were to be filtered through a succession of lenses, one lens beiing affected by the peculiarities of the American environment of crime and social control, another by the particular and shifting expression which the American victims movement gave to that environment, a third by the manner in which the ideas of that movement were imported into Canada, and yet another by the reception awarded those ideas by those who were to become exposed to them. My own interest in all that complicated process is confined to the response of the Ministry of the Solicitor General of Canada. Events will simply be ignored if they made no recognizable impact on that institution.

Victimology and the victims movement could not have had an unambiguous or stable presence in the lives of officials working in the Department. After all, they were not themselves complete or coherent phenomena: they contained prolific contradiction and openness, they were undeveloped and they were still changing. It was a shared anxiety about victims that brought their members together, but anxiety does not have to generate an identity of reactions. District attorneys, the staff of rape crisis centres, and others are not always in concord. Describing the very similar case of groups banded together around the problems posed by drugs and alcohol in the United States, Wiener has written about 'a network of ideology bearers', a network united by a 'common concern' but representing 'different aspirations, perspectives, languages'.[90] It is useful to analyse the American victims movement as just such a network, it being the case that there is an abundance of nuances, themes, structures, and styles of discourse accessible to those who choose to observe it. Moreover, the science and the movement had evolved over a number of years, being monitored, appraised, joined, and deserted by different staff all the while. It was held by more than one official that the entire bearing and character of victimology had undergone a reversal over the course of a decade. One commented, 'victims research started out more against the victims than for the victims—victim precipitation and so on—[but] there's no question now that it's basically a movement, a

[89] *Report of the Canadian Federal–Provincial Task Force on Justice for Victims of Crime*, Ministry of Supply and Services Canada, Ottawa, 1983, p. 2.

[90] C. Wiener, *The Politics of Alcoholism*, p. 17.

cause. A lot of people are toying around with it and see it as a cause of human justice and everything else.'

As staff encountered different facets of the movement, as their own commitments, knowledge, and interests changed, so their interpretations of American developments also fluctuated. There was an undoubted agreement that the victims movement contained some unusual features. It was a young organization, still being zealously championed by an untried first generation. In 1981 it had been chaired by Marlene Young, a woman whom some found charismatic and inspired. It centred on themes and problems that are quite extraordinarily poignant and pathetic. Its supporters manifested little of the distance or weariness displayed by others whom officials meet in their journeys about the criminal justice system. One former official stated, for example, 'Americans working in the crime victim field are inspiring. ... Everybody's marriage breaks up and they devote their lives to it. And those people are, I think, inspiring.' Similarly, an official working at the Department of Justice reflected, 'they're an unusual group, a dedicated type. Unlike meetings of social workers, [people attending NOVA conferences] complain about time lost in social activities.'

There has been no uniform response to such evangelism. Rather, officials' replies have been shaped by the changing interplay of time, setting, biography, and personal position in the social structure that emerged around the victims initiative. In the main, the victims movement was extended appreciable sympathy by those who were to be at the centre of the politics of the initiative. Indeed, it had sometimes been immersion in the affairs of the movement that had led staff to become attached to the initiative: they had developed a recognized competence or had acquired a motivation that propelled them in. It was those officials, too, who would have resisted most strenuously any identification with the bureaucrat of stereotype, the man or woman who sought to eliminate from 'official business love, hatred, and all purely personal, irrational, and emotional elements'.[91] One bitterly spurned part of an earlier draft of this book, observing that I had failed to recognize the vital role played by beliefs and passions, that I had made his colleagues seem to be 'scarecrows hanging in the wind'. Another official remarked that 'to say that they're against emotional commitment is so incredibly false'. For such officials, the victims movement acted as a baffle, a spectacle, and as a source which resonated their concerns. It was not to be dismissed. Yet there was also a clear nervousness. The selfsame official

[91] M. Weber, 'Bureaucracy', in H. Gerth and C. Wright Mills, *From Max Weber*, Routledge and Kegan Paul, London, 1961, pp. 215–16.

who had embraced the idea of emotional commitment revealed some caution about aspects of the movement in the States: 'there are some things that do sort of feed into paranoia. Like there's people who talk about the potential of vigilante groups. ... There's a side of it that's potentially very scary like a witch hunt.' And a colleague reflected, 'some of the Southern groups are quite conservative. They seem very near to vigilante groups. You get the feeling that they want to run down the street and lynch the first offender they meet.' So diffuse and diverse a movement prompted every official to voice some caveats or reservations about some aspects of NOVA and its attendant organizations. There was no complete endorsement of everything that was done in the name of victims.

Moreover, and as I have argued, officials attach importance to the cultivation of proper style and the development of a sensitivity to the demands of an occasion. Emotionality was held by many to be quite seemly, but it was not to be exuded in every setting and it had to be harnessed to sensible talk. Emotion must be tempered by wit, sensibility, and purposefulness:

> There's not very much tolerance for sloppy thinking.... if you continually sort of say, 'well, we must do something about victims', what people are going to say to you is 'maybe you're right. How should we do this?' Now, if you sort of say, 'well, I don't know but we ought to do something', then people are ultimately going to get sick about hearing about it. If you come up with a plan, people may reject the plan, but you're more likely to get an attentive audience. If you simply keep on yelling a phrase, you know, what do you do with that?

It was appropriate to be concerned. It was inappropriate to be gauche. On occasion, the victims movement appeared gauche, there being a shifting tension between the style of speech of the evangelist and the style of the policy-maker. The discourse of the Ministry and the discourse of the movement could jar. At a seminar given by Marlene Young at Carleton University, for instance, a senior Ministry official murmured *sotto voce,* 'there's no point in saying anything. It's a religious meeting.' At a similar meeting elsewhere, exception was taken to what was called the 'preachy' tone of talk. Officials can be preachy themselves, but they believe it necessary to modulate fervour. They are intelligent and reflexive, attending to themselves and their plans. Much of their own talk is a running series of *obiter dicta*, little asides about their own actions and the manner in which they present self. Often, indeed, they objectify themselves by talking about themselves in the third person. They engage in banter, translating into a playful form or game the activities in which they are involved professionally. Their special skill is in the deployment of words, and words are frequently toyed with, experimented with, and admired. There can be a display of considerable role distance,[92] advertising the gulf that occasionally exists between a situated self and the reflecting intelligence that directs it. The result is something of a distinct idiom, what Heclo and Wildavsky describe as the 'usages, manners and deportment of . . . governments'.[93] The idiom is not employed universally, but it makes possible a strain between bureaucratic style and the unremitting seriousness and unselfconscious stance of the evangelist.

On occasion, the work and business in America simply spilled over into Canada without planning. After all, Canadian criminology and politics are awash with American influences and it is quite impossible to draw boundaries or separate bundles of thought. As an official reflected rhetorically, 'where do Canadian criminologists go to school? What books do they study? Canadians—including scholars—watch Amer-[ican] t.v.—etc.' Canadians thus swim in an American sea. And their officials often seek out Americans when projects are contemplated. When the Ministry first began to envisage a major survey of victims and victimization, its staff cultivated an acquaintance with the Americans who had pioneered crime surveys for such bodies as the President's Crime Commission of 1967. Those Americans represented a formidable accumulation of practical and theoretical expertise, and they were eminently accessible. They were brought in bodily as consultants, Albert Reiss of Yale University being one of the most prominent. They were approached as they convened in meetings and seminars. One official, entrusted with the planning of the Canadian victim survey, for instance, went to a Victimization Seminar in April 1976, meeting 'people from universities and government agencies across the United States [who had gathered] to discuss the U.S. Victimization Surveys—surveys on which $56 million (!) has been spent to date'. He reported that he had 'returned with several hundred pages of important documentation, including a number of important internal documents from the U.S. Bureau of the Census'.[94] In 1977 another major effort was made to collect information about the problems and techniques of surveying victims. As I shall show, all that industry was to lead to an importation of American ideas which were dressed unexpectedly with additional thinking about the connections, uses, significance, and contents of survey work. Officials were

92 See E. Goffman, 'Role Distance', in *Encounters,* Bobbs-Merrill, Indianapolis, 1961.

93 H. Heclo and A. Wildavsky, *The Private Government of Public Money,* p. 1.

94 Memo to Director, Research Programs, on *Victimization Seminar—Washington, D.C.,* 27 Apr. 1976.

exposed inadvertently to writing and arguments about victim assistance programmes, their thoughts being turned to novel and unanticipated problems. Waller, for example, began to analyse the limitations of the survey before any Canadian survey had been done, maintaining that it could have only a minor bearing on the framing of policies for crime prevention and assistance to victims.[95]

Sometimes the introduction and use of American material were quite intentional. I have discussed already the routine way in which Canadian policy-makers would scan American publications before preparing proposals to venture into a new area. Thus, at an early stage of my history and when victims started to become a policy issue, an official was charged with composing a précis of salient American findings on victim services. Again, and as I shall show in the next chapter, Irvin Waller was to be particularly active in gathering and disseminating articles and press-cuttings about doings in America. What is important at this juncture is to appreciate that American work on victims and victimology established a reservoir of precedents and warnings for action. Criteria laid down by the Law Enforcement Assistance Administration could be borrowed by the Ministry's Consultation Centre and applied to the funding of Canadian projects.[96] Linda MacLeod could propose that the Pima County Victim–Witness Advocate Scheme be transplanted to deal with the problem of battering husbands in Canada.[97] Another federal official could model one of the very first drafts of a federal initiative on the Brooklyn Victim–Witness Assistance Project and the wider Law Enforcement Assistance Administration Crime Victim Initiative. Such a list of adaptations and lendings can be extended indefinitely. It underscores the purposes to which American work could be put once a decision had been made to develop a policy on victim assistance within the Ministry.

What happened in America does not explain why or how Canadian officials ever arrived at that decision. All of the work of the American victims movement, victimology, and their allies need not have shifted Canadian criminal justice policy. After all, there is much that is done abroad that plays itself out without manifest effect. To be sure, there were a number of projects, rape crisis centres, and transition houses established in Canada itself. But the absolute number of programmes was small, they were scattered across the face of a huge country, and

[95] See I. Waller, 'Victimization Surveys as Guides to Action'.

[96] Minutes, Victims Priority Presentation, Consultation Centre Staff Meeting, 21 Sept. 1981.

[97] L. MacLeod, *Wife-Battering in Canada: The Vicious Circle,* Ministry of Supply and Services, Ottawa, 1980, p. 65.

there was little sign that they were affecting the work of the Ministry of the Solicitor General in the beginning.

Simultaneously, there was a movement of thought in the United States, and there was an institution in Canada, but the meeting of the two demanded practical mediation. It was necessary to import the ideas and inspiration of victim assistance into the Department. That importation drew on American initiatives and it was achieved quite concretely by one principal person in the opening phases of my history.

Movements of thought require practical mediation. Without some person or group serving as a conduit or sponsor, the politics of victim assistance would have remained outside the frontiers of the Ministry of the Solicitor General. Of course, much mediation is obscure, diffuse, and oblique, forming the dimly discernible background of all social life. But the ferrying of ideas can also be very simple and direct. It occurs with the traffic of people. In a sense, everyone acts to merge, fuse, and synthesize organizations as he or she travels about the world. As Strauss observed, 'elements in [the] environment [are] literally inside [an] organization itself, in the form of workers carrying the outside into the work of the organization.'[98] When workers are substantial and powerful figures, that importation of an environment can be very consequential indeed. In the formative years of the Secretariat of the Solicitor General, Irvin Waller was Director General of Research, and he was to channel the thinking of the American victims movement into the very heart of the Ministry. Conversely, and as important, the American victims movement prepared its own path and its own patron by staging a succession of opportunities for conversion, opportunities that worked on Waller. Waller was moulded by the victims movement, profoundly stirred and inspired by its evangelism. They were to evolve together, the one influencing the development of the other. It is with the movement's changing of people, the conversion of Irvin Waller, and his influence on the Ministry that I shall deal in the next chapter. Without Waller, it is possible (but not demonstrable) that there would not have been an initiative.

[98] A. Strauss, 'Interorganizational Negotiation', *Urban Life,* October 1982, Vol. 11, No. 3, p. 352.

IV. The Moral Entrepreneur

Introduction

Victimology and the victims movement are somewhat given to theatrical display, achieving impressions on those who participate in them. It is with that dramatic work that I shall linger, for it was to be vital in the making of the federal initiative.

Lacking full recognition and acceptance in the 1970s, victimologists suffered in a modest fashion from what Berger has called a 'flawed plausibility structure'. Their arguments and perspectives were still to acquire the taken-for-granted quality of simple truths. Their problem was common enough and it evoked a common enough reply. The conventional response of many organizations to such uncertainty is a collective affirmation of commitment: 'the supportive community ... provides specific practices, rituals and legitimations that maintain the faith.'[1] Victimology was not unlike the sect in an unbelieving world. It would be unhelpful and foolish to search for excessively precise parallels between the two. For instance, victimology conforms to none of the criteria which Wilson proposed for the recognition of a sect.[2] Yet there remains a similarity that seems to be shared by all instances of a newly formed and strange world-view in its early stages. It resides in those practices, rituals, and legitimations of the less than perfect plausibility structure.

Durkheim observed of the life of the Australian aborigines:

> The life of the Australian societies passes alternately through two distinct phases. Sometimes the population is broken up into little groups who wander about independently of one another, in their varying occupations. ... Sometimes, on the contrary, the population concentrates and gathers at determined points for a length of time varying from several days to several months. This concentration takes place when a clan or a part of the tribe is summoned to the gathering, and on this occasion they celebrate a religious ceremony, or else hold what is called a corrobbori in the usual ethnological language. These two phases are contrasted with each other in the sharpest way. In the first, economic activity is the preponderant one, and it is generally of a very mediocre intensity. ... The

[1] P. Berger, *A Rumor of Angels*, p. 37.

[2] See B. Wilson, *Sects and Society*, Greenwood Press, Westport, 1978, pp. 1–6.

dispersed condition in which the society finds itself results in making its life uniform, languishing and dull. But when a corrobbori takes places, everything changes. . . . The very fact of the concentration acts as an exceptionally powerful stimulant. When they are once come together, a sort of electricity is formed by their collecting which quickly transports them to an extraordinary degree of exaltation. Every sentiment expressed finds a place without resistance in all the minds, which are very open to outside impressions; each re-echoes the others, and is re-echoed by the others.[3]

It is Durkheim's contention that the experience of such an assembly can give birth to collective representations, each member seeming to confront a social reality that transcends not only himself or herself but the very group. The congregation of so many people who view the world alike can profoundly amplify and anchor personal conviction, transforming it into an impersonal and solid truth. That, after all, is what many conferences are designed to accomplish. They are intended to give majesty and authority to convictions. The idea which is obviously accepted by everyone and is the specific creation of no one ceases to be arbitrary. Moreover, a simple increase in the numbers of people assembled together will bring about a disproportionately large increase in the number of relationships which they can have one with another. As a gathering grows, so there will be a mushrooming of connections that are independent of any one person's will. Small face-to-face groups tend to seem subjective, changeable, evanescent, and unprepossessing. The large meeting is rather more objective and immutable, engendering its own legitimacy.

It is not entirely fanciful to compare university teachers and the members of the victims movement with Australian nomads. The periodic conference can impress on the otherwise solitary academic or practitioner some qualities of the collective life in which he or she participates. After all, teachers can experience a very real isolation when they embark on research, writing and lecturing. It is an isolation which can be reinforced when one contemplates supporting a novel and unfashionable enterprise that others might ignore or condemn.

Victimologists and members of the victims movement do as their colleagues and the aborigines do. They spend a considerable portion of their lives dispersed and apart from the main body of those who think the same thoughts. At intervals, they come together to celebrate their unity. Those meetings are of great consequence to them and they are repeatedly invoked in talk and writing. A social world has been built in

[3] E. Durkheim, *The Elementary Forms of the Religious Life*, reprinted by Collier, New York, 1961, pp. 245, 246, 247.

and around them. As Waller observed, 'an international community of scholars, practitioners and advocates has grown out of a series of international meetings.'[4] A collective history and memory have been established. The brief life of the science and the movement has been punctuated by a small number of remarkable conferences, each of which is described with a distinct respect. It is as if each conference confirmed the advancing maturity of the discipline. More important, perhaps, each conference affirms the viability of victimology, its sheer capacity for survial. Thus Fattah stated:

> While still facing attacks and criticisms similar to those directed at criminology several decades ago, victimology is slowly coming of age in academic and professional circles and is gradually achieving worldwide recognition as an integral part of criminology, as shown by: . . . a series of international symposia on victimology . . ., and an international institute on victimology.[5]

Viano, too, has described the way in which conferences furnished a plot for the evolution of the discipline: '[the] foment of ideas, research, and reform efforts in the area of victimology has now reached a significant momentum. The First International Symposium on Victimology held in Jerusalem in 1973 gave the area of victimology international recognition as a distinct focus of inquiry within criminology. Another major international event—the International Study Institute on Victimology—took place in July 1975 in Bellagio, Italy. A Second International Symposium is to be held [in] September [1976] in Boston.'[6] The meeting at Bellagio was depicted as 'several days of intensive work' whose most significant consequences were the 'pooling of topics, . . . learning what problems interest people of different backgrounds, and . . . receiving the stimulation of others to pursue one's work'.[7] Conferences are thus treated as unusual and significant. They give a history. They are evidence of the tenacity of victimology. They provide a source of cohesion.

Conferences so constituted and so regarded can become decisive turning-points in the lives of those who attend them. Some officials told me of the manner in which their careers had been changed by their participation in the meetings of victimology. A number of people involved in the federal initiative appeared to have realized their common purpose in talk at the 1980 NOVA Conference in Portland, Oregon. It was at

[4] I. Waller, 'Crime Victims: Needs, Services and Reforms', paper delivered at the Fourth International Symposium on Victimology, Tokyo/Kyoto, August 1982, unpublished, p. 41.

[5] E. Fattah, 'Some Recent Theoretical Developments in Victimology', p. 198.

[6] E. Viano, 'Victimology: The Study of the Victim', p. 4.

[7] E. Viano, *Victims and Society*, p. xvii.

that Conference that they formed a joint resolve and a set of strategies for a Canadian victims initiative. Irvin Waller was there and he returned inspired. Again, a senior official in one of the Ontario ministries bent his will towards the problems of victims after attending the first international conference of victimologists at Jerusalem in 1973. Thereafter, he was to plan a series of community-based projects in Canada. A federal official working in the Research Division of the Ministry of the Solicitor General, described the collective excitement which had developed around victims:

There is no question that it's been a movement to some extent. I've sat at various meetings with people, you know, you're sitting somewhere till midnight talking about *victims*. You know, I haven't done that since the Vietnam War! It's a cause in that sense. It's an exciting kind of thing.

But the conference as a *rite de passage* was possibly most powerfully exemplified by the impact which Irvin Waller claimed the Bellagio Study Institute had upon him. The Institute consisted of some fifty people who discussed the problems of victims intently between the first and the twelfth of July 1975. In Waller's own words, it induced a *crise de conscience*, a catalytic crisis[8] that transformed his stance towards victims and the world:

It wasn't until '75 that I really realised that I was involved in a sort of victims issue. That was at the Bellagio Institute in Italy where suddenly everybody came together on victims. I've spoken three times in the last two weeks to Gerd Kirchhoff who I met at the session and who's Secretary of the World Society of Victimology. I've been dealing over the last two weeks on four or five occasions with issues relating to John Dussich about visits he's going to be making here. I met him at that Institute. ... It was organized by Emilio Viano who's been very influential in the victim area: he helped draft the papers from the First International Symposium ... and also organized a big Victimology Conference in Washington about a year ago. But he organized this meeting and it was effectively two weeks together to talk about victims ... I guess it was the first time that I heard anybody else give the arguments about victims being the forgotten people in the criminal justice system and the first time you heard people talk about wanting to set up a World Institute of Victimology. You heard a lot about the victimology movement in Japan. And you found people really committed to doing stuff for crime victims, some of whom were focused on rape victims, some of whom focused on domestic violence situations. But people like

[8] Interestingly enough, I have discussed the Bellagio Institute with other participants. It is my sense that the experience which is provided was variable and personal. Not every member shared Wallers's *rite de passage*. On the contrary, its meanings were situated, intersecting with the biographies and experience of those who attended. Moreover, to outsiders, Irvin Wallers' conversion was not apparent: it was to come later in 1979.

Viano and Mendelsohn were focused on victims generally. Certainly it very much brought together a group of people who were very interested in victims and hadn't talked to each other before. And once they'd talked they discovered they had a sort of mission that they held in common which was to do something for victims. The publications coming out of it. The fact that there was a book. That's where the victimology journal was founded. It was papers delivered at that conference which were the first papers for that journal. Thinking back, it was a moment when you really had a *crise de conscience*, a realisation that there was an issue, primarily a crime victim issue, that you should be in your particular society fighting for.

Between May 1974 and August 1980 Irvin Waller was a senior official in the Ministry of the Solicitor General. As Director General of the Research Division, he supervised the planning and development of research, presiding over the expansion of the Division from its initial staff of three to some thirty when he resigned. He guided the formulation of research and affected policy during the period when the victims initiative and the very Ministry itself were in the making. In that sense, he was a kind of ancestral figure who infused stories about the creation and unfolding of the Secretariat. Some of his colleagues were to call him 'Mr. Victims'. The then Acting Assistant Deputy Minister in charge of the Programs Branch described the crucial 1981 Strategic Overview as a monument to Irvin Waller. And one of those who nursed the initiative in its last stages before public release remarked, 'it's fascinating. Irvin has this master plan and we're little bits of it. Irvin makes all these political leaps. ... Irvin's controlling it all.' Her colleague commented, 'he will still be controlling it all even after he'd left.' Between 1978 and 1980, Irvin Waller established much of the political environment of the federal work on victims and he also laid the foundations of the initiative itself. He may be regarded as the practical incursion of victimology and the victims movement into the Canadian government, having fused the three together. He was the mediating agent. His *crise de conscience* at Bellagio was thus of the utmost consequence for the making of policy.

Irvin Waller as a Moral Entrepreneur

Howard Becker observed that 'rules are the products of someone's initiative and we can think of the people who exhibit such enterprise as moral entrepreneurs.'[9] Someone has to do something before social problems are identified and managed. In the case of Canadian victims, that someone

[9] H. Becker, 'Moral Entrepreneurs', in *Outsiders*, Free Press, New York, 1963, p. 147.

was chiefly Irvin Waller.[10] He was an entrepreneur who worked within a bureaucracy that gave him access to considerable power. He could as readily be identified as an evangelical bureaucrat, one who attempted to do politics from inside a government department, and such a role has many precedents.[11] What was important was Waller's busy and persistent effort. Without him, there might not have been a victims initiative at all. To be sure, the feminists in and around Ottawa supplied an additional and alternative impulse for political action. Yet their unaided plans nearly foundered, leading eventually to a very specific concentration on the battered woman. They encompassed a much narrower conception of the victim, referring only to raped, assaulted, and battered women, and they would almost certainly have omitted the very title of *victim* from anything they did. There were provincial stirrings, especially in Ontario under the guidance of the Ministry of Correctional Services. Yet the generalization of those stirrings, their transformation into a national enterprise, stemmed from a federal preparedness to respond, and it was Irvin Waller who organized that response. The timing of the federal initiative was quite vitally important. If it had been more laggard it could well have foundered on the financial restrictions imposed by a new politics of austerity. It was Waller's driving that moved it along smartly through its earlier stages. Waller was the mouthpiece and representative of the victims movement in the Ministry: he gave victims definition as a social problem, he spun webs of causality around that problem, and he was present, alert, and resourceful at a number of decisive stages in the evolution of policy. He was responsible for condensing and shaping what might otherwise have passed the Ministry by. In Wiener's natural history of policy-making, animating the problem is the first step.[12] It was Waller who animated victims in Ottawa.

Waller's influence was so marked and diffuse that there will be constant reference to it throughout the rest of this book. It is unnecessary and impossible to contain it in this chapter alone. Yet because it *is* so marked, it is important to prise it away from the contexts in which it appeared and expose it to a separate analysis. It is a topic amply meriting its own special place.

The moral career of Waller the victimologist unwound rather slowly. It seemed to be staggered over several episodes, and each episode lacked

[10] Other moral entrepreneurs may be found in the history of the victims initiative, Art Daniels of the Ontario Ministry of Correctional Services being a prime example. But my interest is in the affairs of the federal government.

[11] See D. Dickson, 'Bureaucracy and Morality', *Social Problems*, Fall 1968, Vol. 16, No. 2.

[12] See C. Wiener, *The Politics of Alcoholism*, p. 6.

uniform visibility and significance to the people who talked about it. Waller's standing and influence were matters of quite considerable interest in the Ministry and its environs. They were eagerly discussed, even after Waller had resigned from the Department. People could not agree on the relative importance of the different turning-points in Irvin Waller's public life. And, to compound confusion, the turning-points were subject to continuous re-interpretation as time passed, events unfolded, and the victims became more prominent as a social problem.

Waller was born and educated in England, receiving a BA degree in Mathematics and Economics from Cambridge and advancing to write a Ph.D. dissertation at that university on the release of men from prison.[13] From 1966 until 1974 he worked at the Centre of Criminology, University of Toronto, undertaking further research on the release of inmates as a member of the Hugessen Task Force. It was that earlier work on discharge that led him to attend to victimization in his second book, *Burglary: The Victim and the Public*.[14] He recalled:

> My interest in victims came straight out of *Men Released from Prison*, which was my Ph.D. thesis, published as a book in '74. In the end of that you'll find specific reference to restitution and prevention. ... The second line here says that 'the system almost totally ignores the victim and prevention whilst concentrating on the offender. One can be sure, however, that the victim will be forgotten or possibly given a nominal grant but a similar offence is just as likely to occur in the future'. That was not a random statement. ... I was really talking about prisons at that point but, once I'd looked at overall policy, the immediate thing that came up was doing something for victims and crime prevention. Now that led into the *Burglary: Victim and Public* study which was influenced really by a sort of attempt to look system-wide at what the social service system was doing, at what the justice system was doing, in relation to that one offence, at what the public wanted, and what its impact was on the victim. A major drive in the proposals relating to the burglary study was the impact of crime on the victim—what does the victim want? And that's really the whole concentration of the study.

Burglary: The Victim and the Public was an organized attempt to expel what its authors considered to be the dominant myths of burglary, in particular those myths which represent burglary as a 'vicious stranger-to-stranger crime, where rape, murder and robbery are the eventual aims of "professional" or "obsessed" burglars'.[15] It was a study based upon a survey which furnished the survey's archetypal victim. 1655

[13] I. Waller, *Men Released from Prison*, University of Toronto Press, Toronto, 1974.
[14] I. Waller and N. Okihiro, *Burglary: The Victim and the Public*.
[15] I. Waller and N. Okihiro, *Burglary: The Victim and the Public*, p. 4.

members of Toronto households were interviewed in the spring of 1974. It was reported that those who had been burgled rarely experienced prolonged distress. After a brief spate of upset and fear, most victims sought only to retrieve what had been taken from them: 'what happens is that retributive feelings fade and the major remaining concern in burglary is just getting the goods back.'[16] Losses were found to be quite petty, an average value of $345 being involved, burglaries themselves were uncommon, and personal injury to the victim was even less common. In short, it was concluded that burglary was a minor social problem which could well be resolved by sensible crime prevention measures and an extension of adequate property insurance. It had been inflated beyond reason to demand an unwarranted share of police and judicial resources. Indeed, the gravest social problem was held to be the fear of crime that had developed around burglary, not the immediate impact of burglary itself.[17] Social policy should focus on that issue, dispelling misapprehensions by 'more frequent publicity of the peaceful nature of residential burglary. The police officer called to the house could do more to provide reassurance to the victim by explaining the amateur and non-violent nature of most residential burglars.'[18]

Although focused on burglars and burglary, the project gave Waller a public identity as a person who was writing about the victims of crime. His work on the book took him to Bellagio in 1975. It led to him being singled out by others who had a stake in addressing him as a potential victimologist. He was to be progressively drawn into the skein of meetings which formed the beginnings of victimology, meetings which pointed to a future based on a new moral purpose and a special intellectual career. The project admitted him to the social circles that were being built around the problems of the victim. As important, perhaps, the book generated a public response which prompted Waller to make a public profession of his commitment to the welfare of victims.

The book's publication was delayed. When it did appear, Waller had already moved to his new post and all his utterances had attained a new political salience. In the main, *Burglary: The Victim and the Public* was well enough received in academic journals. Mohr, for example, called it 'an important social commentary with enduring value'.[19] Members of the criminal justice community were not always enthusiastic. As I have

[16] Ibid., p. 47.

[17] For a later assessment and discussion of the book, see M. Maguire, *Burglary in a Dwelling*, p. 138.

[18] I. Waller and N. Okihiro, *Burglary: The Victim and the Public*, p. 105.

[19] J. Mohr, review published in the *Canadian Journal of Criminology*, July 1979, Vol. 21, No. 3, p. 373.

reported, the *Canadian Police Chief* described the book as 'fantasizing' and 'casual'. The lay reaction was hostile, complicated by its organization around a critical editorial in the *Globe and Mail*. Waller recalled: 'the reception given to the book was actually the reception given to an editorial that distorted not only what was said in the book, but what had been said in the Globe and Mail's front page story.' The *Ottawa Journal* was incited to dilate upon the irresponsibility of the government for which Waller worked. It deplored 'the Liberal Government's apparent attitudes towards criminals, coupled with a seeming indifference towards victims of crime'.[21] Letters were written to newspapers. Under the headline, 'Give burglars a break? A mind-boggling view', four indignant letters were published in the *Globe and Mail* of 25 November 1978. One asserted that its writer was 'thoroughly amazed', another proposed that 'we should "destigmatize" these noble men by offering a burglar-of-the-year award', a third suggested that only mass murders might deserve police attention, and the last enquired whether 'moral and ethical values [are] to be weakened or dispensed with altogether for the sake of practical expediency?' Letters continued to be written until well into December 1978. Burglary victims, in particular, protested that they did seek more than restitution. One maintained that if he were burgled again he would hope that the burglar would 'be sufficiently incapacitated to the point where any future possibility of repeating the crime would be a physical impossibility'.[22] Letters were sent to the Ministry and to the Minister. The Solicitor General was asked whether 'thieves that desecrate homes and steal family heirlooms are now to be called "peaceful intruders" and not criminals ...'.[23] It was suggested by another correspondent that 'perhaps we should go to the next step and place signs in our windows—"WELCOME BURGLARS"'.[24] Irvin Waller himself was told, 'it is plain that neither you, nor Mr Okihiro have experienced a burglary in your home. We were appalled at your recommendation that the criminal code be amended.'[25]

Waller composed replies to all those letters and, in doing so, was impelled to make a public declaration of his sympathy for victims and his desire to better their lot. To the *Globe and Mail* he wrote, 'more emphasis should be placed on policies which would reassure, compensate or help the victims recover'.[26] To the letter of one whose house had been

[20] Letter to myself dated 22 Feb. 1983.
[21] Ottawa File, *Ottawa Journal*, 20 Feb. 1979.
[22] Letter to the *Globe and Mail*, 9 Dec. 1978.
[23] Letter to the Hon. Jean-Jacques Blais, 29 Nov. 1978.
[24] Letter to the Hon. Jean-Jacques Blais, 21 Nov. 1978.
[25] Letter dated 22 Nov. 1978.
[26] Letter to the *Globe and Mail*, 9 Dec. 1978.

left in a messy state after burglary, he replied 'we are well aware of the emotional trauma that some victims experience, particularly where a house has been trashed or vandalized'.[27] He did not retract the major arguments of his study, but there did appear to be an obligation to profess his compassion. As he remarked, 'the letters brought home in emotional terms the importance of 5% of responses—I would not change the rational contents of the book.'[28] He had confronted the other archetypal victim, the victim of clinical experience who was aggrieved, upset, and uncomforted. The contrast with the archetype of the survey was quite stark enough for him to reflect on the organized deficiencies of survey work:

> The [National Crime Surveys] have provided some important information on the direct impact of crime. ... However, these measures do not illustrate how the crime is experienced by the victim. ... without discussing their feelings of unhappiness, victims who are traumatized by the event can be the most active writers of letters to the press or to legislators, the most disillusioned with police services and generally the most dissatisfied with criminal justice programs. Press reports, in which burglary victimization surveys are quoted as showing serious events to be rare, tend to generate vitriolic letters to the editor from those who have been traumatized by such events in the past.[29]

All that visible display of sentiment about the character of victimization and the need for assistance to victims was to be characterized by Irvin Waller's colleagues as the major turning-point in his political and professional career. One likened the experience to that undergone by Saul on the road to Damascus. Another remembered that the press had presented 'Irvin as being uncaring about victims and so on. He took quite a beating in the press over that. In reaction to that, he became *very* interested in victims.' Irvin Waller himself would discount the importance of the criticism that attended his book, contending that his policy commitment had been formed long before any significant social reaction has taken place. What is nevertheless evident is the public and professional recasting of Irvin Waller as one who began to protest his concern for victims at the end of 1978.

In a process that was becoming rather over-determined, that public transformation was to be completed a little later when Irvin Waller went to another conference, the 1979 meeting of NOVA in Philadelphia, and came back 'just like a man transfixed'. It was at that meeting that he

[27] Letter dated 15 Mar. 1979.
[28] Letter to myself dated 22 Feb. 1983.
[29] I. Waller, 'Victimization Surveys as Guides to Action', p. 12.

had his first encounter with NOVA and, 'in NOVA I met a number of victims and I had the emotional charge that victims bring. I think they have had a major impact on me. [At that conference] I first met people emotionally involved in a big way. That link was very influential in my getting very actively involved'. Before 1978 most of those around Waller took him to be 'offender-oriented'. After 1978 the public identity of 'Mr. Victims' was fixed, although, as Irvin Waller himself remarked, 'I was also concerned about other issues'.

Burglary: The Victim and the Public became important in another fashion. It came to represent Waller's research and policy agenda for the Ministry of the Solicitor General whilst he was the Director General of its Research Division. After all, the book formed his last major essay at analysis before he became a civil servant, it had propelled him into the stream of events and gatherings of victimology, and it had prompted the public response to which he had made his own answering affirmation. In that manner, the book was a framework of interests, perspectives, and commitments that could be exported to his new post. Waller would describe himself as a political criminologist, one who sought to bring about social reform rather than contemplate the intellectual puzzles of crime and control: 'my interest in criminology has always been a consumer view.' He had moved to the Ministry itself 'because I wanted to see changes', and the changes were listed in his book:

I think if you look at the research programme of the Solicitor General, you will find that the major elements in it were really the things that I'm trying to do in the burglary study. They were public attitudes, they were victim issues, they were crime prevention, public attitudes including retribution. That was the whole major emphasis. Now it obviously had to include police and corrections, but I think without necessarily saying, you know, I have looked at the burglary study and said this is what I should do, once I was involved with the national programme, you obviously have some prejudices that were in the burglary book and were to some extent involved in the research programme.

A perusal of the research priorities flagged in the *Research Program Guides* between 1974 and 1977 certainly confirms that there is a substantial mirroring of the themes in the burglary book. The research programme did contain additional priorities drawn from the debates about dangerousness and capital punishment, diversion, the training of correctional staff, and the like. Moreover, many of the topics included are so broad that they omit little. Crime prevention and public attitudes are very catholic concerns that had been planted in the foundations of the Ministry in 1966. And it will be discovered that crime prevention, victimization, and public attitudes were items on the programmes of other government departments in other countries. The Law Enforcement Assistance Administration in the United States and the Home Office Research Unit in the United Kingdom had given attention to the same themes.[30] The Government of South Australia would appear to have passed through their own very similar history of research and policy. None the less, there is a recognizable affinity between Waller's concerns, his published statement of intent, and the general drift of the Ministry's research.

In 1972 and 1973, in the earliest period of the Secretariat's history, there was a Research Division of one person and very little capacity to formulate or realize plans: the division was 'one, relatively low ranking official—single handedly doing all the "research" work (questions from the House and contracts etc.)'. There was an established programme of corrections research and little else. There could be no preoccupation with victims because 'there was no place to *be* interested in victims'. Waller's appointment in 1974 was the beginning of the great expansion of the Secretariat. With it came the growth of research capacity at the Ministry: 'Irvin was hiring left, right and centre. It was like opening the floodgate.' And with it came a research agenda. Victims were mentioned in the *Research Program Guide* for 1975–6 and in response to the Peace and Security package, a response which I shall discuss in the next chapter. Under the heading of 'Violent Crime, the Dangerous Offender and the Victim', it was announced 'the Ministry has identified violent crime as a priority area primarily because of its strong contribution to public fear of crime and victimization'.[31] Three dependent topics were described: '*Criminal–Victim Relationships*—offences against the person/crimes of violence are of particular interest; the *Victim and the Police*—willingness to report crimes—treatment and handling of victims of violent crimes; *Alleviation of Victim Problems*—alternative methods of assisting the victim—effects of assistance on victim/public attitudes towards the criminal justice system.'[32] But despite that early beginning, it was to be another seven years before victims could be transformed effectively into the special target of a separate initiative. As I shall show in the next chapter, Waller's act of insemination placed victims in the Ministry. It was

[30] In the case of the Home Office, see, for instance: P. Mayhew *et al.*, *Crime as Opportunity*, HMSO, London, 1976; C. Banks *et al.*, 'Public Attitudes to Crime and the Penal System' *British Journal of Criminology*, July 1975, Vol. 15, No. 3; P. Mayhew, 'Opportunity in Crime', *Home Office Research Bulletin*, Issue 2, 1975; J. Vennard, 'Victims of Crime', *Home Office Research Bulletin*, Issue 3, 1976.

[31] *Research Program Guide*, Solicitor General, Ottawa, 1975, p. 13.

[32] Ibid., pp. 13–14. Italics in original.

important. Yet it took time before the embryo grew; many did not know that there had been a conception at all; and a still birth was the most probable outcome for a long while. Waller himself said, 'I was very frustrated outside by what the government was doing and I got frustrated inside and saw some progress but was never satisfied with the progress one made.'

Throughout much of the time it took to nurse victims as a policy issue, Waller was in diligent attendance. Rather like Ariel on Prospero's Island, Waller could be found coaxing, guiding, prompting, and pushing everything forward to the final Act. He may not have been successful in every manœuvre but, as the Director of Policy observed, he 'kept on talking about victims, victims, victims'. Accordingly, Irvin Waller will reappear continually in the history which is to come. This chapter is intended only to introduce him, not to give a full and detailed account of his activities. In particular, I shall refrain from discussing those important plays which were made at very special phases of the history. Instead, I shall concentrate upon Irvin Waller as a builder of networks, as a disseminator of victimology, and as a prompter of action.

The Builder of Networks

During his years as Director General of the Research Division, Irvin Waller was to exhibit considerable industry as the constructor of a social world which turned on victims, the victims movement, and victimology. In so doing, he was engaged in an activity which is familiar enough in Ottawa to have won its own name. 'Networking' is a word which appears with some frequency in the talk of officials. It refers to the process of forging links between the like-minded and the complementary so that information can be exchanged and co-operation nurtured. Networking is taken to be a useful preliminary stage in much policy work, being directed particularly at colleagues in other government departments and in the private sector. Performed properly, it can establish a real enough presence for a piece of policy, serve as a baffle for the policy-maker's own ideas, confer objectivity, and foster busyness. It amplifies, focuses, and creates demands that are independent of the policy-maker's own private sphere of action. It lays the basis of provincial, national, or even international organization. Upon it can be heaped all the activities that accompany the work of social reform: journals, meetings, professional associations, titles, and institutions.

Irvin Waller was a prodigious networker. He was a conspicuous participant in that great chain of conferences that yielded a structure and biography for the discipline of victimology, attending meetings, giving papers, chairing sessions, and arranging yet more conferences. Waller was to become a member of the International Advisory Board to the Third International Symposium on Victimology and, at that Symposium, he was appointed to the executive committee which was formed to consider the creation of a World Society of Victimology. In time, he became a member of the Executive Committee of that Society. In 1980 Irvin Waller was a member of the NOVA Advisory Committee.

He was to be discovered giving papers and press interviews about victims throughout the late 1970s and early 1980s: he talked at Bellagio in 1975 and at Münster in 1979; he convened the March 1980 National Workshop on Services to Crime Victims in Ottawa; he ran a two-day workshop on *Crime Prevention: Victim Assistance, Effective Approaches to Crime Control*, organized by the Advanced Professional Training Institute of Ottawa, and offered at the Holiday Inn in Ottawa on the 7th and 8th of May and at the Bayshore Inn, Vancouver, on the 21st and 22nd of May 1981; in July 1981, he told a symposium on pre-trial services, 'the first priority should be to assist the victim or to get them tied into agencies that can help them';[33] he advocated providing 'assistance recovering financial loss and with the trauma and crisis that crime created' at the meeting of the Probation Officers of Ontario in August 1981; he addressed a plenary session of the John Howard Society of Ontario in October 1981, talking, 'you've guessed it', about victims; he spoke at the 1981 NOVA Conference in Toronto, having been most influential in bringing NOVA to Canada and arranging a special ancillary meeting of American and Canadian legislators to serve as a prologue to that Conference. And there were many other meetings and conferences that he attended, planned, and monitored. As one of his colleagues remarked, 'he's got an enormous amount of energy and a certain amount of proselytising ability or bent, so that when he gets these notions, he doesn't let them go at all.'

Irvin Waller cultivated the people he met at conferences, meetings, symposia, and workshops, becoming an unusually prolific correspondent. Having formed acquaintances, he would pursue them, relaying information about his own and others' work, discussing the development of thinking about victims and the constitution of victimology itself. After every conference, a shoal of letters would be sent to those who had come within Irvin Waller's sphere of acquaintance. Consider the aftermath of a single meeting. After the Third International Symposium a sheaf of correspondence was written. For example, to a counterpart working in the government of another state, Irvin Waller wrote:

[33] *Toronto Star*, 29 July 1981.

I enjoyed meeting you at the Third International Symposium on Victimology and was sorry not to have had longer to talk with you. Given your interests in the relationship between victimization survey research and policy, I am enclosing the two papers which were presented at the Symposium, together with a flyer on the book in which they were based. The one on Victimization Studies as Guides to Action . . . deals with many of the organizational issues relating to how such research can be useful to policy makers.

Other letters were sent to other participants. Waller was manifestly assiduous in stirring, echoing, and supplying the curiosity of those about him. He would survey the world for signs of interest in the problems of the victim of crime and, having detected such a sign, would approach those who had demonstrated it. He would respond to newspaper reports, periodicals, and the publications of the private sector. For instance, he wrote to the Executive Director of the John Howard Society of Ontario:

I have just read the 1978 Annual Report of the John Howard Society . . . and noticed a statement in your report referring to new developments and services to victims. Attached are three reports that may interest you. The little blue book on 'Crime Victims Have Rights, Too' was circulated at the recent Federal Provincial Meeting of Ministers responsible for Justice as an example of some of the major developments taking place in the U.S. . . . I've been to a number of meetings recently both in the U.S. and Europe relating to victim seervices and victimology so I have accumulated a fair amount of materials and contacts. If I can help you further, please let me know.

Irvin Waller was as busy distributing information and ideas about *Burglary: The Victim and the Public*. He made it clear that the book was to serve as a foundation for the evolution of research and policy in the Ministry. Thus, in one letter to an American professor, he announced:

While undertaking the Burglary study in Toronto, I spent considerable time studying and thinking about the issues of victimization. Unfortunately, since moving to the Solicitor General's Department I had not made the time to ensure the victimization survey here took advantage of that thinking. As a result, the Vancouver survey did not build on the Toronto work, but developed separately. Before we engage in further major studies in crime prevention, victim service, orienting criminal justice services to citizen needs, studies of public insecurity, I hope that new initiatives will build on both the studies.

Waller therefore devoted part of his time in office to weaving a net of links between himself and associates, links that were based chiefly on victimology conferences. It was those links which brought him into contact with the developments of victimology and he used them as a conduit to conduct information to the Ministry of the Solicitor General itself.

The Disseminator of Ideas

Withing the space of four or five years, Waller had managed to establish himself in many of the principal centres of victimology and the victims movement. Akin to Flay or Steerpike of Gormenghast, he was privy to the simultaneous stirrings of major sectors of the political organizations that had begun to emerge about victims. He was positioned in a senior post in a strategic government department, attached to the major North American social movement of victims assistance organizations, and entrenched in academic victimology. Even after he had left the Ministry of the Solicitor General, he retained enough influence and maintained sufficient contact to engineer some of the processes that unfolded inside the federal government. Indeed, at a remove, he supervised the movement of a number of ostensibly independent institutions at the time of the NOVA Conference of 1981, shaping actions and responses in an orchestrated sequence. One of his erstwhile colleagues observed, Irvin Waller 'has his hands everywhere' and another stated 'he has a whole lot of connexions and a whole lot of fingers in a pie out there that are very broad'.

Waller was to feed the Ministry with the fruits of his industrious cultivation of ideas and people. In a manner hitherto unknown he constantly distributed press cuttings, reports, and articles about the growing problem of victims. In November 1979, for instance, he copied and circulated an excerpt from the *Ottawa Citizen* entitled 'Car Stolen, wrecked, daughter raped, bills go to mom'. In May 1980 he sent the Chief of the Causes and Prevention Division a memorandum about a Ph.D. thesis written at the University of Michigan and revealing that 'persons in rural areas, in that part of the United States, are victimized as much as people in urban areas because they go and do their shopping and trading in urban areas'. Within a year of his arrival at the Ministry he had distributed an article[34] which, 'although it talks about "witnesses", ... might have discussed "victims". It is an area of research and policy neglect, where some initiatives might be taken, particularly by ourself and Consultation.' Four months later he wrote 'a memo to file', 'Re: Victimization and Social Indicators. *Denis Szabo* brought to my attention that Belgium and France were setting up regional "antennae" for meas-

[34] M. Ash, 'On Witnesses: A Radical Critique of Criminal Court Procedures', *Notre Dame Lawyer*, December 1972, Vol. 48, No. 2.

uring the quality of life. He will be investigating how this relates to criminal justice projects and letting us know.'[35] Only a few days later he proposed a meeting 'on the subject of victimization' to bring 'material together ... As you are aware, my own "Burglary and the Public" in Metro Toronto, included a victimization survey testing a number of methodological issues ...'[36] In July 1975 Waller wrote a general letter summarizing the proceedings of a Washington workshop on victimization surveys. In February 1976 he distributed a photocopy of an LEAA Newsletter and asked that a general review of victimization studies be prepared. And so it went on in a continuous flurry of letters, circulars, and memoranda. On occasion, the materials related to matters at hand, and particularly to the methodological research which was initiated in the mid-1970s on the conduct of victimization surveys. Sometimes there was no obvious occasion which had elicited the materials other than their publication or discovery. But the results were the same. They brought about an unremitting emphasis on victims and the need for a policy on victims. It gave victims a presence in the Ministry. As a former colleague of Waller's reflected, 'the Chinese water torture was employed, I think. When Irvin was here he used to play that theme a lot and ... by frequent repetition, it sort of became part of the intellectual atmosphere, as you say, in the air.' And another colleague alluded to 'the sense of "overwhelmingness" of the I.W. phenomenon'.

The Prompter of Action

Waller was alert, attentive, and resourceful. At a number of major turning-points in the early history of the initiative, it was Waller's prompt action that turned a development towards victims. Much of the rest of this book will be a chronicle of those moves, but it is instructive to list some of them: Waller was to play a central role in securing Government approval for a study of the methodological problems of a national survey of victims in Canada; he confirmed a Ministerial commitment to remedial work for victims in 1979; in 1980 he helped to instil a common awareness and identity amongst those who provided services to victims in Canada; he supported the inclusion of victim assistance as a part of the 1981 Strategic Overview of the Ministry; and he promoted the first Canadian meeting of NOVA in 1981, a meeting intended ceremonially to launch private and official moves to develop programmes for victims. Waller was ever moving things forward.

[35] Memo to File, 3 Sept. 1975.
[36] Memo dated 30 Sept. 1975.

Conclusion

Irvin Waller had spent two years in an untiring campaign to promote victims' rights and he resigned from his post because he concluded that he had failed. He recalled:

I would say there were basically two people who were hooked on crime victims when I worked [in the Ministry]. One was myself and the other was [an official in the Causes and Prevention Division]. I don't think the interest in crime victims went any broader than that. ... I resigned from the Government because I concluded that they weren't concerned about three things: they weren't interested in crime prevention; they weren't concerned with the effective use of resources and corrections area; and they weren't interested in victims. ... I think if you speak to people in the Policy Branch or the Deputy Minister's, I don't think there was any support whatsoever.

Waller spoke about the unrequited needs of crime victims in his leaving speech. He spoke about them in a subsequent interview with the press: 'there's been very little interest in trying to deal with the harm done by crime, despite the fact that it wouldn't cost much to show a little concern for the victims.'[37]

Waller's style is redolent of that of the great Victorian reformers. Indeed, his own biography was not so very different from theirs. His father was a senior British judge and he remembered having continuously discussed matters of crime and law reform at home. What Waller had done was to export some of the manners and pattern of the English 'intellectual aristocracy',[38] an aristocracy given to recognizing a close affinity between social research and political action. There is a closeness of certain political and intellectual circles in Britain that seems to guarantee that the ideas expressed by their members will be practically consequential.[39] So too in Canada. And there are other similarities. Like Chadwick and Kay-Shuttleworth, Waller was indefatigable. He believed in research as enlightenment: the uncovering and propagation of facts being an obvious and indispensable prelude to intelligent action. Like many of the 'leading public servants' of Victorian Britain, he was a member of those organizations that conduct social investigation for purposes of social reform.[40] The statistical societies of the Victorian reformers and the contemporary victimology of Irvin Waller are linked

[37] *Globe and Mail*, 5 July 1980.

[38] See N. Annan, 'The Intellectual Aristocracy', in J. Plumb (ed.), *Studies in Social History*, Longman, London, 1955.

[39] See K. Banting, *Poverty, Politics and Policy*, pp. 6–7.

[40] M. Bulmer, *The Use of Social Research: Social Investigation in Public Policy-Making*, George Allen and Unwin, London 1982, p. 7.

by the 'strong implicit moral assumptions [that are] built into the reliance upon social research as a method of inquiry'.[41] Waller conceived the business of government to be the protection of those who were rendered vulnerable and weak by misfortune. He believed that political action could flow out of research. He engaged in tireless campaigning. He sustained and drew sustenance from an intellectual community of those who were bent on making policy. In all this, 'the social policy process has not changed dramatically since the nineteenth century'.[42]

Waller made a most profound impact on a number of phases of the victims initiative, having been responsible for the implantation of the issues and for much of its later cultivation. Yet it was also held that he had created a series of minor disturbances around the issue that were to complicate its future pattern of growth. The effects of his presence were massive and they remain unresolved, being experienced and debated still by those whom he had left behind in the Ministry. So powerfully did he exemplify the politics of victims that he came to personify them, becoming Mr Victims himself. It became difficult for his colleagues to disentangle their stances towards victims, the man who championed them, and the office which he occupied. Victims came to form part of the very persona of Irvin Waller. One colleague was to comment, 'I never knew what was being promoted, I.W. or the issue.' In turn, officials declared that it was almost impossible to distinguish between the social organization of enterprise and the character of the moral entrepreneur, between the limitations of the office of Director General and the manner in which its incumbent worked. One may suppose that, in such an early period of the life of the Secretariat, when Irvin Waller moulded the very features of the office of Director General, the distinction between post and person must have been fine indeed.

It will be remembered that Waller had resigned from the Ministry in August 1980, having not been promoted to a more senior appointment, and announcing that he had failed in his quest to stir the government into action: 'I left because I did not feel governments were concerned enough about programs to prevent crime or programs that would help victims of crime recover from the experience.'[43] Some officials have asserted that such a failure was inevitable because the quest was not truly Waller's: he was Lancelot, not Galahad. They would claim that the making of policy was not within the brief and mandate of the Director General of Research, that it was not his business to generate a policy

[41] Ibid.
[42] K. Banting, *Poverty, Politics and Policy*, p. 143.
[43] *The Gazette*, Montreal, 1 Dec. 1982.

initiative for victims. Research could provide support and inspiration but the work of translating an idea into policy had to be done elsewhere. As Smith has argued of the general structural position of research in government, 'the social scientist is often an advisor *at one remove*; that is an advisor to an advisor'.[44] Waller had no direct grasp on policy, and it was the removal and translation of the victims issue that eluded him during his years at the Ministry. So intimate was the association between victims and the person of the Director General to become that it proved difficult to detach one from the other. There was seen to be a problem of proprietorship.

The Director General of Research could not make policy immediately. That was someone else's job. He could make suggestions and spur activity along, but he could not assume command himself. His ideas required the sponsorship of one more powerful, centrally placed, and functionally appropriate than himself. As an Assistant Deputy Solicitor General argued, 'if you want the Deputy Minister to get behind something, it needs to have the Assistant Deputy Ministers behind it. Because, if they don't, it's *dead*! Because the group with the real power is undoubtedly the Committee of ADMs and the Deputy.' At the beginning. Irvin Waller did not secure the effective endorsement of a senior official. He tried to move without support and he was balked.

Perhaps his failure arose from impatience. Waller was ahead of the sympathies, processes, precedents, and agreements that move initiatives on: 'maybe its time hadn't come? How long does it take generally for an idea to become a movement/an initiative?' Perhaps his failure arose from style. His lack of success was explained by some of his former colleagues as the outcome of an omission to be programmatic and concise in the making of proposals: it was not enough merely to stress the plight of victims, 'if you can't say, well okay, I'm really excited, tell me five things I should do, then I'm not going to listen anymore, you know . . . If you don't have five things that you should be trying to do, then all you've got is a *theme*!' There was an unwillingness to accept what was defined as such an unadorned theme. As another colleague stated, 'he was hammering victims as somehow an issue in itself.' It was argued that an unfocused zeal tended to estrange some of the more senior officials. One tended to call him 'earnest and unremitting', and those who were unimpressed by the appeal of a victims of policy tried occasionally to avoid him.

In some measure, too, there was a perceived difficulty of ownership.

[44] G. Smith, 'Social Work, Policy, Government and Research', in J. Gandy *et al.* (eds.), *Improving Social Intervention*, p. 228.

The issue would stagnate until it could be transported to the Policy Branch, but, it was claimed, 'he couldn't give it up. . . . if he had instead let it be an [Assistant Deputy Solicitor General's] issue, do you know, it could have gone. Or if it had been realised that at some point you give it to Policy . . . that at some point to actually expedite something you have to recognise . . . that some things are better done by this group and some by this person.' Whatever the merits of this charge, the outcome is the same. There may be something of an inherent dilemma in the evolution of any issue that is identified very closely with a single official. Ironically, sadly, and perhaps importantly, a number of officials have conjectured that it was Irvin Waller's resignation that made possible what he had not been able to accomplish in office. His resignation might have brought about a divorce between the social problem of victims and the person of Irvin Waller.

Victims *were* given a place on the agenda of the Ministry of the Solicitor General by a more senior official who was, in his own words, 'a very different sort of operator'. Almost immediately after Waller's departure, and in the midst of a series of staff changes, a newly-promoted Acting Assistant Deputy Minister ratified victims as a concern: 'I went from being Director of Research to Acting Assistant Deputy Minister and, when I had my first meeting with directors of Programs Branch, victims was put on the list as a thing of high priority.' Waller illuminated the problem of victims but it was another who had the authority to act.

In effect, Irvin Waller had confronted some of the problems that seem to attend academics who enter government work in order to effect political change. His was a recurrent difficulty, encountered elsewhere and with many of the same results. In the United States, for example:

> The social scientist's demand for elite accessibility, though said to be inspired by noble purpose, tends to set the social scientist apart from other employees of the federal government. He sees himself as an advising expert instead of as an employee. The social scientist takes himself seriously as an appointed official playing a political role in a way that most federal workers do not. The federal bureaucracy finding that the social scientist has come to Washington to 'set the world on fire', tends to think that a presumptuous intention, unmindful of the flame that also burns in the heart of the staff administrator.[45]

[45] I. Horowitz and J. Katz, *Social Science and Public Policy in the United States*, Praeger, New York, 1975, p. 154.

V. Victimization Surveys and Peace and Security

In the early 1970s, during the first few years of the Secretariat's existence, it had been the intention of the Solicitor General to play a part in extending and advancing compensation schemes. Eight of the ten provincial governments administered compensation at that time, and he sought to reinforce their work. He argued in 1973:

> The very purpose of the criminal law stems from a desire to provide a means of protection for the public against the few who do not respect the rights of others.... Protection of the public is a multi-dimensional concept involving police activities ...; analysis of new trends in crime; determination of the law's responsiveness to new forms of crime and assurance that the public can be compensated for injury as a result of criminal activity ...[1]

Later, and during the preparations for the Peace and Security proposals especially, Warren Allmand was to recommend a considerable increase in the federal contribution to cost-sharing programmes. In place of the restrictive standards of eligibility which were then enforced, he suggested an appreciable enlargement of the scope and generosity of compensation awards. His ideas were resisted. One of his former officials recalled, 'there was a proposal that the level of funding ... be dramatically raised. It was turned down by the Department of Finance and the Treasury Board and that more or less took the wind out of the sails of anything that could be done in that regard at that time.' And Warren Allmand himself remembered, 'people put up money for all sorts of things and they could have worked it out if they'd tried. It was just lack of interest. No-one was interested.' Criticisms and objections revolved chiefly around the problem of jurisdiction: 'it was shot down because of federal–provincial relations, but that was nonsense because a number of provinces had funds and we could have helped just like Medicare. Justice also felt that victim compensation was their baby.'

In short, the division of labour supporting the Canadian system of criminal justice had denied the Ministry of the Solicitor General access to the victim in his or her role as an applicant for criminal injuries compensation. That role was governed by the Department of Justice and

[1] Remarks made by Warren Allmand, PC, MP, Solicitor General, on introducing Bill C-2 in the House of Commons on 25 Jan. 1973.

provincial Attorneys General. If the Ministry was to have dealings with victims, it had to be through one of the routes prepared by its acknowledged functions. The Ministry exercises control over federal policing and corrections and it plays a diffuse role as the shaper and leader of general policies which have no specific anchorage in provincial institutions and practices. It is with the police that I shall deal in the next chapter. In the remainder of this chapter, I shall dwell upon one facet of the leadership role. It is a duty of the Department to provide enlightenment and intelligence about the character and workings of the criminal justice system. In turn, it is part of the Ministry's task to map the world in which it operates. Victims were first to enter the Department as features of a statistical description of crime.

Victims took a serpentine path into the Ministry, changing their form and significance over time. Instead of instantly appearing as candidates for assistance programmes, they presented themselves originally as data and social indicators. Their vehicle was the crime survey. As a senior Policy official remarked of their earliest guise: 'the work being done on victimisation surveys was totally neutral and was being sold at the time, not on the basis of providing information about victims, but on the basis of providing information in crime trends, on unreported crime, so that it wasn't really advanced as a way of finding out about victims.' It was only after a number of unexpected transformations that the victim of the federal initiative emerged. Those transformations are interesting and important and deserve discussion. They significantly illustrate the part played by research as an item in talk and deliberation, a part that is fluid, situated, and changeful in meaning, lacking an obvious logic of progression. Victim surveys were to be one facet of a more general form of evolution that has been described as not a 'linear order from research to decision but a disorderly set of interconnections and back-and-forthness that defies neat diagrams'.[2]

The Peace and Security Package

Mr. Speaker, the current wisdom is that parliament will pass Bill C-84 and thus abolish capital punishment, though probably by a very narrow majority. At the same time, sir, it is readily apparent that no issue in recent years has so aroused the Canadian public, the vast majority of whom, according to most indicators, favour retention. How can this apparent contradiction between the views of parliamentarians and those of the electorate be explained?'[3]

[2] C. Weiss, introduction to *Using Social Research in Public Policy Making*, Saxon House, Farnborough, 1977, p. 14.

[3] Elmer MacKay (Central Nova), in the House of Commons debate on measures respecting punishment for murder and other serious offences, 25 May 1976.

During the years before 1975, and almost entirely outside the range of this particular history, Ministry officials had been exploring a number of problems in the areas which they regulated. The branches and agencies continually probed issues spawned by the practical work of law enforcement. Thus, in 1972, the Royal Canadian Mounted Police and Policy Planning and Program Evaluation Branch had examined possible responses to organized and violent crime. In 1973 the Canadian Penitentiary Service had become concerned about the custody and management of dangerous prisoners. In 1974, some preliminary suggestions having been made about possible strategies for strengthening gun control legislation, the Management Committee of the Secretariat requested the Assistant Deputy Minister of Police and Security Planning and Analysis to produce a comprehensive study of gun control measures. And, at the beginning of 1975, a gun control study group had been formed with instructions to report to the Deputy Solicitor General by July. Welling up within the broad policy area of criminal violence, therefore, was a scattering of piecemeal developments which might well be amalgamated if a suitable organization could be imposed upon them. Indeed, the Solicitor General issued a statement in March 1975 entitled, 'The Prevention and Control of Violent Crime in Canada: Some comments on violent crime, capital punishment and other related issues.' It was a statement that could be exploited later in the production of policy. Although gun control was to excite considerable hostility when it was eventually proposed in Parliament, there was little about these early stirrings that was politically volatile, and that lack of volatility was quite typical of much work at the Ministry.

I have observed that Solicitors General tend to be regarded as Ministers who confront sporadic crises but rarely attract prolonged and concentrated political attention. Their work is normally supposed to be uneventful enough unless it is momentarily disrupted by one of those sudden disturbances that beset the world of criminal justice. They have been described as 'fire-fighters', attaining visibility only during a short-lived penitentiary riot or a scandal revolving around police wrongdoing. Yet it is apparent that Solicitors General are also concerned with problems that can be quite pivotal to politics. Their domain centres on the control of illegal, wicked, and immoral behaviour, and that behaviour is perhaps the most dramatically charged of all. On occasion, it can lend itself to intense conflict and emotion. After all, fiction, film, television, newspapers, and the pulpit endlessly reproduce and celebrate the interplay between good and evil, making it symbolically fertile, and promising to envelop any who deal with it.

In Canada it is the Solicitor General who plays a strategic part in the presentation and management of much that is vivid, theatrical, and freighted with meaning. He administers the Royal Canadian Mounted Police, a force which is itself a national emblem, whose members have been the heroes of abundant films, stories, and musicals. He administers the penitentiaries, repositories of the villainous and grim reminders of the consequences of wrongdoing. He paroles and pardons malefactors. And, before 1976, he was entrusted with matters to do with the execution of murderers. Kai Erikson announced that, 'in a figurative sense, at least, morality and immorality meet at the public scaffold, and it is during this meeting that the community declares where the line between them should be drawn.'[4] The scaffold is the quintessence of moral symbolism. The practices and ceremonies of execution have always been treated as extraordinary and they have excited extraordinary interest.[5] In some measure, capital punishment is the ritual enactment of awful themes at the very core of politics and morality.[6]

When the time came, arguments about putting an end to executions in Canada were to capture something of that moral insistency. Outside the House of Commons the major institutions of morality and control made declamations about hanging. Churches pronounced their position. Within the House of Commons there was allusion to the Bible and to the moral commands which it contains. Thus a Member of Parliament stated, 'in the beginning, and seeing that man misused his freedom and rejected even His commandments, the Creator determined penalties according to offences, and this is why God said ... "Whoever sheddeth man's blood, by man shall his blood be shed".'[7] Another entered into a disquisition about the stances adopted by the United Church of Canada, the Mennonites, the Canadian Council of Churches, Anabaptists, and the Rabbi Plaut of the Holy Blossom Synagogue in Toronto. He concluded, 'today the state is God's agent in making sure that people in today's society can in fact live out their lives in peace and harmony.... Punishment must follow actions in which God's laws are broken.'[8] Theology and an absolute morality were invoked by only a few Members, but their very introduction in debate was uncommon and it indi-

[4] K. Erikson, 'Notes on the Sociology of Deviance', in H. Becker (ed.), *The Other Side*, Free Press, New York, 1964, p. 14.

[5] See J. Lofland, *The Dramaturgy of State Executions*, Paterson Smith, New Jersey, 1977.

[6] See M. Foucault, *Discipline and Punish*, Allen Lane, The Penguin Press, London, 1977.

[7] Léonel Beaudoin, speaking at the debate in the House of Commons on measures respecting punishment for murder and other serious offences, 26 May 1976.

[8] Jake Epp, speaking at the debate in the House of Commons on measures respecting punishment for murder and other serious offences, 28 May 1976.

cated the special standing of capital punishment as a symbolically-laden process.

The then Solicitor General, Warren Allmand, was convinced of the moral repugnance of executions. He argued, 'killing is certainly reprehensible at all time, but when the state sets out on the most deliberate path to destroy a human life, then perhaps that is one of the most heinous acts of all. When the state indulges in murder, the result is the weakening of the moral fibre of that society ... [it] contributes to the brutalization of the society as a whole.'[9] It is clear that the potent significance of executions could transform the ordinarily tranquil work of the Solicitor General, making it part of a brightly illuminated and combative process. All the lesser tasks and projects of the Ministry could also be transformed in the wake of that larger turmoil about abolition, accelerating activity and giving birth to new ventures. And victims themselves were to become the subjects of one such venture delivered by the abolition debate.

Before 1975 the major turning point in the evolution of the Canadian law on the death penalty had occurred in 1961. Until 1961 all murder had been liable to capital punishment but it was then decreed that a distinction should be traced between capital and non-capital murder. Capital murder was defined as that which was planned, deliberate, and a result of the killer's own act. It also included cases in which the victim was a prison or police officer, special officials requiring special protection. In 1967 a five-year period was fixed in which capital punishment was confined only to the killing of such officials. The five-year period was taken to be tantamount to an experiment, it being hoped that some final decision could be made about the fate of executions when it expired. In 1972, however, it did not seem possible to mobilize sufficient support in Parliament to bring about a final end to the death penalty. Warren Allmand failed to secure total abolition. 'The best I could get past Parliament'[10] was an Act replacing the terms 'capital' and 'non-capital' murder by 'murder punishable by death' and 'murder punishable by life in prison.' The death penalty was retained for the murder of police and prison officers.

In practice, many of those distinctions and classifications were somewhat immaterial. No convicted killer, whether guilty of capital murder or murder punishable by death, had been executed in Canada since 1962. But that very lack of executions had led to an accumulation of problems. By 1975 there were some ten men awaiting punishment by death. One of them was the notorious murderer, René Vaillancourt. And

[9] Remarks made by Warren Allmand on introducing Bill C-2 in the House of Commons, 25 Jan. 1973.

[10] *Globe and Mail*, 3 July 1975.

the Solicitor General charged with reviewing the possible commutation of death sentences was Warren Allmand, a declared abolitionist. He had repeatedly pronounced himself absolutely opposed to capital punishment. In April 1975[11] he had asserted that he would resign if the death penalty were not abolished and, in the same year, he stated that he would prefer resignation to signing an execution order.[12]

René Vaillancourt seemed to be the very embodiment of a callous and deliberate killer. Having bought a motorcar in Montreal with stolen identification papers, he had driven to Toronto and there booked into a hotel and then a motel, giving a false name. Vaillancourt proceeded to steal another motorcar in Scarborough and, on 1 February 1973, robbed a branch of the Canadian Imperial Bank of Commerce in Toronto, flourishing a loaded gun. Vaillancourt was observed by Constable Maitland, an armed police officer, and Constable McCullum, an unarmed trainee officer. He abandoned his motorcar in a dead-end street and, when confronted by Constable Maitland, shot him dead. According to the police officers who arrested him, 'Vaillancourt did not choose to make his escape but pursued the unarmed officer and from close range, made a deliberate attempt to murder him by firing four shots at him. Luckily, he missed.'[13]

Vaillancourt was apprehended, convicted, and sentenced to death. But he was not executed. His case offered a perfect opportunity to those who advocated the retention of capital punishment. Deliberations about the commutation of a death sentence normally tended to proceed without controversy. Vaillancourt's case was not allowed to remain quiescent. According to an editorial in the *Toronto Star* of 27 February 1975:

> There is gathering around him what may become the most violent storm in the history of the capital punishment controversy in Canada. . . . The upholders of capital punishment have chosen their battleground shrewdly. The murder of Constable Maitland was a brutal and cold-blooded crime, and there is nothing about Vaillancourt to arouse any sympathy. . . . In this climate, overwhelming pressure can be built up on the cabinet ministers to make an example of Vaillancourt.

The newspaper proceeded to state that the law on the death penalty was 'an awkward compromise': legislation had prescribed the hanging of those who murdered police and prison officers, required courts to sentence those found guilty to death, and then permitted cabinet ministers systematically to commute their sentences to terms of life

[11] *Toronto Star*, 29 Apr. 1975
[12] Ibid, 25 Aug. 1975.
[13] Ibid., 27 Feb. 1975.

imprisonment. It was around that equivocating policy that arguments began to grow, allowing a Member of Parliament from Vancouver to collect what were claimed to be 110,000 signatures on a petition demanding Vaillancourt's death, police spokesmen to agitate about the stay of execution, and numerous letters to be written to the Solicitor General and to Members of Parliament.

Thus it was that in the first half of 1975 a determined Solicitor General and an abolitionist Cabinet confronted the beginnings of a substantial political campaign to restore the use of the death penalty. Convicted murderers, and Vaillancourt in particular, daily awaited a decision about whether they would be reprieved or hanged. Their waiting was reported and pored over by the mass media. It potently underscored the poignancy of executions, the agony of uncertainty, and the ever increasing need for a definitive judgement about policy. The very continuing presence of the condemned men provided a target for retentionist protest. In its turn, the 'awkward compromise' was becoming more and more awkward, forcing the Liberal Government to act. After all, Vaillancourt was an unsuitable subject for a special display of mercy. His case seemed to demand either a hanging or an attack on the general principle of capital punishment. The Government felt that its situation was becoming difficult.

An execution date of 5 May had been set for René Vaillancourt. When that day came, execution was neither confirmed nor commuted but merely delayed until October. For a while, however, the approach of the 5th of May came to represent a pressing constraint in the timetables of the Ministry and the Government. Warren Allmand recalled that decisions were 'taken in a hurry'. By early April the Ministry had already prepared and circulated draft proposals to deal simultaneously with the issue of the future of capital punishment, the problem of violent crime, and the emerging public reaction to abolition, a reaction exemplified in miniature by the response to Vaillancourt's case. It was held imperative to demonstrate that the death penalty was no deterrent and could be discarded safely. It was also held imperative to manifest visible concern about the protection of the public and the regulation of criminal violence. Many of the ingredients of those proposals were assembled from the scattered pieces of work already in train in the Ministry. Other items were tacked on. Gun control was to be part of the display of concern; parole reform was another part; and increased compensation to the victims of violent crime was suggested as a third part. However, the Department was to be informed that it had no jurisdiction over criminal injuries compensation and should not make proposals in that area.

The Minister of Justice and the Solicitor General agreed to develop a package of laws and administrative measures to achieve the final abolition of the death penalty. There would be compensating amendments to the parole regulations so that those who might formerly have hanged would be required to serve long mandatory prison sentences. And there would be a set of proposals to eliminate crime in general and violent crime in particular. For a while, the proposals were thought to be so politically contentious that no public disclosure was made of them.

It is important to understand how very disputatious and hostile the world seemed to those who had to prepare that package of measures. Organized opposition to the commutation of Vaillancourt's sentence had been the early catalyst of the Ministry's actions. That opposition had persisted and it became generalized. It was voiced principally by the significant groups that composed the normal working environment of the Ministry. It stemmed from the world of criminal justice itself. Such criticism is practically and politically consequential and its forcefulness should be emphasized.

It had been the murder of one police officer and the attempted murder of another that had crystallized the crisis of early 1975. It was a number of police organizations which protested when abolition was mooted. Externally and publicly, there was a spate of police demands for the implementation of the death penalty. In June 1975, for instance, the Ontario Provincial Police Association campaigned for a commitment from the Government. In an advertisement placed in the *Globe and Mail*, the *Toronto Star*, and the Ottawa *Citizen*, the Association recalled the thirty-three police officers and two prison guards who had been murdered since 1967, argued that the federal government was responsible for the creation of an environment in which violent crime could flourish, and asserted 'we believe that capital punishment must be enacted against persons that cause death as a result of premeditated crime.'[14] Some considerable opposition was expressed at the annual conference of the Canadian Association of Chiefs of Police in August. The President of that Association, and Chief of the Victoria, British Columbia, force, predicted that vigilante action would be a 'very real danger' if there were no capital punishment.[15] The Deputy Chief of the Ottawa City Police and Chairman of the Association's Law Amendments Committee prophesied that police might well resort to extra-legal sanctions.[16] A

[14] *Globe and Mail*, 5 June 1975.
[15] *Toronto Star*, 25 Aug. 1975.
[16] Ibid., 26 Aug. 1975.

paper prepared for that Committee stated, 'one thing the criminal element does understand is quick retribution ... we are at a loss to understand why some of our high-ranking legislators cannot understand this fact of life when apparently the criminal can, peace officers can, and from the continued hue and cry from the general public, they can. It is our view that the will of the people should be applied.'[17] And in July 1975 another major organization in the social structure of control, the prison employees' group of the Public Service Alliance of Canada, orchestrated a 'national day of mourning' for Paul Gosselin, a murdered prison officer. It was estimated that 7,000 federal prison workers from forty-nine prisons took part in what was virtually a strike. What is significant about such public protest is that it emanated from institutions for which the Ministry was supposed to have direct or indirect responsibility. It could not be regarded as inconsequential. It represented an upheaval in the Ministry's own immediate territory, a kind of mild mutiny.

All that public protest was echoed and amplified by the private arguments that were relayed to the Solicitor General by his own agencies. He was informed that the staff of the penitentiaries would probably react very negatively to any proposed abolition of capital punishment. Further, he was told that no welcome would be extended to any great increase in the numbers of prisoners serving life sentences: such inmates posed problems of security and control and it was difficult to justify their prolonged incarceration on treatment or humanitarian grounds. The Royal Canadian Mounted Police reminded the Deputy Solicitor General of his moral duty to protect them. The Parole Board alluded to a very real public concern which could be allayed only by the safeguard of a lengthy minimum sentence for murder.

Other bodies outside the system and world of criminal justice took up those themes. Warren Allmand was asked to resign by the Leader of the Opposition in July, it being argued that he had introduced legislation that he was not prepared to enforce.[18] In August the Association of Municipalities of Ontario voted to reinstate the death penalty for premeditated murder and murder committed during a robbery.[19] Opinion polls uniformly reported a massive public opposition to abolition.[20] And so it went on as a miscellany of very different institutions produced a stream of criticism and demands that repeatedly stressed their hostility to abolition.

[17] Ibid., 26 Aug. 1975.
[18] *Globe and Mail*, 3 July 1975.
[19] *Toronto Star*, 7 Aug. 1975.
[20] See, for example, the *Toronto Star*, 4 May 1976.

To be sure, editorials in major newspapers, the Canadian Civil Liberties Union[21] and, eventually, the Liberal Party Convention in November did express their support for the Cabinet's dissatisfaction with the death penalty. The Party Convention, indeed, passed a resolution that was to be a most faithful anticipation of legislation that was to come. The resolution encapsulated the Solicitor General's major concerns:

Be it resolved that a) the Liberal Party believes the purpose of the criminal justice system is the protection of society and views with concern the increasing incidence of violent crime. b) protection of the public be improved by adopting a package of measures to tighten bail, temporary absence and parole provisions with respect to dangerous offenders, to increase the penalties for violent crime, to abolish capital punishment while at the same time ensuring the security and protection of the public by providing for life sentences with substantially increased non-parolable periods, to establish a more effective gun control system, and to step up efforts to combat organized and violent, drug-related crime in Canada.[22]

Those few editorials and the party resolution were unusual. Almost all the other visible and audible signs of political response were contrary to the Government's purpose. It was as if those who assembled the package were surrounded by angry voices condemning and threatening what they did. Of course, it *was* possible occasionally to discount some antagonism. For example, Warren Allmand told people dining at an American Bar Association luncheon that opinion polls were insensitive devices that could not measure considered thought: 'personally, I do not think the government can be guided by the results of such surveys. [They] dodge the event itself—an act of extreme cruelty as part of a sordid and dismal ceremony at dawn, in hideous surroundings, an act beneath the dignity of the state.'[23] But it was not thought possible to disregard those representations altogether. After all, opposition was being fathered by the three groups which are especially salient to a Solicitor General: spokesmen of the electorate, institutions of law enforcement, and members of the House of Commons. They seemed to imperil the Government's prospects of re-election, the Ministry's capacity to implement policy, and the Cabinet's ability to control the passage of legislation.

Abolition was held to be a precarious issue in Parliament. Warren Allmand had been unsuccessful in his attempt to repeal capital pun-

[21] *Globe and Mail*, 6 Apr. 1976.
[22] *Resolutions Report*: Liberal Party of Canada Convention 1975, p. 15.
[23] *Toronto Star*, 9 Aug. 1975.

ishment in 1972. A renewed effort was no more certain in 1975. The matter was to be decided by a free vote of the House of Commons, and the Cabinet could be sure only of its own intentions. Indeed, Warren Allmand repeatedly expressed anxiety about the prospect of failing again. In February 1976, for instance, he declared that his Bill might not be passed.[24] In April 1976 a poll of Members of Parliament disclosed that 99 were in favour of the Bill, 98 were against, 27 were undecided, and 37 refused to give an answer.[25] In short, the Parliamentary process had to be managed with considerable delicacy if defeat were to be avoided. A newspaper article observed, 'as things are now, a bout of flu among those opposed to capital punishment on voting day could mean several hangings this summer.'[26]

The bundle of proposals surrounding abolition was therefore constructed with some trepidation. Frequently repeated were injunctions to mollify the public. Circling around the problem of the death penalty and preoccupying the Ministry were references to the fear of crime, public confidence, and strategies of crime prevention. In all this talk was the unquestioned assumption that the elimination of hanging could be purchased only by offering a wide range of reassurances and compensations. Parliamentary action would have to take the form of a balance of measures, abolition being achieved by satisfying demands for retributive punishment, deterrence, and protection. It was quite explicitly designed to be a kind of compact with the public. As Warren Allmand argued, 'we can't do it alone, there are so many other issues that are related.... We're studying proposals from all over now on the parole system, security in the system, protection of guards, gun control. It's a package for protecting society against crime...'[27]

When it *was* publicized, Government policy was treated as a tacit contract by the media which made it known to the world. The *Globe and Mail*, for instance, argued 'if hanging is to be abolished, the public needs assurance that there will be protection from those who have already struck once.... the new bill must be looked at critically to see if it supplies the assurance of protection that has been so sadly lacking in recent years.'[28] And the *Toronto Star* observed 'the government's planned legislation should overcome the fears Canadians have about abolishing capital punishment...'[29] So construed, proposals to end executions had to be

[24] Ibid., 5 Feb. 1975.
[25] Ibid., 19 Apr. 1976.
[26] *Globe and Mail*, 28 Feb. 1976.
[27] *Toronto Star*, 12 July 1975.
[28] *Globe and Mail*, 26 Feb. 1976.
[29] *Toronto Star*, 6 Feb. 1976.

accompanied by a substantial counterweight. Their very title, the 'Peace and Security Package', conveys their protective and reassuring intent. Indeed, presentation was so central that it has been claimed that the author of the title, Ron Basford, was rewarded by immediate promotion from Inland Revenue Minister to Minister of Justice.[30] And the package itself was published in a striking folder that was blue on the outside and crimson within, housing copious explanatory notes and a 22-page press release. Its principal components were two Bills: C-84, 'an Act to amend the Criminal Code in relation to the punishment for murder and other serious offences', and C-83, the substantial counterweight, 'an Act for the better protection of Canadian society against perpetrators of violent and other crime'.

I have stated that diverse pieces of work on violence, dangerousness, and gun control were already in train before the Peace and Security legislation was named or considered. But all that activity was to undergo a sudden acceleration after the Government had decided to proceed with the abolition of capital punishment. There was an abrupt change in the customarily measured pace of work. Officials began to put proposals together in the middle of May, drafted recommendations for the Government in the Autumn, prepared draft legislation by December, and laid two Bills before Parliament in February. Within the Ministry of the Solicitor General, the process was superintended by the Ministry Steering Committee on Violent Crime which met for the first time on 12 May. Its work was compressed into no more than a few weeks, giving rise to a prevalent sensation of urgency and rush.

It was in this fashion that a flood of ideas, suggestions, drafts, and papers came to be written into the Peace and Security Package. It was the recollection of officials that the Ministry of the Solicitor General was encouraged to come up with initiatives, '*any* initiatives'. One member of staff recalled that various proposals were 'thrown into the Package in an *ad hoc* manner and then justifications and legitimations were developed to explain their relevance to the abolition of capital punishment. The whole operation had been hasty.' And another official remembered:

> The key thing there was the political trade-off really that was going on when the Solicitor General of the day wanted to abolish capital punishment primarily, and in order to do that he wanted to offer on one hand the abolition, on the other hand 'we're doing all these other things to protect the Canadian public'. Which was fair, but we were really given almost *carte blanche* at that time to come up with ideas that we thought had been neglected, things that could be done...

[30] See R. Gwyn, *The Northern Magus*, p. 176.

At the various meetings and deliberations within the Ministry and between the Ministry and the Department of Justice, there was discussion of a great sweep of ideas, embracing almot all the projects and ideas which were then prevalent in criminology, penology, and criminal justice policy. At one meeting of 12 August on 'measures to control violent crime and ensure public safety', the following topics were reviewed as possible measures: applications of the notion of 'defensible space', a paper being in preparation on research findings in the area; gun control; the adoption of voluntary guidelines on the display of violence on television; wire-tapping; team policing; bail supervision projects; the inquisitorial system and self-incrimination; tactical emergency response teams in prisons; the training of prison staff; the building of new, special prisons, parole and its effect on deterrence; increasing the size of the parole board; increasing the amount of parole supervision; improvement of communication between law enforcement agencies; an inquiry into the causes of crime; models of alternative sentencing; the use of mental health institutions; and the sentencing of dangerous offenders. And other ideas were aired at other meetings. There was an abundant willingness to scrutinize and accept almost any plausible candidate for inclusion in the package of measures to prevent crime. A large net was cast and much was considered, but there was very little time. The Peace and Security Package was virtually omniverous. Consider the recollection of one official who talked about the way in which one component was constructed:

> People were searching around for something that might be positive, that might have an impact on crime prevention. And people had vaguely heard about work in the U.S. in this area [of crime prevention through environmental design]. It was a bit faddish at the time, just beginning to be a fad. And I'd been at work about three weeks and I was just trying to figure my way around the building and Irvin popped into my office and said 'I need a short discussion paper on this stuff called crime prevention through environmental design. Why don't you do something and we'll discuss it?' So I went and read a couple of articles and thought for a little while and figured out how to use a dictaphone and tried out my new secretary and it was all very exciting. So I dashed something off on the dictaphone, put in a few commas, and sent it to Irvin, thinking it would be discussed. But there was a tremendous flurry of activity of course and somehow or other it never got discussed. And when I got this communications thing that was released, here's this thing on environmental design, which as far as I know, was not discussed with anyone. Fortunately, all I said was that it would be worth looking at.

The willingness to accept crime prevention through environmental design could extend to victimization surveys. Thus it came about that the compilation of the Peace and Security Package gave Irvin Waller his opportunity. Ministry officials tend to refer back to that period of search, talk, evaluation, and drafting as 'Irvin's Opportunity', as if it were the capitalized heading of a chapter in a novel. An important Government Bill being hurriedly prepared and with omnibus provisions is a powerful engine for the furtherance of many small and large projects that have been in waiting. It moves them on. So one official stated, 'a Bill like Peace and Security can get money for things like victims.... Irvin got victims into Peace and Security.' Another official stated, 'Peace and Security was an opportunity and a happenstance. Irvin Waller pushed victims in.' A third official stated, 'victims were tacked on to the Peace and Security legislation.... It was a very useful vehicle for hanging good causes on. And I think that's how the victims stuff really came up.' A fourth official stated it was 'like he was waiting in the wings to pounce'. A fifth official stated, 'there had been some initial concern with victims but not really very much. Very little had been done.... Irvin came bouncing in one day saying that we have an opportunity here to get some reaction to some of the ideas that we've been discussing.' And Irvin Waller himself stated:

> I think if you look at the Peace and Security Package, you'll find there a lot of the ideas and ideology in the Burglary book. There's a heavy emphasis on victims ... I think the Peace and Security Package was supposed ... to do great things, good things: 'we're going to prevent crime, assist victims ...' I think the specifics like the victimisation survey or the public attitude research, I don't think we really sort of consciously said, 'this is a fantastic thing. You have to do it'. I think they said, 'this seems to be a good thing. We'll go along with it and see what it produces'. So it was really an opportunity to get money to do these things and to get money—people and money. And in federal government terms they were a pittance. A tiny wee drop in the bucket.

Crime surveys were not an explicit part of the Peace and Security legislation but they were an item in the larger portfolio of projects that was submitted for funding under those laws. They appear to have been included only in the later stages. The recommendation was to be made that there should be three victimization surveys and annual public attitude surveys over five years. It was argued that the crime survey would enable policy-makers to eliminate fear, decrease the volume of crime, and make intelligent assessments of the effects of particular programmes and strategies. But that argument was not expanded or phrased in minute detail. The applications and justifications were to be developed later, after approval, when officials had the time and sanction to explore them. As one who was centrally involved remarked, 'we essentially just said "victimization surveys do these kinds of very general things and it was mostly give a true incidence figure or a better incidence figure". But there was very little specification beyond that. We didn't really have time to think carefully about it.'

So Crime Surveys were awarded broad Government support as early as October 1975, emerging again in February 1976 as one of a set of 'crime prevention measures', and being presented as a series of 'studies every eighteen months over the next five years to assess more accurately the incidence and effects of crime on victims.'[31] Thereafter, surveys were to be again transformed. Once the first wave of activity had passed, and victimization surveys had been injected into the Peace and Security plans, officials began to embark on the patient work of reviewing what had been done elsewhere and what was possible in Canada. One important official recalled, 'it took several months simply to piece together just what had happened in the U.S. because ... they had a very severe publication lag and they were not able to get things out quickly.' The pace of work steadied. As time went by, so proposals became increasingly tentative and cautious, refined to become a careful examination of the methodological problems of sampling so vast and sparsely populated a nation as Canada. The submission that was eventually approved centred on the preparation and pre-testing of a 'victimization methodology'. It then moved slowly through the committees of the Ministry, being presented to the Research Projects Committee on 12 May 1976, receiving endorsement four months later, and passing to the Policy Group in early 1977. What was ultimately agreed was the allocation of some $200,000 to 'methodological studies basic to the development of a victimization research program'.[32] Irvin Waller observed, 'it involves large sums of money and it [is] also highly visible due to its relation to violence in the old "Peace and Security Package".'[33]

Victims therefore entered the thinking and research of the Ministry in a quite specific guise. They were not founts of knowledge about the dark figure of crime. Neither were they deserving supplicants. They were, instead, aids and indicators in the evaluation of crime prevention programmes that had been designed to allay public fear about the possible effects of the abolition of capital punishment.[34] The Peace and Security

[31] *Press Release, Peace and Security, Protection against violent crime*, Department of Justice and Solicitor General Canada, Ottawa, 24 Feb. 1976.

[32] 'Victimization Studies: Reverse Record Checks', paper presented to the Research Projects Committee, undated.

[33] Memo to Acting Director, Research Programs, 19 Apr. 1977.

[34] It is interesting that the South Australian Government contemplated a crime survey in a very similar setting. See *Report of the Committee of Inquiry on Victims of Crime*, p. 27.

Package provided an unambiguous and dominant context, a special mandate, which gave significance to all its materials. And it was entirely obvious that victims had been introduced in that context and no other. Thus Irvin Waller insisted that there should be no doubt about the connection between survey proposals and crime prevention. In November 1976 he wrote:

> I have read the Ministry paper 'Objectives of Canadian Victimization Surveys' ... The paper seems to me interesting, clear in research terms and position, but leaves many questions on objectives unanswered and does not make our expectations explicit ... What specific benefits will occur in relation to crime prevention and when might they occur. Will they relate to violence as depicted by Peace and Security ... ?[35]

It became entirely routine to phrase discussion about surveys in a way that stressed their bearing on crime prevention. After all, it is the convention in Ottawa that civil servants do the will of politicians, and politicians had talked of prevention. Moreover, financial accounting demanded reference to the budgetary authority that allowed expenditure to take place. It had been money allotted to crime prevention that allowed expenditure to take place at all. Thus victimization took on a very precise meaning: it was a state that was to be mapped epidemiologically, and its mapping was intended to allow the consequences of projects to be measured and the deployment of police and other resources to be planned.[36] The primary goal of Canadian federal government work on victims was described repeatedly as the provision of support to law enforcement agencies in their monitoring of different strategies.

It was only gradually and crescively that other themes began to infiltrate the original, simple characterization of Canadian surveys. In the Ministry, two officials became ever more immersed in the writings and arguments that Americans had produced, becoming exposed not only to their thoughts about methodology and crime prevention but also to a host of other concerns that had not previously been scrutinized by federal officials and had never been inserted in the Peace and Security Package. In something of a standard stage in the natural history of policy-making, officials were learning about a sphere of action, reinterpreting their earlier ambitions as they did so.[37] As one of the two officials

[35] Memo to Acting Director, Research Progams, 8 Nov. 1976.

[36] See J. Evans and G. Leger, 'Canadian Victimization Surveys', *Canadian Journal of Criminology*, April 1979, Vol. 21, No. 2.

[37] See C. Weiss, 'Research for Policy's Sake', *Policy Analysis*, Fall 1977, Vol. 3, No. 4.

recollected, 'because we were getting contacts with U.S. people over victim surveys, we were accumulating information about victim assistance as a side issue. We were accumulating stuff about victim services.'

Moreover, as time passed, so there was a decline in the once strict subordination of the projected survey to the Peace and Security proposals. Contexts slipped and changed. What had once been pressing came to seem like an ever more remote past. Solicitors General were appointed and dismissed. New preoccupations began to loom. As the days of the Package receded, planning a survey inevitably came to acquire its own autonomy. It emerged as an important activity which could not remain the captive, unchanging creature of an earlier reform. Indeed, Canadian officials were beginning to acquire considerable sophistication and expertise in matters of surveying. They knew more. It became apparent to them that the goals which they had first accepted were confining and mean, outlined in haste and lacking a proper foundation. It is so with all research: initial proposals invariably appear naïve as information, experience, and knowledge begin to pile up.

Above all, that prolonged period of reflection and enquiry forced officials to detach themselves from others' work and examine it quizzically. In a simple dialectical movement, what had first aroused and crystallized interest and then justified argument became an object to be criticized. The criticisms arose out of the very materials that were appraised. Hence one of the two officials entrusted with the survey stated:

> I spent quite a lot of time just reading, of course, and spending some time in the U.S. asking people at the Census and the National Academy.... Victim needs emerged as a focus after Peace and Security. I don't think anyone had a clear notion that they would become a part of it. It was only when we started to look at what was actually being collected and thought that, if all we got was what the U.S. had been publishing, it wasn't worth it. So then we said, 'What can we add to that?' ... We said, 'okay, what we need is impact of crime because that gets at victim needs. It gets at financial loss. It gets at physical loss...' While the debate about abolition gave us an *entrée* into it, and while Irvin as Director General at the time wanted to be as responsive to that as possible, wanted the survey to concentrate more on violent crime than it wound up doing, the responsibility for the design of it was left with me. And it was my view, after reviewing the work done in the U.S., that the best use of the instrument and the money would be to get at the range of objectives that we'd specified in our publications.

It is instructive to examine those publications, writings, and drafts to note how the goals of the crime survey were to evolve over time. In February 1977, for instance, the survey was firmly grounded in the mandate and framework set by Peace and Security. Notes for a meeting at that time began with a review of the Peace and Security legislation.[38] In September 1977 crime prevention was presented as the sovereign function of information extracted from any survey. In a paper offered to the Thirteenth Annual Conference of the Atlantic Provinces Criminology and Corrections Association in September, it was argued, 'as you know, the prevention of crime is of special concern to the Department of the Solicitor General. Consequently the question of the utility of victimization surveys for crime prevention activities has been of major importance to us in deciding whether the Department should become involved with such surveys.'[39] Within thirteen months the aims of the survey had been enlarged to embrace 'the planning and evaluation of a wide range of criminal justice programs and policies, particularly those related to crime prevention, to the delivery of services to victims, and to police/community relations'.[40] By June 1980 the context and significance of surveys had changed radically. A departmental policy paper argued that 'over the past few years the Ministry has had an extensive program of research and demonstration projects designed to stimulate services for crime victims. These include victimization surveys carried out to collect better information on the experiences and needs of victims...' Finally, in June 1982, the Ministry's National Program Consultant on Victims was asked on a radio programme what the use of the victimization survey might be. He replied, 'you know the major focus is Victims of Crime... assisting victims of crime is basically what the information is for.'[41] To be sure, crime prevention work is designed to reduce the number of victims. But there may be detected a steady shift in emphasis away from crime prevention and towards the provision of services to victims. The meaning and purposes of the survey were not stable. They evolved as the experiences of officials changed and as the social organization of expertise and knowledge began to develop.

In one sense, it may be argued that all that was changing was the context of argument that surrounded the survey. The actual design and application of the survey could have remained very much as they were despite the copious talking that took place. Crime prevention remains a priority of the Ministry and it was given prominence when the press

[38] Notes for 28 Feb. 1977 meeting.

[39] J. Evans and G. Leger, 'Crime Prevention and the Uses of Victimization Survey Data', 1977, pp. 1–2. (The very title is significant.)

[40] Information note: The Federal Department of the Solicitor General's Victimization Research Program, 10 Oct. 1978.

[41] 'Midnight to Three', CKEY Toronto, 2 June 1982.

announced the beginnings of the survey in 1981.[42] Not that much changed. Yet it does seem that there was also a gradual accretion and transformation of tasks so that crime prevention was partially displaced and complemented, allowing other concerns to become attached to what had once been a simpler vehicle. As I have observed, processes achieve their meanings in emergent fashion, policy in the Ministry being a moving platform. In the brief history of the Ministry, the Peace and Security Package is now seen as a relic of a kind of Departmental Middle Ages, long superseded by other, more recent problems. The programmes and missions engendered by the Package have taken on a life that is somewhat independent of it. Many of the staff who work on them were appointed after the days of the Package.

Conclusion

I cannot trace all the unwindings and repercussions of the Peace and Security legislation and its offspring, the victimization survey. That would require its own lengthy history. What my rather limited focus can reveal is only the bulkier features of the nascent victims initiative. And I can discern three prominent effects of the abolition era.

One consequence of the successful Peace and Security initiative was the establishment of victims as a central topic and problem in the work of the Ministry. Hitherto, victims had been a peripheral matter. They could now be awarded attention. It was Peace and Security that provided the opportunity and it exacted a price. Victims were allowed to enter policy-making processes, but the route they took and the character they assumed were a little odd. There were some who considered crime prevention an inappropriate and deforming context for a survey of victims. Thus an internal memorandum of Statistics Canada observed:

> The stated prime objective is not to estimate victimization rates, but rather to provide an analytical tool to be used in improving crime prevention methods. I am not fully convinced that an adequate case has been made for the feasibility of using the survey results in this fashion. This may not be a relevant comment, since the sponsor of the survey is the Solicitor General, not us, so it is the Solicitor General who has to be convinced of the value of the survey.

However curious the birth of victims may have been, their appearance in the wake of Peace and Security meant that they no longer had to be the subject of desultory speculation and isolated promptings. They had become a major enterprise favoured by Cabinet, allocated resources and

[42] See, for example, the *Globe and Mail*, 14 Dec. 1981.

meriting attention. The Ministry could announce that it was solidly committed to the exploration of problems posed by the victims of crime. Any subsequent research or proposal could be constructed on that basis, no longer requiring a detailed and exhaustive defence. The survey could come to represent a vital and continuing project around which satellite projects and interests were able to form. It was the beginning of a scheme of policy and action.

In its turn, the survey was eventually to become a little detached from its origins. Thus alienated, it was itself free to be used in arguments about other matters. There were new policies and problems that preoccupied the officials of the Ministry, and they bestowed fresh meaning on the survey. So salient and solid a feature of Ministry affairs tends to be converted into a political resource. It can underpin the rhetoric employed to support ideas that are still untried and unsupported. Thus the survey did not only breed lesser ventures about it. It was also treated as a source of legitimacy, becoming itself objectified, exploited, and demoted in the process. It was in this manner that the survey was ultimately to be clumped with other developments, forming the core of a wider federal initiative on justice for victims.[43]

Thirdly, the four people who were to be set to work on the survey and the allocation of several hundreds of thousands of dollars added an imposing cluster of skills and resources to the Programs Branch. It brought about an important direction and bending of effort. It led to the building of a small social world inside the Secretariat, a world given its identity by the problems of victims. People were imported to advance ideas about victims. Most important was an official who was appointed in August 1976 to work for the Research Division on a miscellany of projects. He was described as having 'a strong background in methodology, and has, since beginning . . . acquainted himself with the issues involved in Victimization research'.[44] That official's principal duty was to develop work on the survey, being encouraged to think and learn about victimization, and constituting an increasingly significant source of competence and influence. The division of labour within the Programs Branch gave that official an animating role, transforming him into an amplifier and accelerator of policy. He acquired commitments and sunk intellectual capital. He discovered, revealed, and created features of the area that he was asked to chart, being himself changed as he did so. A small dialectic then came into play with the growth of the social world

[43] For a parallel development in South Australia, see *The Report of the Committee of Inquiry on Victims of Crime*, p. 13.

[44] 'Victimization Studies: Reverse Records Check'.

concentrated on victims. A moderately self-contained body was created, modifying its own goals and environment, developing stocks of knowledge, and coaxing others to attend to different projects. Irvin Waller was later to claim, 'the way the Canadian survey developed was very different from what I intended—largely because my energies were diverted elsewhere'.[45] The survey experts were to pass progressively beyond the reach of others. Thus a senior expert described how the new official was transformed:

> [He] was hired to work in the Causes and Prevention section and one of the key things at the time was the victimisation survey. I didn't particularly worry about his competence at survey design and analysis. He wasn't hired specifically for that. But he was hired to work in that section. It's true that as soon as he came aboard that was the main thing we were doing, and he and I were involved very closely on the development of the victimisation survey in particular. It's one of the few examples of . . . research *clearly* having a key role in the development or the bringing to consciousness of an issue . . . Because [the official], to his credit, as he was reading and working on the developments of the victimisation survey, did have his interests expanded and he started to collect information on victim assistance programmes and a whole range of things that was done in the U.S. He developed this expertise and clearly a very strong personal interest, and he'd been around long enough at that point, so when this interdepartmental committee on family violence started [see Chapter IX], he was just given responsibility for that. He knew a lot more about it than I did, and had a whole lot more interest in aspects of it than I did. There was no point in me being on it.

The official modestly called himself a 'worker bee', and stated 'I guess we've come to the appreciation that things really don't get on the front burner until somebody gets people together and just keeps after people. The way with victims, I realised, to get them more on the front burner, was to really push.' And as he learnt more and cared more, so he acquired a stake in the problem and began to 'feel strongly about things like family violence'. It is clear that when staff are allotted particular projects, social worlds begin to grow, lending considerable guidance and thrust to the propulsion of an issue, forcing it on to a new stage and giving it a motive power of its own.

It is also clear that the dialectics of this process can be ever further complicated by the identification of issues with particular social worlds. The members of little worlds typically elicit responses from the officials around them, influencing their conduct and inviting replies in return.

[45] Letter to myself, 22 Feb. 1983.

That interplay can come to possess its own history which is rather independent of the issue which is under development. The social world will become an object that is surveyed and assessed in ways that affect its future. The fates of initiatives will come to hinge on the manner in which those processes are finally resolved. The Secretariat is small enough, and its members are exclusive enough in their functions, for particular enterprises to become associated with particular people. In this sense, the members of a social world seem frequently to stand for an initiative at large, representing in their persons that segment of the division of labour that they have been elected to fill. Projects then become the creations and protégés of named individuals, and their reception is often interwoven with the wider play of friendships and rivalries in the Ministry, in Ottawa, and in Canada. The original appearance of the initiative had been associated with Irvin Waller. By the end of the 1970s victims were identified with a separate and small group. But their influence and reputation were still very parochial. They were not a force affecting the Secretariat as a whole and they had not yet touched the Deputy Minister or Solicitor General. As an official remarked, 'I'm not sure this expertise was widely recognized outside the Programs Branch [and, in that early period] the Research Division was not successful in interesting the Minister and the Policy Branch in the prospect of a victim's initiative.' That was to come.

VI. The Police

Mandates and Perspectives

In March 1981, at a relatively late stage in my history of the initiative and at a time when the first proposals were being cautiously drafted, there was some apprehension about possible political responses to the Ministry's plan to declare an interest in the victims of crime. After all, it had only been a year since the Province of Quebec had not attended the National Workshop on Services to Crime Victims, it having announced that the federal government had no authority to bury itself in that area. And six years before, the Solicitor General's proposals about criminal injuries compensation had been rebuffed. Many existing schemes for victims did lie within the orbits of the federal Department of Justice and provincial Attorneys General, and there was an active guardianship of established rights and claims. In exploratory anticipation, one of the early essays at a proposal for an initiative considered 'possible opposition' and cited 'provincial governments—intrusion on their territory'.[1] In this instance of victims, and in almost all other matters, the officials of the Ministry are obliged to reflect upon problems of mandate. The phenomenon of victims was hedged with border disputes.

Wiener has talked of 'establishing turf rights' as an indispensable prelude to the successful animation of a social problem.[2] The Solicitor General's 'turf rights' are secure enough in one important tract of the criminal justice system. The Royal Canadian Mounted Police enforces federal law and serves as the principal police force of eight provinces and two territories. It is accountable to the Solicitor General, and that accountability offers a very broad and uncontested entrance into the practical affairs of law and social control in Canada.

The members of any police force are typically scattered, they have frequent and varied dealings with the public, and they have numerous functions heaped upon them.[3] So it is with the Royal Canadian Mounted Police. It would be difficult to prepare an exact and complete description of that body's work. It is a force that undertakes all the ordinary and

[1] 'Victim Services', 13 Mar. 1981.

[2] C. Wiener, *The Politics of Alcoholism*, p. 20.

[3] See E. Cumming, I. Cumming, and L. Edell, 'Policeman as Philosopher, Friend, and Guide', *Social Problems*, Winter 1965, Vol. 12, No. 3.

predictable duties of the peace officer. Thus one official definition of its objectives runs, 'to enforce laws, prevent crime, maintain peace, order and security'.[4] But the RCMP has also acquired a number of ancillary functions because of its centrality in Canadian policing. The RCMP has many officers, they are widely dispersed, they have elaborate support, a great range of duties, and a complex division of labour. The RCMP has come to occupy a tutelary role in the Canadian criminal justice system, providing advice, reinforcement, and assistance to other forces. It mans the Canadian Police Information Centre, Crime Detection Laboratories, Criminal Identification Services, and the Canadian Police College. It has come to assume a kind of diffuse responsibility for policing at large. Thus another definition has portrayed the RCMP as 'catalysts in marshalling a holistic approach to crime'.[5] Definitions of the Force are generous and they seem to exclude little. They furnish the makings of an extensive mandate for action by the Federal Government. As the Auditor General of Canada observed:

> The RCMP environment is ... complicated by its role in providing assistance and services to all police forces in Canada. This role has evolved over the years primarily because of the national scope of RCMP activities and the federal government's use of the Force as a channel for providing centralized police support services throughout Canada.[6]

The Royal Canadian Mounted Police has become something of an expeditionary force for the Ministry, planting claims in all the different parts it visits. The problems it confronts can become problems for the Ministry itself.[7] The Force acts as a form of peripatetic mandate, and much Ministry policy has been attached to its doings.[8] It has become prudent and conventional to graft many new policies on to police work. Thus, in time, it happened that the very spread of services to victims was achieved by following the paths which a structure of police-based services would prepare. The Canadian initiative was to be anchored partially but not wholly in the police. It was otherwise in some states: in the United Kingdom, victim support schemes tend to cluster around voluntary organizations; in the United States, there was a growth of programmes

[4] *Estimates for the Financial Year ending March 31, 1981*, pp. 28–30.

[5] *Notes for a Speech by the Solicitor General of Canada, The Hon. Bob Kaplan, P.C., M.P., at the Canadian Congress on the Prevention of Crime,* Winnipeg, Manitoba, 13 July 1981.

[6] *Report of the Auditor General of Canada to the House of Commons, Fiscal Year Ended 31 March 1981*, Ministry of Supply and Services Canada, Ottawa, 1981, p. 288.

[7] See, for example, the arguments offered about the Solicitor General's interest in the problem of child abuse, a problem largely referred to provincial authorities: Warren Allmand's Speech on a Private Member's Motion with Reference to Committee Respecting Abuse and Neglect, House of Commons, 6 Dec. 1974.

[8] It should be observed that the RCMP does not necessarily see itself in this role.

around the courts and the offices of district attorneys. The Canadian move towards the police reflected the bias of mandates and institutional bonds as much as the logic of victim needs.

When a victims initiative was mooted at the very beginning, it was argued that 'police-based victim services seem the most feasible for the Secretariat to select as a) the Ministry has direct operational responsibility in policing; b) the Secretariat has responsibility for police policy; c) the RCMP has already requested assistance in this area.'[9] And the official who had originally been appointed to advance the survey stated that the initiative was devised not only to be 'a humanitarian exercise and nice improvements, but it's very much related to some of the fundamental kinds of mandate in the Ministry: policing—the evolution of policing away from law enforcement to a full service role ... '. It was in this manner that the shadow of the Royal Canadian Mounted Police appeared to offer a sheltered space in which projects and ideas might prosper.[10]

In the latter half of the 1970s there could be discerned the first stirrings of an interest in programmes for victims and the rudiments of a mandate borrowed from Peace and Security and the other founding documents of the Department. Any further developments were most likely to grow in and around the protected places provided by the police. And so it came to pass. But when the time actually came, the forces to have the very first dealings with the Ministry were not linked with the RCMP directly. They were independent municipal forces from Alberta, Ontario, and British Columbia. Perhaps that is not so remarkable. The RCMP is a substantial bureaucratic organization draped across the face of Canada. It has a complicated chain of command. It has its own intricate internal and external policy environments. It tends to change slowly. By contrast, the municipal police forces of Canada are abundant and versatile. Their decision-making is a relatively uncluttered process. There is always the possibility that some force somewhere will embark on innovatory work that will be seized later by a larger constabulary. As an RCMP Staff Sergeant involved in policy formulation reflected:

> There's no question that Calgary and Edmonton got the views of the victims initiative very early. And I think that part of that is because of the size of their departments and that they're in *one* location. There's considerably different pressures for them. And there's a whole range of things dealing with manpower

[9] 'Towards a Strategy for a Victim Justice System', undated.

[10] See, for instance, G. Norquay and R. Weiler, *Services to Victims and Witnesses of Crime in Canada*, p. 84.

and your rationale for getting manpower that different police organizations use. . . .

Yet if the Royal Canadian Mounted Police did not start the work of developing projects, it was the Ministry's connection with the Force that licensed its participation in the affairs of the municipal departments. The Solicitor General's interest in the RCMP gave him a kind of tacit legitimation by analogy. It was an authority based on claims to a leadership role in the organization of police matters. Dealings with municipal and provincial forces could not be grounded in any strong assertion of right. They had to be conducted with some little caution of their own. Obeisances had to be made. In one instance, it was reported that a provincial ministry 'indicated that they personally saw no problems ... with federal government involvement ... but would have to discuss the matter with senior officials'.[11]

Although the police offered a mandate and a point of entry, even into municipal forces and provincial territory, there was a price to be paid. A clear organization is imposed on any activity that uses the police as a means of access to the criminal justice system. The police mandate is also a scheme of perspectives, giving shape to what takes place in its name. The institutional structure of action set limits on what could be done and what could be known.[12] It focuses the responsibilities and interests of the Ministry, illuminating some sectors and obscuring others. As an official of the Department argued:

'It's a constraint in that it limits the way you can look at things, and it would help us to define who we would be concerned with as victims. It limits the kind of programmes that we can fund within our frame. I don't think that's particularly a constraint. I think it's probably a help. It kind of sets some limits because otherwise it's a totally impossible task.'

The outcome has been that much, if not all, of the Ministry's management and cultivation of the problem of victims was mediated by policing. And that mediation gave a special character to work. The Solicitor General has never had a diffuse commitment to victims. His Department neither sought nor acquired one. In the area of violence to women, for example, it is the terrain touched by police work that predominantly concerns the Ministry. Thus in 1979 two social workers asked an official about 'the policy and objectives of your department in

[11] Memorandum to File: Evaluation of the Victim Services of the ——— Police Department, 1 Dec. 1980.

[12] See J. Edwards and R. Batley, *The Politics of Positive Discrimination*, Tavistock Publications, London, 1978, p. 35.

regard to family violence, with particular reference to spouse abuse'. He replied:

> As far as I know this Ministry has focused primarily on improving the role of the police in crisis intervention situations. As you probably know, Health and Welfare Canada takes the primary responsibility at the federal level in assisting the provinces with the cost of providing the social services noted in your letter. Because of the mandate of the Ministry of the Solicitor General, our interest in spouse abuse has centered largely on issues related to law enforcement. Crisis intervention, of course, has been a large part of the routine work of police officers for many years.

When the time came, police work gave authority and definition to the Ministry's response to the victims of crime. It also played an early and quite substantial part in extracting that response. After all, the problems of victims are an integral feature of the everyday experience of police officers. Victims represent a kind of personal client, although the police have other clients and require no physical victim at all. And victims are the principal source of an officer's knowledge of the occurrence and character of criminality. They give order to policing. What is interesting is that the Canadian police seem to have stressed two major facets of victimization, prising them away from the mass of incidents and problems that compose their world. It is an enormous mass whose scale and properties should be explored before the mounting of a police reaction is discussed.

Victims and the Police

On inspection, there appears to be very little that is not of legal or practical concern to police officers. In the sphere of law-breaking, they are supposed to exercise diffuse control: apprehending criminals, dramatizing deterrence, preventing crime, and displaying a reassuring presence.[13] They are numerous and widely scattered,[14] it being their business to conduct a running surveillance of conduct everywhere. And they also act as a useful resource to those who summon them, preparing to venture anywhere. Their work is predominantly 'reactive', answering calls from the victims and witnesses of crime. In the United Kingdom and the United States, some 80 per cent of policing is initiated by members of the public.[15] A study of a municipal force in Ontario suggests that that

[13] See P. Manning, *Police Work*.

[14] See D. Gibbons, *Society, Crime, and Criminal Careers*, Prentice-Hall, New Jersey, 1968, p. 67.

[15] See A. Reiss, *The Police and the Public*, Yale University Press, New Haven, 1971.

proportion may be rather smaller in Canada.[16] But there is a general and widespread public resort to police officers in matters of crime.

In other areas, the police represent a more general remedy for certain problems. Their work is not confined to thief-taking. Thus Bittner has suggested that 'the role of the police is best understood as a mechanism for the distribution of non-negotiably coercive force employed in accordance with the dictates of an intuitive grasp of situational exigencies'.[17] It is his argument that the police are the only body of officials, often invoked as a 'last resort',[18] who are licensed to bring force to bear on those myriad crises and difficulties that beset everyday life. They are the final dispenser of solutions to the entanglements and problems which complicate social relations. In many situations, there may simply be no-one else who is accessible, willing, competent, or authoritative enough to settle disputes or unravel complexities. In the case of assaulted women, for instance, Linda MacLeod has written, 'the public in general looks on the police department as the only all-purpose emergency and protection service available 24 hours a day. As a result, the police most often receive the first call for help when victims look outside the home for protection or assistance.'[19] And Bob Holmes has stated of child abuse, 'in rural areas, because there are most often no other social agencies to deal with these problems, the child's protection depends directly upon police officers responding to reports or suspicions of an abused child'.[20]

The work done by the police has another colouring. Not only is it greatly dispersed, it also takes officers into the unlovely, disreputable, and repulsive sectors of social life which many people avoid. It is the 'dirty work' of society, that portion of the division of labour which has been shunned by those who wish to refrain from contaminating themselves with immoral and unpleasant things.[21] Police talk often consists of 'war stories' which harp on the nastiness that abounds in their world. Confronting the pain of victims, needing to reassure and comfort those who have been hurt, the police constitute a service to victims *faute de mieux*.[22] Moreover, doing the dirty work of society, they encounter a great

[16] See R. Ericson, *Making Crime*, University of Toronto Press, Toronto, 1981.

[17] E. Bittner, *The Functions of the Police in Modern Society*, National Institute of Mental Health, Maryland, 1970, p. 46.

[18] See R. Emerson, 'On Last Resorts', *American Journal of Sociology*, July 1981, Vol. 87, No. 1.

[19] L. MacLeod *Notes for a Brief to the Standing Committee on Health, Welfare and Social Affairs on Family Violence*, 25 Jan. 1982.

[20] R. Holmes, 'The Police Role in Child Abuse', in J. Eekelaar and S. Katz (eds.), *Family Violence*, Butterworths, Toronto, 1978, p. 417.

[21] See E. Hughes, 'Good People and Dirty Work', in *The Sociological Eye*, Aldine-Atherton, Chicago, 1971.

[22] See M. Maguire, *Burglary in a Dwelling*, p. 137.

span of social problems, being obliged to devise remedies for those who have become victims in very diverse ways. They deal with the vagrant, the homeless, the battered, and the abused. In Hamilton–Wentworth, Ontario, for instance, the Regional Police Community Services Section was required to contend with a series of attacks on Asians in 1976. Their solution amounted to the provision of a victims services unit, although it was described as a 'Race and Ethnic Relations Program'.[23] It was a local response to a local problem, but it was directed at the needs of victims.

The Police, Surveys, and Crime Victims

Initially, and quite characteristically, exchanges between the Ministry and the police tended to come to the politics of victims in a somewhat oblique fashion. Work done in the beginning was only retrospectively identified as a part of a general project of victim assistance. A federal initiative cannot be itself until its time has come: it must always be something else until political sanction has been given. Subordinate to the declared intentions of Government, it is always decked in the trappings of the context in which it was born. No approval had yet been given for the provisions of services to the victims of crime.

It will be remembered that the Peace and Security Package had first offered victims a firm place in the schemes of the Ministry of the Solicitor General, victims themselves being defined as possible indices of the effects of crime prevention strategies. In 1976 an official who superintended the development of the survey had written, 'victimization surveys . . . will be consequential for deployment strategies as well as for a range of other crime prevention services provided by police forces'.[24] And, in 1981, Wood and Sim's catalogue of federal initiatives classed 'systematic victimization studies' under the heading of *Preventive Policing (1976)*.[25] So it was in this context that victims were formally associated with police work. After all, crime prevention undertaken by the police had been inscribed in the Department's mandate from the first, and the police represent the reach of the Ministry into the criminal justice system. Interchanges between the police and Ministry officials therefore began by crystallizing around the surveying of victims and the conduct of prevention projects.

The Canadian population is relatively small and it is scattered across

[23] See 'The Police and the Community: Policing a Multicultural Community', Hamilton–Wentworth Regional Police, Ontario, undated.

[24] 'Objectives of Canadian Victimization Surveys', October 1976, p. 8.

[25] J. Woods and H. Sim, *Highlights of Federal Initiatives*, p. 38.

a vast land area of some three and a half million square miles. From Vancouver in British Columbia to St John's in Newfoundland, it is three and a half thousand miles. Without continuous social intervention, the different regional and functional portions of the Canadian criminal justice system could part. The officials of governments, prisons, police forces, courts, and voluntary organizations form a rudimentary social world, sometimes called the 'criminal justice community', which is quite deliberately produced and maintained in a series of busy social exchanges. The Ministry itself underpins that world. The Regional Consultants, Planning and Liaison Division, Consultation Centre, and Communications Division organize a continuous stream of workshops, meetings, committees, and journals in an effort to foster coalitions and associations within the criminal justice community. Officials seem always to be journeying about Canada, affirming the interest of an otherwise distant Ottawa, gathering local information, and spreading news about federal affairs. A number of social circles have emerged in and about the many conferences that give organization to the officials' year, circles with their own venues, characters, dialect, gossip, and reputations. It was within the meetings of the criminal justice community that the police and Ministry officials first talked informally about what was afoot. Police officers learned of the Department's new concern with victims and surveys. Officials learned about police-based victims assistance projects that had begun to touch on their own expanding plans.

At first, it was Irvin Waller's impression that the Royal Canadian Mounted Police favoured the survey proposals that had been lodged in the Package. In July 1976 he wrote to a colleague in the Programs Branch that the Deputy Commissioner of the RCMP was 'potentially a strong supporter of the activities of the Research Division' and that he had 'expressed considerable interest in the Victimization work'.[26] Later, questions put by the RCMP indicate that the Force entertained some doubts about the utility and relevance of a survey: in February 1977 the official superintending the survey was told that it seemed to be a costly enterprise which might be difficult to justify in terms of its satisfaction of needs and the enhancement of police planning and procedure.

The Royal Canadian Mounted Police *were* prepared eventually to endorse the survey, but it was to be three other forces which gave a particular welcome to the evolving structure and crime prevention work. One was the Hamilton–Wentworth Regional Police which co-operated with the Department in its programme of testing survey techniques in

[26] Memo dated 27 July 1976.

1978. The other two were municipal forces from Alberta and their links with the Ministry's Secretariat were mediated by the informal social circles of criminal justice. The chief official responsible for the survey was himself an Albertan. Another official, then working in the Law Enforcement Section of the Ministry, had had a connection with the two Albertan departments before entering the Department. It is evident that informal communication prepared the way for the association that was to develop. The Chief of one of the Departments, the City of Edmonton Police approached the official of the Law Enforcement Section in 1975 before the contents of the Peace and Security Package had even been disclosed. He stated, 'it is my understanding that the Solicitor General's Department is planning to undertake a Victimization Survey on a Canada-wide basis. I am very interested in a research effort of this nature and would be willing to consider a measure of support to the project.' Similarly, the Calgary Police Department expressed themselves anxious to assess the effects on attitudes and victimization of a forthcoming experiment in team policing. The official of the Law Enforcement Branch asserted that 'these developments ... provide us with an enviable opportunity to advance our research in the victimization, public attitudes and team policing areas'.

Edmonton presented itself as one of the very first sites for exploring the practical problems of survey methodology,[27] it having been decided that the scale and costs of a Canadian national survey were so daunting that some techniques had to be introduced to save labour and money. Although the Canadian population is much smaller than the American, there could be no commensurate reduction of sample size because the survey was intended to search for a number of comparatively rare crimes. It was only the large sample that could unearth serious crime and offences of violence. One tactic proposed to remedy the problem of expense was telephone interviewing, and it was in Edmonton that it was tested because 'of the degree of co-operation the police were willing to provide'. Successful telephone interviewing was thought capable of achieving savings of some 70 per cent. The Ministry ascertained the usefulness of a 'reverse record technique', a technique that compared the replies given in telephone and personal interviews with data made available in police reports. The second task of the reverse record check was the examination of the capacity of a questionnaire to supply the kind of information needed for a national survey. It was concluded that there was no sig-

[27] This small section borrows from G. Catlin and S. Murray, *Report on Canadian Survey Methodological Pretests.*

nificant difference between the response rates of the two methods of interviewing. Further, it was discovered that there was little difference between the recalled rates of victimization for the two samples. Finally, the interviewers were themselves asked about the efficacy and practicability of the questionnaire which they had administered. It was found that those surveyed had not considered some of the items criminal or important, and suggestions were made about their deletion in succeeding questionnaires.

The City of Edmonton Police had offered themselves to the Ministry because, quite independently, there had arisen in that department an interest in the victims of burglary and other crimes. The Chief of that Department had been anxious throughout much of the 1970s to establish a Victim Service Unit, having attended meetings in the United States and monitored the doings of the victims movement in that country. It was not until 1979 that the City awarded him extra funds to found a unit. Employing a sergeant, two constables, and three clerical workers, the Unit was designed to compensate for the 'conspicuous absence of any consideration for the crime victim'.[28] Passing through a number of phases,[29] it advanced progressively from an initial concentration upon house and shop break-ins to the victims of robbery in November 1979 and, in April 1980, to the victims of assault and injury. It was intended to enhance liaison between the police and the public, refer victims to 'community resources that might provide additional assistance',[30] offer information about the progress of investigations, and help in the early return of stolen property. Its report claimed that 'the terror generated by the criminal act and the fear of repetition ... are responsible for the subsequent need to comfort and counsel victims. ... Most victims are more frightened than many people realize.'[31] The Ministry of the Solicitor General was eventually to give $49,570 as the first instalment of a contribution to the Police Force's operation of a Citizens' Participation and Support Project in its Victim Services Unit. The project was devised to recruit, train, and maintain a force of volunteers who would deliver services to victims.[32]

[28] Victim Services Unit, *Final Report,* Edmonton Police Department, Edmonton, 1980, p. 1.

[29] Based on *Report of the Police Community Relations Laboratory on Victimology*, 23 Apr. 1981, Edmonton Police Department—Victim Services Unit.

[30] Victim Services Unit Information Card.

[31] *Final Report*, p. 47.

[32] Based on News Release issued by the Ministry of the Solicitor General: The Hon. H. A. (Bud) Olson on Behalf of the Solicitor General of Canada Announces $49,570 Contribution to Edmonton Police Department Victim Services Unit. 30 Apr. 1982.

The Department let it be known that it sought to sponsor police-based victim service units as part of its general promotion of crime prevention programmes. Thus an inspector of the Calgary Police Service was 'informed by a member of the Federal Solicitor General's Department that substantial amounts of funding are available to Police Departments in Canada which have existing Victims Service Units that they want expanded or for starting new units'.[33] That Calgary Unit had followed a course that mirrored the development of the Edmonton Victim Service Unit. Indeed, the two departments have tended to vie with one another in their introduction of new schemes and policies. The Calgary Unit had also emerged independently, having been championed by one who had also been attracted to work undertaken in America: 'a proposal was put in by a constable in 1977 to establish two clerical positions to provide information from police reports to victims. His idea had come from the still-fledgling movement in the United States.'[34] The Unit was to expand, wane, and then expand again. Originally, in 1977, 'its activities were mainly clerical providing property crime victims with verification of incident for insurance purposes, and with a telephone number to call should victims wish to provide the police with more information pertinent to their case'.[35] It also restored stolen property to the victims of crime, thereby relieving the work load of the Police Service's property section and contributing to better relations with victims; offered one central location for those who wanted information about the state of their case; and informed victims about their rights in law. After a while, the Unit appeared to have become atrophied. A proposal was made to resuscitate and enlarge the programme, it being argued that the Unit had degenerated into little more than a mechanism for sending letters. A reformed scheme might have marked effects on the Police Service's capacity to prosecute offenders and obtain evidence about incidents:

From talking to victims of crime, it still comes out loud and clear, that they will only offer their services once as a witness because of the coldness of the Judicial System. This also includes the Police Service. As you know the witnesses who become involved in this system are expected to drop everything that they are doing and go to Court, sit through countless remands, have their cars tagged and towed. No provisions are made for their children or countless other inconveniences. Again, putting yourselves in the shoes of the victim, and as a witness,

[33] Inspector L. McQueen, 'Victim Services', undated, p. 4.

[34] Letter to myself from E. Reimer, Deputy Chief, Bureau of Field Operations, Calgary Police Service, 24 June 1983.

[35] J. Muir, *Needs and Services for Crime Victims*, Victim Assistance Unit, Calgary Police Service, January 1982, p. 2.

how many times would you put up with it before you turned a blind eye to crime, vowing never to get involved again?[36]

It was intimated to Inspector McQueen that the Department hoped to treat the Calgary Unit 'as a catalyst ... which could then be used as a model for other Police Departments wanting to start Victim Service Units'.[37] The Consultation Centre mediated the relations between Calgary and Ottawa, busying itself with the problems posed by a federal department becoming involved in Albertan territory, but the official appointed to advance the survey was also to play a critical part in drafting proposals. He had become the official within the Causes and Prevention Division who was entrusted with the supervision of projects affecting victims. He had acquired considerable knowledge of the practical research and writings of victimology and the victims movement, knowledge which stemmed from direct enquiry or the indirect filtering of ideas. In November 1980 he referred Inspector McQueen to the experience of other units, one being the Edmonton project. There was a discussion of American schemes, including those sponsored by the Law Enforcement Assistance Administration, and, indeed, the Calgary Unit did come to resemble the victim–witness programmes of the United States. It was noted that while other jurisdictions such as the United States have many such programmes, the only ones in Canada apparently were in Calgary and Edmonton.

By the end of 1980 the Consultation Centre had prepared a proposal within the 'priority area *Preventive Policing*'. The magnified Calgary Unit was to continue informing victims about their legal rights and provide liaison with the social services. But it was additionally planned to offer advice about crime prevention, provide baby-sitters, help with the repair of damaged property, deal with insurance problems, and establish a volunteer-based system of counselling.[38] The Department was to spend $203,500 over three years,[39] $98,500 being devoted to the employment of a civilian co-ordinator and a further $105,000 to an intensive evaluation of the programme. The Solicitor General himself commented, 'the victim of crime has all too often been the forgotten person in the criminal justice system'.[40]

Channelled into the realm of policing, the Peace and Security pro-

[36] Inspector McQueen, 'Victim Services', p. 3.

[37] Inspector McQueen, Victim Services Unit—Amendment I', 31 Oct. 1980, p. 2.

[38] *News Release*, Solicitor General of Canada, 22 Apr. 1981.

[39] See *Toronto Star*, 12 June 1981.

[40] *News Release*, Solicitor General of Canada, 22 Apr. 1981.

posals seemed to achieve three major effects. First, in its investigation of the methodological problems of a future Canadian national survey, the Department introduced a number of small exploratory studies that were organized around the use of police records as tests of reliability and recall. Its interest in victims and victimization became a subject of talk in the social circles of the criminal justice system. Simultaneously, there arose a few police-based victim service units that had been inspired by American example, and their organizers were to make themselves known to the Department. The police and officials came together in and about the problems of victims, their relations being loosely-coupled and mediated by the social structure of criminal justice. There never was an identity of interest or knowledge between the Department and the forces, but a working congruence of aims. At that stage, the dominant policy context for action was quite unequivocally set by the Peace and Security Package and the conventional mandate of the Department. Victims and the police were bound together in an approved entity called 'preventive policing', and it was in the name of preventive policing, not victims, that interest was expressed and funding given. Quite typically, it was not claimed that help was being extended to victims because they were vulnerable and benighted. It was filtered by the Department's theme of preventive policing and assistance to victims became a little complicated in the process. Peace and Security made it possible to further schemes favoured by people inside and outside the Department. It allowed an implementation of some of the advice that had flowed into the Ministry alongside the writings on the American surveys, advice that some Canadian police departments had also acquired and also heeded. At a distance, the American victims movement affected two Canadian institutions and it affected their interplay with each other. And thirdly, the experimental victim services could stand as objective evidence of emerging interests and commitments that were external to Ottawa. A whole succession of policy documents and memoranda could point to the variety and scale of police-based programmes as proof of a growing demand for services, the makings of a national movement, and the extent of the Department's investment in the field. Thus, in their analysis and list of schemes for the victims and witnesses of crime in Canada, Norquay and Weiler could make extensive reference to:

> The critical role played by police in the provision of services ... Interest on the part of police in serving victims and witnesses of crime is part of a general broadening of the scope of police activities.[41]

[41] G. Norquay and R. Weiler, *Services to Victims and Witnesses in Canada*, p. 95.

Included in their catalogue of happenings, police projects were described as components in the:

victim/witness service field [that] is on the verge of considerable development and expansion in Canada. Governments, it is hoped, will respond . . . by planning and implementing programs . . .[42]

The Police and 'Domestic Crisis Intervention'

'Domestic crisis intervention' is the phrase that has been adopted to describe the role played by the police and other agencies in the regulation of conflict and violence in the family. Most frequently, it is understood to refer to the formal management of wife-battering. It is unusually fraught work and has become a component of ideological debates about the policing of gender in Canada. It is taxing, delicate, and volatile, laden with ambiguities and possibilities of misadventure. Troubling to the police, and of concern to women's organizations, it not only emerged as an independent sphere of policy but also as a problem that came to bear on the initiative itself in intricate fashion. It represented the coming together of feminist politics and the Ministry's development of policing strategy, a synthesis which housed mildly antagonistic strains. As I shall argue, feminism supplied another major policy framework that organized events and ideas in the realm of victims. Complementing and contradicting movements that were in progress elsewhere, it shaped some of the most prominently marked stages of the initiative.

Family disputes loom large in that area of policing which Bittner described as the settlement of problems by the use of 'non-negotiably coercive force'. After all, the family is the social arena within which many people spend much of their lives. It is distinguished by the intimacy and continuity with which people face one another. Its relations tend to be densely interwoven, stretching over long swathes of time and highly detailed and emotionally charged. It provides a running context for action, bestowing significance and magnifying the meanings and implications of any utterance and action. Even the pettiest of acts can reverberate within the elaborate contours of a family's history. What might seem trivial outside, limited inside a finite and segregated province of meaning, can become indefinitely extended and embellished in the family. Moreover, the family is one of the most enclosing institutions, engrossing and monopolizing the attention of its members. Arguments and problems are amplified and complicative in that setting, ramifying

[42] Ibid., p. 106.

over time and across many faces of experience. They are both intensive and extensive, feeding on themselves. If only because the members of a family tend to see each other so often, there is a greater probability of their doing harm to one another. One Royal Canadian Mounted Police officer has written of the 'horrendous history of family violence'.[43] Of the 499 murders committed in Canada in 1974, some 32 per cent of the victims were members of the killer's family.[44] More generally, between 1961 and 1975, 27.4 per cent of all murders took place within the immediate family and just over half of those victims were married to the offender.[45] As Linda MacLeod once asserted:

> Wife battering is a fact of life in families across Canada. Women are kicked, punched, beaten, burned, threatened, knifed and shot, not by strangers who break into their homes or who accost them on dark streets, but by husbands and lovers.[46]

According to Levens and Dutton, much domestic crisis intervention is a most equivocal part of criminal law enforcement. It is an aspect of 'order maintenance', an 'ambiguous and problematic police function involving the management of interpersonal behaviour with few specific guidelines as to what order is or how to establish it'.[47] The assessment of any social setting is a difficult feat. It is complicated when judgements are made to support practical action, and it is even further complicated when the scene turns to crime and deviance. As Matza once remarked, those who are deviant tend also to become devious. Deviant situations often attain murky and misleading appearances, and those who are to be discovered in them intend frequently to conceal what they are doing. In the case of family violence, confusion is possibly at its greatest. Family structures are especially elaborate, private, and dense. They are usually grounded in unspoken assumptions and secret knowledge. The police may be summoned when there has been no clear breach of law and when their authority is problematic. they act not as simple thief-takers but as 'the poor man's social worker'.[48] They are required to analyse, under-

[43] G. Bell, 'Inter-Spousal Violence: Discovery and Reporting', in J. Eekelaar and S. Katz (eds.), *Family Violence*, p. 209.

[44] United Way, Social Policy and Research, *Wife Battering, a Review and Preliminary Enquiry into Local Incidence, Needs and Resources*, Vancouver, 1976, p. 40.

[45] See J. Hogarth, *Battered Wives and the Justice System*, University of British Columbia, 1979.

[46] L. MacLeod, *Wife-Battering in Canada*, p. 6.

[47] B. Levens and D. Dutton, *The Social Service Role of the Police—Domestic Crisis Intervention*, Solicitor General Canada, Ottawa, 1980, p. 6.

[48] See B. Levine, 'Domestic Crisis Intervention', *Canadian Police College Journal*, 1978, Vol. 2, No. 2.

stand, and judge intricately figured histories whose evolution and character are obscure. They are asked to make inferences about the responsibility and influence of people in all that opaque morass. Statements made and requests issued may always be withdrawn or repudiated. And situations cannot be neatly undone but will survive and develop after an officer has departed. What makes decisions additionally acute is the tendency of family disputes to embroil those who intervene. Six of the forty-one police officers killed in Canada between 1961 and 1973 were murdered whilst dealing with domestic complaints.

Despite the unsettling and difficult character of domestic crisis intervention, it seems that the Canadian police have found themselves caught up in it for a significant portion of their time. Inevitably, the victims whom they encounter are often battered women. In Vancouver, an analysis of incoming calls for police assistance revealed that just under half, or 46.6 per cent, were appeals for a social service and between 5.5 per cent and 6.5 per cent were for help with domestic disputes.[49] A reasonably similar figure of 4 to 5 per cent was offered for the police of London, Ontario.[50] It is not usually regarded as a welcome or honourable part for policemen to play. Many police officers do not define it as 'real policing', it is messy, and confers little distinction. It was claimed of the police of London and Middlesex County in Ontario, 'there is an overriding belief among the agents of the criminal justice system that the police and courts should not become involved in this area and that when they do become involved, everything possible should be done to discourage the victim from pursuing full court intervention'.[51] Indeed, it has never been clear that 'full court intervention' is universally sensible as a strategy. As one official was to observe of American strategies, 'there is growing recognition among women's groups and criminal justice officials that the option of unconditional arrest of men who batter their wives is more convoluted than had previously been assessed'.[52]

The awkwardness, dangerousness, and volatility of domestic crisis intervention made it problematic for police officers, their administrators and, in their turn, the officials of the Department of the Solicitor General itself. The beginnings of an interest in police-based victim services also embraced work on family violence. Indeed, a preoccupation with

[49] B. Levens and D. Dutton, *The Social Service Role of Police,* p. 24.

[50] W. Reitz, 'Evaluation of Police Family Crisis Training and Consultation', *The University of Western Ontario Psychology Department Research Bulletin 289,* April 1974, p. 1.

[51] P. Jaffe and C. Burris, 'Feasibility Study on Improving the Justice System's Response to Abused Women in London, Ontario', December 1980, p. 8.

[52] Memorandum on LEAA Meeting to Evaluate Funding of Victim Oriented Services, 10 Sept. 1981.

domestic crisis intervention actually preceded the more general work on victims. But the one could feed on the other. As a paper prepared by the Ministry argued, 'by dealing with victims of crime, many agencies may discover that a high percentage of their cases are family violence cases, and shift their resource allocation so that they can better respond to the needs of battered women'. There was never a wholesale drift towards the problems of family violence. Yet once more in the name of preventive policing, and not as an initiative explicitly addressed to victims, the Ministry did start to busy itself with special projects and training programmes for the police.

In 1974, for instance, the Department became involved with an ambitious programme that had started four years earlier in London, Ontario. At first, the Chief of Police had responded to newspaper reports and local criticism about the deficiencies and complexities of the police reaction to family disturbances. It had been alleged that 'police officers feel they neither have the time, competence, nor societal mandate to deal with such problems'.[53] Having secured funding from private foundations, the Chief of Police instituted a scheme in 1972 to train all junior officers in the strategy of policing family violence and, in the following year, the force was provided with a complementary family consultant service. If the situation seemed to warrant it, and if one or more members of the family agreed, a consultant would be dispatched to bring additional aid to bear. Starting with three consultants, two men and a woman, and available at unusual hours, the scheme was used extensively and with police approval. In its first six months the consultants were invited to act on nearly 700 occasions. They continue to be employed heavily, either dealing with matters themselves or referring cases to a variety of local agencies.[54] Their principal duties have been to make assessments of family needs, co-ordinate different social agencies, enhance community appreciation of the social service role of the police, and promote the training of police officers. The Ministry became involved as patron and financier when private funding began to decline in 1974. Much later, it again encouraged the development of work in London by providing money for research on the legal and social services available to the victims of family violence. In August 1980 Peter Jaffe of the University of Western Ontario was awarded a contract to produce a report on the feasibility of 'improving the justice system's response to abused women'. By 1982 the service was wholly funded by the municipality of London.

[53] P. Jaffe and J. Thompson, The Family Consultant Service with the London (Ontario) Police Force', in J. Eekelaar and S. Katz (eds.), *Family Violence*, p. 216.

[54] Family Consultant Services with London Police Force, *Annual Report 1974*, London, 1975.

Similarly, and building in part upon the work undertaken in London, the Ministry sponsored a proposal to employ a mix of volunteers and paid workers to embark on the Restigouche Family Crisis Intervention Project. Supported again as a preventive policing scheme, it was argued that:

> The problem of domestic disputes is one that is continually laid at the door of the police. Police in general . . . are ill-equipped to follow up on these problems. . . . Research shows us that the police involvement in this type of incident is probably one of the most dangerous activities he will perform in his career.[55]

At the time of its drafting in early 1979, the Restigouche proposal was conceived unequivocally as a means of easing the trials of police officers engaged in perplexing and taxing duties. In particular, it was intended to dispel the difficulties that ensued after the police officer's initial intervention in a family dispute. The police were sometimes at a loss about how to proceed, and there was a sense that local social service agencies were ill-coordinated and inadequate in their response to family violence.[56] The project was designed to organize volunteers to handle family crises when social workers and others were unavailable; enlarge information and knowledge that were before the local RCMP detachments and town police; integrate the work of social welfare agencies; increase the range of skills that could be deployed around the problem of domestic disturbance; and divert a number of cases away from the criminal justice system. Staff Sergeant Bob Holmes of the RCMP was consulted.[57] Holmes, who may be described as one of the quiet animators of the victims initiative, informed his colleagues about work elsewhere: 'it was learned that a program in London, Ontario, was operating very adequately in alleviating some of the pressures on that community's police service',[58] and a proposal was laid before the Ministry and accepted. In February 1980 it was announced that $97,500 would be provided to assist the scheme. Some months later, in December, it was agreed to expend a further $70,000 on an evaluation study of the programme. The special significance of Restigouche, New Brunswick, was held to be its rural setting, making it an interesting site for an experiment in the use of dispersed volunteers who would be a relatively inexpensive and decentralized source of assistance. In an area with a

[55] Proposal: Restigouche Family Crisis Intervention Project, 17 May 1979.

[56] See 'Hey, What about Me?', *Liaison*, April 1983, Vol. 9, No. 4, p. 21.

[57] Interim Progress Report Prepared for the Ministry of the Solicitor General: *Restigouche Family Crisis Interveners*, by J. Dupuis and G. Daigle, 31 Oct. 1980, p. 3.

[58] *Tribune*, 10 Sept. 1980.

population of only 40,000, the programme was answering seven calls a month.[59] The scheme was thought to represent a major economy, saving the time of the RCMP and police salaries. It was argued that 'police are now able to turn the problem of domestic crisis over to a trained intervener which allows police to return to their primary duties'.[60]

In large measure, 'domestic crisis intervention' was a topic classified by the Department with the policy frameworks of preventive policing and the administration of the police at large. Its history as a social problem was to be given a twist and a greater political prominence when it was grasped as an issue by women's organizations who held that it exemplified important truths about women. In the late 1970s and early 1980s, there was an important confluence of policies and politics and feminism began to address the problems of victimized women. Canadian feminist politics are so important that I shall examine them in their own chapter. What they accomplished in the instance of crisis intervention was the transformation of a burdensome and hazardous operational problem of law enforcement into an illustration of the existential situation of women. For a while, and briefly, domestic violence acquired a new framework of meaning and a new direction in policy. It is with those matters that I shall deal in Chapter VIII.

After 1980, as a result of a Government commitment made in *Towards Equality for Women* and the Speech from the Throne, crisis intervention drifted into policies to protect and aid battered women. What had once revolved around the revision of police tactics moved over to the support of female victims of criminal violence. One official concerned with the development of policing strategies recalled:

> For reasons unrelated to victims policy, wife battering and child abuse were pursued. ... People in charge of wife battering came to say, 'hey, now I'm a big actor in the issue of victims!' At first we weren't interested in battered wives but in family crisis intervention. But Status of Women were forging ahead and they succeeded in adding women to victims. We went with the flow. We weren't looking at wife battering in our earlier incarnation but we got with it none the less.

In later chapters I shall argue that the history of the social problem of violence against women was largely independent of what had gone before. It embraced distinct political ambitions, emanated from a special set of ideologies, was populated by its own cast of characters with their own scripts, and it was given structure by its own acts and scenes. Folding

[59] Ibid., 10 June 1981.
[60] *Campbelltown Graphic*, 11 June 1981.

into the activities of the federal government of Ottawa, it was mediated by the work of the different departments and agencies, by their plans and by the policies which they were nursing. It was to affect the emerging and tentative interest in the victims of crime. At that stage, it will be remembered, victims were the subject of a policy that dare not speak its name. What was done was done in the name of preventive policing. It could only be a gradual and exploratory movement, indirect in its objectives and methods. By contrast, the politics of violence against women were established in their own name, they were conspicuous, pressing and turbulent. The drift towards victims was jolted forward in its collision with those politics. There was a sudden confluence of interests and effort, each flow absorbing something of the other, and each offering a framework and a set of conditions and opportunities for the other. The progress towards services for victims was catalysed in the interests of women. A Staff Sergeant working in the Crime Prevention Centre of the RCMP stated, 'over time . . . the women's movement and their increasing emphasis on crimes against women in the family created the need for a member of the force to pay attention to that area and it naturally fitted into many of the things that I was doing'.

After 1980 attention was given to battered wives. What had once been promoted under the heading of preventive policing then became a series of policies to restrain family violence. The first subsidy of the London Family Consultants had been designed to enhance techniques of policing. In late 1980 that programme was represented somewhat differently: '——— briefed the Committee on the purpose and relevance of the project. He pointed out that the area of Family Violence had been identified in the House of Commons as well as the last Speech from the Throne'.[61] In 1978 the Restigouche Family Crisis Interveners had been supported as a scheme which would advance preventive policing. In December 1980 its evaluation was justified by the official responsible for victim matters becaue 'it relates to Ministry objectives of community involvement and preventive policing, and the problem area itself is directly relevant to the high priority concern of family violence'. But by this later phase, sponsoring officials had developed a fairly clear conception of their interest in the victims of crime and were tending to treat many of the items that came before them as the components of an evolving whole. One chief sponsor stated:

Through the Consultation Centre and over the years we've spent a good deal of money on victims. I don't know if anybody's ever added it up but I would be

[61] Extract from the Minutes of an unnamed Committee, undated, p. 4.

surprised if it was much less than a million dollars trying to get work going in that area. We spent a lot of money and a lot of our effort in the area of family dispute intervention. Now we came at that from the perspective of serving one of our clients, namely the police, who were very concerned about it and didn't know how to cope with that kind of call. So we came at it from that particular direction. That was our 'in' if you like, that made it a priority to respond to. But I think we quite consciously framed our work more broadly than simply looking at the police. Not only because that would make better research but also because we had the notion of victims issues in mind.

Indeed, in time, when the notions of victims issues had been approved politically, family crisis intervention and family violence underwent yet another twist. The Department was to describe the Restigouche Family Crisis Interveners Project as 'part of an ongoing program of research and demonstration projects to promote innovative police-based policies and programs to assist victims of crime in Canada'. That linkage and context were announced in August 1981 when the aims of a few had been realized, when political sanction had been given to a victims initiative, and when all those little beginnings and transformations had been awarded a new, retrospective meaning. In 1980 it was not at all certain that there was an ongoing programme to assist victims of crime in Canada. What *was* certain was that those in the centre of the social circle turning on victims in the Programs Branch had come to wish that such a programme could exist. Whether it would emerge, by what agency, and in what form were matters that were entirely unresolved.

Conclusion

The staff of the Ministry had to move warily in the terrain about them. In many areas, they were the 'Feds' and treated with some suspicion. But the Royal Canadian Mounted Police are the clear and undisputed responsibility of the Department, and an implied syllogism has enlarged the Solicitor General's sphere of interest to encompass all policing in Canada. It may have been politic and civil to exchange courtesies whenever the Ministry busied itself in a province or municipality, but no serious challenge to its authority and standing was issued. Police forces in Canada experienced operational difficulties, and the Ministry replied, advancing police strategies, and the politics of victims as they did so.

In this sense, the history of Canadian policing is an expression or refraction of the history of criminal justice policy as it passed within the sphere occupied by the Department. The police were the willing vehicles of a complicated transformation that was to envelop the victims of crime. Within that field described by policing, the Ministry engaged in substantial building, the style and contents of its achievements being mediated in complex ways. It funded projects that responded to the policy concerns of crime prevention, preventive policing, and the victimization survey, concerns that had been filtered by the lens of the Peace and Security proposals. It answered requests and proposals that stemmed from the police officer's practical problems. Whatever the private objectives and campaigns may have been, the working structures of policing and the legitimating structures of policy gave shape to what was done. And it is evident too that those objectives and campaigns were themselves to be progressively moulded by the emerging experiences and outcomes of projects.

The support of crisis intervention had not been intended principally to disclose truths about battered women. Indeed, it had not been couched in the language of victims and victim assistance at all. That was to come as the projects evolved and others became absorbed in their workings. As with much else, when projects are launched into the world, they can become the preoccupation and the object of others whose involvements and very presence may not have been predicted. Thus it was that the activities of Peter Jaffe and the London Family Consultants were applauded by the London Status of Women Action Group:

> Domestic violence is becoming an almost daily feature of our local news. Its victims are most often women and children. . . . For this reason, it is particularly encouraging to learn of Dr. Peter Jaffe's recent research into family violence here in London. . . . We urge thorough discussion and consideration of all the report's recommendations.[62]

In time, indeed, after a very short while, the Ministry had surrounded itself with a solid environment of accomplishments. It had given objectivity to its preoccupations, collaborating with others to create a network of events and processes that could answer back and move it forward. It was a network whose parts affected one another, Edmonton influencing Calgary, Calgary and London influencing Restigouche, the whole being supplied with ideas and connections from the Ministry and other institutions grounded in the victims movement. As the pivotal official remarked, 'there's no question that there's a lot of influence in the day to day work with the researchers and in the meetings. . . . So I'll go and talk with the police chief and his officers etcetera and I'll say, "here's what we learned at other places, here's what I think is in it for you if

[62] Letter to Co-ordinating Committee on Family Violence, 12 Mar. 1981.

you collect that information". So you influence it in a three-way or multiway programme development.' The network began to acquire its own autonomy, working on the Department as an independent and authoritative agent.

In return, the projects and conferences delivered a considerable quantity of useful working information about the management of police-based victim assistance projects. In the period of a few years, the Department had learned much. Almost invariably, the replies it received suggested that assistance projects were reasonably inexpensive, effective, and locally and politically popular. Newspapers endorsed what had been done. In Restigouche, for example, 'The Voice of Restigouche' announced:

> The unique family crisis intervention program initiated one year ago ... is proving to be both effective and practical in solving problems faced by families in need of assistance.[63]

It called the project 'unique and innovative',[64] declaring that 'police and probation services are enthusiastic and hopeful about this project ... proud precedent setters'.[65] In an editorial, it maintained 'the police forces and probation services in the county are to be commended for initiating a well-needed and long overdue crisis intervention program'.[66] The *Dalhousie News* stated, 'the Restigouche Family Crisis Interveners is a unique project, not only in Canada but in the whole of North America'.[67] It proceeded to discuss the part played by the Solicitor General in funding the scheme. When a department is most commonly identified with 'fire-fighting' and the control of institutions that generate bad news, programmes like those of Restigouche, London, Calgary, and Edmonton are a source of unusual commendation.[68]

In July 1981 the Department of the Solicitor General and the Ministry of Justice jointly submitted a memorandum to Cabinet on 'Justice for Victims of Crime'.[69] Historically, the Department could point to the long catalogue of projects which it had sponsored. A substantial sum of money had been committed to justice for victims of crime and just over a third had been allotted to schemes revolving around crisis intervention and the preparation and training of police officers, and most of that allotment

63 *Tribune: 'The Voice of Restigouche'*, 10 June 1981.
64 Ibid., 10 Sept. 1981.
65 Ibid.
66 Ibid.
67 *Dalhousie News*, 17 June 1981.
68 See, for example, L. Krotz, 'What About the Victims?', *Quest*, June/July 1982.
69 *Solicitor General Annual Report* 1981–2, Minister of Supply and Services Canada, Ottawa, 1983, p. 5.

had been spent on victim service projects in Calgary and elsewhere. Thus almost all the funding had been devoted to police-based projects and those projects, in their turn, could be translated into concrete evidence of a long history of assistance to victims. At a time when there was talk of austerity, when, in Wildavsky's phrase, 'the fact that something has been done once vastly increases the chances that it will be done again',[70] it was useful to produce a history of work with victims. What had started as preventive policing and crisis intervention could be reviewed and presented as the precursor of an initiative. After all, little other work had been done, what there was did more or less centre directly on victims, and those who approved police-based programmes were interested in advancing federal enterprise in the victims area. Many of the projects, and particularly those that had been drafted towards the end, did actually lend themselves very successfully to such a transformation.

Symbolically, all that activity could be read by those who viewed it as the stirrings and beginnings of a larger undertaking. The origins of each project may have been discrete but, evolving, they started to merge and play with one another. As they evolved, so their sponsors and participants started to acquire motives, experiences, and knowledge that prompted a revision of the meanings of what had been done. There was a new self-consciousness. Research was undertaken and, as Skogan once remarked, 'from the researchers, practitioners learn that there are victims that they never see and problems that they do not know about'. Specific needs and local histories began to become generalized and anonymous, features of a wider process. People who were close to police projects started to discern a movement of ideas and policies that were more extensive than domestic crisis intervention, preventive policing, and reverse record checks alone. The development of ideas was willed. It was carefully nurtured by those people who had been steeped in the American victims movement and sought to work in the name of victims in Canada.

So it was that victims began to loom as a political entity in their own right. A Staff Sergeant of the RCMP reported in 1981:

> It seemed to explode when I came back to the Crime Prevention Centre in June [1980]. ... I was gone for one year. Up until that time, we were doing these things but it was always a struggle. It was like running your head into the wall all the time. You kept meeting resistance and you'd meet it everywhere. But now, with the change and the slight alteration of the labelling process, nothing changed in what we were doing. It's how we said it. When we talked child abuse, that's a medical label and that's a very difficult concept within criminal justice. When we talked wife battering, that also was perceived as being a social

[70] A. Wildavsky, *The Politics of the Budgetary Process*, p. 3.

problem. It wasn't perceived as being a criminal problem. So that was a difficult process. ... We all know that we had investigated children when they got murdered and raped and all that, but they were pretty rare. ... Much of the problem was one of communication, of creating words that were common understanding. And that's what the victims' services do. Going across the country and hearing over and over again from police officers out in the street who were saying, you know, 'well, what about the victims? And yes, you're talking about the battered woman, but she's only one of the victims. What about the elderly? And, yes, you're talking about child abuse, but what about the victim of robbery?' And then, slowly, it became clear that really all we're talking about is all victims. And while special interest groups would like to see the words and policies and everything centre around their particular needs, I think for advancement we really need to provide words of labelling that are more common to all, that people can pay attention to.

VII. The Province and the United Nations

Introduction

I have alluded to the difficult relations which occasionally exist between the federal and provincial governments of Canada. At times, indeed, it has seemed as if the very political coherence of the nation was endangered. Faint echoes of that larger discord have sometimes been heard in the reaches of the criminal justice system itself. To be sure, I have also alluded to the problems which attend any description of federal–provincial and interdepartmental relations. Officials make rhetorical and political gains by referring to those relations in particular ways, and it would be unwise to replicate political talk without providing a political context. In the quiet of committees and task forces, away from public declamation, much intercourse has been peaceable enough most of the time. A number of officials did, in fact, protest that my reference to argument was 'somewhat overplayed'. In the event, too, the matter of victims was to be managed without much controversy.

Yet discord is not entirely illusory. There have been occasions when argument became aggressive. In the past, it will be recalled, the Department's attempts to foster diversion programmes were frustrated in a number of areas; there was some hostility to the introduction of victim–witness projects in the courts; the Solicitor General had been barred from involvement in the administration of criminal injuries compensation schemes; and Quebec had declared roundly that the federal government was not entitled to become interested in the provision of aid to victims.

On inspection, many of those quarrels and boundaries disputes cannot be reduced to federal–provincial relations alone. The matter is more complicated. Much of the censure and proscription actually emanated from lawyers in official positions working in and around the courts of provincial jurisdiction. As an official remarked, 'the hostility ... was not necessarily attributable to federal–provincial relations, but lawyers' ownership *re* what happens in *their* system'. Those lawyers were no less guarded in their relations with provincial colleagues, and I shall illustrate their position later in the chapter. But it must also be appreciated that the stance of provincial lawyers can fold into the larger structures of federal–provincial relations, becoming inseparable from them. For practical purposes, it may be a little immaterial wh rately be ascribed to a lawyer's attachment to his Constitution's allocation of federal and provincial there and it can infuse the activities of officials. I presence exercised the staff of the Ministry of the So is always possible that quarrels will become uncontro upwards to engulf ever more senior officials and a wider a of institutions.

In reply, the members of the Department were manifestly a ious that their actions could not be read as threatening to the provinces. After all, much is at risk when the nature of provincial government can be understood chiefly through its contrasts with federal rights and duties. 'Federal–provincial relations' have become a theme that is endlessly discussed in the talk and writings of the Ministry. It is carefully inspected for its bearing on every plan that is projected. On occasion, it is as if the Department's dealings with the provinces map out a Balkans of the Canadian criminal justice system: one maladroit move always promising to lead to a much wider disturbance.

It was consequently emphasized that the provinces must not be upset. There was a constant attention to the protection of face, to courtesy, and to solicitude. In every paper will be found a routine reference to the preservation of amicable federal–provincial relations. Amicability is paramount and much will be done to achieve it. The criminal justice system would be unworkable without it. Thus, those who drafted the Strategic Overviews of the Department were required to list the effects which any new proposal might have upon provincial governments. The Director of the Policy Branch recommended caution when he put plans about the victims initiative before members of the Consultation Centre. He stated that neglect of federal–provincial relations 'would clearly get us into trouble'. When a report was prepared in 1981, it was announced that 'the fact that so many of the practical program proposals and implications of initiatives in this area fall under provincial jurisdiction requires sensitivity to be shown by the federal government in launching a major initiative which some of the provinces may perceive to be an intrusion on their own priorities and responsibilities'. When Cabinet approval had finally been given to the initiative, the Director of the Policy Branch wrote 'projects can only be funded with the concurrence and the real commitment of the provinces and communities involved. . . . I cannot stress strongly enough the importance of coordination in this area and the necessity of playing a supportive but not overly directive role, since most potential victim services fall within provincial juris-

n.'[1] And so it went on throughout the history of the victims initiative nd in almost every important document that signalled its progress.

By extension, the business of propelling federal actions into provincial space is an appreciable problem demanding detailed consideration. A successful federal–provincial enterprise becomes admirable for many reasons: it is a persuasive demonstration to the provinces that such things are possible; it is a pattern of future action; and it is more generally significant in the context of a tenuously united federal state. As important, the acquisition of a provincial partner will enlarge and affect federal plans: it is evidence of the acceptability of national projects to at least some provincial figures; it ensures that a provincial voice will be heard in federal planning; it releases some of the jurisdictional restraints on federal activity; it enables a province to share or assume command of an otherwise solely federal process, thereby altering the appearances of action; it allows things to be done by a province that could not be done by a federal department; it knits the segments of the criminal justice system together into a working whole; and it is for these reasons that it is rhetorically potent in the construction of arguments for use in Ottawa.

The building of any initiative is therefore immeasurably reinforced when a visible provincial partner has been secured. The federal victims initiative was itself accelerated and strengthened by the unexpected pronouncement of a provincial Minister in October 1979. There was a remarkable effect when Gordon Walker, Ontario Minister for Correctional Services, spoke on victims' rights at the very first meeting of Ministers Responsible for Criminal Justice. His was a substantial contribution to the birth of the federal initiative. As Irvin Waller remarked:

> The political name associated with the victims movement in Canada is Gordon Walker. Two years ago there was a meeting of Ministers. I sat in the back, somewhat horrified by the amount of time spent on constitutional issues. I had heard of Gordon Walker but never heard him speak. Gordon Walker probably doesn't realise the importance of the remarks he made. Quebec became interested. The Federal Government became interested. . . . Gordon Walker was the first to speak publicly about crime victims. He had great courage in doing so. Gordon Walker for me is the politician who precipitated out the beginnings of a victim movement in Canada.[2]

Gordon Walker's speech is interesting in many ways. It illuminates how the coincidental meeting of timetables can lead to major changes in

[1] Letter to Regional Consultants, 9 Sept. 1981.

[2] I. Waller, Remarks addressed at the opening session of the Conference of the National Organization for Victim Assistance, 14 Oct. 1981.

policy and planning. As Art Daniels, then Executive Director of the Community Programs Division of the Ontario Ministry of Correctional Services, remarked, 'two organizations were working on similar things that just converged at that time'. It also illustrates how separate histories flowing together can form contexts for one another, being employed by officials to develop action. Gordon Walker and his Ministry were attempting to advance their own work in Ontario, but his statement was seized in a great embrace by the Federal Department of the Solicitor General, and that embrace was as eagerly returned. A provincial declaration of interest in victims was useful and timely in the autumn of 1979. It proved to be a major engine, making possible a public commitment of federal intentions. Yet it might well have passed unnoticed only a few years before. Indeed, Art Daniels observed of that speech of October 1979, Gordon Walker 'had said nothing particularly new'. What was important was the place, the audience, and the possibility of a federal response. The little history of the politics of victims in Ontario was an aspect of a complicated dialectical interchange: it achieved significance as a context for federal action within the wider framework which the evolution of federal action had itself prepared. Reciprocally, the federal reply was incorporated in the unfolding history of policy in Ontario, given meaning by that policy and used to push it onwards. As an Ontario official reflected, 'after that speech, Irvin discovered that he had a soulmate, and Mr. Walker wouldn't let it go either. You've got to give him full marks. He was banging it through his field.' I shall try to explain how some of these exchanges came into being.

Victims in the Provinces

Since the late 1960s, and across the breadth of Canada, federal, provincial, municipal, and private sector organizations have worked on a miscellany of programmes for victims. Their history has been very brief and it has yet to be written. There is great uncertainty about how many programmes there are, what they are intended to accomplish, how they arose, and what they actually do. Even within the provinces themselves there has been some uncertainty about the volume, structure, and content of activity. For example, it was stated in a 1982 Report of a provincial committee, 'once the Ministry has a more complete picture of what victim needs are in this province, what this Ministry and other ministries and community groups are doing, and what this Ministry should be doing, then it will be in a position to respond to the federal position in general and to specific federal initiatives'. The character of victims services was being established and discovered throughout the history of the initiative. As each stage of the initiative passed, so new groups and projects were encountered, injecting wholly novel histories and structures into what could be said about Canadian schemes. Indeed, one of the principal effects of the initiative was to lay bare what was happening. The initiative built its own past and environment as it proceeded.

In one of the few reviews of victims services, Norquay and Weiler describe the rediscovery of the Canadian victim as a process that took place in the 1970s.[3] Their report lists no project that was founded before 1970: it traces the growth of Canadian rape crisis centres back to British Columbia and Ontario in 1974, and it offers an even briefer pedigree for concern about wife-battering.[4] To be sure, the institutional response to child abuse is much older, having arisen in the nineteenth century, but it is a response which used to deny that abused children were the victims of *crime* at all.[5] Another small survey of programmes was based on approaches to 600 agencies and an examination of published sources. Printed as a *Victims Services Directory* in 1981, it gives the earliest project as the Vancouver crisis centre that was started in 1969.[6] Almost all the programmes catalogued seem to have been aimed at two principal populations, abused children and assaulted women, and it may be presumed that they were not conceived initially as elements in a movement to assist the victims of crime at all. Under various classifications of services to women, the *Directory* lists two of the 3 programmes begun in 1969–70, two of the 4 begun in 1971–2, eight of the 13 begun in 1973–4, four of the 8 begun in 1975–6, five of the 8 begun in 1977–8, and nine of the 15 begun in 1979–80. Eight of the projects received funds from a municipal authority, four from private bodies, twenty-three from provincial governments, four from federal departments, and two from federal–provincial cost-sharing agreements. The *Directory* is incomplete, but it conveys a clear impression that most programmes were promoted by bodies other than federal departments, that they are young, and that most centred on the provision of help to battered women, a provision that would probably not have been greeted as help to victims. Again, it was said of

[3] G. Norquay and R. Weiler, *Services to Victims and Witnesses of Crime in Canada*, p. 17.

[4] Linda MacLeod has pointed out that groups of nuns in Quebec had organized refuges for battered women as long ago as the 1930s. Their work is usually ignored in the standard histories of assistance to women.

[5] It is interesting that the newly dominant emphasis on criminal victimization had begun to encourage Children's Aid Societies to undertake criminal prosecutions in the 1980s.

[6] N. Tomasson and M. Johnson, *Victims Services Directory*, British Columbia Police Commission, Vancouver, 1981.

Quebec in 1982 that the province 'is only beginning to reflect and to act in the area of victims of crime. Initiatives taken in this regard are few and of recent date, with the exception of the fields of violence against women and children, and of compensation.[7]

Officials in the federal government tended to acquire a somewhat haphazard knowledge of all that was stirring in Canada. To be sure, as an official argued, 'there were enclaves in Health and Welfare, Status of Women, Sol. Gen., Justice and other departments', but it was not until the beginning of the 1980s that a network of information began to form. It was not until that time, too, that those enclaves would have talked about victims *as* victims. Their members would have discussed family violence, assaulted women, abused children, and applicants for criminal injuries compensation. In the late 1970s work with victims seemed to have emerged with great suddenness and in numerous guises; there was no organization devoted to the preparation and dissemination of information of what had been done; the work was not clustered together either politically, institutionally, or semantically; and most organizations had only a most rudimentary knowledge of one another's doings. The staff of many programmes were and are too few and too busy to canvass the world about their activities. Moreover, the federal government had only begun to become attentive to victims and it had only a marginal political and financial stake in what had happened. It was the case that numerous articles, books, and reports about victims were deposited in the libraries and offices of different departments. Irvin Waller had stocked the library of the Ministry of the Solicitor General. The official appointed to forward the survey had filled three large filing cabinets with copies of American and Canadian writings about the victims of crime. But much information remained dispersed and uncollated, available to only a few, not having been forwarded to the Ministry and staying outside its intelligence. After all, for most of the time, there was little purpose served by gathering and forwarding it. The Department had not always been expressly concerned with victims. Neither had it been the major source of funds for transition houses, rape crisis centres, and criminal injuries compensation schemes. The evolution of a greal deal of practical work on Canadian victims was thus effectively invisible and inconsequential to the Department.

There had to arise something substantial and conspicuous, central to the Department's own mandate and scheme of relevance, before provincial work became pressingly critical in the affairs of the Solicitor

[7] M. Baril *The Victims of Crime in Quebec*, A brief presented to the Federal–Provincial Task Force on the Victims of Crime, May 1982, p. 1.

General. Not every influential event has to be melodramatic, but politics is often theatrically staged and theatrically exploited, and Gordon Walker's speech did give immediate stature and presence to provincial sentiment. It was a notable turning-point, invoked on numerous occasions, and palpably important in the advancement of the federal initiative. It is for that reason that I shall concentrate on the politics of victims in Ontario.

Ontario and Ottawa

Ontario is Canada's second largest province and its third largest territory, occupying about a ninth of the country's land mass. It is the most heavily populated province, possessing a third of the people of Canada. It is the most heavily industrialized province. With Quebec, it looms large in the criminal justice system: the triumvirate of Quebec, Ontario, and the federal government dominating the politics of Canadian crime. As West and Snider remarked, 'in a constitutional sense, there is no Canadian criminal justice system but rather ten provincial ones. This constitutional variety can be overplayed, however, in the sense that the two central provinces ... compose about three quarters of the total population, and the federal government provided much of the total justice revenues ...'[8] Further, Ontario is also the province that physically encircles the city of Ottawa, and relations between the federal government in the capital and the provincial government in Toronto are an odd blend of practical complexity, political separateness, geographical propinquity, and social intimacy. An official working in the Department of the Solicitor General will probably live in Ontario; pay taxes to Ontario, the City of Ottawa, and the federal government; be governed by Ontario in some segments of his or her life and by Ottawa in others; have friends or relations working in provincial governments; may be a member of a federal–provincial task force, working party, or committee; may well, indeed, have worked in provincial government himself or herself; be largely ignorant of victims schemes in and around Ottawa unless special curiosity or need propels him or her to them; and may have close knowledge of a victims project in Calgary, Vancouver, or Winnipeg. In all this, there is an overlapping series of zones of relevance which make the Ontario government sometimes very near and sometimes very far.

[8] G. West and S. Snider, 'Justice Policies and Justice Politics in the Canadian State: Recent European Theories', unpublished paper, April 1981, p. 16.

Victims in Ontario

The great bulk of Ontario's institutional work on victims was conducted under the Community Programs Division of the Ministry of Correctional Services. Officials of the Justice Secretariat, the co-ordinating and policy-developing group that serviced the provincial Ministries, recognized some little paradox in that Ministry busying itself with victims, but the provincial Ministry of the Attorney General and the provincial Ministry of the Solicitor General displayed uncertainty about the propriety and wisdom of substantial organized assistance to victims. They were reluctant to undertake an appreciable expansion of the province's involvement with such work. In 1981, and as a response to federal and provincial movements of policy, the Ministry of the Attorney General cautiously approved victim–witness services, announcing that pamphlets should be prepared to appraise victims about the aid that was available. It recommended that the police should superintend the provision of counselling and practical help to those who had been distressed by crime and had suffered loss or damage to possessions. But it also expressed major reservations about the harm that would be done to the criminal justice process by the introduction of volunteer or lay schemes of victim support. The Crown Attorneys and officials of the Ministry were evidently concerned about the manner in which victim assistance might subvert the courts and criminal justice:

> There is a very great danger that 'psychological' support to victims could endanger the integrity of the Crown's evidence at trial. Any volunteer group that is to come into contact with witnesses prior to their testifying would have to be carefully instructed by the police so as to prevent the compromising of a witness's later evidence. In all but the most extreme cases the police should first obtain a statement from a victim before arranging for contact with emotional support services. It, therefore, is important that the overall coordination of these services be with the prosecution who will be in a position to determine the proper time and circumstances for their intervention.... We feel that any Victim/Witness Services should never be turned entirely over to volunteers or to any agency other than the police or Crown Attorney if the public is to be assured of the continued integrity of our criminal justice system.[9]

That argument was to reverberate through significant portions of the history of the initiative, defining positions and protagonists. It urged the exclusion of untutored outsiders from the courts and courtroom processes. It made the areas in and around the courts most inhospitable.

Not only was the neighbourhood of the court uninviting territory

[9] *Report of Committee on Victim/Witness Services*, Ministry of Attorney General, Ontario, 25 Feb. 1981, pp. 3, 6.

for those who were not lawyers or police officers, but the Ministry of Correctional Services had no sovereignty there. On one occasion, for instance, the Ministry had tried to make a modest foray into the courts and it had been rebuffed. The Probation and Parole Services of the Ministry had sought to fund a project that would have been administered by a private sector agency but it became apparent, as the agency reported, 'that money for a Victim/Witness Assistance Program would not be forthcoming from the above source, because the Ministry of Correctional Services has no legal mandate for Victim Services'. If that Ministry was ever to become the patron of victim assistance projects, it would have to move into the spaces that other departments could not or would not choose to occupy. The Ministry's particular responsibilities led it to impart a distinct emphasis to the schemes which it introduced. Victim assistance in Ontario was to become an adjunct of probation and the organized treatment of offenders in the community. In that guise, it could become the property of the Ministry.

Until the late 1960s the Ministry had been named the Department of Reform Institutions, and its *Statement of Purpose* had then claimed as its main function the holding 'in custody for the prescribed periods those persons sentenced by the courts to its jurisdiction'. That simple custodial objective was to give way before the larger North American campaign of 'decarceration' and 'deinstitutionalisation'.[10] A new *Statement of Purpose* announced, 'the emphasis should be on helping offenders develop and maintain responsible and acceptable behaviour within the community rather than on short-term custodial care'. Reflecting on the transformation which he had accomplished, the Executive Director of the Community Programs Division observed:

> Trends reversed dramatically. Critics of the justice system questioned the impact of institutionalized programs. The costs of institutionalization in terms of economics and social justice were being re-defined and alternate ways were sought for dealing with the offender, not in an institutional setting, but, in the community. Programs were introduced which would remove the inmate from the institutional setting sooner, such as the temporary absence program, work release, volunteer work in the community, effective discharge planning, and stepped-up use of parole. All these programs were directed toward the decarceration of the inmate population.[11]

It was in 1974 that the Ministry began to link decarceration with

[10] See, for example, A. Scull, *Decarceration*, Prentice-Hall, New Jersey, 1976, and D. Garland and P. Young (eds.), *The Power to Punish*, Heinemann, London, 1983, especially the chapter by S. Cohen entitled 'Social-Control Talk: Telling Stories about Correctional Change'.

[11] A. Daniels, 'Future for Alternatives', *Correctional Options*, Fall 1981, Vol. 1, No. 1, p. 2.

the succour of victims. Building upon the emerging emphases of de-institutionalization and community programmes, and reinforcing the much older practice of making restitution orders in the courts, the Ministry supported a project proposed by the Mennonite Central Committee, the social service agency of the Mennonite and Brethren in Christ Church. Mennonites had been linked with the Ministry since the inception of the Volunteer Probation Program in 1969.[12] Together, they shared an elective affinity which promoted certain themes. 'Community' entered in the guise of a local voluntary group. Decarceration was secured by arranging for victims and offenders to meet one another and become peaceably reconciled. Reconciliation resonated particularly Christian ideas: 'the persons involved in initiating the project ... saw the need for Christians to assume a peacekeeping stance, whatever their vocation.'[13] The Victim–Offender Reconciliation Program (or VORP) was modelled by its organizer, Mark Yantzi, after a prototype in another Mennonite community in Elmira, Ontario. It answered a special need of the Ministry. One of those who had worked in the Ministry during the early phase of those programmes recalled that released offenders were thought to present a risk to the community and victims which they had left behind:

> Victims started with the introduction of a wider notion of community programmes. For example, when I first started with Correctional Services, I was working in an institution. We would release men on temporary absence, and one of the contacts we made (we made two contacts) was from the security end of it. That's when we started to consider the victim.

Victim–Offender Reconciliation Programs thereby provided some assurance that the returned offender would not do harm outside the penal institution which he or she had left. That assurance was perhaps necessary. Of the 54,200 persons who completed various kinds of sentence in 1978, about 42 per cent were again inmates on probation or in other programmes of the Ontario Ministry of Correctional Services by the end of 1979.[14] The programmes saved the Ministry the expense of housing those who might otherwise have been incarcerated. They amplified particular arguments about the moral accountability of the offender, arguments to which I shall return. References to the victim's gains were to emerge a little later: 'the project was initiated as a means of encouraging the offender to take responsibility for correcting the material and

[12] *Victim–Offender Reconciliation Program*, Probation and Parole, Cambridge, Ontario, 1980.

[13] W. MacPherson and M. Yantzi, *Victim–Offender Reconciliation Program*, Kitchener, 1979, p. 3.

[14] *Crime in Ontario—Questions and Answers*, Provincial Secretariat for Justice, Toronto, undated, p. 28.

emotional damage that had been created, [but] the director of the project, Mark Yantzi, soon realized that it held benefits for the victim as well.... Increasing the victim's involvement in the criminal justice process soon became an explicit goal of the Victim Offender Reconciliation Project.'

In October 1978 the Ministry acquired a new Minister, Gordon Walker. It also established a Community Programs Division with Art Daniels as its Executive Director, a man described by a former colleague as 'Ontario's moral entrepreneur'. It was after that time that the stress upon decarceration became most pronounced. As Art Daniels argued, 'with the emphasis now in community programming, the organization is viewed as a service to the community providing community assistance, underlining old fashioned values of work and restitution'.[15] Some of the work that was then initiated revolved around victim–witness schemes based upon models developed in America. For example, I shall discuss how the Brampton Victim–Witness Assistance Program, inaugurated in September 1979, was originally inspired by a report in *Federal Probation* about a project in San Mateo, California.[16] It was a practice of officials to scout for ideas in the United States, joining NOVA and visiting different programmes. In June 1980, for example, a member of the Community Programmes Support Services Branch reported to the Justice Secretariat about his inspection of the Victim–Witness Assistance Office in Boulder, Colorado: 'attached you will find copies of the materials I obtained from the Boulder project which I feel—after discussing the matter with Art—likely best meets the needs at this time in "selling" the program...'

Victim–witness programmes had been established in Brampton, Rexdale, Windsor, and Kitchener. It was evident that they served a distinct demand and a special population. After all, not every crime furnishes a known and compliant offender. And some victims have no wish to be reconciled with those who have hurt them. It was claimed that battered women in Ontario had no desire to do so. But it was Victim–Offender Reconciliation which was to be the predominant theme in the Ministry's work with victims.[17] It too borrowed from America.[18]

[15] A. Daniels, 'Future for Alternatives', p. 3.

[16] That report was to influence other projects in Canada. It affected the work of the John Howard Society of Saskatchewan, for instance.

[17] See T. Dittenhoffer and R. Ericson, 'The Victim/Offender Reconciliation Program: A Message to Correctional Reformers', *University of Toronto Law Journal*, 1983, Vol. 33, No. 3.

[18] The Kitchener scheme borrowed from the Night Prosecutor's Program in Columbus, Ohio.

All but eight of the thirty programmes supported by the Ministry in 1980 centred around it. Programmes were operating or contemplated in Windsor, Kitchener, Toronto, Sudbury, London, Belleville, Picton, Trenton, Renfrew, Pembroke, Kingston, Guelph, Stratford, Burlington, Atikokan, Kirkland Lake, and Peterborough. VORP was taken to be a personal extension and exemplification of the more general conception of the Community Service Order, victims acquiring both an individual and a corporate identity. Thus Art Daniels remarked, 'I always see victims in a box sort of thing. You know, you've got the victim as a community, the victim as an individual receiving service, the victim as an individual receiving money, and the victim as an individual receiving money and service.' And Community Service Orders were an extension of probation. Art Daniels stated, 'I was coming at it from a probation stance.' The Probation Service was to be the ultimate superintendent and support of many of the schemes. *Pari passu*, the community service order and decarceration were facets of the maintenance and defence of community, an important entity whose preservation was a concern of the Ministry. It had, after all, initiated a Community Programs division to forward projects in the name of the community. Another Victim–Offender Reconciliation Program, based on the example of the Kitchener–Waterloo project, was committed to '[involving] community people in work with problems that normally lead into the criminal justice process ... [and identifying] crime that can be successfully dealt with in the community'.[19] The idea of community is pivotal. The Victim–Offender Reconciliation Projects enshrine the contention that returning responsibility to the community is meritorious in its own right. It takes initiative away from government and state bureaucracies and restores it to the people. It gives authority to those who act out of compassion or duty rather than as paid functionaries. And it is cheap. As Gordon Walker argued:

> The type of program we are hoping to implement would rely heavily on volunteers. As you are aware volunteers, besides being an economic necessity in the justice system, bring a host of skills and a depth of motivation that could never be encompassed by even the most dedicated paid staff, and their individual perspectives give great potency to all community programs.[20]

At a time of austerity, programmes devoted to victims were economi-

[19] 'VORP Victim Offender Reconciliation Program', Langley, British Columbia, undated.

[20] Gordon Walker, 'Victim/Witness Assistance', Address to Provincial Court Judges, Metro Toronto, 23 Feb. 1979.

cal, popular, and demonstrative of government solicitude. They gave salience to compassion. They emphasized 'the biblical teachings on peace and justice'.[21] They could be self-supporting. By extracting a surcharge on fines or by using the revenues of prison industries, it was argued, some several tens of thousands of dollars could be raised. The outcome would be an inexpensive and politically attractive initiative:

> The 1980s will pose serious problems for Government. Undoubtedly, the most difficult challenge will be to find ways of meeting the public's expectation that Government continue to provide the services necessary to meet community needs, despite rising rates of inflation and shrinking sources of revenue to pay for Government programs. ... The danger is that the same Governments which, during periods of prosperity, are seen as benevolent bestowers of services will be perceived in times of constraint as hard-hearted villains, indifferent to the very public whose dollars they administer. Governments which hope to survive must find innovative and low-cost ways of providing services that will demonstrate that the Government cares about the citizenry. An area which has been neglected in Canada and which has great potential for development at minimal cost in the 1980s is the area of victim/witness services.[22]

Gordon Walker

Gordon Walker was the Minister through whom and about whom the Ontario policy on victims began to evolve in the late 1970s. His was a special scheme of political perspectives that lent itself to a major reformulation of criminal justice. In this sense, victims' rights and community service in Ontario were but working extensions of his larger radical conservatism. There was to be a remarkable marriage between Gordon Walker's thought and the ambitions of his staff in the Ministry of Correctional Services. One senior official remarked, 'I had just been waiting for some Minister to come to beat the gong at the right time.'

Gordon Walker had been trained as a lawyer at the University of Western Ontario and Osgoode Hall Law School. At the age of 30, in 1971, he was adopted as Conservative Party candidate for London North. Only two years later, he was to become parliamentary assistant to the Revenue Minister, Allan Grossman. Then he lost his seat in the election of January 1976. He was to explain his party's poor showing as the outcome of the Conservatives' drift to the left: 'how the voter must be frustrated with our party appearing as socialist Conservatives....

[21] K. Harley, *Program Guide: Victim Offender Reconciliation Program and Community Mediation Service*, Kitchener, 1981, p. 5.

[22] *The Challenge for Government in the 1980s*, undated, unattributed, Toronto, p. 1.

Frankly, I have to think there's no time more right than the moment to have our party return to its original base.' He proceeded to assert that the Conservatives had abandoned themselves when 'the public is looking for an alternative to bureaucracy, statism, burgeoning welfare, public sector strikes and erosion of the work ethic'.[23]

Those themes of the uncontrolled expansion of the state and the pauperization of welfare recipients were to be continually argued by Mr Walker. In May 1976, for instance, the Western Ontario Progressive Conservative Policy Conference agreed that the able-bodied welfare recipient should work to qualify for financial assistance from Government. Gordon Walker himself argued that 'it would be an incentive to get off the welfare treadmill'.[24] During his period without a riding, Mr Walker was held to have established himself as the 'outspoken element of the [Conservative Party's] right-wing conscience'.[25]

Gordon Walker re-entered the Ontario Legislature as Member of Parliament for London South in June 1977. Inside the Legislature, he was to again reiterate his aversion to profligate Government spending and the damage done by bureaucracy.[26] It was considered that he had made himself eligible for a Cabinet post, representing as he did a practical opportunity to 'restore some of that right-wing fervour' to the Government.[27] And so it came to pass. On 23 October 1978 he was appointed Correctional Services Minister, a post that he was to hold until April 1981.[28]

One immediate problem confronting his Ministry was prison crowding. There were reports of problems at the Barrie jail;[29] the Minister was constrained to order portable cells to house the excess population of the jail at Sault Ste Marie;[30] and, in May 1979 he was required to respond to a riot of the inmates of the Guelph jail.[31] Gordon Walker repeatedly expressed his criticism of the manner in which large numbers of offenders were sentenced to imprisonment. He held that overcrowding stemmed, in part, from an unwillingness to explore alternatives. In November 1978 he talked of his disappointment with judges who were reluctant to sentence first offenders to community service instead of terms of imprison-

[23] *Globe and Mail*, 9 Jan. 1976.
[24] Ibid., 3 May 1976.
[25] Ibid., 13 Nov. 1976.
[26] Ibid., 20 Dec. 1977.
[27] Ibid., 18 Aug. 1978.
[28] Mr Walker was to remain Provincial Secretary for Justice for some time after April 1981.
[29] *Globe and Mail*, 25 Oct. 1978.
[30] Ibid., 21 Nov. 1978.
[31] Ibid., 9 May 1979.

ment.[32] But he was not a Minister with responsibility for the courts and sentencing policy. His jurisdiction embraced prisons, probation, and community corrections, and major reforms had to be worked in that area. The need for a policy was great because, within days of his appointment as Minister, Gordon Walker was informed that he had to cut some eight million dollars from his budget and he did not know how he was to do it.

Community Service Orders and decarceration become linked to population pressures in the Ontario prisons and the financial problems of the Ministry. Of course, that linkage was not inevitable and it could never be simple. It was brought into being by willing officials and politicans who confronted rather precise difficulties. It is possible that the great prison builders of the nineteenth century would never have dreamed of coupling those matters together. They would have strained to create more prisons. Gordon Walker did not have the means to build on a grand scale and he did not wish to do so. Moreover, between the decision to build and the actual provision of space there is always a long lapse of time which prevents any rapid response to a problem.[33]

What helped to encourage the association between crowding and community programmes was a budgetary crisis, a sense of urgency, and a loss of faith in the prison as an engine of rehabilitation. It is evident that Gordon Walker accepted that jails did not increase the sum of human happiness. Quite the reverse. He represented imprisonment as a waste of time, money, and labour. Not all inmates could or should be set free: there was a case to be made for incapacitating the few who were dangerous, but most of the others should be released and set to productive toil. To the John Howard Society, for example, he asserted:

> Your society has shown imaginative leadership in its intermittent program. In fact, you are the only community which has in place a system whereby people serving weekend sentences report to you for supervised work on the Welland Canal, rather than reporting to the jail. I think this is a most commendable idea. It is better than having weekend inmates sitting around in jail doing nothing useful for their misdemeanors.[34]

It is in this juxtaposition of ideas about prison population, decarceration, community service, and useful labour that the coherence of the emerging Ontario policy may be found. It will be recalled that Gordon

[32] Ibid., 22 Nov. 1978.

[33] See A. Blumstein, 'Prisons: Population, Capacity, and Alternatives', in J. Wilson (ed.), *Crime and Public Policy*, ICS Press, California, 1983, p. 235.

[34] Remarks made by the Honourable Gord Walker to the Annual Meeting, John Howard Society, St Catharines, 27 Feb. 1980.

Walker had maintained his opposition to the pauperization of those who received welfare payments. Recipients should be required to work, and the system that would regulate them and direct their efforts was named 'workfare': 'the government-sponsored gravy-train must come to the end of the line, and welfare must no longer be almost a career choice for those without high ambitions.'[35] The very discipline of work was commendable and it was the duty of the state to instil it. Gordon Walker was Minister in charge of the state's correctional services, and he was to apply some of his beliefs in his own realm. Transcribed into penal policy, workfare was to become a blend of community service, remunerative prison industry, and personal restitution. People passing through the courts and penal system were divided into distinct populations. Those who had to be incarcerated would be obliged to be industrious: 'it is better than having them sitting in their cells reading comic books. . . . The time has come to place more of the correctional cost burden on the inmates and less on the taxpayers of Ontario.'[36] Those who could be released should be discharged. Others who might formerly have been committed would now be free. Instead, they would be set to work on productive and sensible projects: 'putting an offender on probation to repay his debt to society through community service, makes more sense than bed and board at the taxpayers' expense.'[37] The structural and intellectual connections between workfare and community service are quite intelligible: both constituted an exchange of benefits rather than the imposition of a dependent helplessness on the client.[38]

Those thematic unities had been stressed in the Minister's meetings with his officials. It was put to him that there was a coherence of purpose in all that had and might be done, a coherence that could be extended even further to reach the victims of crime. The Minister's staff had seen the possibilities of the American victims movement and they had been touched by its enthusiasm. They contended that the penal embodiment of workfare should be expanded to include the provision of services to the victims of crime:

> Mr Walker is a conservative in both philosophy and politics. And this helping the victims was a good conservative stance. And he was really pleased with this C.S.O. programme. And he was really pleased with this self-sufficiency, like having inmates working in the community rather than lounge around in the jails. So it was a natural conversion for him when we started talking about victim

[35] *Globe and Mail*, 28 Nov. 1978.
[36] Ibid., 26 Mar. 1980.
[37] Ibid., 22 Nov. 1978.
[38] Ibid., 28 Nov. 1978.

services. We sort of put it before him: the scenarios and some of the American victim-witness assistance programmes, and he said, 'well, that's really very, very good'. He wanted to make some impact himself, you know, and here was an organization that was doing very well. He said, 'I want to do something that gives me notoriety and I can put my *imprimatur* on it'. We said, 'what we're offering you in Community Service is a kind of workfare that's marketable because we're dealing with people who're able'. And we reduced populations by using alternatives. And we were worried about people remanded in custody, and he worked on that one.... Our questions are economic and social. Our jails: we can't overfill them, we can't build quickly enough.

It must be understood that there had been some little controversy about Gordon Walker's earlier conception of workfare. When it had been first mooted, it was alleged that he intended to force the poor, disabled, and overburdened into labour. A number of the representatives of women, in particular, argued that workfare was calculated to oppress the abandoned or single mother with dependent children. One columnist described how Mr Walker had become identified as 'the "latest Tory bully-boy" or the "thoroughly nasty man" who is about to throw welfare mothers and children out into the streets, shovelling snow or picking up litter. Indeed, if there was ever a case of a politician growing instant horns, Gordon Walker has done it.'[39] And another observed, 'maybe Walker doesn't suffer empathetic pangs for the misfortunes of others. From his cosy perch as a cabinet minister, he recently was heard pronouncing about the province's 175,000 welfare recipients. Those bums should get out there and shovel snow or be cut off their benefits, said this genius of social philosphy.'[40] Gordon Walker was to protest that he had been misinterpreted and, having repeated some of his criticized defence of workfare, asked 'does that show that I was insensitive and uncompassionate? Does that suggest I was proposing disabled people or deserted mothers be put to work?'[41]

Restitution to victims did not attract the odium of workfare. After all, offenders were not usually described as morally deserving: they were 'people who're able', and they were people who had engaged in wrongdoing. The beneficiaries of restitution *did* commend themselves as worthy and unambiguous objects of compassion: they had been neglected by a criminal justice system that committed far too much to the offender, and they merited sympathy. The contrast could be quite poignant. One official recalled how Gordon Walker had been visibly moved by an

[39] H. Winsor in the *Globe and Mail*, 1 Dec. 1978.
[40] M. Landsberg in the *Toronto Star*, 6 Dec. 1978.
[41] Letter from Gordon Walker, *Toronto Star*, 6 Dec. 1978.

account of the distress felt by a family of victims in San Mateo, California, the victims whose suffering gave rise to the programme that was adopted as a pattern for the Victim–Witness Assistance Program in Brampton, Ontario. The description on which that account was based compared the fates of different people in their passage through the criminal justice system: 'there are few rights for victims and witnesses ... and no paid advocate, like an attorney. While Ron and Neta grieved over their losses, Carl Tapirs waited comfortably in his cell, watching a football game on his television set.'[42] The story that Gordon Walker heard was almost identical, only the names had been changed:

At the moment of his arrest John Sullivan was given his rights. With a butcher knife and without provocation he had just attacked a family of total strangers. He had smashed into a house ... and killed a two year old boy, seriously injured the boy's mother and mortally wounded the unborn child in her womb. Sullivan was arrested near the scene of the crime and he immediately punched a policeman in the eye. His rights were protected however and the police treated him with restraint... Within hours, John Sullivan, booked and charged with murder and eight other crimes was receiving free legal advice. In the months that followed Sullivan received free medical attention for his drug abuse symptoms. Although in custody he was provided with minimal comforts, nourishing meals and courteous treatment. There was a constant safeguarding of his rights and a competent attorney to serve as an advocate of these rights. For his victims, the Mendoza family, there was no comparable protection.... At the Mendoza's home, pools and splashes of blood, a caved in wall and broken window and bloody footprints over the carpets traced the killer's rampage.... Tony and Anne [Mendoza] received little advice on what to expect in court and had no paid advocate to assist them. While they grieved over their losses John Sullivan waited comfortably in his cell, confident in the skill of his legal aid lawyer and watching a football game on T.V.[43]

An official who had also attended the meeting and had heard about Carl Tapirs/John Sullivan was to remember:

We would go to Judges' Seminars and conferences and tell them what our new ideas were. And ... Don Page who was really pushing the programme on victim-witness assistance [was there]. And I said, 'you do a speech to the Judges because Mr. Walker will be there and he'll be listening'. And we went through this scenario with this guy in San Mateo. It's beautiful. The guy's a Spanish guy and he has a trucking company and he loses his company. You know, the

[42] D. Helbush and D. Mandel, 'Aid to Victims and Witnesses', *Federal Probation*, December 1977, Vol. XXXI, No. 4, p. 3.

[43] D. Page; 'Victim/Witness Assistance', Address to Provincial Court Judges, Metro Toronto, 23 Feb. 1979.

whole scenario where the guy loses everything. The offender's getting hospital treatment. He's already killed this guy's wife and kids. You know, it's a perfect story which we gave to the Judges and said we're interested in helping the victims of crime. And Gordon Walker said at that point, 'That's a good thing. I could use that'.

Later, Gordon Walker himself talked at Brampton about the anguish of the victim of crime, alluding to 'the fear ... the mental and physical nausea', the financial loss, the mystification, the unwelcome publicity, and the embarrassment that can follow on the heels of an offence.[44] It was his argument that there was a fundamental and disturbing imbalance between the attention devoted to the offender and the indifference extended to the victim: 'as you can see, the victims of many crimes are indeed the forgotten losers of the criminal justice system.'[45]

Antipathetic to an increase in government spending, bureaucratic expansion, and the slothfulness of prisoners, constrained by a declining budget, Gordon Walker endorsed proposals to compensate victims by direct and personal reparation. The immediacy of Victim–Offender Reconciliation Programmes would be salutary for those who had tried to deny the damage they had wrought.[46] The final responsibility would be assumed by the offender, the man or woman who had caused the injury in the first instance. Gordon Walker proposed not to increase government compensation to victims: 'we have enough government and pay enough taxes as it is.'[47] Devolving moral and financial liabilities was a means of demystifying the criminal justice system, forcing the offender 'to deliver justice to his victim'.[48] It demystified the criminal, leading, as one of Gordon Walker's former officials stated, to the discovery that the offender 'is not an organized criminal but a 17 year old person who does not have horns on his head'.[49] It restored the balance beween defendant and victim.[50] A senior Ontario official commented that policies for victims 'fitted well into the "sock it to the offender" philosophy which [Walker] brought to the Ministry of Correctional Services'.

The increasing prominence of the victim was thus a facet of delegating

[44] *Helping the Victims of Crime*, an Address by the Honourable Gord Walker, Q.C., Minister of Correctional Services, to the Brampton Rotary Club, 11 June 1979.

[45] Ibid.

[46] Remarks made by the Honourable Gord Walker to the Canadian Crime Victim Compensation Boards, 21 Aug. 1980.

[47] Remarks made by the Honourable Gord Walker ... to the Annual Meeting of the John Howard Society.

[48] Ibid.

[49] P. Sonnischsen in 'Midnight to Three', CKEY Toronto, 2 June 1982.

[50] See L. Butler, 'Making Right the Wrong', *Today Magazine*, 28 Mar. 1981.

and grounding corrections in face-to-face encounters. It removed some of the bureaucratic and institutional intermediaries that had stood between an offender and his victim. It recommended, by extrapolation, a decline in the role of the state and a campaign for the recognition and legislation of victims' rights. Gordon Walker came to champion the idea that victims should be entitled to be consulted about charges, to speak in court, and to be compensated.[51] He was to be applauded for his advocacy. The *London Free Press* observed:

> Walker is right. Making the offender responsible for restitution, making him aware of the damage he has done and guaranteeing that the victim's loss or pain is fully recognized by the courts all make good sense.... He should press ahead energetically and enthusiastically with his ideas and concerns for the victims of crime.[52]

Indeed, victims seemed to form an opportune area for an ambitious politican with limited scope for innovation. An official reflected, 'he saw the victim field as almost the only one in which (to use his favourite phrase) he could "get some ink" since almost every other issue would be claimed by one of his colleagues on the Cabinet Committee on Justice—and usually by the Attorney General.'

Gordon Walker's defence of victims' rights tended to affront some central strands in legal reasoning about the interplay between the state, crime, and prosecution. Long ago, Blackstone had argued 'public wrongs, or crimes and misdemeanors, are a breach and violation of the public rights and duties due to the whole community, in its social aggregate capacity ... since besides the wrong done the individual, they strike at the very being of society'.[53] In that fashion, crime is much more than the local concern of the person who has been harmed. It is an offence that extends outwards to engulf society, it attacks a metaphysical or corporate victim, and that attack is held to justify an abrogation of a person's right to control the passage and direction of actions taken by the police and courts. It has been argued that the agents and representatives of criminal justice have a right and duty to intervene even when no individual victim has been detected or named. They are the arms of a greater body whose interests transcend that of the personal victim. As Reiss and Bordua once observed, 'the police in a sense are a service without clients. The police serve the public as a collectivity rather than distributively. Enforcement

[51] See the *Oshawa Times*, 28 Aug. 1980.

[52] *London Free Press*, 23 Aug. 1980.

[53] W. Blackstone, *Commentaries on the Laws of England*, Clarendon Press, Oxford, 1778, Book IV, p. 5.

must be initiated when there is no victim and/or complainant.'[54] In that context, and with that interpretation, some took Gordon Walker's urgings to be fundamentally subversive to the conception and administration of criminal justice. There was to be a tension flowing from those contradictions, a tension that entered relations between the various criminal justice Ministries of Ontario. The attempt to lodge victims' rights in practice and law was resisted, and it has been argued by officials that one of the aims of the speech of October 1979 was to gain a wider audience and external allies. As one official recalled, 'there was a political turf war for a while between the Attorney General and Correctional Services'. But it was as much a legal counterpart to the conflict between the Roman Catholic Church and Nonconformism: a conflict about the rights and quality of intercession, the ability of a supplicant to speak for himself or herself, and the part played by doctrine and due process in ceremony. In a manner, Gordon Walker was the Martin Luther of the victims movement. His battle was to reverberate through the later history of the victims initiative. It was to be fought on the Federal–Provincial Task Force on Justice for Victims, some of whose members roundly declared 'the Criminal Courts are not designed to "settle the score" between the victim and the offender. That is the primary purpose of the civil process. The criminal process is designed to determine, having given the accused a proper opportunity to defend himself whether or not the Crown has proved his guilt beyond a reasonable doubt, and if so to impose a sentence which protects the public.'[55] If there was going to be a change, it would require a mobilization of support. If the change affected the Criminal Code, the support would have to be furnished by a federal department.

The Speech

Gordon Walker's speech to the very first Meeting of Federal–Provincial Ministers Responsible for Criminal Justice was not the only occasion on which he had pleaded for the victims of crime. As I have reported, he had spoken on the matter many times, victims being one of the emergent priorities of his Ministry. Gordon Walker had already made an address on victims in Brampton in June 1979. He was to talk about victims after October 1979. There was little that was really novel in the speech that

[54] A. Reiss and D. Bordua, 'Environment and Organization: A Perspective on the Police', in D. Bordua (ed.), *The Police*, John Wiley, New York, 1967, p. 30.

[55] Early draft of the Federal–Provincial Task Force Report on Justice for Victims: 'The Integrity of the Criminal Justice System', undated, unattributed, p. 14.

was to become such a benchmark in the making of the initiative. As one Ontario official commented, 'Mr. Walker had already given a few speeches and had received a good press in emphasizing offender responsibility and concern for the victim. He'd flown a few of these trial balloons and it had all gone really well. If you go further back, you'll see that in other speeches.'

The October speech was designed to reflect Gordon Walker's preoccupations. It seems that its successive drafts wavered uncertainly around the question of how much stress should be given to the victims of crime. The very first versions tended to emphasize retribution to the offender and it was only after some discussion that they drifted back towards a focus on victims: indeed, one senior Ontario official described the first draft as 'incredibly bad'. In turn, it appears that some officials attempted to reverse that drift, trying to 'talk [the speech writer] out of too much victim justice ... but it really captured the flavour of Gord'. Another official recalled that the speech was devised to introduce the possibility of major changes in the criminal justice system: 'we wanted a simple speech without exaggeration which would quickly capture people's attention.'

The meeting itself was recognized as a significant episode in the history of the Canadian criminal justice system. It was the 'first time in Canada all federal and provincial responsibilities within the criminal justice system met as one body'.[56] Such an assembly was without precedent. It signalled the emergence of an interest in the work of the system as a whole. It recognized that 'the activities of the various components of the system could dramatically affect one another'.[57] It encapsulated and symbolized all the complexities and tensions of the relations between federal and provincial governments, relations made peculiarly fraught at the time by talk of secession and federal intrusiveness. It may not have been an occasion of the greatest moment to the larger world. It received modest interest from the press. But it was of considerable consequence to those who worked within the fragile structures of law enforcement in Canada. It was a necessarily theatrical event.

What is of some analytic importance is the apparent insignificance of Gordon Walker's speech to many of those who observed and reported that conference. It is an insignificance that reflects two interesting qualities of the process which I am trying to explore. First, and clearly,

[56] *Ministerial Statements, Agenda, Communiqué and other Related Documents*, Federal–Provincial Conference of Ministers Responsible for Criminal Justice, Ottawa, 25–6 Oct. 1979, Solicitor General Canada, Ottawa, 1979, p. iv.

[57] Ibid.

meaning is a situated accomplishment. Victims were not a matter of concern to most of those who attended the meeting. The participants tended to be bound up in problems of the Criminal Code Review, the accountability of the RCMP, the Canadian Human Rights Act, Cannabis, Duplication and Overlap, and the like. It is more than likely that the 1979 Conference will be remembered chiefly for its effect upon the progress of the Young Offenders Legislation or the reform of judicial statistics. It is perhaps largely within the framework of this particular history of an initiative that Gordon Walker's speech was so critical. And, secondly, the apparent general insignificance of what was said points clearly to the manner in which meaning can be bestowed by those who need meaning in what is before them. Significance was collaboratively created and emphasized by members of the network that had settled on the social problems of the crime victim.

Gordon Walker's speech was not on the printed agenda of the Conference. Neither were victims. It was listed as one of a number of 'other Ministerial statements'. It was not included in the press release which was eventually issued on 26 October. Victims were not mentioned in the opening remarks of Senator Jacques Flynn or Allan Lawrence, the Solicitor General of Canada. After the Conference, Gordon Walker's observations secured a twelve-line paragraph in a lengthy summary of what had taken place. They were reported briefly in the *Montreal Gazette* of 26 October and at rather greater length in the *Toronto Star* on the same day. Most of the other newspapers preferred to attend to the question of the legalization of 'le pot'.[58] In short, the speech was one amongst many: it merited reporting but it was not singled out as momentous. Its political presence was shaped by those who had drawn up the Conference's agenda and press releases, and their bias had been determined by what they had known of the speeches that were to come. To the wider world, the speech did not seem to deserve special attention. There were other processes in train and there had been no preparation for a redirection of interest. As one Regional Consultant recalled, 'there was no warning that it was going to take place and no feedback. I never got any response or heard anybody who went jumping up and down saying, "Wow! Did you hear that Gordon Walker speech? Was it ever fabulous!"' But he then proceeded immediately to say, 'the next thing I heard was that when Ottawa wanted to do something on victims, they were then using that as justification.' In that fashion, the speech was to become of intense interest to one small group seeking to advance a project, and its historical stature continued to grow thereafter.

[58] *Journal de Montreal*, 26 Oct. 1979.

Gordon Walker spoke for some twenty minutes on victims. He began:

As we work our way through the agenda, particularly the items concerning the criminal code, might I suggest we give special attention to the needs of the victims of crime. The Criminal Justice System makes the offender its centre of attention. The resources of the police, the courts, the legal profession, the correctional system, the law itself all focus inordinately upon the offender's needs. His rights are well articulated and well protected—as they should be. By contrast, the rights and needs of the crime victim pale into insignificance. Too frequently victims are forgotten by the criminal justice system. For them, justice is often a bitter and costly disillusionment. That, I suggest, is not how it should be. We have been attempting to correct this balance in Ontario, with some success, through our Criminal Injuries Compensation Board and our new Corrections Program, but we're really only scratching the surface of an inequity that deserves a strong and integrated effort among all jurisdictions ... It seems to me ... that we should try to tilt the scales of justice, pivoted as they are on the criminal code, more in favour of crime's victims.[59]

There was a local, immediate, and marked response amongst the members of the federal circle who had sought to further the interests of victims. One senior Ontario official remembered that there had been rather little provincial interest, one or two heads had been seen nodding around the table, but those from Ottawa were somewhat unkindly described as having 'an orgasm of delight'. The official who had been appointed to service the survey claimed that this display of provincial interest was important because 'it looked like the victims issue ... was not going to be well received in the provinces. I mean ... maybe that would have dissuaded Policy Branch from going ahead on this, you know. So ... there was a province out there saying, "Hey, can we get going on victims!"' A province had made a call for 'an integrated effort' and it seemed incumbent on the federal government to reply.

The first practical consequence was that the Solicitor General *did* reply. His answer represented another of Irvin Waller's opportunities. Irvin Waller sat close to the Minister: 'they made that speech and then suddenly the Feds had to look good, so they couldn't just shut up. So we then drafted a reply very quickly.' Irvin Waller wrote the bulk of Allan Lawrence's response: 'I was well prepared. I don't think it's very difficult for the average academic who knows an issue to respond in two or three minutes on the sort of issue that those guys are discussing.... It was an issue I'd been interested in for a long time.... Lawrence did a brilliant

[59] Introductory Remarks by the Honourable Gord Walker, Q.C., Provincial Secretary for Justice and Minister of Correctional Services, to the Federal–Provincial Conference of Ministers Responsible for Criminal Justice, Ottawa, 25–6 Oct. 1979.

job on it. He used everything I said and put in a few things of his own on federal-provincial concerns and fiscal restraint.' The Minister was to read out Irvin Waller's draft reply, adding the phrase 'without increasing the budget' to the first sentence in the last paragraph:

> ... we believe the problems Mr. Walker to have raised on crime victims in Ontario to apply throughout Canada. Only 6 million out of 3 billion dollars we spend in Criminal Justice go directly to crime victims. [In our document *Selected Trends in Canadian Criminal Justice*] we see crime victims as one of the areas where small amounts of money can have major benefits.... A major emphasis in the research program of my Ministry is to study the extent of victimization. We are presently spending $300,000 on research in this area alone. We hope to provide information on more effective ways of assisting crime victims and helping them protect themselves.... I would like my research division to increase its efforts to provide knowledge on the plight of crime victims without increasing the budget. We need more effective ways to reduce the effects of crime and particularly identify measures that can provide them with cogent assistance to meet the financial loss, physical injury, emotional trauma and fear of crime that too many experience.

Thus it came about in October 1979 that victims were defined by a federal minister as a federal concern before an audience of all his peers. He described the research that had taken place as the discovery of information bearing on assistance to victims. He had promised to amplify and extend his research effort. There had been no warning and no preparation. But, as Irvin Waller reflected, 'what's important was that victims had become part of the agenda.... I tried to get them on the federal agenda for that meeting and did not succeed. But the moment the provinces put them on the agenda, then it became a federal agenda.' In one of the most significant political forums of the Canadian criminal justice system, and before every one of his political colleagues, the Solictor General of Canada had pledged himself to advance the cause of victims. It was now very loosely established as a Departmental policy issue, no longer merely an aspiration of some members of the Programs Branch but something close to a commitment. And even if the substance and extent of that commitment had not been mapped properly, Irvin Waller did proceed to regard it as binding. Others were to define it as a beginning, the political overture which gave work its legitimacy. The Deputy Solictor General maintained that it was at the October 1979 meeting that the Department's plans were first 'crystallised' and the initiative was truly started. A former policy analyst at the Department called that occasion 'the first real concrete articulation of the issue'. And the official in charge of the programme of research on victimization asserted, 'well, we really seized on it and made use of [Gordon Walker's] statement in talking to other officials in the federal government. The statement that he made, we embraced, because it could have been written by one of us.'

In every document and statement that came to feed the growing initiative, Gordon Walker's speech was cited as evidence of the existence of strong provincial support for joint federal–provincial action. It was to be mentioned in the paper prepared for the Joint Justice Committee: a draft outline, prepared in April 1981, referred to the speech as one contribution to the pressure that was being exerted on the federal government. It was proof of the 'increased public profile of this issue'. It was to be used by the *ad hoc* federal–provincial working group that considered victims. It was to appear in the Cabinet submission of July 1981. It was listed in the very first paragraph of the Federal–Provincial Task Force Report on Justice for Victims. As a part of the 'Origins, Mandate and Participants' of the Task Force, the 'theme of improved assistance for victims of crime was stressed by a number of Ministers at the October 1979 Conference of Ministers responsible for criminal justice'.[60] Those involved had acquired a most solid provincial buttress for any future work. Public declaration and provincial affirmation had bestowed a firm political status on the victims of crime.

The Workshop of March 1980

In the immediate aftermath of that momentous meeting, there was some indecision about what should be done next. It was clear that the newly achieved prominence of assistance to victims offered further possibilities for action, but there was no certainty about what that action should be. The responsibility for victims seemed to have remained locked inside the Programs Branch. Policy Branch officials were not yet involved, they had not been wooed, and ideas were too ill-defined to merit being placed before them. What had to be done appeared to turn on the development of research on services to victims. Yet apprehension existed that too little was known to allow even that step to be taken. There was talk with an official from the Planning and Liaison Division, and she recalled:

> In October 1979, [Irvin Waller] got victims put on the agenda at that meeting. Gordon Walker, the Minister for Ontario talked at that meeting about victims and ... Irvin somehow got Lawrence to say ... that this Ministry was interested as well, and I think talked about the research that would be going on in the

[60] Canadian Federal–Provincial Task Force *Report*, p. v.

Ministry. And Irvin called a meeting.... At that meeting, we went round in circles about what we should do as a result of that.... The notion of a conference or workshop came up at that first meeting that Irvin called. We did go around in circles, with [the official who serviced victimisation research] saying that we should do more research before we have a meeting.

And that servicing official himself said:

I remember sitting and reading and in fact I remember saying, 'geez, I don't know. It's not much time to organize all this and everything else', and Irvin saying, 'but ... remember, you've got to strike while the iron's hot, okay? It's the time. So let's do it!'

The outcome of that first meeting of 7 November 1979 appears to have been somewhat inconclusive. There had been no firm resolution. The official from the Planning and Liaison Division continued:

At that meeting, we went around in circles about what we should do.... I can't remember how that meeting was left. It was, I guess, what's called '*exploratory*'. And then I ... because she wanted not to do what she was then doing, decided I would be pro-active (I think is the word). So I wrote a little memo saying, why, this is what happened. And then nothing happened. Then one day, in passing, I said to Irvin, 'my heavens, Irvin, what's happening?' And he said, 'nothing, nothing ever happens. Get on with it'. And I all wide-eyed, I said 'super!' Which is what I'd hoped would happen. I thereupon set about organizing this victims conference.

That 'little memo' of 14 November referred back to the meeting of the week before, trying to make sense of those rather indecisive deliberations:

It was felt that it would be ... useful to meet with some 'key' people from across Canada in an effort to explore the current range of activities, create awareness about gaps in service and the possible directions which victims services might take. This kind of get together could lay the groundwork for future federal and provincial initiatives.... the meeting could be seen as 'exploring the state of the art in victim services'.[61]

Irvin Waller's own intention had been to 'get people together to make them think victims'. It was to be a major exercise in networking and stock-taking, an effort to build the beginnings of a social world. It was purposed to hold a Workshop on Services to Crime Victims in March 1980 before the expiry of the financial year. The initiative was traced back to the October 1979 meeting and approval was given on those grounds in January 1980. It was at that stage that a most important process was set in motion. The Department's Regional Consultants

[61] Memo to file, 14 Nov. 1979.

were requested to identify provincial ministries, projects, programmes, organizations, and persons 'who might be considered for invitation to a workshop on victimization'. The Consultants began to report back local intelligence about work in victim assistance. The Prairies Regional Consultant, for example, informed the Ministry about a Victim–Offender Reconciliation Project in Winnipeg and the work of the John Howard Society in Regina, Saskatoon, and Moose Jaw. And this colleagues did likewise. What is palpably significant about that quest is that it was the first orderly search that had ever been undertaken to discover who it was that was providing services to victims in Canada. It led to a modest rewriting of history: as projects and people were encountered, so the character and past of Canadian schemes had to be reassessed. That search was officially conducted by the staff of the Department of the Solicitor General of Canada and in the Solicitor General's name. It was given organization and unity by the word 'victims', a word that had not hitherto been widely employed as a source of definition. People were not being solicited about their aid to women, children, or any other group: they were being classified together as joint participants in a Canadian venture, a venture described by a common preoccupation with victims. One official recalled that such categorization occurred 'not without some resistance', and that resistance was to persist after March 1980. But there is political import in the very fact that it was a concern with victims that brought people together. Those invited were told that 'there is a crucial party who tends either to be forgotten, or used primarily to aid in the process of the criminal justice system—the victim'.[62] Perhaps for the first time, Canadians were being encouraged to conceive of themselves as sharing an interest in the victims of crime.

The search unearthed an array of Canadians. It disclosed the importance of police projects and the interest taken by women's organizations. It was to reveal the dominance of the Department of the Solicitor General of Canada and the Ministry of Correctional Services of Ontario in the early stages of policy formation.

The man who serviced victimization research drafted a speech for delivery by the Deputy Solicitor General in which allusion was made to the imbalance between the care extended to the offender and that offered the victim. Victimization was described as potentially traumatic, causing physical, emotional and financial distress. It was held imperative to reassure the victim that he or she had not been forgotten. And finally the Deputy Solicitor General argued, 'the development of better services

[62] Letter from Deputy Solicitor General, 8 Feb. 1980.

Table 2: *Workshop on Services to Crime Victims, 24–25 March 1980: Canadian Participants*

Ministry of the Solicitor General of Canada	14
Federal Department of Justice	4
Status of Women Canada	2
Advisory Council on the Status of Women	2
Privy Council Office	1
Federal–Provincial Relations Office	1
National Health and Welfare	1
Law Reform Commission of Canada	1
Royal Canadian Mounted Police	2
Ministry of Correctional Services, Ontario	4
Other provincial Ministeries	8
Probation, court, and social services	5
Police forces	11
Crown Attorneys and the Canadian Bar Association	3
Criminal Injuries Compensation Boards	2
Workers Compensation Board	1
University	3
Canadian Association for the Prevention of Crime	1
Elizabeth Fry Society	1
United Way	1
Church Council on Justice and Corrections	1
Mennonite Central Committee of Canada	1
Canadian Council on Social Development	1
	71

to crime victims will demand the cooperation and coordination of many private and public agencies, and of all levels of government'.[63]

The programme itself was bifurcated, the morning of the first day being given over to talks delivered by members of the American victims movement known to Irvin Waller and established in their field. There were papers given by the Program Manager of the Victim–Witness Unit of the Law Enforcement Assistance Administration, the Executive Director of the New York Victim Service Agency, and the Pima County Victim–Witness Program, representing another infusion from the United States. On the second day, it was the Canadian experience that was reviewed, recapitulating much of the history that I have reported: Sergeant Bill Hutchinson of the Calgary Police Service and Staff Sergeant Bob Holmes of the RCMP discussed police programmes; Linda

[63] Notes for Opening Remarks by the Deputy Solicitor General of Canada to the Workshop on Services to Crime Victims, Ottawa, Ontario, 24 Mar. 1980.

MacLeod, then of the Canadian Advisory Council on the Status of Women, and Flora MacLeod talked about family violence and assaults against women; Art Daniels of Ontario described 'comprehensive victims assistance programs'; and there was a discussion of financial aid to victims. Concluding the Workshop, the then Assistant Deputy Minister, Programs Branch, 'suggested that the most effective follow-up to the meeting might be for participants to attempt to stimulate increased awareness of victim's needs and, where possible, encourage the development of appropriate victim/witness services when they returned to their communities'.

The gathering of some seventy Canadians was a major catalyst. It represented another occasion on which people stopped, stood back, and reflected on what they were doing. For many, it led to a redefinition of the significance and direction of their work. It was to be regarded as a process of discovery in which people with similar pursuits found each other for the first time. And it reinforced the Canadian network of those who were sympathetic to the development of a policy on victims. The official from the Planning and Liaison Division remembered, 'there was the sense of discovery because people did come who were eager to come. They came and they felt they'd learned things.' Art Daniels stated:

> We all realised that we had a lot of commonality. That meeting was good. I didn't get any feeling that, you know, 'it's our programme' or 'we in Corections own it' or it belongs to the police or it belongs to the Crown level. I guess it's something we can all work together on. It's not federal, it's not provincial, it's not police, it's not courts, it's not corrections, it's something that we can all have a hand in. And I felt really good about that meeting. It was a *positive* meeting.

In short, victims were obviously beginning to emerge publicly as a jointly shared object in which many people had a stake. They were attaining form as a visible concern in the lives of officials and voluntary groups across Canada. People were starting to learn about one another and coagulate into the first, tentative makings of a national network. As Irvin Waller argued, 'we used the Ontario people. We used the odd police project in Calgary and Edmonton and we used the victim compensation board people. We began to get a broader base.' Moreover, all that movement towards consolidation had occurred very conspicuously under the auspices of the federal Ministry of the Solicitor General. It was yet another vivid display of the Department's assumption of an increasing responsibility for victims and their care. The very engagement of the Department and the groupings which it organized signalled that policies were stirring. To the astute, the comments of the Deputy Solicitor

General and the Assistant Deputy Minister, coupled with the earlier statement of Allan Lawrence, gave the appearance of a prelude to action. Thus the Senior Adviser on the Status of Women at National Health and Welfare Canada stated 'the whole field has emerged and become visible only within the last eighteen months'. Her comments were made in the summer of 1981, and they suggest that victims were born as a political entity in the period dominated by the Ministers' Conference and the Workshop of March 1980. People started to locate themselves and their problems within that emerging field that had been shaped by victims. The representative of the Elizabeth Fry Society who had attended the Workshop wrote:

> As I listened to the various panelists, particularly the speakers on family violence, I was struck with the fact that many female victims suffer from similar problems as female offenders—lack of services; poor knowledge as to rights and the legal process; being confronted with a system largely staffed by men. Just as services to female offenders suffer from chronic funding problems, so do interval houses for battered women, and rape crisis centres. The conference on victims raised a startling question—when does a victim become an offender? For those of us who work with offenders and want to prevent crime, services to victims offers another relatively unexplored field of service.[64]

Again, and quite typically, the Workshop later became part of the historical and rhetorical furniture of the Department, another benchmark in the apparent evolution of a drive towards an initiative on victims. It was evidence of the Department's readiness to commit labour and resources to the problem, itself indicative of a drift in policy. It demonstrated that there was a growing tide of demand for some sort of federal initiative. It documented the breadth and scale of interest in the problems of victims in Canada. And the Ministry made all those matters objective and public by issuing a *Report of the Proceedings*[65] in a series published by the Department and in the Department's own very distinctive cover. The report was written by Richard Weiler, a private contractor, and it was prefaced by the customary warning that it did 'not necessarily reflect the views or policies of the Solicitor General of Canada'. None the less, a report had appeared with all the trappings of Departmental authority. It gave the parentage of the Workshop as the 'concern expressed at a federal–provincial conference of Ministers responsible for criminal

[64] *CAEFS Newsletter*, Canadian Association of Elizabeth Fry Societies, Newsletter No. 5, May 1980, p. 9.

[65] *Report of the Proceedings: National Workshop on Services to Crime Victims*, Ministry of Supply and Services, Ottawa, 1981.

justice'.[66] It signified that victims were part of the Department's legitimate territory. It reiterated the Deputy Solicitor General's ambition to support the co-operation and co-ordination of segments of Canadian society in their striving for 'victim justice'. It was itself completed in the hope that it would 'increase awareness and stimulate interest in services to crime victims'.[67]

It was as if the politics of victims were beginning to acquire substance and form. *Something* was happening, and it raised the question of what the Department should do after the spring of 1980. After all, there was abundant unfinished business, expectations had been created, and the Deputy Solicitor General and Assistant Deputy Solicitor General had publicly re-emphasized the Solicitor General's argument that action should be taken. Officials could quote those speeches to one another as proofs of a promise made before them and in public. In a characteristic dialectical movement within the world of the Department, a number of people had helped to draft arguments which were then vetted and approved, rehearsed publicly, and thereafter cited by those self-same people as motives for their own future activities. The Workshop, its *Report*, and its speeches were components of an environment that officials were beginning to construct around themselves, an environment which forced them to respond. It seemed as if processes had acquired a momentum which could not be readily disrupted. The future role of the Department appeared to be undergoing definition. In reply to that environment, and to further those processes, Irvin Waller prepared a memorandum for the signature of the Assistant Deputy Minister of the Programs Branch. He argued that the growing importance of family violence (an importance which I have already discussed in brief) and the problems of the victims of crime warranted the writing of a policy paper on victims. The Assistant Deputy Minister, Programs Branch, accordingly despatched a memorandum to the Assistant Deputy Minister, Policy Branch, arguing that 'a more comprehensive policy paper on services to crime victims would appear useful as a follow-up to the recent workshop on this topic that was held by the Ministry. We found that there was a good deal of interest in this area and it will likely become increasingly important to identify what the role of the Ministry (and of Justice?) should be.' There was a clear invitation for one thing to be allowed to lead to another, pursuing a logic that was being traced from phase to phase and within a framework that all the stages seemed to prepare. In that invitation, and in its acceptance, were the germs of the trans-

[66] Ibid., p. 1.
[67] Ibid., p. 1.

formation of victims into a policy issue processed and superintended by the Policy Branch. It was only a beginning. The Workshop and the events that preceded it were still the nurselings of the Programs Branch. The Ministry officials who organized and attended the Workshop were almost entirely drawn from the Research Division, the Causes and Prevention Division, the Consultation Centre, and the Planning and Liaison Division. There is a record of only one number of the Policy Branch being present, and it may be concluded that the policy implications of the Workshop were as yet correspondingly modest. The transformation of victims into a policy issue was to be arduous, and it was to incorporate other strands, but it was about to start.

Following the Workshop, and building on it, the Department returned to Richard Weiler. He and Geoffrey Norquay of the Canadian Council on Social Development were commissioned to undertake the first major survey of 'the emerging system of services to victims of crime in Canada'.[68] They were instructed to discover what was happening in Canada, how American projects might act as a pattern for Canadian work, and to 'identify possible adjustments to existing policies and programs relating to services for crime victims in Canada'.[69] Over 800 organizations were polled and 300 replied, offering the makings of a map of the Canadian victims movement. Although the book was not to appear before the summer of 1981, drafts had circulated before that time, and the very processes of questioning and writing had become sources of illumination and order in their own right. The experience of being asked about the provision of 'any specialized services for victims or victims as witnesses' enforced a self-consciousness on members of organizations. When it was published, the report talked of the manner in which Canadian society had 'gradually begun to rediscover the victim' during the 1970s. It identified victim–offender reconciliation projects, transition houses for battered women, rape crisis centres, and police-based services as the principal carriers of assistance to victims. It catalogued projects new to the Department or outside its reach. It referred to the Kitchener–Waterloo Victim–Offender Reconciliation Project as an important experiment. More particularly, it offered as instances of exemplary schemes the Restigouche Family Crisis Interveners Program, the City of London Family Consultant Service, and the Victim Service Unit of the Edmonton Police Department, acknowledging the part played by the Programs Branch of the Ministry. The Secretariat itself was described as 'active in

[68] G. Norquay and R. Weiler, *Services to Victims and Witnesses of Crime in Canada*, p. 1.
[69] Ibid., p. 17.

the promotion of victim services through demonstration projects and in the area of research and evaluation of some existing projects'.[70]

The Programs Branch had asked consultants to hold a looking-glass before itself and before Canada and it saw its own face there. The Branch was told of its own prominence, of the rapid expansion of services in Canada, and of what was to come. Teleology became manifest, officials being advised about the future for which they should prepare themselves:

> The victim/witness service field is on the verge of considerable development and expansion in Canada. . . . It is likely that advocacy for greater attention to victim needs will increase as such groups as rape crisis centres and transition home coalitions and federal and provincial advisory bodies on women and the elderly press their various points of view. Governments, it is hoped, will respond to these representations by planning and implementing programs that respond in a sensitive, creative and above all, co-ordinated fashion to the needs of crime victims and witnesses in our society.[71]

The United Nations

There was one other important process that was structurally and symbolically akin to the little history of the October 1979 meeting, the Workshop, and their aftermath. At much the same time and with some of the same people, there was a parallel progress of the Canadian delegation to the Sixth United Nations Congress on the Prevention of Crime and the Treatment of Offenders held in Caracas, Venezuela, between 25 August and 5 September 1980.

I have remarked that the world of Ottawa and its environs is rather small. There was only a comparatively modest population from which the fifty-strong Canadian delegation, the largest at the Congress, could be drawn. Almost inevitably, the delegation was to be affected by people who had been active in the processes surrounding the emergence of interest in victims. By the time the delegation was starting to form, the American victims movement was some six or seven years old and four years had passed since the founding of the little social circle that revolved around the survey and victimization research in the Department. There was a scattering of people who had begun to know one another. They were to touch the delegation at a number of points and in different ways.

People continuously move about as they pursue their interests in Ottawa and beyond. The criminal justice community is constituted by conferences and forums where people meet as they pass from stage to

[70] Ibid., p. 84.
[71] Ibid., p. 106.

stage and from role to role. Ideas endlessly seep and spill from one setting to another, travelling with officials and those who consort with them. Thus, the March 1980 Workshop had been attended by three people who went on to participate in the very much more local Workshop on Victim/Witness Programs and Services organized by the Ottawa Branch of the Ontario Association of Corrections and Criminology in June 1980. Others were to be found in the meetings of the John Howard Society. Again, five of the Canadian delegation had attended the March 1980 Workshop. And even if they were not delegates, there were others in the victims network who became involved in the consultations that preceded the delegation's departure for Venezuela. The official who serviced the Ministry's victimization research stated, for example, 'people preparing drafts came to me and I gave them material to read and I talked to them for an afternoon'.

People stepped across the boundaries of one history and joined another, bringing with them concerns about crime prevention, family crisis intervention, victimization surveys, the provision of services to crime victims, and the like. It was as if the delegation permitted an old cast of actors to take new parts. Of course, new scripts define and constrain action. The actors were never wholly and doggedly given to the pursuit of a policy for victims. They had other preoccupations. Besides, most members of the delegation were not of the network. Yet, just as the preparations for the March 1980 Workshop had led to a search across the face of Canada, so the copious consultations conducted by the delegation disclosed themes that were just emerging in Canadian criminology, criminal justice policy, and corrections. In particular, when the delegation eventually examined itself and issued a report about the Congress, it discovered that its members shared an interest in victims, and that interest was to become a fact of some political significance. The very standing and constitution of the delegation endowed its conclusions with gravity.

The United Nations Congresses on the Prevention of Crime and the Treatment of Offenders have been held every five years since the first meeting in Geneva in 1955. Each Congress has received a Canadian delegation, and the responsibility for mobilizing and organizing the Canadian representatives has been assumed by the Department of the Solicitor General in consultation with the Secretary of State for External Affairs since 1965. The Department had to contend with very characteristic diplomatic problems when it began to gather the Canadian delegation together in readiness for the 1980 Congress: there are eleven Canadian governments, two territories, and a number of private and international organizations lodged in Canada, each with a stake to conserve and a dignity to defend. The co-ordination of all those bodies demanded very substantial administration in its own right, it being vital to conduct consultations and make appointments only with the proper display of respect. Thus it was announced in June 1978 that it was intended to preserve the 'pattern of Federal–Provincial cooperation in these congresses'.[72] To that end, a National Consultative Network was established, regulated by a small management committee, and composed of representatives of the Departments of External Affairs, Justice, and the Solicitor General. Provincial Deputy Ministers in charge of Corrections were asked to name people who could form part of that Network and liaise with its management committee. It was incumbent on the Network to deliberate about the objectives of Canadian participation, the preparation of working papers, the arrangement of prefactory meetings, and the composition of the delegation itself. The internal politics of the Canadian state ensured that the successful completion of those dealings was to be almost as important as any of the subsequent transactions of the Congress itself. It was necessary to plan for the 'full participation of the provinces, territories and non-governmental organizations; regional and national consultation seminars; ... [and] early appointment of a Canadian Delegation to permit delegate participation in preparatory meetings and in the development of Canadian positions'.[73] So early, broad, careful, and solicitous a procedure considerably enhanced the stature of the delegation and its arguments. It was to produce a massive group of people who became an extraordinary, miniature parliament of the Canadian criminal justice system. Importance was conferred on all that was accomplished simply because it was such a parliament. As one of those who organized it reflected, 'the very fact that this exremely mixed delegation which heavily represented provincial jurisdictions, territorial jurisdictions and quite a bit of private sector input, and that the delegation against all the indications came together with a more or less common view, they thought conferred some legitimacy on its conclusions'.

The delegation was not the only cumbersome administrative artefact. The Congress was itself unwieldy, having entailed lengthy planning and liaison. Its agenda had been established soon after the ending of its predecessor. At the beginning of 1977 it was determined that the Congress

[72] 'Information Note: Sixth United Nations Congress on the Prevention of Crime and the Treatment of Offenders', 5 June 1978.

[73] *Report of the Canadian Delegation to the Sixth United Nations Congress on the Prevention of Crime and the Treatment of Offenders*, Ottawa, December 1980, p. 5.

should attend to five topics: crime trends and crime prevention strategies; juvenile justice; crime and the abuse of power; 'de-institutionalisation' of corrections; and norms and guidelines in criminal justice. It may be observed that assistance to the victims of crime did not have a place amongst those topics, although some ingenuity would have allowed it to be smuggled in as an aspect of crime prevention or 'de-institutionalisation'. From the very start, the deliberations of the delegation and the Congress were constricted, turned towards a set agenda.

There were elaborate preparatory discussions about the Congress and its agenda before the delegation ever left Canada. In July 1978 Topic I was examined by a United Nations Inter-regional Meeting of Experts in Ottawa. In November of that year a National Consultation Meeting was again held in Ottawa, being attended by representatives of federal and provincial governments. And in 1979 there began a succession of regional consultation seminars on the topics prescribed for the Congress. Superintending those seminars were special advisers, a Staff Sergeant of the RCMP, one of the major quiet animators of the victims initiative, being commissioned to administer Topic I, crime prevention. The Chief Adviser was a Senior Policy Analyst of the Department of the Solicitor General, and he was ultimately to become quite vital to the success of the initiative. The first regional seminar was held at Clear Lake, Manitoba, in September 1979. Thereafter, there were twelve regional seminars supported by the Ministry and two special consultations with the Canadian Bar Association and the Candian Association of Chiefs of Police. Finally, a special National Seminar on the abuse of power and norms and guidelines was conducted in Winnipeg in March 1980.

The delegation itself was appointed in a most gingerly manner, being composed of a representative from each province and territory; the Solicitor General and Deputy Solicitor General of Canada; the Parliamentary Secretary to the Solicitor General; the Assistant Deputy Minister, Policy Branch; officials from the Department of Justice, Correctional Services of Canada, the National Parole Board, and the Royal Canadian Mounted Police; Parliamentary Advisers, Special Advisers, Non-Governmental Advisers, Topic Advisers, and Other Advisers; five Canadians representing International Non-Governmental Organizations; and fourteen Canadians attending as Individual Participants. The delegation was to have its own preparatory meetings in Ottawa, and other federal departments were invited to send observers. There was thus a scrupulous regard for all the political groupings that compose and fringe the loose and inordinately complex Candian criminal justice system.

Victims were mentioned only intermittently in that collection of meetings which formed the prologue to the Congress. They had to be insinuated in a somewhat devious guise before they were considered at all. After all, the seminars were organized by topics and the topics precluded extended discussion of victims and victims programmes. In Manitoba, at the very first meeting, one person did submit an address on the 'Humanist Perspective on Crime Victims', an address that deplored the excessive concentration on criminals in films such as *Looking for Mr. Goodbar* and *Bonnie and Clyde.* But that person was an American, the wife of a professor who had talked about Topic I, Crime Prevention Strategies.[74] In the Saskatchewan Meeting of November 1979, the fear of victimization was mentioned in conjunction with a larger analysis of crime prevention.[75] I could discover no other reference to victims in the consolidated reports of the consultation seminars. It was only much later, when the Canadian delegation faced the task of formulating a position on the topics, that victims were put forward as a subject. The Chief Adviser proposed its inclusion as part of the Canadian response to the area of 'norms and guidelines'. It was then that the suggestion was made that victims might become a specific topic on the agenda of the Seventh United Nations Congress on the Prevention of Crime in 1985.[76]

At the Caracas Congress there was again no formal, public deliberation about victims. The grid imposed by the agenda seems to have excluded such talk. There *had* been a draft intervention prepared to introduce the subject of the victimization survey as a facet of the Solicitor General's work on crime prevention.[77] That was all. It was not what was said in the public forum of the Congress that was later to be appropriated as part of the history and justification of the federal initiative. Rather, it

[74] Report of Seminar 1 on Crime Trends and Crime Prevention Strategies, in *Briefing Book III: Reports of Consultation Seminars*, Ottawa, 1980.

[75] Regional Consultation, Saskatoon, 16–17 Nov. 1979, in *Briefing Book III.*

[76] It is interesting that in 1983 Irvin Waller, by then no longer in the Ministry but a Professor of Criminology in the University of Ottawa, should have drafted a 'declaration on the protection and assistance of victims of crime' for eventual adoption by the United Nations. The declaration was written under the auspices of the World Society of Victimology and the Task Force on Victims of Violence of the World Federation for Mental Health. It recommended that states should be obliged to provide legal rights relating to protection from crime, recovery from victimization, and justice for victims and witnesses. It sought to lay down standards for the delivery of services that flowed from those rights. Irvin Waller suggested that the declaration could become 'a major initiative for the 7th UN Congress on the Prevention of Crime ... in 1985. It could be discussed in 1984 at the meeting of experts on Victims of Crime tentatively scheduled for Canada—which is "preparatory" to the UN Crime Congress.' *Declaration on the Protection and Assistance of Victims of Crime: Background and Statement*, 14 June 1983, p. 3.

[77] *Report of the Canadian Delegation.*

was the retrospective discovery that victims could be regarded as one of the themes that unified the reflections of the Canadian delegation. It was the RCMP Staff Sergeant, the quiet animator, who said:

> [Victims] never got entered into the United Nations Congress at Caracas, but in the follow-up meetings within the Ministry of the Solicitor General and with provincial representatives from all over the country, it became clear that the people involved were all prepared to say that this should be a growing concern for the next five years and should be a major focus for the next United Nations Congress in 1985. Well, that became adopted, circulated and the people within the Ministry of course supported that position ... and suddenly there was a bit of a ground swell starting.

At a distance, it is a little difficult to establish how that discovery was made, when it came to be made, and how many people made it. It would be foolish to hazard much. It is certainly the case that the Solicitor General did not consider the topic of victims important enough to be mentioned in his recapitulation of what had taken place at the Congress.[78] Yet the delegation did formally declare that victims were a kind of tacit theme. The Staff Sergeant must have contributed something. The agent of discovery is evident enough: he was the Chief Adviser to the delegation and it was his proposal that led to the inclusion of victims in the report. It may be that his influence and authority are sufficient explanation. Perhaps, too, Weick has illuminated a part of the process when he commented 'members of organizations spend considerable time negotiating among themselves an acceptable version of what is going on'.[79] The sheer effort to make sense of the Congress may have allowed victims to become visible. The delegation agreed that the meeting's omissions were almost as significant as its resolutions. They held that it was part of their task to recognize what was immanent in the Canadian criminal justice system, anticipating the future as well as capturing the past.

At a follow-up meeting held in October 1980, it was argued that, although they had not been on the agenda or discussed formally at the Congress, victims qualified as a neglected problem which should be listed in the delegation's report. It was maintained that 'present efforts were either insufficient or inadequately focused in terms of the emerging importance of [the items on that list]' and that 'the objective in identifying those issues is to reinforce the priority given to present activities

[78] Notes for an Address by the Hon. Bob Kaplan, Solicitor General of Canada, on the 6th United Nations Congress ... to the Second Annual Clear Lake Seminar Sponsored by the Manitoba Society of Criminology, Clear Lake, Manitoba, 13 Sept 1980.

[79] K. Weick, *The Social Psychology of Organizing*, p. 13.

with respect to some of them and to draw the attention of the criminal justice community to the need to take new initiatives with respect to others'.[80]

Thus it was that another body, housing all the different factions, strata, and segments of the criminal justice system, made a firm recommendation that victims be treated as a candidate for policy development. What is important is that the Canadian delegation's recommendations were taken seriously enough to be incorporated into the routine planning of federal timetables and committees. The Head of that delegation, the man who could implement its arguments, had asserted that he wished:

> to stress the importance of between Congress follow-up. If the Congress consisted only of two weeks' discussion every five years and then was forgotten, it would not be useful. The lessons we learned at the Congress must be applied in our own systems and in the light of our own situations in order to have relevance.'[81]

As a matter of course, the reports and recommendations of delegations to United Nations Congresses entered the agendas of the Joint Criminal Justice Committee. Victims were forwarded with them. Their paternity in the United Nations Congress was impressive. It was noted that they were one of the six areas advanced for priority attention. More generally, it was noted that 'the general perception among federal officials involved in the Congress was that the working relationship with provincial officials was very positive and should be maintained'.[82] A willing compliance with the delegation's suggestions was one obvious way of maintaining those positive relationships, adding to the stature of victims as a social problem. Victims were mooted in September as a topic which might engage the Joint Justice Committee's interest and it was again noted that Ontario (and Newfoundland) had raised questions about the position of victims in the criminal justice system.[83]

It was in that manner that victims were formally conducted into the procession of committees that were to culminate in the federal initiative. The rest of this book will follow their future journeyings from committee to committee. I shall describe how a paper was presented to a Meeting of Deputy Ministers Responsible for Criminal Justice and from thence to

[80] *Report of the Canadian Delegation*, pp. 30–1.

[81] Notes for an Address by the Honourable Bob Kaplan, P.C., M.P., Solicitor General of Canada, on the 6th United Nations Congress on the Prevention of Crime and Treatment of Offenders.

[82] Follow-up to the Sixth UN Congress on the Prevention of Crime and Treatment of Offenders, unattributed, undated, p. 2.

[83] Possible Issues for Joint Criminal Justice Committee, 30 Sept. 1980.

the Meeting of Ministers that followed in its wake. That paper endorsed victims as a group requiring political attention. Not only did it refer to the Canadian delegation as a source of authority and as a pressure on the federal government. It also modelled its argument on the Joint Justice Committee's memorandum on the follow-up to the Congress. It approved that memorandum's identification of 'two major options concerning the federal government's approach to the general question of victims'.[84] The paper was a linear descendant of the delegation's report and it was to have a pronounced effect. In another chapter I shall discuss how the May 1981 Meeting of Deputy Ministers instructed the Department of the Solicitor General to prepare a policy review of the implications of the United Nations Congress. The Department was also requested to work with officials from Alberta, Ontario, Saskatchewan, and British Columbia in the writing of a working paper on 'assistance to victims'.

Conclusion

Towards the end of 1979 and at the beginning of 1980, the people who manned the Canadian criminal justice system assembled in two major gatherings that were to affect the course of the victims initiative. Those gatherings were august and memorable, bestowing legitimacy on anything that was resolved in their name. They contained representatives of provincial governments, bodies whose co-operation was essential to the very preservation of a federal state and a national system of criminal justice. At neither meeting were victims included on the official agenda. Indeed, at the United Nations Congress there was to be no public discussion of victims at all. What did transpire was that victims nevertheless achieved a presence which was made momentous by its momentous setting. In the instance of the October 1979 Meeting a forceful Minister from a powerful province voiced his concern about victims, and the federal Department of the Solicitor General made its own answering commitment to the service of victims. The United Nations delegation was reported to have reached a consensus. It was the will of a number of participants that that should be so. The Meetings of 1979 and 1980 were allowed to assume a particular significance in the very special history and talk of the victims network. Their occurrence, subsequent use, and bearing followed a pattern described by Weick: 'organizations have a major hand in creating the realities which they then view as

[84] Draft Outline: Victim Justice—Options for a Federal Approach, 6 Apr. 1981.

"facts" to which they must accommodate.'[85] The meetings became realities that gave salience to certain courses of action. To be sure, officials did not enjoy a complete freedom to do as they pleased. Gordon Walker's speech came unheralded, surprising the staff of the Department of the Solicitor General. And, although the United Nations Congress follow-up report did seem to conjure victims out of thin air, the delegation was apparently united in its satisfaction with what it had achieved. What certainly happened is that officials' accounts gave focus, brilliance, and emphasis to the Meetings. Victims were beginning to acquire an explanatory legend, a story, that guided them on to the agendas of central committees, committees that might well propel them towards Cabinet and political acceptance.

[85] K. Weick, *The Social Psychology of Organizing*, p. 13.

VIII. Women

Introduction

In South Australia and the United States women were the midwives of the politics of victims. So too in Canada. Women's organizations were to be of cardinal importance in shaping the development of the Justice for Victims of Crime Initiative, and their role demands thorough exploration. They formed the only structured pressure group that could be discerned outside the formal boundaries of the criminal justice system. In a sense they were the sole expressions of anything resembling conventional public opinion in the entire early history of the victims policy. Positioned in and about Ottawa, working together to present an intricately figured political display, they exercised a diffuse and critical influence. So widespread did their presence seem to be that it touched almost all the little histories that I have narrated so far, moulding the development of policies in Ontario, the arguments that directed victimology, and the politics of domestic crisis intervention. Urged to point to a public clamour for their proposals, officials turned to women as the only audible political lobby in the otherwise silent environment of federal and provincial government. Women had been awarded an entrenched place in the institutional structure of Ottawa, being required to monitor new proposals and ideas for their bearing on the status of women. Lacking substantial power and capacity to make policy or implement programmes in their own name, they had to question, exhort, and plead with other departments whose activities affected them. Women were politically consequential in a setting which contained no other corporate representatives of the victim.

In a politically unstructured world, the women's movement *was* relatively audible, and it helped to spur the victims initiative onwards. But an entity which possessed character enough to spur policy could not immediately be controlled or dismissed by any other group it met. It could not be absorbed smoothly by the social circles and ideology that had grown up around the victims of crime. Women's organizations had their own ideas, having possessed an independent history with a distinct train of accomplishments, characters, and campaigns. They had never been designed to champion victims at large. They lacked the responses and vocabulary to deal with victims at large. Victims had no political meaning for them. They were, however, prepared to deal with violence against women, and that perspective and commitment brought them close to and apart from the champions of victims.

In the other little histories, people had described victims as alienated witnesses, social indicators, components of crime prevention programmes, forgotten parties, participants in a process of mediation and reconciliation, and men and women who had been bruised, traumatized, upset, and frightened. When the events and processes of victimization were encountered by women's organizations, they were defined inevitably by new schemes of relevance peculiar to those encounters. Victims were most marginal to the institutional politics of women. When I questioned members of the women's movement in and around Ottawa and Toronto in the summer of 1981, I was given the impression that a substantial number of them were not especially knowledgeable or especially curious about general developments in the politics of Canadian victims, had heard little of what was stirring, and required briefing. To be sure, part of their response was supposed to test me in order to discover what sort of person I might be. Part flowed from the character of my questioning: talking to women who had a mandate to speak on behalf of women, women who felt they had an obligation to focus on women in their answers, it is not surprising that rape and battering should surface as a theme. But part also suggested that members were structurally and existentially distant from the victims movement itself. They had not necessarily identified that movement as salient to their history or interests. If they *did* talk about victims, it was not in the language of the victims movement or the criminal justice system. They preferred to speak of violence against women. And that is not particularly remarkable. There are other forms of victimization that have been subject to similar local colouring. Thus child abuse is not always treated as a problem of victims, crime, and criminals but as a form of family pathology or private conflict. In the United States the Attorney General's Task Force on Family Violence reported 'a large proportion of family violence is committed by people who do not see their acts as crimes against victims who do not know they are victims'.[1] So too with the women's movement in Canada: that movement had not grown up within the criminal justice system and it did not seek that system's reform as its primary objective. There is more than one way to consider violence against women.

An official of the Ministry put it to me that there are 'enormous rifts and in-fighting among various groups' but there is 'certainly a repetition of themes across feminist organizations'. My problem has been to re-

[1] *Report*, Attorney General's Task Force on Family Violence, Washington DC, 1984, p. 5.

cognize a few of those themes and parcel them together in a way that will reveal interesting properties of the victims initiative. My solution cannot fail to be partial, guided by pragmatic criteria. I propose to concentrate upon a solitary strand of ideas that have become associated with a small number of feminist intellectuals and policy-makers. In a sense, I shall make an analytic incision into the movement, attempting to disclose and accentuate particular arguments. The incision will lay bare only a part of one feminist subculture, and I am mindful of its atypicality and the likelihood that it will be disowned by many women and some feminists. What has encouraged me to dwell on that strand is its accessibility, being reproduced in journals, books, and speeches; its apparent authority; and its seeming acceptance. The strand did appear to influence some policy-makers: it entered documents and speeches in Ottawa, and I rarely witnessed it being challenged. On the contrary, that group of intellectuals was consulted, cited, and appointed to advisory posts. If I rely on what they said, it is because many policy-makers and politicians have done so before me. There were undoubtedly others active in the women's movement, but they were less vocal and prominent in the history of the victims initiative, and their influence is less easy to detect. I am content to illustrate trends, not map them in their entirety, and the strand will serve as an example of what occurred.

The arguments of that strand claim baldly that feminism resides in an understanding of the way in which relations between men and women become distorted in a society variously called sexist, patriarchal, and capitalist. Deformations abound, but their most crude and overt expression is in the outright physical assaults which men launch against women. Rape and wife-battering are not to be classified with offences against men and boys. Their political significance is distinct. They disclose special truths about the position of women in conditions of oppression, and their assimilation within a general victims initiative was thought to demand the neglect of those truths. Many feminists, and representatives of the intellectual subculture in particular, would hold that rape and battering lose their meaning if they are removed from the politics which the women's movement had organized.[2] Clark and Lewis, for example, argued of rape:

> No other subject better illustrates the terrible price women pay for living in a fundamentally sexist society, and it is not accidental that the issues which

[2] Let me repeat that many women, many policy-makers, and some feminists would dissociate themselves from this vision. For example, one very important shepherd of the victims initiative told me, 'I was a spokesperson for feminism and yet felt that . . . a synthesis of feminism with a more global theory would be possible'.

most deeply concern feminists have all revolved around the female sexual and reproductive function. The logical end of such concerns is an analysis of rape.[3]

In the 1970s and during the early period of the history of the initiative, it was apparent that victimized women were not always championed because they were victims but because they were women; feminism was not directed at victims but at women; and it was feared by some that the victims initiative itself could become a distraction and rival to the women's movement. By extension, feminism fed some contradiction into the emerging initiative. One of the principal propellants of policy was also to be a source of strain, turning against that which it had unwittingly brought into being. It was to be an odd and complicated relationship, feminism forming the involuntary principal flank of the victims movement.

Victimology, Victims, and Women

The feminist subculture I propose to examine has come to settle on the body. The body's iconology and practical politics have become strategic. The Canadian women's movement has itself been explained as a campaign devoted to the right of women to 'have control over their own bodies',[4] control being identified with the female body's special ability to produce children. Rape, abortion, birth control, and sex education are issues which have come to organize and refract phases of feminism. Rape, particularly, has been defined as a vital staging of sexism. It symbolizes 'the most extreme example of the abuse of a woman's body and her integrity'.[5] It reveals the brutal, fetishistic, and objectifying qualities which disfigure relations between the sexes. Instead of being aberrant, rape is taken to be a stark 'act of over-conformity by a man trying to fill society's expectations of him'.[6]

Rape is extremely educative, 'a microcosm of what passes for "normal" sexual relations between men and women'.[7] As a metaphor, it signified and stimulated the growth of one portion of the Canadian women's

[3] L. Clark and D. Lewis, *Rape: The Price of Coercive Sexuality*, p. 30.

[4] R. Kasinsky, 'The Rise and Institutionalization of the Anti-Rape Movement in Canada', p. 152.

[5] D. Schram, 'Rape', in J. Chapman and M. Gates (eds.), *The Victimization of Women*, Sage Publications, Beverly Hills, 1978, p. 54.

[6] R. Kasinsky, 'The Rise and Institutionalization of the Anti-Rape Movement in Canada', p. 151.

[7] L. Clark and D. Lewis, *Rape: The Price of Coercive Sexuality*, p. 30.

movement.[8] It was to become the focus of much theatrical and publicized activity. Women wrote about rape, proclaiming its power to reveal the foundations of sexuality. They marched.[9] They fought to 'claim the night'[10], demonstrating in those places and at those times which women normally shunned. One recalled, 'I had what is unfortunately a rare experience ... I walked along dimly-lit streets without fear. I was not afraid because I was in the company of at least 800 of my sisters'.[11] They organized self-defence classes.[12] In Vancouver they orchestrated a latterday version of charivari or rough music,[13] moving to the homes of men accused of rape and chanting, 'We know what you did. We know who you are. We're watching you. We're going to fight back'.[14] They formed vigilante groups to patrol university campuses.[15] They criticized proposals to reduce the penalties for rape.[16] In short, rape was to be a catalyst of some moment. As a member of the National Action Committee on the Status of Women reflected: 'it was an issue that women could focus around and, as women's self-awareness increased, women started to feel like these were offences against them'. Rape and strains of feminism thereby began to amplify one another, lending political meaning and urgency to the understanding of what happened.

Little of this agitation centred on the Department of the Solicitor General of Canada. Rape and wife-battering entered its domain only obliquely as a problem in policing. After the publication of Linda MacLeod's *Wife-Battering in Canada*, a group from the Advisory Council on the Status of Women did visit the Solicitor General and received support for the initiation of measures to control violence against women. But policies and programmes in the realm of violence tended to implicate other departments and governments. Thus the provision of finance to transition houses and rape crisis centres is a matter for provincial government, National Health and Welfare, and the Secretary of State.[17] The

[8] See E. Fattah, 'Victimologie: tendances recéntes', *Criminologie*, 1980, Vol. XIII, No. 1.

[9] *Toronto Star*, 4 Nov. 1977.

[10] *The Citizen*, 19 Sept. 1981.

[11] J. Curry, 'We Took Back the Night', *University of Toronto Women's Newsmagazine*, October 1981, Vol. 2, No. 2, p. 6.

[12] 'Women Learn Self-Defence!', in the *University of Toronto Women's Newsmagazine*, October 1981, Vol. 2, No. 2.

[13] See G. Pearson, *Hooligan: A History of Respectable Fears*, Macmillan, London, 1983, pp. 197 ff.

[14] *Globe and Mail*, 15 Mar. 1980.

[15] *Toronto Star*, 8 Nov. 1978.

[16] Ibid., 24 Jan. 1981.

[17] National Action Committee on the Status of Women, *Overlapping Jurisdictions: A Pitfall in Supplying Services to Women*, A Paper Prepared for the Canadian Advisory Council on the Status of Women, unpublished, undated.

problem of rape itself was characteristically debated in arguments about the propriety of clauses in legislation, Bill C-52 being particularly salient. It was therefore to become an issue for the federal Department of Justice, and lobbying and criticism were generally directed at that Ministry.

C-52 was intended to be an omnibus Act, designed to rationalize and amend the Criminal Code and certain 'other Acts in relation thereto or in consequence thereof'. Presented on 1 May 1978, it was to occasion some scandal. In retrospect, officials of the Department of Justice concluded that the Bill had been drafted hastily and without proper consultation. What caused special offence was the portion of the Bill which touched on changes in the law on rape. Under Section 148, it was proposed to retain the provision of 'spousal immunity', an immunity which made it possible in law for a husband to have forcible intercourse with his wife. There was further concern about Section 149 and its reference to severe psychological damage flowing from indecent assault.

The Canadian Advisory Council on the Status of Women commended much of C-52, but it argued 'in effect, the law allows a person cohabiting with a spouse to indecently assault her or his spouse with impunity, thus sanctioning the idea that a person is the property of her or his spouse'.[18] The National Action Committee on the Status of Women approved a policy recommendation in March 1978 that there should be 'removal of the husband's exemption from the charge of rape by his wife'.[19] The National Association of Women and the Law declared that 'the most serious deficiency in Bill C-52 is its failure to eliminate the immunity from prosecution for rape committed by a husband against his wife'.[20] And the Association advanced other criticisms as well.

There was to be substantial lobbying. Encounters between women and officials at the Department of Justice became abrasive. One report stated:

> On Friday afternoon ... a delegation from the National Association of Women and the Law ... met with Justice Department officials, ostensibly to discuss our recommendations on sexual assault amendments. After having been told to expect two or three people, we were a little startled to see 9 Justice lawyers show up, at least two of who had evidently prepared themselves at a liquid luncheon. Only one had read our report. With such a large group of fine legal minds

[18] M. Rioux and J. McGadyen, *Background Notes on the Proposed Amendments to the Criminal Code in Respect of Indecent Assault, (Bill C-52)*, Canadian Advisory Council on the Status of Women, Ottawa, 1978, p. 18.

[19] *Index of Policy Recommendations*, National Action Committee on the Status of Women, Toronto, undated, no page numbers.

[20] National Association of Women and the Law, *Sexual Assault Offences: a response to Bill C-52 ...*, Ottawa, 1978, p. 6.

assembled, the propensity for showing off was great ... As a parting shot, one fine legal mind giggled that removal of the spousal exemption might result in himself being charged with sexual assault for pinching his wife ...[21]

Of another meeting, a former senior official of the National Action Committee on the Status of Women stated that forty women had attended:

I should think that meeting probably shook Justice up quite a bit because they don't usually get exposed to groups who feel strongly. Apart from all the male lobbies ... the business organizations and so on who've got their permanent lobbies there all the time, to have a bunch of furious women there is rather surprising.

C-52 lapsed at the end of the Parliamentary session and it was not received the next year.[22] A new Minister of Justice, Marc Lalonde, announced in March 1979 that he would prepare a new Bill 'following representations I have received from women's organizations and various other groups'.[23] His successor, Jean Chrétien, announced in his turn that 'spousal immunity' would disappear; 'this "spousal immunity" from rape derives from the traditional belief that marriage meant irrevocable consent to sexual intercourse. If the new law is to protect the integrity of the person ... marriage should no longer mean forced sexual submission'.[24] The argumentation and lobbying were to go on. Resurrected as Bill C-127, proposals were made to abolish spousal immunity and to emphasize the violent rather than the sexual in rape. The Committee Stage of the Bill seems to have been particularly taxing. When it was complete, it was said 'many of the 20 MPs involved in the often acrimonious, sometimes hilarious and occasionally serious debate looked as if they desperately wanted to leave town before they hit someone—most likely one of their own parliamentary colleagues'.[25] The Bill was ultimately passed by the House of Commons on 4 August 1982.

What is significant about the campaign and the reverses of the Department of Justice is that officials of that Ministry were to become so rudely and abruptly acquainted with the sentiment which women felt about rape and sexual assault. Officials had been unprepared for what happened. They had been discomfited. Ever afterwards, they were to be

[21] *National Association of Women and the Law Newsletter*, September 1978, pp. 8–9.

[22] House of Commons Debates, 20 Dec. 1978.

[23] House of Commons Debates, 6 Mar. 1979. See R. Carrière and C. Lamontagne, 'Viol au Canada—un Débat Renouvelle', *Deviance et Société*, March 1979, Vol. 3, No. 1.

[24] J. Chrétien, *Information paper: Sexual Offences Against the Person and the Protection of Young Persons*, Ministry of Justice, Ottawa, December 1980, p. 13.

[25] S. Riley, 'The Joy (and Politics) of Sex', *Maclean's*, 9 Aug. 1982, p. 16.

solicitous about the victimization of women and the political response of women's organizations. It was partly for that reason that they were prepared to join with the Department of the Solicitor General in the construction of a federal initiative when the time came.

Further, the discomfiture and eventual pliability of the Department of Justice were awarded some significance by feminist organizations. It was eventually to become apparent that the criminal law and law enforcement were areas in which women might achieve something. They were areas that were particularly suitable for exploration by a new generation of young, feminist lawyers who were located in and about Ottawa. Mary-Ann Nixon, one of those lawyers, reflected, 'those problems became issues [because of] the increase in the number of professional women who were able to articulate [them]. Prior to that, we didn't have a lot of women in the legal profession much before the early '70s. . . . The women in the legal profession were . . . women who were most aware of it.' That awareness of possibilities was to grow gradually. At first, the politics of rape had been the local concern of a small number of women's groups. The events of 1978 and after seemed to declare that those politics could be developed further. They were a signal for concerted action and around them were to emerge an organization and a body of writing. Thus Christine Blain, legal adviser to Status of Women Canada, recalled:

> I was both quite active in Women and the Law and the local Rape Crisis Centre at the time and had been working on the issue of sexual assault for some time, as had a couple of other members of my group, and we could see that this issue was coming up. . . . Once the Bill was introduced, it became clear that the Government was willing to act in this field, so women's groups decided that they'd better act on this thing and not something else. We in Women and the Law Group formed this committee, starting in May '78, as soon as the Bill [C-52] came out. We met regularly, at least once a week, for an entire evening or a whole day, until October to hash out a policy.

Battering, too, was available to acquire an iconic character. It was again but one strand of the women's movement that turned to battering as a mirror of 'the patriarchal system',[26] a documentation of the power that men exercised over women. Women had cared for women long before the renaissance of feminism in the 1970s.

Further, many feminists defined violence very broadly, indeed somewhat metaphysically, as a structural problem which ramified into employment, educational, and political practices: they did not always

[26] E. Flynn, 'Report of the Discussion Sections of the Second International Symposium in Victimology', p. 45.

care to dwell minutely on the problems of physical assault alone. And it was the case that some of the newer transition houses were not founded as parts of a feminist project. For instance, the geographically remote Yukon Women's Transition Home was opened in March 1980 without an explicit political or ideological mandate: 'the philosophy underlying the service . . . was initially not clearly stated but rather evolved through the implementation of management policies and in house administration'.[27] But the Yukon House was remote and it was associated with the rather special needs of Indian women. It may have been rather exceptional and it certainly excited censure from segments of the women's movement. It was observed in a review of services to battered women, 'another problem is that the transition home is not feminist; feminists feel apart'.[28]

Although not all feminists turned to battering, and not all women who did turn were feminist, there was an affinity between services to assaulted women and arguments within feminism. Many transition houses were to be obviously rooted in the defence of women against patriarchy. One of the first homes to be built in the second wave was the Battered Women Support Service scheme in Vancouver whose education co-ordinator, Debra Lewis, had once remarked, '[hatred of women is evident] in the systematic violence against women and in the more subtle forms of manipulation, ridicule and everyday discounting of women as full human beings'.[29]

Transition houses could represent an opportunity for women to exploit their experiences as women as they succoured women who had been hurt by men. They had the makings of levelling institutions, celebrating a community of practical experience, rejecting the intercession of experts, stressing the importance of works, and affirming the solidarity of those who suffer. Their arguments are not remote from those of the Protestant dissenters who sought to build small, perfect societies in the midst of a larger corruption. Consider some of the assertions presented to a Consultation on Wife Battering organized by the Canadian Advisory Council on the Status of Women. Each assertion refracts recurrent themes. In a discussion centred on work in British Columbia, it was agreed that 'violence against women is endemic to our society, that the reality of women's experience is denied by the professional views of wife

[27] A. McLaughlin, *Kaushee's Place: Yukon Women's Transitional Home; Final Report of a Three Year Demonstration Project*, Whitehorse, 1983, p. 13.

[28] L. Gerstman, 'Yukon' in *Symposium on Inter-Spousal Violence* by Gerald Daigle, unpublished, 1981, p. 2.

[29] T. Hilborn, 'Debra Lewis', *University of Toronto Women's Newsmagazine*, October 1981, Vol. 2, No, 2, p. 6.

battering, and that the woman is constantly faced with "solutions" provided by the official service system which actually make her situation worse'.[30] An analysis of the task force that was struck by the United Way in British Columbia in 1977 talked of 'the subversion of women's experience and the perpetuation of violence against women by a definition of the problem which does not take women's reality into account'.[31] A report on government initiatives in Québec concluded with the statement that 'women working out of the women's movement must be given credibility with respect to the problems surrounding wife battering, and ... women must remain in control of any changes in the area'.[32] An examination of the federal government's response to battering complained that 'most of the people that women who are battered have to deal with, have interests in the patriarchal system which keeps women subordinate, dependent and so defined as appropriate victims'.[33] A paper on the Regina Transition House claimed 'feminist support services must begin to attack the subordination of women in our society on as many different levels as possible. Women who work in transition houses, as well as women who come to the houses for help, are victims of violence in our society.'[34] The thesis is unequivocal. Battered wives are not to be regarded as mere victims. They can be helped and explained only by women schooled in feminist ideas and practices. It is only in the frameworks supplied by feminism and the experience of women that they acquire their full meaning.

It may be seen that rape and battering have acquired moral and political importance. They have been subject to strong proprietorial claims. They cannot be grasped as if they were innocent of implications for power and policy. Their rescue and reconstruction by women, and by particular groups of feminists especially, was an event of some moment, and attempts to give them alternative meanings were treated as rival political strategies. In particular, the question of the culpability of women victims injected the possibility of confusion into the dialectics and politics of sexual morality. If women were declared guilty of some form of contributory negligence, men could be freed of some blame, and the moral lines between the sexes would no longer be quite so distinct but ambivalent and difficult to trace. Victim-precipitation was to become an issue for some feminists, further discouraging the very use of the word

[30] *Wife Battering is Everywoman's Issue*, Canadian Advisory Council on the Status of Women, Ottawa, 1980, p. 12.

[31] Ibid., p. 15.

[32] Ibid., p. 17.

[33] Ibid., p. 21.

[34] Ibid., p. 23.

'victim'. Precipitation blocked analysis and action. As Diane Wood of Status of Women Canada argued:

While it may seem simplistic to say that the basic problem for women as victims is one of attitudes, it is no less true. It is also no excuse. Those of you involved in direct service of one kind or another, as well as those involved in policy development ... know full well that the most frustrating obstacles are those in peoples' minds—not only the attitudes of women and men toward each other in the victim/victimizer relationship, but the attitudes of people in the criminal justice system, social services, counselling, family members, religious advisors, and the community at large. The common element running through these acts of violence is that somehow the victim has brought it upon herself, somehow she is responsible for the victimization, perhaps she likes it, and that most certainly, in some way the victimizer is blameless.[35]

Those who are prominent in the politics and ideological work of the one strand of feminism would further remove women from victimology and the victims movement. They would claim women as their own, part of a campaign which celebrates and defends femininity. The very classification of rape and battering has become a political matter. Their alignment with burglary, theft, and the abuse of male children can bring about a loss of distinctiveness, a sexual neutrality, and a forfeiture of control and authority. Clustered with other crimes, they would no longer signify and convey special truths about the nature of sexist society. Those truths are capable of exciting deep emotions and profound sentiments, and they are not sacrificed carelessly. Thus one report of a conference organized by the Calgary Status of Women Action Committee stressed the reactions of women to a paper about infibulation: 'the description caused several women to faint, and others to leave the room to vomit or escape. From the podium, bodies seemed to slump in syncrony to the pain and violation Russell described; women turned to each other, hugging to comfort and share their suffering.'[36] Again, the same report touched on the conference's response to a debate about rape: 'all of us mentioned the powerful emotions it had engendered in us; the anger, disgust, frustration ...'[37] In another article on the same conference, it was stated:

'There was a good component of emotional support', said Hartsook. 'Feelings were emphasized, even in the large group. It was very heavy though, too serious

[35] D. Wood, 'Speaking Notes: Women as Victims', paper delivered at the 33rd International Course in Criminology, Vancouver, British Columbia, 6 Mar. 1983, p. 4.

[36] J. Ridington and G. Errington, 'Women in a Violent Society', *Kinesis*, June 1978, Vol. 7, No. 6, p. 12.

[37] Ibid.

both in content and in factual information'. 'At times you just had to leave because it was too heavy', said Judy Bader, a Prince Albert social worker. 'It was very stimulating'.[38]

Rape and battering are freighted with feeling. They are infused with significance. It was not in a context of victims that the feminists of the one strand recognized the assaulted women. In fact, they would maintain that they had been active long before any general victims movement had begun. So it was that senior officials of the National Action Committee on the Status of Women told me of their 'real resistance' to the word 'victim' and their lack of interest in victims at large. Their concern was with women who had been violently attacked. And there was something else involved as well. The feminist stance tends to support Mary Douglas's observation that 'a heavy social load ... is carried by apparently innocent-looking classification systems'.[39] *Victims* seemed to be taken by some to suggest passivity, defeat, and defilement. Thus a member of the National Action Committee argued:

I think it's not a good idea to be identified with the victim sort of issue because you're fighting from a down position and I don't think we should do that. If we're going to be victims, then maybe it's as poor women, as uneducated women, as native women. I think a lot of people point to the fact that everybody in the world is either male or female and you can be a multiplicity of other things but you must be male or female.

That argument is quite significant, revealing a most fundamental bifurcation of the physical, social, and symbolic world. The sexual division is the one supreme ontological fact to the feminist. It embraces questions of biology, sociology, and economics: 'the population of normal persons is [above all] a morally dichotomized population.'[40] A moral dichotomy demands protection. It would be wrong and foolish to replace it by lesser rankings and methods of stratification. In this sense, the victims movement is conceived to be *trivializing*, replacing a major ontology by a minor one. It has a capacity to introduce ambiguity into classification schemes and most people would wish to avoid such a threat.[41]

Hence it came about that, in the beginning, organized feminism was sometimes loath to accept the categories, benefits, and costs of the victims

[38] *The Network of Saskatchewan Women*, May–June 1978, p. 8.
[39] M. Douglas, preface to *Rules and Meanings*, Penguin, Harmondsworth, 1973, p. 11.
[40] H. Garfinkel, *Studies in Ethnomethodology*, Prentice-Hall, New Jersey, 1967, p. 122.
[41] See R. Scott, 'A Proposed Framework for Analyzing Deviance as a Property of Social Order', in R. Scott and J. Douglas (eds.), *Theoretical Perspectives on Deviance*, Basic Books, New York, 1972, p. 22.

movement. The National Co-ordinator of Status of Women Canada stated:

Although we have been supportive of this victims services business, we're very leery of it and we think that the lack of willingness to deal quite separately with battered women, women who were victims of rape and what not, may be a big mistake. In fact, this preoccupation with victims came along in no way related to the demands that were being made by women's groups on the Government. Not at all. They had a separate historic track. ... The reasons why women are attacked and the reason why women are battered within the family are quite different from the reason why someone is assaulted on the street. I mean it's different. It's embedded in our society. ... It has to do with a sexist, patriarchal society. It has to do with a lack of economic power. It's different from break and entry victims, victims of assault in bars, and what not. It's qualitatively different.

Aspects of the Social Organization of a Feminist Response

I shall deal cursorily with the very recent history of a few salient Canadian feminist institutions that addressed the problem of violence to women. I shall attempt to provide just enough detail to make their contribution to the victims initiative intelligible. Feminism is yet another instance of a separate, important, and largely uncharted stream of events that flowed into my own area of interest. It is difficult to offer an adequate account of the origins and structure of those events. Indeed, it is not even apparent that they *were* obviously structured and coherent. I shall try merely to create a simple description that will carry my analysis a little further forward.

It seems that the institutionalization of special Government departments, rape crisis centres, and the more radical transition and interval houses is quite new. It is certainly more novel than the history of feminism proper which may be traced back to the politics of suffrage before the First World War. Work was being done with battered and assaulted women before the 1970s, but it was not until that decade that violence came to the fore as a markedly feminist problem. Thus a former President of the National Action Committee on the Status of Women reflected:

Violence has only just turned up within the last three or four years. There's always been abortion and those kinds of issues, but violence, harassment, battery and also the whole business of child battering and so on which is a kind of tangential concern, they're coming in a great deal more. Part of it is because women in those situations or women concerned with women in those situations have formed organizations, the R.C.C., the battered women's services, which weren't in existence more than five or six years ago. And so a good deal of concern has come from them. All those things weren't talked about ten years ago. Looking back what we hadn't had is rape crisis centres and so on. [We had] the good old professional women's clubs and the women's institutes who've been working merrily away on some of the issues which are very much the concern now and have been all along. You know, equal pay and employment ...

Perhaps the emergence of a specific, organized response to physical violence was inhibited by the urgency of other crusades directed at inequalities of educational and economic opportunity. Perhaps rape, incest, and battering were hidden, taboo problems that could not be ventilated publicly without a new courage and the invention of a new language. Perhaps, too, the origins of a rekindled feminist reply to violence should not be sought in Canadian society and Canadian women's associations but in the United States. Like much else, the inspiration for the more radical rape crisis centres and transition houses came from abroad, England being one source but the United States being the prime mover. As I shall show, many Canadian organizations were patterned after American examples, and it is possibly to the radicalism of America in the 1960s and 1970s that analysis should turn. One of the very first shelters stemming from the women's movement was established in California in 1964,[42] but it was in 'the 1970s [that] feminists, community activists, and former battered women increasingly responded in a new way, providing emotional support, refuge, and a new definition of "the problem" '.[43] Perhaps there has also been something of a tendency to generalize violence into a metaphysical matter, a kind of metonym, so that the anchored, practical problems of the assaulted and raped woman were obscured. A Ministry official, knowledgeable in these matters, argued, 'it is partly because all discrimination against women is seen as a form of violence' that the stress on some modes 'apart from other less sensational forms of violence is feared for its potential to misrepresent the importance of less obvious' problems. Violence can, indeed, be defined most liberally. Consider the frontispiece to a report on battering published by the Canadian Advisory Council on the Status of Women:

DO YOU SEE YOURSELF AS A VICTIM OF VIOLENCE AGAINST YOU? Have you ever felt battered by a T.V. commercial, being put down by your boss, by a movie or newspaper article, being the token woman on a board, committee or council, having your appearance questioned positively or negatively, being asked

[42] S. Schechter, *Women and Male Violence: The Visions and Struggle of the Battered Women's Movement*, Pluto Press, London, 1982, p. 55.
[43] Ibid., p. 56.

how to manage having a full-time job and a family, having your face slapped in an approving sort of way, having your face slapped in a disapproving sort of way, being pushed, shoved or kicked, having your hair pulled, having forced sexual activity or forced sexual inactivity? If you can answer yes to any of these, THEN YOU ARE A BATTERED WOMAN. WIFE BATTERING AFFECTS EVERY WOMAN, NONE OF US IS EXEMPT.[44]

So diffuse an analysis of violence tends to deflect people away from specific problems to a more general onslaught against oppressive structures and symbolic brutalities. It is not an invitation to linger with one, minute form for very long. It was only when attention was devoted to simple practical projects, and that attention was coupled with a renewed radicalism, that the institutionalized reaction grew. The one strand of the feminist response tends to refract themes that were central to American radicalism in the early 1970s: decentralization of control; distrust of professional authorities who claim to know about their clients' problems;[45] an extolling of knowledge acquired through personal experience;[46] an emphasis on the spontaneous group that is organically embedded in a community; and an identification with other oppressed groups. As Ettorre remarked, 'we are concerned with the dialectics of power', and 'this analysis is capable of linking up all forms of human oppression, human struggle and human division'.[47] The works, writings, marches, demonstrations, exercises in self-defence, petitions, and charivari that I have described were all performed in the 1970s. They were accompanied by 'networking' and the building of rudimentary social structures. In 1979 Dorothy Smith wrote:

About three or four years ago I think feminists started talking about networks and networking. I think each of us thought we'd invented the term. . . . Networking is the making of linkages between individuals which connect up sources of information, support, competencies and other resources. . . . Our practical work took up specific problems such as rape, health, violence against women, or local organizational work in women's centres. . . . These were the practical forms of struggle. What we learned from these was fed back into the networks and the arenas. This was how we got our understanding of the shape of oppression in society.[48]

[44] Excerpt from a presentation given on 7 Mar, 1980, by Joyce Hayden, Trudy Don, and Connie Chapman, in *Wife Battering is Everywoman's Issue*, Canadian Advisory Council on the Status of Women, Ottawa, 1980.

[45] See K. Millett, *Sexual Politics*, Rupert Hart-Davis, London, 1969.

[46] See B. Stone, *Sisterhood is Powerful*, Pathfinder Press, New York, 1970.

[47] E. Ettorre, *Lesbians, Women and Society*, Routledge and Kegan Paul, London, 1980, p. 162.

[48] D. Smith, 'Where there is Oppression there is Resistance', p. 12.

In this manner, rape crisis centres and transition houses were central to the development of the strand. They were themselves creatures of the 1970s, having been sired by feminism and the victims movement of the United States. The Quebec nuns were active before, but their labour was not accepted as part of the struggle and it was not written into the history of the movement. Most accounts return to a much later period.

One of the very first rape crisis centres was established in Vancouver in 1974,[49] and it borrowed from the example of Seattle Rape Relief across the border in Washington State.[50] Its constitution was grounded in an emerging feminism: the centre's handbook explained 'we saw ourselves dealing not just with a crisis but with the whole area of sexual politics between men and women (where rape is an extremely important violent instance of sexual power-tripping)'.[51] The centre was to operate at all times of day and night, being manned by shifts of two women who offered counselling, practical advice, and assistance in escorting victims to hospital, to police stations, and to court.

Rape crisis centres were to multiply throughout the 1970s, but 1975 was the fulcrum on which political action turned. Canada had endorsed the United Nations' designation of 1975 as the International Year of Women and as the start of the Decade for Women. A National Plan of Action had been drafted and commitments had been given. In their turn, the departments of the federal government had moved into policy-making for women, the International Year being the symbolic marker that 'furnished ideological and organizational bases and womenpower to tackle ... problems of women'.[52] National Health and Welfare supported the construction of a network of information and practical exchange, financing a 'National Assister', a newsletter, and aid to new centres. The Secretary of State sponsored the first national conference of representatives of rape crisis centres. Within three years, in 1978, twenty-five centres were reported to be functioning.[53]

Rape crisis centres were to be one of the very few organized champions of the victim to be discovered outside government, but their capacity to lobby and make themselves known was limited. Not only were there repeated crises and disputes about funding, evaluation, and control,[54]

[49] See *Helping the Victims of Sexual Assault*, p. 37.

[50] See R. Kasinsky, 'The Rise and Institutionalization of the Anti-Rape Movement in Canada', p. 160.

[51] It is interesting that the centre nevertheless expressed a willingness to admit men and boys who had been sexually assaulted.

[52] M. Amir and D. Amir, 'Rape Crisis Centres in Ontario', p. 4.

[53] See R. Kasinsky, 'The Rise and Institutionalization of the Anti-Rape Movement in Canada', p. 164.

[54] See S. Tafler, 'Two sides remain far apart in rape crisis centre dispute', *Globe and Mail*, 5 Feb. 1982.

a series of political and constitutional tensions bedevilled the internal organization of the movement itself. Ontario's centres did band together in a loose coalition, but no national association emerged and no single voice spoke for those who worked with rape victims. The individual centres themselves had to subsist on meagre resources and modest numbers of staff. There has rarely been the surplus of money and labour to support a conspicuous politics of rape relief. As the salaried member of one centre argued:

It's always the money and the time. What we're finding ... is that all we can do at this point is maintain ourselves. Because of the financial situation, we're not able at this point to play a very active role. We're not able to get out ... as much as we'd like because most meetings take place during the day. They take me out of the office, which means that there's nobody here to answer the 'phone.

None the less, there has been some activity. In Ontario, for instance, members of the Ottawa Rape Crisis Centre lectured to schools. They organized 'claim the night marches' each year. Rape crisis groups have set up information booths, held seminars, and demonstrated.[55] The fifteen rape crisis centres of Ontario lobbied a sympathetic Gordon Walker and received $485,000 for a three-year programme.[56] Agitation prompted the Toronto Board of Police Commissioners to create an all-woman task force to investigate street attacks on women and children.[57] Above all, the very fact that women's organizations existed was to be most important, and I shall discuss its effects below. That fact furnished some of the elements of a symbolic environment that was to be used in time to come.

The more radical transition houses are also quite recent. According to Linda McLeod, the first houses of the new wave were opened in Alberta and Vancouver in 1972. Two more houses opened in 1973, 4 in 1974, 14 between 1975 and 1977, and 14 in 1978.[58] In British Columbia alone, the growth and novelty of transition houses has been marked. The first house was incorporated into the services of the Vancouver Resources Board and then, eventually, into those of the provincial Ministry of Human Resources.[59] By June 1979 6 more transition houses had been founded in British Columbia.[60] Two years later, it was reported that

[55] See the *Globe and Mail*, 4 Nov. 1977.

[56] *Toronto Star*, 1 Apr. 1980.

[57] *Globe and Mail*, 13 Aug. 1982.

[58] L. MacLeod, *Wife-Battering in Canada*, p. 48.

[59] *Family Violence: Report of the Task Force on Family Violence*, United Way of the Lower Mainland, Vancouver, 1979, p. 9.

[60] M. Ostrowski, *Legal Process for Battered Women*, United Way of the Lower Mainland, Vancouver, 1979, p. 8.

there were another 16 houses operating in the province.[61] They were designed to ease the transition of women who had fled homes or relationships in which they had been beaten or abused. The houses were to become refuges or sanctuaries, providing support, advice, and liaison with legal and social services. The newer transition houses thus afforded women an opportunity to remove themselves from the world to take stock of their situation.[62] And, by extrapolation, they also came to represent a physical counterpart to the space which feminism had wrested from sexist society.

The rise of transition houses has been prodigious, lacking collective organization and coherent records. Linda MacLeod listed 89 houses at the very end of 1979, and referred to another 12 that were planned to open in 1980.[63] In late 1981, I traced references to 108 houses: 1 located in the Yukon; none in the North-West Territories; 11 shelters in Alberta, 8 having been inaugurated since 1975; 23 in British Columbia; 6 in Saskatchewan; 3 in Manitoba; 33 in Ontario; 20 in Quebec; 8 in New Brunswick; 2 in Nova Scotia, 1 having opened in September 1978;[64] and 1 in Newfoundland. Figures disclosed to the National Health and Welfare National Clearinghouse on Family Violence in 1982 produced a record of 130 transition houses.

At the time when the federal initiative was being conceived, most of the houses were only a few years old. Many were but a few months old. During that critical period of conception, they had not managed to attain a collective identity, become the centre of a cohesive politics, or achieve a working unity. As a Ministry official observed, 'attempts to encourage coordination failed largely because there are widely discrepant ideologies across and within transition houses'. No national association of transition houses emerged during the 1970s and early 1980s, despite attempts by the Canadian Advisory Council on the Status of Women. It is revealing that, on 16 October 1981, representatives of the transition houses at the Conference of the National Organization for Victim Assistance were unable to discover a common position or a method of discovering a common position when they were approached about approving the birth of a Canadian national organization for victims. They were to flounder a little, declaring that they had been taken by surprise and required time for discussion and consultation with their parent organizations.

[61] G. Daigle, *Report of a Symposium on Inter-Spousal Violence*, p. 2.

[62] See Feminist Services Training Program. . . . *but why do they stay? A Handbook about the dynamics of Wife Battering*, no place of publication, undated, p. 10.

[63] L. MacLeod, *Wife-Battering in Canada*, p. 49.

[64] K. Richardson, 'Halifax Transition House Opens', *Status of Women News*, December 1978, Vol. 5, No. 2, p. 4.

The National Action Committee on the Status of Women

Knitting rape crisis centres, transition houses, and other women's organizations together into a loose coalition was the National Action Committee on the Status of Women. It was that body which lent some order to the otherwise diffuse and inchoate politics of Canadian feminism. It had attained a presence in Ottawa, entering into a symbiotic relationship with particular officials and institutions in the federal government. The interplay between the National Action Committee and the initiative's authors was part of the rhetorical construction of an environment for policy, an environment used by both groups in a collaborative staging of necessity. Weick has claimed that 'the outcomes of organizing are reasonable interpretations of a slice of experience; these slices being treated as amenable as well as prescriptive for future activities'.[65] One effect of the National Action Committee was to supply the materials for a 'reasonable interpretation' which could then be 'prescriptive for future actions'.

The Committee grew out of a meeting that was held in Toronto in 1966. The representatives of some twenty women's organizations convened to review the situation of women in Canada. Their review was conducted in a context of nascent feminism:

> There had been President Kennedy's Commission in the United States, Betty Friedan and Germaine Greer's books, and consciousness raising groups were being formed. The women agreed that more information was needed, and recommended a Royal Commission on the Status of Women. This was appointed by the Government in 1967.[66]

Thereafter, those who had attended the meeting were to maintain something of a parental interest in the Royal Commission and in the fate of the Commission's findings. The Royal Commission reported in 1970 and the Ad Hoc Committee of 1966 met again. Having concluded that the Commission's report had been neglected by Government, the Ad Hoc Committee lobbied Ministers about the implementation of what they believed were its more important recommendations. They also secured Government funding for a conference on the 'Strategy for Change' in Toronto in early 1972. The Ad Hoc Committee reconstituted itself as the National Committee, and proceeded to press Government to execute the Royal Commission's findings and take action generally to

[65] K. Weick, *The Social Psychology of Organizing*, p. 47.

[66] *The National Action Committee on the Status of Women*, Unattributed, undated leaflet issued by the Committee.

advance the position of women. The Committee was to grow. By 1981 it was composed of 160 rather diverse voluntary organizations whose common commitment was to women. Amongst them were the Young Women's Christian Association, the Imperial Order of the Daughters of the Empire, church organizations and, latterly, rape crisis centres and transition houses. The Committee had dedicated itself to a 'feminist perspective, for a cooperative, non-violent, conserver society'.

The National Action Committee publishes a monthly journal, convenes an annual meeting in Ottawa which is coupled with a lobby of Parliament, and attempts to disseminate feminist intelligence about women. It is an organization of organizations, a federation, which may have little immediate impact upon individuals. As a past President argued:

> I don't think half the constituents know that the parent body exists so that inasmuch as they don't hear about it, it may not influence them unduly. I mean, there are women's organizations, big ones, which are themselves federations, and there are organizations like the United Church of Canada and the Anglican Church, and I'm quite sure if you go to the average congregation, they will never know about NAC and their own Status of Women organizations. It just doesn't seem to filter down.

The influence of the National Action Committee was to be upwards or sideways towards a searching audience in Government. In the history of the victims initiative, it was waiting officials who gave substance and urgency to the recommendations of the Committee. It was their response that dramatized the Committee's representations about violence, an instance of a form of dialectics that the Pragmatists had analysed: 'mind and world [are] two factors in the process, necessarily related through the process, neither having any existence independent of the other.'[67] The importance of the Committee's approach to violence was contingent on the reaction of people in the Ottawa departments, a reaction that was itself shaped by the emerging experience and personality of the victims initiative.

I have remarked that there is a metaphysical strain in feminism that describes violence as diffusely engrained in many of the encounters that pass between men and women. That strain translates physical assault into the visible outcrop of a much wider system of oppression.[68] It is

[67] D. Rucker, *The Chicago Pragmatists*, University of Minnesota Press, Minneapolis, 1969, p. 28.

[68] See D. Klein, 'Violence Against Women', *Crime and Delinquency*, January 1981, Vol. 27, No. 1. D. Klein; 'Can this Marriage be Saved?', *Crime and Social Justice*, December 1979, Vol. 12.

argued that the very possibility of assault is prepared by the scripts which men and women receive in a sexist society. Male roles embody aggression, female roles passivity: 'rooted in a social structure which is characterized by male domination, the socialization processes of the male and female act to mold women into victims and provide the procedure for legitimizing them in this role'.[69] More generally, economic, educational, political, and other practices conspire to subjugate women. Those practices are girded by a pervasive structural intimidation, and efforts to reform or remove them are themselves portrayed as attacks on violence. As a Ministry official argued, 'violence has always been a feminist issue in that all discrimination against women is seen as a form of violence'. In this sense, the women's movement itself has always been levelled against violence. On a more pedestrian plane, however, the movement has not been very preoccupied with violence. The National Action Committee has not done much about gross assaults on women. A perusal of its publications and accumulated policy recommendations reveals that it has become engaged with the problem of physical attacks recently, peripherally and outside a context set by the victims of crime. As its former President observed, manifest violence became a concern only during the late 1970s.

Of the fifteen publications listed by the Committee in 1981, one, published in 1978, addressed the issue of pornography; another published in that same year reviewed the supply of services to women; and a third commented on a film called *How to Say No to a Rapist and Survive*. The other publications tended to dwell on problems of human rights, pensions, employment opportunities, and the portrayal or women on television. None of the works on violence to women appeared before 1977.

Policy recommendations adopted at the Committee's annual conferences concentrated quite disproportionately on problems of marriage, employment, and education. It may be seen that gross physical violence was a marginal issue. Resolutions dealing with violence constituted a mere 3 per cent of the total, dwarfed by those concerned with employment and discrimination (49 per cent), income tax and income support (13 per cent), family law (8 per cent), and family planning and abortion (9 per cent). Those resolutions on violence were to be discussed at later conferences only. And some dealt with matters that might be described as idiosyncratic to any major interest in the problems of victims. The earliest, passed in 1977, deplored the sexist depiction of men and women

[69] *Rape Prevention Resource Manual*, compiled by the British Columbia Rape Prevention Project and the British Columbia Police Commission, no date, no place of publication, p. 13.

in a film about rape and it censured both the film and the agencies which bought and showed it. All but one of the remainder touched on the campaigns to change the law on rape, and, in particular, those clauses dealing with the admission of the victim's previous sexual history, spousal immunity, and the problem of resistance. The National Action Committee classified those resolutions under 'violence' and did not make use of the word 'victims' at all.

In short, it seems that physical violence to women has not really been pivotal to the main thrust of Canadian feminism. Those who sought to weld arguments about battering, rape, sexism, feminism, and patriarchy into a coherent whole are but a minor tributary of the feminist movement, a tributary with a small following. Women did ultimately make an impression as a lobby, but what happened cannot be described as the straightforward activities of a pressure group compelling a government to respond. The case was much more complicated, reflecting the tangled interdependencies of advocates, policy-makers, and symbolic environments. Women exerted an influence chiefly because officials in Ottawa

Table 3: *Resolutions and Recommendations Adopted at General Meetings, Annual Meetings and Conferences of the National Action Committee on the Status of Women*

	Year									
	1972	1973	1974	1975	1976	1977	1978	1979	1980	1981
Education/Training					4	2				
Employment/ Anti-Discrimination/ Human Rights	10	6	1	9	12	30	31	14	20	15
Family Law	1			1		14	1	6		
Family Planning/ Abortion	5	5	4	2	3	6	2			
International		1	2	1	2					
NAC/Campaigns Funding	3	1	1	6	6		1			14
Status of Women	5				1					
Taxation/ Income Support		1			8	10	15	5		
Violence					1	3	2	2		2
Child Care	7	2		3		2			4	1
Social Services/ Health										4
Constitution										8

and the provinces acted retrospectively to give solidity and force to their arguments. Influence was conferred retroactively when things started to move in the politics of victims.

Let me pursue that argument. On one level, it is clear that lobbying did take place, but political action was sometimes difficult to organize and its results were uncertain. Thus the National Action Committee's annual conference is held in Ottawa, and a meeting with politicians is one of its components. Those formal discussions with Members of Parliament and Cabinet Ministers do not appear to be managed with great ease. Reports and interviews suggest that women lobbyists tend to feel patronized by male politicians. In 1979, for instance, a delegate wrote of 'the Liberals, led by Lalonde, [being] a maddeningly disdainful lot'.[70] And in 1978, despite the interest of some Ministers, the National Action Committee's confrontation with Cabinet was a little awkward: one Minister '(bless his heart) was his usual patronizing and paternalistic self, reassuring us we were on the right track in our efforts at achieving equality for women'.[71] Ministers were described as doodling and staring at the ceiling and, with the exception of Monique Bégin, 'the contribution of the other cabinet ministers to the meeting was virtually non-existent'.[72]

At other times, when people are not assembled together in Ottawa, the National Action Committee has to face the considerable organizational problems of mobilizing volunteers without substantial funds in a geographically immense country. The Committee is constrained to use busy women who are preocupied with careers and families. As a past President remarked:

> We're not equipped to do the lobbying at the time and place with the personnel. The voluntary movement just doesn't have the resources. Now, it's helped by the research done by the Advisory Council and other government bodies, but the physical fact is that, to get a delegation or a brief together, to get people up in Ottawa at the right time and the right place, takes money and an awful lot of people—not an awful lot, but some expert people to do it. And what happens is that NAC's executive, all of whom have full time jobs except for a couple of old ladies like me, have to make time out of their jobs or lose time or whatever, and put together what may appear to be a hit-or-miss kind of brief because of the shortage of time and so on.

The situation was different with some members of the movement. It is undoubtedly the case that individuals were extremely active in mount-

[70] J. Burke, 'A Delegate's Diary', *Status of Women News*, Summer 1979, Vol. 5, No. 4, p. 5.

[71] 'Cabinet meets NAC', *Status of Women News*, June 1978, Vol. 4. No. 4, p. 2.

[72] Ibid., p. 3.

ing a campaign against violence to women. For example, Lorenne Clark and Debra Lewis are names which may be encountered repeatedly in any inspection of the politics of violence. It was Lorenne Clark and Debra Lewis who wrote *Rape: The Price of Coercive Sexuality*, one of the very rare Canadian books in the area and much cited in consequence. It was that work which argued that rape is merely an elaboration of the fundamental sexism of Canadian society; that rape was offensive because it was an attack on men's property rights in women; and that the response of Canadian males has been to blame the raped woman, to deny the problem and evade responsibility. *Rape: The Price of Coercive Sexuality* was identified as useful reading by the National Association of Women and the Law;[73] it formed the basis of a position paper written by Lorenne Clark for the National Action Committee;[74] and it was described by Ridington and Errington as 'excellent'.[75]

Lorenne Clark herself was to become most energetic in promoting the cause of the victimized woman, speaking at conferences,[76] writing, and lobbying. She was commissioned by the Department of the Solicitor General to compile a bibliography of works on rape.[77] She was the chief architect of the National Action Committee's stance on violence, becoming prominent in that period when the Committee became concerned about the law on rape, drafting the position paper in which it was argued that women are property and that rape is an onslaught against property: 'rape laws ... reflect the view that it is normal for men to coerce women into sexual intercourse, and that it is wrong for them do so if and only if they have no right to exclusive enjoyment of the sexual property they enjoy'.[78] She was to become Vice-President of the National Action Committee in 1978, organizing its very first sessions 'on issues under the general banner of violence against women'[79] at the Committee's Annual Meeting of that year. She was to propose resolutions on the law of rape in 1978, introducing that subject for the very first time. More particularly, she was to sustain some of those symbiotic relationships which did so much to advance feminism in Canada. A colleague reflected, 'it wasn't so much the book as the legwork Lorenne was doing. She was always talking to one bureaucrat or another.'

[74] L. Clark, 'Rape—Position Paper', *Status of Women News*, November 1977, Vol. 4, No. 2.
[75] J. Ridington and G. Errington, 'Women in a Violent Society', p. 12.
[76] See for example, the *Globe and Mail*, 2 Oct. 1978.
[77] L. Clark and S. Armstrong, *A Rape Bibliography, with Special Emphasis on Rape Research in Canada*, Ministry of the Solicitor General, Ottawa, 1979.
[78] L. Clark, 'Position paper'.
[79] L. Clark, 'Workshops on Violence Against Women', *Status of Women News*, June 1978, Vol. 4, No. 4, p. 13.

Debra Lewis had also been busy. She was the co-author of *Rape: The Price of Coercive Sexuality*. She had been a founding member of the Toronto Rape Crisis Centre, education co-ordinator of Battered Women Support Services in Vancouver, and a part-time instructor in Women's Studies in Vancouver Community College. She had animated the Vancouver rough music. She had lectured across the breadth of Canada. But Lorenne Clark and Debra Lewis did not change the Government's position unaided. Throughout much of the time that they were agitating, their words and acts were unheeded. As a centrally placed official in Ottawa remarked in the middle of the most active period of the initiative: 'they weren't involved in this ... they weren't visible.' Visibility grew later and with hindsight. It was coaxed into being when it was needed. Luminosity was *bestowed*.

What the Committee, Lorenne Clark, and Debra Lewis did accomplish was a dramatic role in a theatre of politics built by Ottawa officials. The lobbying, marches, books, and petitions were not the simple causes of action by Government. Their significance and causality were *conferred* in a highly intricate negotiation. It was not immanent. Dewey once argued, 'an object or event is always a special part, phase, or aspect, of an environing experienced world'.[80] So too with feminism.[81] In the social circles that revolved around victims in Ottawa, where realities followed the drift of argument, the meaning of the feminist campaigns flowed out of the special experienced world of the policy-maker. Further, it flowed backwards. A political community of substance and permanence never really evolved around the social problem of violence to women. Neither did the campaign achieve direct effects. The function of Lorenne Clark, Debra Lewis, the National Action Committee, and others was to provide the appearance of an external demand that could be developed when it was needed in the deliberations and arguments of Ottawa. The campaign was mediated, amplified, and used by policy-makers whose choice made it potent. It became a dramaturgical resource which was invoked when it became timely to do so.

Feminism accomplished a dramatic role in a theatre of politics, aiding the presentation of a particular reality. Unlike most other episodes in the history of the victims initiative, the agitation about violence to women was performed by a reasonably complete cast of actors which included representatives of the public. One of the policy analysts working on the victims initiative remarked in 1981:

[80] J. Dewey, *Logic*, Henry Holt, New York, 1938, p. 67.

[81] Conversely, of course, the significance of Ottawa was given a special shape in the experienced worlds of feminist circles.

It was important to establish that there was public concern for the issue and public support for the issue. That's difficult of course because there aren't ... marvellously articulate lobby groups out there constantly writing us letters ... but I can produce a number of recommendations that have been submitted to our Department, Health and Welfare and Justice, saying that we would like you to do this, this and this. So we could say with complete honesty that there *has* been pressure from women's groups.

The significance of the National Action Committee was that of a symbolic buttress. It was not what the Committee and its companions achieved in direct confrontation with Government. Neither was it its uncertain power to mobilize the votes of women. It was the preparation of a helpful political set. And the dramaturgy of the matter was appreciated by feminists. As a member of the National Action Committee executive committee remarked, 'we have our range of crazies who can be called out. We give clout. Status of Women would be lost without us.' And one of her colleagues said, 'women in Government love being pressured. That's the only way they can continue to exist.' Thus it is the power of women to dramatize politics that is important. When they are required, their actions will be noticed, relayed and magnified, creating an effect 'beyond all expectations'.

It was very often in this guise that the campaign entered the initiative. There are a number of instances of the National Action Committee being cited in Ottawa committees, and particularly in the Interdepartmental Committee on Family Violence whose history I shall trace in the next chapter. For example, the Minutes of the Interdepartmental Committee's meeting of 17 March 1980 refer to the 'NAC meeting with Justice department officials in which Lorene [*sic*] Clark put forward the recommendation that women from women's groups working in the area of wife-battering be incorporated on crisis intervention teams dealing with family violence.'

However, it must be appreciated that the interplay between women and organizations inside and outside Ottawa is a little more indefinite and complex than a simple exploitation of symbolic resources. After all, women clearly play a part in moulding the policy proposals which require their support. They are the major constituency of a number of federal institutions, Status of Women Canada being one of the most strategic, and their deliberations and assertions are heeded. Frequently, their influence is most pronounced on those agencies and departments that have the greatest direct responsibility for women. Those agencies, in their turn, feed the mediated demands of women to other organizations inside Ottawa. As buffers, relays, and monitors, they need their women's constituency, and they must appear to respond to its demands. The National Action Committee thereby fuels the representation made by Status of Women Canada in its dealings with a political environment. Thus Maureen O'Neil, the National Co-ordinator of Status of Women Canada talked of its policy on violence being based on 'resolutions that had been made from women's organizations to Government over the preceding three or four years'.

It must also be appreciated that women in Government share a larger world with those outside. They all read and talk about a joint universe of feminist problems. It was the National Co-ordinator again who remarked that work on violence was not 'a response only to pressure because the analysis that led the women's organizations to put pressure on the Government comes from a common source of information that we're all operating from'. In this sense, feminism is made up of a world in common and worlds apart, cohesion and division reflecting the settings in which speech and action occur. On occasion, there seems to be a unity of feminism, but part can oppose part in antagonism and, more complicated still, part can be allowed to oppose part as a useful constraint. In deliberation, for example, the censure of women's organizations can always be quoted as a motive for action or inaction. The Interdepartmental Committee on Family Violence, in particular, was directed by a sensitivity to the concerns of women's groups. One of its draft documents rejected the proposal that the Committee should sponsor a review of writings on violence because of 'feelings among women's groups that it is not further studies that are required, but rather that immediate changes are needed'. The same document later argued that a major research project on battering would meet with 'some criticism from women's organizations that such studies are only a means by the government to avoid or delay the taking of action on the problem of wife battering'.

Status of Women Canada

Lodged in the federal government and acting as the somewhat unwilling engine of the victims initiative was Status of Women Canada. That organization had emerged to co-ordinate the implementation of the recommendations of the Royal Commission on the Status of Women, a Commission that had been established 'in response to urgent requests by some 31 women's organizations'.[82] It was the task of the Commission to

[82] F. Paltiel, *Status of Women in Canada—1972*, Report of the Co-ordinator Status of Women, Information Canada, Ottawa, 1972, p. 1.

enquire into measures that might 'ensure for women equal opportunities with men in all aspects of Canadian society'. The Report examined a great swathe of matters including the criminal law, employment, immigration, and marriage and divorce. At the time of its inception and drafting, and when it was eventually tabled in December 1970,[83] there had been little interest in the problem of women as victims of violence. The principal themes centred on employment and equality of opportunity, not rape and battering. But the Commission's brief had been wide and 167 recommendations were made to Parliament, amongst them the founding of a federal Status of Women Council which would report to Parliament about 'the progress being made in improving the status of women in Canada', 'establish programmes to correct attitudes and prejudices', and 'propose legislation, policies and practices to improve the status of women'.

Endorsing the Report, the Prime Minister declared in March 1971 that he would give priority consideration to its findings. He also asserted, 'we have already appointed within the Privy Council Office a highly qualified person whose responsibility it is to ensure informed and co-ordinated action with respect to the report'.[84] That person and her staff were to become Status of Women Canada. An Interdepartmental Committee was established to consider the recommendations which had been directed at the federal government, and it reported in 1972.[85] Moreover, a Cabinet Minister was awarded the additional responsibility of co-ordinating Government policy on the status of women. Some of those policy recommendations were to be implemented, others were not, but none touched on victims.

In 1976, partly as a gesture to the United Nations Decade for Women, Status of Women Canada was enlarged and detached from the Privy Council Office to become an independent agency. The United Nations World Plan of Action had recommended in Paragraph 34 that governments should instate women's bureaux to accelerate the achievement of equal opportunity. Status of Women Canada was to be just such a bureau.[86] Its mandate was no longer merely to co-ordinate the execution of the Royal Commission's Report. Instead, it had acquired a general monitoring role, required to:

[83] *Report of the Royal Commission on the Status of Women in Canada*, Information Canada, Ottawa, 1970.

[84] Quoted in F. Paltiel, *Status of Women in Canada—1972*, p. 3.

[85] See J. Munro, *The Status of Women in Canada 1973*, Information Canada, Ottawa, 1972.

[86] Based on *Government Machinery on the Status of Women*, undated, no place of publication, Status of Women Canada, p. 4.

ensure that federal legislation, policies and programmes take into consideration the concerns of women. It recommends policy changes to other federal bodies and provides liaison with other federal departments, with provincial governments, advisory councils, and with national women's organizations.[87]

Neither the Minister Responsible for the Status of Women nor Status of Women Canada was empowered to make and enforce policies on women. Rather, they were required to work through other departments, using as their authority the Government's commitment to improve the lot of women and being able to refer to the Government's directive that all policy development must accommodate the interests of women. In particular, they could cite the decision of 26 February 1976 which had determined that all Cabinet documents must include a section on status of women considerations whenever appropriate.

It may be understood that the position of Status of Women Canada is a little odd: it has no direct power to devise and execute policy, but it does have an impressive mandate to exert vicarious influence. Its impact must always be mediated by other departments, and its own work has been translated into the onerous labour of exhorting and reminding them of their obligation to remember women. Officially, that process of admonition takes the form of letters from the Minister Responsible for the Status of Women. At intervals, the various Ministers of the federal government will be urged to take action on the policies they have in train.

As a matter of course, the Minister and his or her National Co-ordinator further impress upon departments their duty to consider women in Government documents and policy proposals. Their prompting has significance. After all, it was the Government itself that licensed it. The need to take into account implications for women in proposals to Ministers was seen as important. Indeed, it was just such a piece of enforcement that led to the injection of victimized women into the 1981 Strategic Overview, an injection that prepared the foundations of the initiative itself.

Unofficially, the work of promoting the ends of Status of Women Canada is conducted, in the phrase of Louise Holmes, one of its officials, 'under the desk and over the 'phone'. It is work that tends to flow along lines of influence established formally and informally for Status of Women Canada. As a result of two recommendations of the Royal Commission,

[87] *Federal Government Mechanisms for the Status of Women: Status of Women Canada*, document prepared for the Interdepartmental Committee on Family Violence, undated, unattributed.

a structure has been built to extend the agency's reach. In 1972 it was reported:

New positions in National Health and Welfare, Manpower and Immigration, Treasury Board, and the Solicitor General's Office will provide special advice on status of women implications for departmental policies and programs. These interlocking structures ... constitute a network for effective communication and action to ensure sound co-ordinated action on the part of the Federal Government in response to the challenge presented in the Report of the Royal Commission.[88]

In practice, and in the region affected by this history, that network was enlarged by Status of Women Canada to envelop all potentially sympathetic women working inside the Ministry of the Solicitor General. And, when the time came, the Ministry was itself to appoint Linda MacLeod, author of *Wife-Battering in Canada*, to the post of policy analyst in 1981. One of the reasons for her appointment was to advertise the Ministry's recognition of the special needs of women in an area of emerging policy: 'I was hired because of a history of problems with women's groups in this area. Women's groups are not very keen on a broad generic topic called victims. They're very afraid that particular types of victims like rape victims and battered wives will be forgotten in the shuffle. I think it was helpful to have me there ... as a kind of reassurance that we would definitely continue to emphasize those groups.' And Maureen O'Neil, the National Co-ordinator, Status of Women Canada, remarked, 'there happened to be people at the Solicitor General who in fact are knowledgeable in this area. If [Linda MacLeod] weren't there, I would have less hope for this being useful for women.'

It was in this fashion that Status of Women Canada was connected formally with the Solicitor General, the Deputy Solicitor General, and its own implanted adviser; it was joined informally with women officials at large (although one commented 'this is news to me'); and, as a victims initiative began to appear, it also acquired links with a special official who had been placed to signal the Department's particular solicitude for women. Relations were diffuse, persistent, and sometimes a little vexed. One of the Department of the Solicitor General's women officials recalled that Status of Women Canada tended not to work by making specific and official overtures. Instead, there were numerous, unrecorded, personal contacts on the telephone and in face-to-face meetings. In all those many unreported encounters, there was a reiteration of the Department's responsibility for the interests of women.

[88] F. Paltiel, *Status of Women in Canada—1972*, p. 8.

Conclusion

So it was that assaults on women were transformed by a strand of feminism into an icon of the larger problem of violence against women in Canada. But violence to women did not engender a group called crime victims and there was a substantial reluctance to associate abused women with other victims and with an initiative whose coherence stemmed from very general problems of victimization. Simultaneously, however, the institutions which were charged with the defence of women in Ottawa had to work through the very departments that were about to foster a victims initiative. The mediated policy-making of women's organizations was to be enormously complex and frustrating; supporting and disturbing the plans of others; being used as a symbolic resource; and providing an alternative system of relevance. For a while, the ambitions and actions of very different groups were to come together in one setting, the Interdepartmental Committee on Family Violence. It is with that Committee that I shall deal in the next chapter.

IX. The Interdepartmental Committee on Family Violence and the Speech from the Throne

Introduction

I have already offered a modest account of how family violence fed into one of the initiative's other little histories. On one occasion, it will be remembered, the feminist response to wife battering merged with the Department's reply to problems of domestic crisis intervention, leading to a systematic shift of policy frameworks and perspectives. There was to be one other major encounter between the political history of family violence and the evolution of the victims initiation: the two met together in the Interdepartmental Committee on Family Violence, they underwent a kind of mild collision, and they swung off one another with an added velocity. The guardians of each history sought to understand one another's actions through lenses provided by their own experiences and purposes. There was some confusion, but the intitiative was accelerated in the process. In particular, it acquired an early authority from the politics of wife battering. At that time, violence to women was a salient and ratified policy issue. Victims were not. It was to be the assaulted woman who moved the initiative forwards in two critical episodes in 1981. Part of her influence was to be channelled through the Committee, and it demands description.

It is always difficult to establish the precise authorship and development of a successfully presented social problem. So it is with wife-battering in Canada. Battering is as old as marriage and it has attracted a fitful succession of responses. It was the effective transformation of family violence into a policy issue that was quite novel: 'only recently has the problem of wife battering come to the fore, like a skeleton emerging from the obscure closet to which it has been relegated.'[1] That transformation was remarkable and it has been given a very particular history by those who work in political institutions devoted to women. Being consequential people, their judgement is itself politically consequential, infusing accounts and affecting action. They hold that wife-battering grew to prominence in the 1970s as a result of its sponsorship

[1] 'Research Project on Wife Battering', no named author, *c.*1980.

by the expanding women's movement. Family violence had been dramatized first in England[2] and the United States,[3] becoming illuminated in Canada from about 1973 onwards as segments of the women's movement began to organize around its relief and exposure. A close interdependence has been traced between feminism and the politics of violence. Thus the first Co-ordinator of Status of Women Canada stated, 'as the women's movement rallied to rescue battered wives and helped them to reorient their lives, governments began to take account of the problems'.[4] And her successor, Maureen O'Neil, reflected in 1981, 'five years ago it would have been hard. The problem would still have been there, but there weren't many people who knew about it. ... All this comes out of the women's movement.' Such a lineage gave feminists a special stake in battering: it was their problem. As one of the founders of a special support group for women argued, 'the first public action goal ... [is] to publicly redefine wife battering as a woman's issue and so to assert the expertise and credibility of women in this area'.[5]

Previous chapters have touched on the manner in which the Government of Canada became caught up in the politics of women. In particular, it will be recalled that the Government committed itself formally to participate in the United Nations World Plan of Action for Women: 1975–85 had been declared the Decade for Women, and the member states of the United Nations were asked to honour it by preparing statements about how they intended to incorporate women more fully into economic, social, and political life. As a document commissioned and eventually endorsed by the Government, the Canadian plan of action became a major mandate. It gave gravity to policy proposals, affecting victims on the margins. As the official entrusted with forwarding victimization research in the Ministry observed, 'it brought [victims] to a higher level of priority'. The promotion of victims had not been planned or intended, but it followed in the wake of the larger stir about women.

Those charged with drafting the National Plan of Action formed themselves into little clusters of working parties, one principal area of concern being women and the family. In its turn, the problems of the family were subdivided into smaller topics, child abuse becoming the

[2] V. Dwyer, 'Interspousal Violence: A Response', Second World Conference of the International Society on Family Law, 13–17 June 1977, unpublished, undated, p. 5.

[3] See M. Van Stolk, 'Wife Beating', *Royal Canadian Mounted Police Gazette*, 1982, Vol. 44, No. 5, p. 7.

[4] F. Paltiel, 'Shaping Futures for Women', *Women's Studies International Quarterly*, 1981, Vol. 4, No. 1, p. 22.

[5] J. Barnsley, 'Vancouver Women's Support Service for Battered Women', in *Wife Battering is Everywoman's Issue*, p. 23.

focus of one group and family violence being selected as the focus of another. Family violence meant something particular and special to the women's organizations of Ottawa. It was, as a former policy analyst of the Department of the Solicitor General argued, 'a code word for Status of Women Canada, meaning wife battering, not child abuse or elderly abuse'. Importance was attached to the defence of that meaning. For example, the Report of the Canadian Advisory Council on the Status of Women deplored the tendency of the federal government to lose battering as a distinct problem. Before 1979, 'the focus was very generally defined as "family violence" and the term wife battering was not used.'[6] After 1979:

> Regardless of the growing public consciousness of the realities of wife battering and recent attempts to develop a more explicit focus on battered wives, the federal response demonstrates patterns [that] include: 1. the substitution of family violence for wife battering. Wife battering is not an acceptable description of the issue. It is persistently subsumed under 'family violence', 'inter-spousal violence', etc. ..., with a strong focus on the impact on children, rather than women. 2. the reliance on professionals for leadership on the issue. Women themselves and women's groups are not seen as experts to be consulted nor are they seen as legitimate or effective recipients for grants, research contracts, etc.[7]

'Family violence' is a phrase with political and semantic ambiguities, and its meaning has been contested in Ottawa. Its disputed significance must be appreciated in all that is to come. It was to plague the Interdepartmental Committee when it was finally convened. It was to influence the meetings that helped to prepare the National Plan of Action. When certain women, acting as the representatives of women, talked of 'family violence', they meant wife-battering and rarely anything else. When certain Ottawa officials, acting as the representatives of major Government departments, talked of family violence, they could mean assaults on the elderly, men, women, or children. The Ministries of Justice, the Solicitor General, and National Health and Welfare have the stewardship of very large policy areas that include women but are not confined to them. National Health and Welfare, in particular, has paid special attention to the needs of children. Their definition of families and family violence is generous in proportion. When they are required to chart the world for policy purposes, it is usually that more generous definition that will be applied. As a senior policy adviser of Health and

[6] 'The Federal Government Response to Wife Battering', in *Wife Battering is Everywoman's Issue*, p. 18.

[7] Ibid., p. 19.

Welfare Canada, a woman, and a member of the Interdepartmental Committee argued, 'I have had an abiding interest in the family as a totality [although] that does not mean that I accept assigned social roles within it . . .'. Family violence is generally regarded as the inflicting of injuries in family settings and women are its common but not its sole victims. It is a conventional and defensible use of the term, suited to the practices of the three departments.

What is obviously critical is that those departments sometimes act as the agents and instruments of Status of Women Canada, the Minister of State with Special Responsibility for the Status of Women, and others. They mediate the special concerns of women's politics with words and ideas that are somewhat foreign to them. When women themselves act as the political agents of women, they may find that they have to work within a set of structures, contexts, and styles of discourse that are quite peripheral to their own politics. In the history of the Interdepartmental Committee, ambiguity was multiplied because the phrase 'family violence' was often used quite literally although it had emanated from an initiative that was supposed to contend with the problem of battering. The problem was exacerbated too, as I shall argue, because the initiative was described in a confusing fashion. In a sequence of refractions, the phrase was interpreted first one way and then the next as it passed through the different frames of the policy process. The genesis of the initiative I am about to describe may have justified the narrow meaning of the term, but the words were equivocal, instructions were unclear, and they changed their usage as they moved from one policy domain to another.

The working parties dealing with the family were housed inside Health and Welfare Canada, and their selection of a focus, name, and problem may have flowed out of a structured combination of a setting, an institutional mandate, a special place in the division of labour, and a sense of what was timely, important, and unexplored. One group, Working Group '3' chose family violence as its topic. One of its members was Linda MacLeod, later to be the author of *Wife-Battering in Canada*, and later still to join the Ministry of the Solicitor General to work on the victims initiative. As a Planning Officer within Health and Welfare Canada, her duties were to 'monitor social trends in Canada, relate them to international trends and suggest their policy implications. . . . to represent the branch on the Departmental Committee for Status of Women concerns'. That Departmental Committee had already suggested that battered women should be considered by a working party, Linda MacLeod being one of their advocates.

The working party report itself attributed the new prominence of battering to 'the re-emergence of the women's movement', a growing public sensitivity to violence, and a current interest in 'environmental factors which create stress'.[8] It met during that important period when there was appreciable agitation about the law on rape and about Bill C-52 in particular. It was apparent that the more eminent women's organizations had acquired a stake in the campaign to change the law on spousal immunity, previous sexual history, and consent. The National Action Committee, The National Association of Women and the Law, and other bodies seemed to be in competent control of the issue. Moreover, rape lent itself to a campaign to reform the Criminal Code, becoming a matter principally for the Department of Justice and not for Health and Welfare Canada. As a later paper reflected, 'a) work was already in progress in the area of legislative reform related to sexual assaults and pornography. b) a great deal of work was being done in relation to child abuse ... c) the significantly neglected area was wife battering.'[9]

However, feminist discussions about rape *had* achieved one significant effect. They had tended to draw the gaze of officials towards the problem of violence to women at large. Battering came into focus as the social problem of rape attained stature. Further, National Health and Welfare had assumed federal responsibility for the victims of one form of family violence, abused children, and the conjunction of women and the problems of families invited a pooling of its interests in an investigation of violence against wives. As Linda MacLeod observed, 'Health and Welfare as a Department was already concerned with child abuse, and wife battering therefore seemed to fall naturally within the departmental purview.' As important, those in the neighbourhood of the working party were beginning to promote battering as a potential policy area:

> The issue had a history in that it had been identified in a preliminary way by United Nations discussion groups and was increasingly visible as an issue which women's groups in England and the U.S. were bringing to the fore. ... Freda Paltiel [a prominent member of the working party] had been very centrally involved for a number of years in women's issues, and had a good network of international contacts, so the extent of concern with the issue may have been amplified by her influence.[10]

[8] National Plan for the Status of Women—Working Group '3'; Report: *Research into Family Violence*, undated, p. 1.

[9] *Research of Wife Battering*, undated paper prepared for the Interdepartmental Committee on Family Violence, p. 2.

[10] Letter from Linda MacLeod to myself, 7 July 1982.

National Health and Welfare had already acquired an investment in the problem through its co-funding of programmes. There were a few signs that the largely unorganized transition houses sought action but generally, as an official of Status of Women Canada put it, 'nothing was going on'. In short, there were stirrings and possibilities that were ill-formed and nebulous. A problem existed, but its structure, quality, and remedy were undefined.

All that was written and said by the working group was 'very vague because we didn't know what to do with it'. And one of the members remarked of the group's report, 'it roams all over the place but it gave us the proper jumping-off place for a lot of things'. Working Group 3 was to introduce the issue of family violence into the National Plan of Action, yet it did so without certainty or precision. It had recognized a region in which work might be done but it did not propose what that work should be. Instead, it advocated a research project to clarify the problem. Amongst the measures it suggested was 'research first the socialization of violence on situational facilitating factors and on the sources of structural stress with particular emphasis on family "pressure points"'.[11] Entering the ensuing Plan of Action on the Status of Women, that recommendation was transformed into 'the government will research the following areas of vital concern so that new policies can be developed: ... violence against women by the Departments of Justice, the Solicitor General, Health and Welfare Canada and in conjunction with provincial governments and women's organizations who have expertise on the subject.'[12] It will be noted that 'family violence' has become 'violence against women', although that was a translation that was to be changed again. It will also be noted that the principal departments were Ministries that had already developed their own pre-occupations with violence, families, and victims.

Towards Equality for Women was approved by the Government in December 1978 to become the 'federal government's commitment to women'.[13] It was binding. As Maureen O'Neil reflected rather flamboyantly, 'we have only to wave the number of the cabinet document to get people to do something.'

On 15 February 1979 Maureen O'Neil wrote to the Ministry of the Solicitor General that each Minister was obliged to present plans for the implementation of *Towards Equality for Women*. Proposals were to be sent

[11] *Report of Working Party 3: The Family, Social Services, Health and Nutrition*, undated, p. 8.

[12] *Towards Equality for Women* p. 12.

[13] Ibid.

to Status of Women Canada by 1 April. In his turn, the Deputy Solicitor General informed the Assistant Deputy Solicitor General, Communication and Consultation, that the Department's research programme would be affected:

[The Government] has requested a major study ... into violence against women, its pervasiveness, the reasons for the apparent tolerance by spouses and communities, the reasons for violence in the family and ways to reduce violence in general and violence to women in particular.

The Assistant Deputy Minister was to draft a plan by the end of the month. In the meantime, Canadian newspapers had begun to refer to the Government's undertaking to embark on a major study of violence against women.[14] It was agreed that the Department's expert on victimization research should convene a meeting on 26 March to discuss how the different Ministries should proceed. In preparation, the official supervising the national survey of victims 'reviewed our own research program to date to see what has already been done that might assist representatives from the three ministries in jointly planning and implementing the research study called for'.

The call to the Ministry of the Solicitor General was answered by those officials who had acquired a competence and interest in matters that touched the problem of violence to women most nearly. They were the members of the social circle that had been working on the victims of crime and the policing of domestic crises. They were obviously eligible to deal with research on battered women. Together with staff from the Departments of Justice and Health and Welfare Canada, work was begun to implement the Government's programme. They did so in terms that were familiar to them, terms that stemmed from their experience, their pursuits, and their capacities. They tended to think of victims and victimization research. All that had been accomplished so far could become a foundation for planning the major study. The politics of battering thereby acquired the momentum of another history and another social problem. In time, too, members of the circle replied in the older, more ambiguous and potentially troublesome language of 'family violence'. There were to be problems of boundaries, categories,

From the very beginning, talk about the study oscillated between references to 'violence against women' and 'family violence'. All kinds of documents and the members of all organizations oscillated. The more detailed were the descriptions of the projected research, the more equivo-

[14] See *The Citizen*, 8 Mar. 1979 and 14 Mar. 1979.

cal they were. Consider the founding document of the study, *Towards Equality for Women*. It recited:

> A major study on *violence against women*, will be conducted jointly by the Departments of Justice, the Solicitor General, Health and Welfare Canada, provincial and territorial governments, in consultation with women's organizations which are expert in the subject. This study will focus on violence between spouses, violence against women, violence in the family, and crisis assistance in communities and will be presented to Cabinet by 1981.[15]

That recommendation was to be quoted liberally in the meetings and papers that led to the striking of the Interdepartmental Committee. It was a mandate, an instruction, and an authority. Yet it will be observed that the recommendation is a little vague and confusing, a product perhaps of its origins in Health and Welfare Canada, a department with responsibility for the well-being of all Canadians. The title of the study is clear enough: research is to be about violence against women. The statement is italicized for emphasis, and it is set in a document issued by Status of Women Canada and called *Towards Equality for Women*. But there is ambiguity thereafter. When an explanation of the study is advanced, violence against women becomes one topic amongst others. It is no longer the sole problem. It may remain the most important theme, but it would seem that the overall objective of the research was actually not a simple one. Prima facie, there can be no other reason to produce such a catalogue of tasks. The casting of violence against women as a special sub-category suggests that it is somehow significantly different from 'violence between spouses' and 'violence in the family'. The nature and consequences of that difference are not disclosed but room appears to have been created for men and children to creep in. After all, it is implied, they are people involved in the separate category of violence in the family, people who might not be covered by the 'phrase violence against women'. And 'spouse' is an androgynous word which could well refer to men as well as to women. The recommendation contained a number of terms which were ill-chosen if the major study was supposed to dwell exclusively on the problems of women. A licence was given to imagine that the research was expected to be a rather general investigation of diffuse forms of family violence.

Those who discussed the study sometimes talked of women, sometimes of families. The working group examined a topic called 'research into family violence' and, very early on, an official of Status of Women Canada drew the Deputy Solicitor General's attention to an American

[15] *Towards Equality for Women*, p. 14.

study 'because your department is singled out [by the Government] in relation to a major study on *Family Violence*'. The letter summoning officials to the meeting of 26 March did so under the heading: 'NATIONAL PLAN OF ACTION ON THE STATUS OF WOMEN:—Research on Violence Against Women.' The subsequent report of that meeting was headed 'NATIONAL PLAN OF ACTION ON THE STATUS OF WOMEN:—Study on Family Violence', and it proceeded to explore the 'Cabinet's directive for a major study on family violence (especially against women)'. In short, it appears that family violence and violence against women were taken to be different but substantially interchangeable labels. When the Interdepartmental Committee was itself struck, it was to be called the Committee on Family Violence and the multivocal character of its title become one of the sources of its failure to progress.

The Interdepartmental Committee on Family Violence

Campbell and Szablowski remarked that there is an 'implicit three-tiered hierarchy among government committees'. Wedged between standing committees of Cabinet and departmental committees are interdepartmental committees. Often formed on the instructions of Cabinet committees, they have 'become the principal means of communication and deliberation in the federal bureauratic establishment'.[16] Although a research project on violence to women quite patently implicated the competences and interest of more than one department, the striking of an interdepartmental committee could also be read as a sign of the scale of the Government's commitment to a resolution of the problem of battering. It gave family violence a presence in Ottawa.

The composition of the little group of eight that were invited to meet on 26 March prepared much of the structure and pattern of development of the Interdepartmental Committee. It embodied diverse interests, conceptions, and movements of policy that were not always central to the politics of battering. Consider its membership. It was a meeting of the representatives and bearers of a number of the little histories which I have narrated. There were those who had acquired a commitment to the surveying of victims, victims assistance programmes, domestic crisis intervention projects, schemes for the aid of abused children, and a victims initiative at large. Two had pressed their departments for years to establish battered children as the object of a policy initiative. One described himself as a voice crying in the wilderness. Many of those

[16] C. Campbell and G. Szablowski, *The Superbureaucrats*, p. 148.

present were members of the social circle that was attempting to galvanize a politics of crime victims. They were on the verge of re-organizing the world with new categories. *Victims*, as one committee member had observed, 'simplified the question of who it is we're talking about ... while special interest groups would like to see the words and policies ... centre around their particular interests, for advancement we need to provide words of labelling that are common to all'. But it will be recalled that the Interdepartmental Committee was not the offspring of those who cared for the word 'victims' at all. Indeed, 'victims' was unacceptable politically. As Maureen O'Neil of Status of Women Canada had argued, 'I just think it's ridiculous to think that you lump into one policy grouping services for people who've had their houses broken into and people whose alleged loved ones have beaten them.' That then was one source of irritation.

A second, related source reflected the apprehension that the inspiration of the women's movement would be displaced or ignored. Not only were feminists concerned about the symbolic engulfment of women by the wider definitions of family violence and victims, they were also anxious about their marginality on their own committee. They were anxious about the usurpation of the practical experience of women by the professional competence of experts from different departments. *Towards Equality for Women* had not referred to the inclusion of members of Status of Women Canada on any committee or project that might be initiated. The agency had no research capacity of its own. At the beginning, indeed, Status of Women Canada was not even invited to send a representative to the Interdepartmental Committee. It was not until 11 June that one of its officials was added to the Committee's list for the distribution of papers.

Two months later, Maureen O'Neil requested that one of her staff be included as a full member of the Committee. It was concluded that Status of Women Canada sat on the Committee as an 'act of politeness'.

Finally, the very words 'family violence' lent themselves to an ambiguous reading. Status of Women Canada insisted that they referred to the battering of wives. Others extended their meaning to embrace battered husbands, the injury of children, and the victimization of the elderly. Thus, listed in the Department of the Solicitor General's review of the history of research on family violence were neuropsychological studies of violence, work on police training and domestic crisis intervention, research on child abuse, rape and rape crisis centres, and delinquency. It was a review that aggregated miscellaneous studies and gave them a new, retrospective description of work on family violence. Some of the problems that had been studied were pertinent to the strict definition of family violence, others were not, but it is apparent that a most catholic interpretation was applied. One of the people present at the Ad Hoc Committee's first meeting of 26 March wrote to its Chairman, 'one of the most important outcomes ... was the clear realization of different perspectives on Violence in the Family. Even the terms used and the emphasis given differ.' When 'family violence' had been delivered to Cabinet, it had borne very specific feminist connotations. Released again and distributed amongst the various groups which touched on victims, it achieved a variety of quite discrepant meanings. Maureen O'Neil from Status of Women Canada observed, 'there was an important variation in ideology on that committee between how one viewed the family as an institution and what benefits there were in the family to women.'

The Ad Hoc Committee and its later incarnation, the Interdepartmental Committee, were the first major opportunities for the carriers of the multifarious little histories to meet. Meeting, they discovered how very indexical was the language they had been employing, how specific and historically bound were their ideas about victims, and how the very word 'victim' was to be in contention. All those matters had to be negotiated and resolved.

The Striking and Evolution of the Interdepartmental Committee

At the very first meeting of 26 March 1979, the Ad Hoc Committee transformed itself into an interdepartmental committee of the three Ministries. Status of Women Canada was not fully incorporated into the new body. Instead, it was to be consulted 'before deciding on the actual scope and design of the study'. It seems that the first meeting moved immediately into a survey of the task which Cabinet had prepared for it. It seems also that the special, situated meaning of 'family violence' was not fully grasped on that occasion. At the head of the Chairman's notes is a general description of the committee's territory and mission, and it is a description that took discussion some little way beyond the frontiers established tacitly by the women's movement and the National Plan of Action. 'Family violence' was interpreted quite literally but also in a manner that was consonant with the explanation offered in *Towards Equality for Women*: the problem was reported by the Chairman as 'violence between spouses/against women', and the observation was made that 77 per cent of the victims of 'spouse killings' in Canada were women, 23 per cent men. Whilst the bulk of the remainder of the notes was confined to orthodox matters within the frontiers, dealing with transition houses, the notification of incidents of wife-battering and the like, that initial allusion to violence against men was a little inauspicious.[17] It was not really the suffering of men that the committee was supposed to examine.

By 4 April the Acting Deputy Solicitor General of Canada was able to inform Maureen O'Neil that the Department's agencies had been approached about their plans for women and were prepared to implement the recommendations of the National Plan of Action. The Royal Canadian Mounted Police, for example, proposed to continue and expand its programme of training police officers in domestic crisis intervention. The Interdepartmental Committee itself was reported to have been struck 'for the purpose of developing options and recommendations for the study'. Further, Maureen O'Neil was informed that the Department actually had a history of research in the area of family violence, including a review of the literature on rape in Canada and a research report on child abuse. All that work 'will be most useful for planning the study on violence against women that was requested by Cabinet as part of the National Plan of Action on the Status of Women'.[18] Uncertainties and ambiguities were manifest in the prećis of work. To be sure, as I have argued, the Ministry's Programs Branch had simply cast back over what had been done, parcelling it together with new and untried names, and presenting the resulting list as research on family violence. The cataloguing was clearly and inevitably makeshift, an *ex post facto* gloss on events and plans that had not previously been identified with family violence. But it was a generous gloss that included much that would trouble women.

From the start, there were signs of strain within the Committee. It was a body that had been required to absorb and reconcile a mass of conflicting politics and ideas. Status of Women Canada was the original author of the Committee, but it was also structurally marginal to many of its early deliberations, and it was unable to execute any of the Committee's recommendations except by proxy. Tension resulted, but much of it was quite deliberately unrecorded. As Maureen O'Neil reflected, the Committee was 'very careful . . . to keep [conflict] out of the minutes because that's too tricky ground'. Yet it was impossible to banish references to conflict from all the papers. It was apparent from the beginning that there were pervasive problems of definition, discourse, approach, and ownership. In one of its first papers, the Committee acknowledged:

[17] For further material on husband-battering, see S. Steinmetz, 'Battered Husband Syndrome', *Victimology*, 1977, Vol. 2, No. 3. D. Gaquin, 'Spouse Abuse—Data from the National Crime Survey', *Victimology*, 1978, Vol. 2, No. 3.

[18] Status Report on Interdepartmental Committee on Family Violence, 4 Apr. 1979.

Because of the complex and emotional nature of the issues associated with women battering and because of the extensive amount of information that is already available, there is likely to be some controversy on the question of what study should be undertaken. . . . this Committee has found that many experts believe that enough knowledge is already available on many issues to justify immediate policy action.[19]

It was around such arguments that the Committee's deliberations were to hover, never really to advance further. Throughout the talk and writings of the Interdepartmental Committee may be discovered a disagreement about the character and context of battering. Moreover, the Committee was small initially, containing only eight people, people who had participated in the histories I have described. Its members were to be the guardians and bearers of different positions, embodying in their persons a whole sweep of institutional developments. The clash between ideas was mediated by their representatives. Conflict became personal, revolving around the alleged traits and bearing of individuals. But it is interesting that those traits also tended to condense departmental and political stances. It was as if particular members enacted tableaux vivants or morality plays, celebrating special virtues and special vices. Their characters were established in part by the histories to which they had contributed and in part by the structure of the setting in which they were displayed.

In their first draft list of recommendations, prepared in May 1979, the Committee mapped the different forms which a research study might take Amongst them was a literature review which could lay bare 'unpublished Canadian material relevant to the study; . . . involve "users" in the study; . . . increase communication; and . . . ensure that the researchers are fully acquainted with the policy and operational issues.' It was conjectured that such a review might be regarded as a stalling device by women's organizations. A second proposal envisaged a miscellany of little projects administered by the three departments, projects that would explore the workings of criminal justice and the provision of social services to battered women. However, 'it is possible that there could be some criticism from women's organizations that such studies are only a means by the government to avoid or delay the taking of action on the problem of women battering.' Thirdly, it was suggested that the Committee could establish a Task Force which would consult and deliberate in order to outline problems and recommend policy. Fourthly, the Committee might

[19] National Plan of Action on the Status of Women: Recommendations for the Study of Violence Against Women, Draft 1, 23 May 1979, p. 4.

organize a National Consultation on Women Battering, akin to the Consultation conducted in Washington in 1978,[20] and designed to produce concrete proposals about a range of specific topics. A National Consultation would be extended to all the principal groups and organizations that dealt with battering, its preliminary talks being intended to achieve legitimacy and representativeness. Further the breadth and length of the Consultation would attract the publicity that spurs Governments into action.

The Interdepartmental Committee was to endorse its own last proposal, suggesting that a National Consultation should be organized and that financial support should be extended to a number of minor studies that the Consultation would identify. It seems that the major study was not to be a piece of reflective, academic enquiry. It was intended to be a pre-eminently political instrument. The criteria advanced for its assessment were the satisfaction of a constituency of women's organizations; the accomplishment of manifest legitimacy; visibility; and the pressing of Government.

There was a remarkable accord about these recommendations although, as a Departmental official later observed, 'I'd like to look behind the agreement'. The Senior Advisor, Status of Women, National Health and Welfare, stated, 'the background and purpose are acceptable with minor editorial changes'; the Co-ordinator, Status of Women Canada, remarked, 'I believe the paper sets forth most of the ideas I would like to see go forward from the Committee to the individual deputy ministers'; and the Senior Policy Analyst of the Department of the Solicitor General said, 'I think this is quite an effective presentation. My comments are relatively minor and I agree completely with the recommendations.'

The first phase seemed to have passed efficiently enough. The summer intervened, a new political party took office on 4 June, and uncertainties arose about the survival of the Interdepartmental Committee's mandate and the intentions of the new Conservative Government. A June meeting was postponed until September and the Chairman busied himself by redrafting his recommendations to include all those little insertions which his fellow members had proposed. The new Minister Responsible for the Status of Women sought to proceed energetically with the project on violence to women. In reply, the new Solicitor General announced that recommendations had been prepared and that the Government would

[20] See *Battered Women: Issues of Public Policy*, A Consultation Sponsored by the United States Commission on Civil Rights, Washington, DC, 30–1 Jan. 1978.

be considering them in the near future. After all, the Interdepartmental Committee had been struck under a Government of the Liberal Party:

However, the Committee needs to consult further with relevant women's organizations before these recommendations can be finalized. An ideal opportunity for such consultation will be at the September meeting of the Joint Federal and Provincial Councils on the Status of Women where a Committee representative will discuss their draft recommendations. We therefore expect that a discussion paper on the matter will be finalized by late September and that a Memorandum to Cabinet will be prepared.

In September the Interdepartmental Committee again convened to be told that the Joint Federal and Provincial Councils on the Status of Women had endorsed the recommendation for a National Consultation. And, in fact, the Consultation was in a state of early preparation. Two members of the Committee had drawn up tentative plans outlining possible lists of invitations to federal, provincial, and nongovernmental organizations, a meeting place in the Government Conference Centre in Ottawa, a date, the payment of expenses, and the use of translators and interpreters. It was further agreed to rewrite the recommendations which the Chairman had drafted. The new version 'can serve as the background Discussion Paper for our proposed Cabinet Memorandum'.

The Discussion Paper

At a much earlier stage, in April and May, at the beginning, the committee had taken to exploring the terrain about it. It had obeyed Government's instruction to consult women and women's organizations, groups which were simultaneously clients and sources of authority. There were not actually many bodies with enough expertise and interest to draw them deeply into talks with the Committee. After all, I have observed that violence was not a pressing and general concern of most Canadian women's organizations. It was the preoccupation of a few, and Gene Errington, British Columbia Co-ordinator for the Status of Women and Co-ordinator of the Women's Research Centre in Vancouver, was one of them. It will be recalled that Gene Errington had been co-author of a report on the 1978 Calgary Conference on Women in a Violent Society, a report which was unequivocally feminist. Her argument had concluded that:

In the face of such overwhelming evidence of misogyny, it became very difficult to find a place to begin either to analyse or to work. Using concepts of patriarchy seems to work best; it affirms our conviction that we cannot release women from victimization so long as the patriarchal system continues.[21]

Gene Errington was impeccably feminist. She began to receive the Committee's papers in May 1979. More important, she was to become defined as the private sector expert and representative on matters of battering. In time, she would be quoted as an authority by Cabinet Ministers and before Standing Committees of the House of Commons.[22] Together with Joanie Vance, formerly the National Assister of the National Association of Canadian Sexual Assault Centres, she met with members of the Committee in consultation about 'the types of issues which should be included in the study'. It was reported that 'Status of Women Canada arranged (and paid for) a half-day consultation between representatives of the IDC and two women experts in the field of violence against women. Each woman was chosen for her expertise, one in the area of rape victims, one in family violence.'

Gene Errington was to become quite central to the structure of the Committee's work. She was awarded a six months contract by Status of Women Canada to 'develop further' the background Discussion Paper, and she joined the Committee to take part in its deliberations and promote its enterprise. Her inclusion reflected conventional practice in Ottawa. The staff of the Canadian Advisory Council on the Status of Women were ineligible to serve as consultants or provide advice because 'it was supposed to be a nonpartisan group, it's supposed to be outside'. Some outsider had to be drawn in, a person who had 'political credibility amongst feminists'. As a Departmental official commented:

And, just the way government always has to, they always have to have internal experts to kind of check out the accuracy of what lobby groups are saying, that's one of the things that governments do. So they had to bring in someone who already knew it because so much was happening that they didn't have time to develop their own expertise. They had to bring in someone who already had some.

It was at that point in the autumn of 1979 that the Committee started to become undone. Indeed, a Departmental official commented, 'it had problems even "becoming"'. The incompatible elements of which it was composed began to part from one another. Members asserted that unresolved disputes about the political economy of gender had led to argument. One stated, 'it was whether or not we should be making

[21] J. Ridington and G. Errington, 'Women in a Violent Society', p. 12.

[22] See 'Speech by the Honourable Judy Erola to the Standing Committee of the House of Commons on Health, Welfare and Social Affairs on the matter of Family Violence'.

statements or doing policy papers that focused on the general inequality of women and how wife-battering is a kind of sub-set of that or whether wife-battering was merely a kind of behavioural deviation in some families caused by alcoholism.' And another argued, 'some people wanted to see it in the context of violence against women as a problem and others wanted to see it in the context of family violence.' In a difficult and deeply embedded process, personal and intellectual disputes began to play with one another, merging into one another, and replacing one another as the life of the Committee wore on. It was not always easy to discern whether debates were the form donned by particular individual animosities, or whether the animosities flowed from debates: 'personal dislike always gets interpreted in terms of, "well, we hate [this person's] position" because you can't just admit that you don't like [him or her].' There was a distinct tendency for the members of the Committee to engage in discussion and planning off-stage. As one official recalled, 'it was productive off-scene rather than on-scene.' Factions seemed to form:

I couldn't stand the people. What seemed to happen about that time was that some of the members, there seemed to be a sort of inner cabal, and every time we had a meeting, it looked as though the agenda and the conduct of the meeting had already been run through by some of the members. Those of us who had not been involved in the initial run-through were getting more and more dissatisfied with the situation.

Conflict was to crystallize around papers prepared by Gene Errington and Status of Women Canada, papers that were based on the narrow definition of family violence and the feminist conception of battering. Not all the Interdepartmental Committee's members declared themselves ready to endorse quite radical statements about the nature of violence and the position of women.

The first such document was 'a rough draft of a discussion paper' composed by Gene Errington in early October. Its intention was to give a frame and focus to the work of the Committee as it moved towards the organization of a National Consultation on wife-battering. At the very beginning was a lengthy quotation from a publication of the Canadian Advisory Council on the Status of Women:

Wife battering is a social disease spread by powerlessness and dependence. All women in our society experience a degree of physical, psychological or spiritual violence because our major institutions are based on a power model within which women are generally subordinate. . . . Wife battering can be seen as a prototype of the violence all women experience. The modern nuclear family—the arena for wife battering—embodies, develops and nurtures 'female' and 'male' roles . . .

Battering was thereby set unambiguously within an environment established by feminism: it was a powerful representation of the fate of women under patriarchal control, obtaining its special qualities from the social construction of gender in the family. The document proceeded to review the progress made by the Interdepartmental Committee, noting that it had met four times, consulted with Status of Women Canada and 'selected representatives from other relevant women's organizations', and had endorsed the proposal to found a National Consultation. Battering itself was described as a process which had been largely unrecorded and unanalysed in Canada. Yet it was palpably a major social problem, constituting just under a third of cases of homicide, a substantial reason for many divorces, and an appreciable part of police work. It was held that the institutional reply made by the Canadian government had been less than adequate: law enforcement agencies in particular tending to define battering as a private affair which did not concern them. The battered woman was consequently unsupported and frequently unprotected, her problems either ignored or subjected to attempts at mediation which would bring her back to the man who oppressed her. The problem was exacerbated by the geographical and social isolation of the victimized woman, an isolation which removed her from sources of help.

The document reported some of the actions undertaken by the federal government, referring to the work of the Research Division of the Ministry of the Solicitor General and the training programmes initiated by the Royal Canadian Mounted Police. It alluded also to the lobbying and agitation performed by women's groups outside Government and proposed that the Committee should compile a list of the recommendations which those groups had made. It then reiterated the arguments put forward in the earlier paper of May, advocating the foundation of a National Consultation.

The recorded response to that document was guarded. Health and Welfare Canada reported its unease with the use of the narrow definition of the family and family violence. One representative asserted:

> Although no definition of family violence has been widely accepted; it is generally thought to include in addition to conflicts between spouses or between parents and their children, any acts carried out with intention to cause physical pain or injury between children themselves, between adults and their aged parents, sexual oppression or exploitation, e.g. incest and self-inflicted injury, e.g. suicide.

Another representative offered approval of the paper but suggested that law enforcement and social service agencies had actually embarked on extensive experimentation with new policies and programmes. Moreover, there was some unhappiness with the criticism of mediation work: 'it would seem a retrograde step to suggest that marital violence can be dealt with more effectively in Criminal Court with its attendant publicity.' In short, 'the portrayal of the family service system as ignorant or insensitive to women's social and economic situation is unfortunate and distortion of the relationship of this service sector to the social problem of family violence.'

It is clear that officials came to the Committee with different assumptions and stocks of knowledge about violence and the provision of services to battered women. Perspectives and purposes were shaped by the institutions in which they had arisen. They were not readily transformed into conceptions that were subversive to those originating contexts, being a mirror of practical knowledge, local social structures, and constitutional responsibilities. I have already described the three Departments as the custodians and occupants of areas of established policy. The narrow definition of family violence was not likely to be accepted without reservation, particularly when it challenged the quality and character of the departments and their dependent agencies. Thus Health and Welfare Canada would not move smoothly to a criminalization of social problems. It did not embrace the breaking of families. Neither did it exclude children and the aged parent from family services. There arose a pronounced tension which threatened to unmake the Committee.

That first document was not developed further. It was agreed that a statement by the new Conservative Prime Minister acted as an effective renewal of the Committee's mandate. On 18 October he had stated on the fiftieth anniversary of the Persons Case that his Government was committed to righting the inequalities of women:

> The interdepartmental committee on family violence is working towards national consultation to find solutions to the problem of family violence, of whom the chief victims are women. This committee was begun under the former government and I consider its work to be a priority in coming to grips with the problem of violence against women.[23]

A Cabinet discussion paper being no longer needed, it was held that there were no remaining impediments to the planning of the National Consultation. Thereafter events began to move rapidly and the undocumented, penumbral activities of the Committee started to become less obscure. The fragmentation and disarray of the Committee's social relations revealed themselves in the progressive disintegration of its inter-

[23] The Prime Minister speaking in the House of Commons, 18 Oct. 1979.

nal political structure. The Committee's Chairman had been engaged in tentative talks with the Canadian Advisory Council on the Status of Women about their possible supervision of the Consultation, a supervision which they were not really empowered to undertake, being outside Government and unable to superintend portions of the Government's work. As an Advisory Council official remarked, 'we sort of said we wondered why he was even coming to us, and it was all very bizarre'. The suggestion that the Council be involved was rejected by Status of Women Canada. The Chairman was told:

> I am concerned with what I see as a weakening of the government's mandate on this issue by turning over to the Council our responsibility to prepare specific government policy . . . it is important that we, as the government, carry through our responsibility as outlined in the National Plan of Action. I believe that we are agreed that the time for recommendations is past and that we are primarily committed to action which governments alone can carry out.

There was a proposal that there should be a meeting between Status of Women Canada and the Interdepartmental Committee to review the 'original intent of the IDC' and determine 'the most effective action to take toward a concrete policy'. Within two weeks Status of Women Canada had convened in its own offices a meeting of the Interdepartmental Committee in order to discuss what had taken place at the 'mid-way point' of Gene Errington's contract. It was stressed that the study on family violence 'flows from the National Plan of Action' and that 'my Minister is interested in seeing some concrete action'. The draft agenda of that meeting of 27 November 1979 had as its first item a report on 'Consultation facilities and timing' by an official of Status of Women Canada. Further, the Chairman's detailed plans for the National Consultation were discussed and rejected. It had been suggested originally that the Consultation should be staggered over three phases, the first concentrating on the preparation of formal papers, the second on conferences devoted to the four Consultation topics, and the last on the making of recommendations to the appropriate levels of government 'for "official" reactions'. But that plan was not to be implemented. According to an account prepared for the Assistant Deputy Minister, Programs, by his staff:

> Instead, the decision appears to have been (there is some ambiguity here since no formal decisions were taken) that G. Errington's paper . . . would be polished and then sent to federal and provincial government departments, with a view to slating it on the agenda of the next Federal/Provincial Conference of Ministers

Responsible for Criminal Justice. This represents a major shift in ICFV mandate. Since such a 'Consultation' could have a 'political profile' rather than being research in focus, ______ resigned as chairman of ICFV and M. O'Neil took over position.[24]

From that time, dominion over the Committee passed from the Department of the Solicitor General to Status of Women Canada. It was agreed that 'IDC will be chaired by Status of Women Canada'. In a sense, as an official commented, it may have been passed on 'because it was on its death bed'. The Committee floundered. Its various members failed to discover agreement on projects which would advance policy and understanding in the realm of violence to women. Squabbles broke out about people failing to disclose their departmental plans, about secretiveness and collusion. There were complaints about the duplication of work. By January, one of the representatives of the Department of the Solicitor General observed:

I am increasingly despondent regarding the possibility of all the actors on the committee ever agreeing with one proposal. ... it seems clear that it was the feeling of most of the group that no study was needed at all and that the group should be turned into a lobby group to put pressure on the various departments to spring money for more women's programming, with which decision, none of the ministry's representatives or the representatives from NHW welfare grants were in agreement (we are the only males in the group!!!) Seriously, I question our further participation in this group, given the events of the past month.

In February 1980 the Committee was invited to consider a discussion document drafted by Status of Women. *Some Considerations and Suggestions for Work on the Issue of Wife Battering* argued that a violent family situation injures a woman and her children; that women should be entitled to flee from a violent family; that a woman and her children constituted 'a viable family unit'; that men should not be considered eligible members of a family until they refrain from violence; and that 'wife-battering is a socio-economic problem in its construction, dynamic, and consequences. It is widespread, systematic, and long-term.' Moreover, 'the formation and situation of the family in our society allows and makes acceptable violence occurring within it.' It was argued, by extension, that there must be a questioning of the practice of placing the nuclear family at the centre of policy and law, of the definition of who constitutes a warranted member of a family ('when and under what circumstances is family membership revoked'), and of wider policies towards women. The

[24] Background Information on Mandate of Interdepartmental Committee on Family Violence, 15 Jan. 1980.

exploitative part played by the family led Status of Women Canada to declare that 'we do not recognize "husband-battering" as a socio-economic problem. Society does not enforce his dependence within the family'. The role of the Interdepartmental Committee itself should be to work towards the provision of a theoretical framework for action, the identification of goals, and the formulation of solutions. Its work would be advanced in an 'ongoing consultation with women and women's groups who are working on this issue'. The co-ordination, inspiration, and thrust for these efforts would emanate from Status of Women Canada.

Gene Errington tabled a paper at much the same time, presenting it to a meeting of the Committee on 12 February 1980. 'Research on Wife Battering' echoed and amplified many of the arguments put forward by Status of Women Canada. It proposed that 'projects will be undertaken specifically in the area of wife-battering'. Departments would ensure that 'research should be consonant with the basic assumptions, goals, and strategies adopted by the IDC'.

The two papers were melded together to compose a background paper and an additional section was offered on 'Departmental Activities in Progress'. The Department of the Solicitor General was not listed as a Ministry sponsoring any current activity.[25]

The focus, themes, and omissions of those documents collectively constituted the *casus belli* that broke the Interdepartmental Committee. On 8 February one of the members representing the Department of the Solicitor General wrote:

> I am getting steadily uneasier about the self-conceived mandate of this committee. Originally, this committee was struck to plan the research into family violence mandated to Justice, NHW and ourselves by Cabinet in reponse to the status of women report. The committee increasingly seems to see itself as the coordinator for all programs associated with family violence. Moreover, it smacks increasingly of a lobby, in that the more militant feminists on the committee see themselves in the role of pushing the respective departments in the direction of committing more and more resources in this problem area. This is a very far cry from the original function of this committee and I am wondering how far we want to participate in this kind of activity. . . . I do not see participation in a lobby group as commensurate with my function; I do not see much balance of judgement among a number of members of the committee, and I am aware that ______ and ______ who sit on the committee are uneasy as well.

A little later, he was to write again. His complaints were addressed to the new background paper, and they were twofold. First, he objected

[25] 'Interdepartmental Committee on Family Violence', undated.

to the 'lobbying or, perhaps, even ... "coercive undertone"' of the Committee. To some of its members he observed, the Committee was beginning to seem unwarrantably imperialistic, attempting 'to force priorities upon individual departments'. 'I am sure that our Ministry will decline to be bound by any *restriction* as to how we conduct our research'. Generally, 'I find the extreme feminist tone of this document offensive. I am not prepared to accept that everything feminine is fine and good and everything masculine congenitally wrong. ... I do not share the notion that the crisis centres are the fount of all wisdom.'

His fellow representative from the Department of the Solicitor General also wrote in response to the paper. Noting that the current 'draft ... fails to mention any of ... the projects ... that are in progress of being completed by my Department', he submitted another list of the Ministry's activities. He appealed for 'explicit recognition of the mandates and priorities of individual departments, and not just those of the IDC'. He protested that men were competent to pronounce upon the problems of family violence: argument should 'be revised because it presently creates the impression that the only qualified researchers are women who work in transition houses etc.'. He defended Departmental autonomy: 'it must be clear that the project manager within each Department is the one who is responsible for selecting what studies are to be carried out by his or her Department and who the most qualified and suitable researcher is for each project.'

In short, the usually quiet and neutral reporting of the Committee's affairs had been shattered. That remarkable commotion arose out of the collision of a number of problems. A powerful Interdepartmental Committee devoted to goals flowing from the women's movement had been required to act through large, general departments which shared neither the goals nor the inspiration of that movement. There were almost inevitably quarrels about clients, discourse, responsibilities, territories, and control, quarrels which were to culminate in charges of imperialism and intrusiveness. Status of Women Canada could not act without the departments, and the departments expressed no wish to act in the manner required of them. There was an accompanying challenge to the authority and expertise of Departmental officials to work on matters concerning women. It will be recalled that segments of the women's movement had expressed levelling sentiments, extolling the grounded experiences of women who confronted the problems of women. The Canadian Advisory Council on the Status of Women Consultation on Wife Battering, for example, had recommended that the problem of wife-battering should be redefined by 'increasing women's control':

'Women working on the grass-roots level must be seen as experts and must be involved at the planning and implementation stages in any government-initiated action in the area of wife battering.'[26] Departmental officials tended to interpret that injunction to turn to women and women's organizations as a political definition of the social sources of competence, a definition that excluded men. An acceptance of that injunction could threaten the very legitimacy of the role performed by critical members of the three departments. They felt it necessary to assert that men were competent to interpret the social reality of women. And to compound all those problems, the departments had come to form appreciable ambitions and investments of their own. They were reluctant to relinquish autonomy and subordinate their various tasks to a general programme based upon a narrow conception of the nature of family violence. The champions of the victims of the other little histories protested their independence.

The Department of the Solicitor General was not the only Ministry to voice unhappiness about a perceived invasion of territory. National Health and Welfare also retained its commitment to the broad definition of family violence. One of its officials serving on the Committee reported that the Social Services Division of Health and Welfare Canada 'would attach priority to those areas which reflect several dimensions of the problem of family violence'. On 13 February 1980, and in reply to the background paper, she stated, 'family violence specifically includes abuse of mates, children, parents, elderly and other household members. . . . Rather than focus all of our attention on wife battering, we would anticipate the support of research projects in [other] areas.' Listed were the effects of family violence on the children who witness it, adolescent suicide, attacks on the elderly, the sexual abuse of children, and institutional battering. In effect, Health and Welfare Canada had replied to the ambiguities of the phrase 'family violence' with their own historically situated description. Theirs was not to be the narrow conception. In February 1980, and within a week of one another, two of the three departments had expressed an extraordinary dissent.

The Committee, under the chairmanship of Status of Women Canada, tried to repair some of that damage in March. At a meeting on 21st of that month it was agreed to include a summary of the work done by the Department of the Solicitor General:

> It was further agreed that the background paper be restructured to include in the body of the paper under work plans only those projects that are concerned

[26] *Wife Battering is Everywoman's Issue*, p. 26.

with wife-battering. Other projects related to child abuse, general court programmes, and so on will be included in the appendix. ... Health and Welfare will prepare in the future a policy-oriented paper on Family Violence from the departmental perspective.

A new paper was also drafted. Entitled 'Research on Wife Battering', its opening paragraph read:

Family violence is generally understood to mean repeated assault, to greater or lesser degrees, by one family member against another. It can, and does, include violence against children, the elderly, the handicapped and women. Data demonstrates that in all cases one of the common factors shared by all victims is that they are without socio-economic status, they are financially dependent, oftentimes on the perpetrator of the assault. In violence between spouses, it is generally men who beat women. There appear to be exceptions, but men in abusive situations have the economic option of leaving.

The revised paper proceeded to argue that a good proportion of murder victims are female, and most were killed inside their own families. Other cases of violence do more harm to women than to men. It was in that context, the paper asserted, that the Government had approved a recommendation intended to remedy the 'social phenomenon of wife battering', a recommendation that had sired the Interdepartmental Committee itself. Moreover, the Committee's subsequent consultations with Gene Errington and Joanie Vance had confirmed that, whilst other areas of violence had been generously studied and busily controlled, wife-battering had been allotted a mere $19,380.85. It was clear 'that focus on the global issue of family violence does not result in sufficient attention to the situation of the battered wife'. Therefore, it was concluded, departments should include in their research plans 'specific projects related solely to wife battering' and 'such research should be consonant with the basic assumptions, goals, and strategies adopted by the IDC'.

The new draft appeared to be conciliatory. The official who had been so upset by its predecessor was at first mollified, declaring 'it is far superior to its antecedent. ... I take it from the revised paper that the ICFV sees itself now more as a generator and coordinator of research on the topic. I believe that this role is quite proper and I think this paper is an excellent start to what should be an important project.' But the appearance of conciliation was soon taken to be deceptive. It transpired that the revised paper did not replace the offensive draft but merely acted as its supplement:

It appears that my recent comments ... were founded on an incorrect premise; apparently the paper I commented on was to have been an annex to the main paper ... not a replacement for it. ... I request that you assign another officer to represent this Branch. I feel I can contribute less and less and I think we would be better served by another officer taking it on, preferably a woman, with whom the ICFV would be more comfortable.

The proposal that a woman should replace the official was not well received by his female colleagues. One commented, 'here's where "our" men tried to manipulate *their* women ... I felt this was a naive move.' No woman was found as a substitute. The other representative of the Department was also affronted by the draft. As the man who had sponsored victimization research, and research on domestic crisis intervention in particular, he dismissed the assertion that only $19,380.85 had been devoted to work on wife-battering. Such a claim would be possible only if an indefensible system of classification were employed: 'the logic ... seems to have been to exclude all projects that were not dealing *solely* with wife battering; e.g., to exclude projects if *both* child abuse *and* wife battering were examined.' That principle of classification effectively prevented the inclusion of all the work that had been done on crisis intervention: 'I find this logic unacceptable, and I fear that to try to justify further research on wife battering on this basis will be seen by ... our Departments as a deliberate attempt to distort the government's previous involvement in the area.' Further, the official expressed continuing concern about what he conceived to be the imperialism of the Interdepartmental Committee: 'it is stated that IDC support for projects in this area by Departments is needed as an additional step in project approval. This would give a "veto" role to the IDC which is different from the "coordinating" function which I believe had been previously agreed to.' The defence of departmental autonomy required a renewed examination of the Committee's 'overall role and mandate'.

That expression of suspicion and discontent effectively ended the Department's participation in the affairs of the Committee. At a meeting held in the Ministry on 28 March 1980 it was determined that the Policy Branch should send one person to act for the Department as a whole, other officials attending when necessary. The contraction and change of membership conveyed a number of signals: they were a token of the Department's wariness 'until the role of this committee is clarified'; they pointed to a decrease in support for the work of the Committee; they indicated that the Committee was now defined as a body that was busying itself with policy and not with research, a definition conveyed by the earlier resignation of the Committee's first Chairman; and significantly, they gave warning of the Department's intention to shunt violence against women into an area where the Solicitor General exercised a greater authority: 'violence against women will likely require a policy paper for the next meeting of ministers.' It will be recalled that the Committee had agreed in late November 1979 to present its recommendations to the next Federal–Provincial Conference of Ministers Responsible for Criminal Justice. In effect, acting on that decision freed the Department to take independent charge of a problem that had become mired.

Thus, in the spring of 1980, the Interdepartmental Committee lost almost all its practical consequence for the Department. The Solicitor General did proceed to compile police statistics on the incidence of wife-battering. A Departmental representative attended a few more meetings. But the Committee came to assume only a spectral presence in the affairs of the Department. It lingered on for a long while, but its meetings became less and less regular, unmonitored by the officials of the Solicitor General. Indeed, those officials were unsure when the Committee died or whether it had died at all. The last reported meeting of what Maureen O'Neil had called 'that interminable committee that could not and would not come to grips with the issues' was on 21 May 1981. The National Consultation was abandoned. There was no National Task Force. And the major study of violence against women never took place. Yet all that talk about wife-battering was to have very real political consequence in two areas, and I shall discuss them before the end of the chapter.

One group on the Committee concluded that others had been simply reluctant to move things forward. Problems had been created by those who did not share a woman's understanding for a woman's plight. The eventual intercession of Status of Women Canada and the assumption of the Committee's chair by women were but efforts to give life to an otherwise sluggish body. By contrast, officials from the Department of the Solicitor General took the urgency and scale of the Committee's task to be a major encroachment on their territory and liberties. Their authority as experts, their sovereignty and their past accomplishments all seem to have been slighted. In all this process of imputation, the one group could do little more than confirm the suspicions of the other, its actions eliciting responses which amplified mistrust and increased conflict. It was a conversation of gestures that became so divisive that the Committee could no longer remain intact.

A former policy analyst of the Department of the Solicitor General reflected, 'they were getting absolutely nowhere. They had this mandate but they were getting nowhere. They were totally spinning their wheels and finally ... they gave up.' What remained was a powerful Cabinet directive to act on the problem of violence to women, the need to produce a visible and reassuring response to that directive, the unsated ambitions of a number of people keenly interested in victims and assaulted women, and a mistrust between departments. What happened next may be understood as a limited answer to that new combination of events.

There was fission: the history of the social problem of family violence divided to take two distinct paths. In one direction, the politics of battering sheered away from the Interdepartmental Committee, becoming the subject of a new little history that took family violence before a new body, the Standing Committee on Health, Welfare, and Social Affairs. As an explicit reaction to Linda MacLeod's *Wife-Battering in Canada*, the Hon. J. Robert Howie, Member of Parliament for York–Sudbury, moved a successful private member's motion that the Standing Committee should examine 'intrafamily violence and in particular ... address the issue of battered wives and dependents'.[27] Beginning its work in early 1981 and reporting in May 1982, the Committee reshuffled some of the elements and actors of the other little histories that I have recounted. It took evidence from the people I have introduced and who were prominent in the politics of policing, domestic crisis intervention, and battering. It was briefed by the Departments of Justice, Health and Welfare Canada and the Solicitor General, by Status of Women Canada, and by the Royal Canadian Mounted Police. It produced a report which achieved some celebrity because a number of Members of Parliament greeted its theme with deriding laughter at a time when CBC reporters were present. There was a scandal to which the Government replied with a show of alacrity. The politics of battering thereby became prominent, acquiring its own trajectory and independence. For those who were nursing the emergent victims initiative, those politics were timely, salient, and relevant. Battering became part of an environment for action, folding back on the policies developing about the victims of crime. Its passage through Parliament was to be cited in talk about the funding of projects by the Department of the Solicitor General. In one instance, an Associate Regional Consultant argued for an application for money, 'the case for funding is especially compelling in light of the present recommendations in front of the Canadian Parliament for assistance and support for programmes which relate to battered women.' When the Canadian Association of Chiefs of Police mounted its Police Week in 1982 around the theme of 'we are all victims of crime', evidence presented to the Standing Committee was quoted in speeches across Canada. The Report

[27] Private Members' Motions, House of Commons Debates, 13 Feb. 1981.

itself touched on the affairs of the Solicitor General in one place only, recommending that 'members of the R.C.M.P. who act as provincial or territorial police should receive training which is specifically related to answering calls in cases of wife battering'.[28] When it was presented in May 1982, it received the endorsement of the Prime Minister.[29] By that time, however, the focused politics of battering began to pass outside the sphere covered by this book.

In another direction and in another guise, battering took a separate course, merging with the developing victims initiative. It was to be reabsorbed by the departments that had once constituted the Interdepartmental Committee. In June 1980 the Minister Responsible for the Status of Women was still pressing the departments to proceed with their work on the Committee: 'my officials in Status of Women Canada advise me that, whereas the interdepartmental committee has been a bit slow in getting off the ground, work is now progressing.' But there was no progress and no movement. It will be recalled that the Ministry of the Solicitor General had stationed a kind of policy watchman on the Interdepartmental Committee, abandoning full participation. Instead, the Ministry's Policy Branch had begun to shepherd the problem of the incomplete initiative on women into its own domain. Together with the Department of Justice, it was in the very first stages of advocating a paper on 'wife assault and the criminal justice system', a paper which finessed the major problems of the Interdepartmental Committee. It was preparing what proved to be a kind of liminal phase of the victims initiative. During that transitional period, it could be argued that the Government's emphasis on the need to attend to women was being busily obeyed, questions about the now barren Interdepartmental Committee could be given a reply, and the problems of the warring departments could be eased. The transitional character of the proposal to issue a paper may be read in its wording. The Departments of Justice and the Solicitor General agreed:

> For officials from the Ministry of the Solicitor General in collaboration with Justice and in close consultation with the ICFV, to produce a policy paper on battered wives and the CJS to be presented at the next meeting of Ministers Responsible for Criminal Justice. This policy initiative should be viewed as a logical extension of [ICFV's] effort. Given that the paper will focus on the criminal justice sector rather than the broader range of interests of the ICFV, the lead role should be assumed by the Solicitor General and Justice, in con-

[28] *Report on Violence in the Family: Wife Battering*, Standing Committee on Health, Welfare and Social Affairs, House of Commons Canada, May 1982, p. 19.

[29] See *House of Commons Debates*, 1 June 1982.

sultation with the ICFV. Until recently, relatively little attention was given to the CJS to meeting the needs of crime victims. The victim has often been described as the 'forgotten person' because the focus of the CJS was directed primarily at the offender. During the past decade, however, there has been a rapid expansion ... in programs, services, and research relating to the victims of crime. Hence, there would also appear to be a need to develop a more comprehensive policy paper dealing with other kinds of victims as well. Although the present policy paper will focus on battered wives, it could be viewed as an initial step in the eventual development of a national strategy on the CJS and victims.

There were delays. In June it was declared that 'unfortunately Joint Justice has been preoccupied with more pressing issues and has been unable to review the proposal to date'. The paper on wife-battering and the criminal justice system appears never to have been written. Instead, talk about the paper became the vehicle by which women were ferried into the emerging victims initiative. Women became one of a number of eligible groups who merited concern. The feminists' foreboding about the loss and displacement of categories was partially confirmed. Women were to fall within a general class of people called 'victims' although they were to remain a separate class. Some of those who had sought to champion the battered women were mollified by that separation. One claimed, for instance, 'wife battering has been singled out within the general "rubric". I don't know that this defeat was as large as [all that].' But other women did not give their full support to the victims initiative. One remarked, 'I'm not persuaded that the initiative is going to do anything for family violence. It's a big trendy routine.'

The Departments of Justice and the Solicitor General had detached women away from their anchorage in the Interdepartmental Committee. Thus free, women brought with them a dowry of an important charter and a useful history which could be inserted into any new proposal. When a report was prepared for a most important meeting of the Joint Justice Committee in April 1981, the work of the Interdepartmental Committee was noted; the involvement of the federal government in funding rape crisis centres and transition houses was mentioned; and reference was made to pressures from 'women's organizations in Canada ... which have actively lobbied for changes in legislation'. It was predicted that 'federal government efforts in the area of family violence and violence against women may give rise to public demands for a more all encompassing effort with respect to victims generally'. The work done for and by women had the unintended consequence of providing a rhetorical foundation for a wider policy on the victims of crime. It became a stage in a career that was unanticipated and not particularly desired, women being translated into an object within an alien frame. To be sure, some recompense and security were purchased by the appointment of Linda MacLeod as a policy analyst in the Ministry , an analyst with a special interest in battered women. The internal frontiers of the initiative were to be policed, Linda MacLeod acting, as Maureen O'Neil of Status of Women Canada phrased it, 'as a limited guarantee that these issues will be dealt with in an appropriate fashion'.

Battering had clearly become one component amongst many, joining the provincial demands expressed by Gordon Walker, the pooled demands of the Canadian delegation to the Sixth United Nations Congress, work performed on the victimization survey, and the example set by the United States. In short, women had been enveloped but their envelopment also offered a kind of strength. They could borrow from the rhetorical materials supplied by the other little histories. They had at last become the object of unconditional attention from the social circle built around victims. The price of that attention was the loss of a number of the distinctive political and practical objectives sought by the women's movement. The battered woman forfeited some of her special urgency. The reward was that such a loss enabled the departments to respond to women in their own way. The Departments of Justice and the Solicitor General began to organize a response that was shaped by their very particular assumptions, practices, and mandates. They transformed the battered woman into one who could be managed, a workable material that was suited to their situated activities. So transformed, much could be done. As a policy analyst remarked, 'women's concerns were put in a context which fitted with departmental mandates so that these concerns could receive a greater attention than they [otherwise] might [have done].'

Those who had promoted the separate interests of women were obliged to accede to what had happened. After all, they lacked the machinery to produce and execute policy and there would not be many other opportunities for action. Maureen O'Neil of Status of Women Canada remarked:

> None of this was ever said explicitly [but] since they had this other victimization thing under way, they said 'well, we can include [battering] within that', and after a year and a half of doing nothing through that Committee essentially, it seemed to me better to say, 'okay, let's make the most of that initiative and let's not just exhaust ourselves.'

The Interdepartmental Committee seems to have ended with a whimper, petering out unobtrusively and quietly. One of its members recollected, 'they wrote a letter ... to Trudeau and said that there would not be a major report: "After looking at all the research that had been done and that has been proposed by the various departments, we are satisfied etc. etc." I went to one meeting of the inderdepartmental committee which was sort of their final meeting and at that point it was decided that there would be no report, they would simply write a letter. ... I know the letter was drafted because I saw the draft but I don't know whether it was actually sent. I presume it was.'

The Speech from the Throne

All the events which I have described were to weave an environment of constraints and justifications for action. From time to time, the busy work and talk of officials would result in the creation of an artefact made significant by the agreed conventions of policy and politics in Ottawa. In turn, that artefact would be recognized and treated as a constraint upon action. Indeed, that was to be its function. Policy commitments, public declarations, publications, and projects were quite deliberately evolved to shape and direct the future course of bureaucratic activity. In this manner, Ottawa organizations 'enact' their own environment: 'they have a major hand in creating the realities which they then view as "facts" to which they must accommodate.'[30] It is this dialectical process that is at the very heart of Canadian policy-making. Officials energetically translate their behaviour into objective and external facts which compel them. Their doing so mirrors a number of concerns: constitutionally and practically they cannot embark on major undertakings without a political sanction that must be won or imposed; they must have, by extension, 'good reasons' for everything they do; and they must erect frameworks of explanation which can co-ordinate, guide, and account for co-operative work within and between departments. Of course, as I have argued, officials are not at liberty to will their own world. They are monitored, regulated, and accountable. That is why they require accounts. Moreover, their alienated artefacts almost invariably become the preoccupation and sometimes the property of others, passing outside effective control to acquire an independent life which folds back on action in unexpected ways. Yet it remains that policy is regarded as artful statecraft, the business of manufacturing an approved logic and history for desired decisions.

Pre-eminent amongst those artefacts in Canada is the Speech from the

[30] K. Weick, *The Social Psychology of Organizing*, p. 1.

Throne. That Speech announces that the recurrent planning cycle of the federal government has begun again. It draws into itself major themes from the process of deliberation and consultation that elapsed in the previous year, projecting them forward as 'a broad direction from Cabinet ... and overall policy priorities' for the year that is to come. The Speech from the Throne distils the decisions of Social Policy Committees, special meetings of Cabinet, Priorities and Planning Committee reviews, Strategic Overviews, and diverse soundings to produce a conspicuous and publicized introduction to the political year. As its most manifest commitment, the Speech establishes broad obligations for the Government which is its author. It sets the tests by which the Government has permitted itself to be judged.

The Speech is intensely and explicitly political in design, intended by Government and ministers to advertise and promote their concerns. Its rhetorical purposes are transparent, supplying a broad base for the construction of policies and programmes. However, the Department of the Solicitor General itself tends to derive only a tangential benefit from that base, almost invariably being forced to structure its proposals so that they can find some roots in the statements and priorities deposited by others. The Department is not taken to be one of the principal Ministries in Ottawa. Indeed, it is junior to the Department of Justice within its own sphere. It is represented on the Priorities and Planning Committee by the Chairman of the Social Policy Committee.[31] During the formative years of the initiative, that Chairman was the Minister of Justice. And crime tends to touch the Speech from the Throne almost never at all. It had affected neither during the entire span that preceded the formal announcement of the victims initiative. Projects formulated inside the Department must be organized on a platform prepared by others, taking their shape from the problems of women, the elderly, the handicapped, natives, and the young. The Speech from the Throne can thereby propel the policies of the Department of the Solicitor General, but it also gives them an odd guise on occasion.

There is something of a conventional order to the Canadian Throne Speech: it typically contains two parts, one emphasizing three or four central themes, the other constituting what concerned officials call a 'grab-bag of items' which address a miscellany of lesser political problems. It is that grab-bag which attends to federal-provincial relations, the representations of prominent lobbies, and the interests of political parties.

[31] See R. Van Loon, 'Current Policy and Expenditure and Policy Management System in Ottawa', *Canadian Public Administration*, Summer 1981, Vol. 24, No. 2.

Inserted in it are the approved conclusions to all the consultations conducted by the Privy Council Office in the months before April. On 14 April 1980 the Speech from the Throne included a section called *Putting People First*, a section which discussed the effects of inflation, the problem of interest rates, pensions, employment programmes, affirmative action, and, finally, violence against women. It was stated:

The serious problem of violence against women will be addressed along with other amendments to the Criminal Code, and efforts will be made in concert with the provincial and territorial governments to improve health and social services for women who are victims of violence.

It was an overt Government promise that could be remembered in the writing of proposals to aid the victims of crime. The Ministry of State for Social Development recognized it as a Government commitment which demanded a response in the Strategic Overviews. It was given prominence in the proposals that were put to the Joint Justice Committee. In sum, it was taken to be a federal commitment which required a visible answer. As one who drafted the early versions of some of the papers noted, if there were a failure to meet the needs of victims, there might be 'a loss of faith in the government's promise [in Speech from Throne] and elsewhere to take action in the family violence area'. The Speech was to form the last important segment of the rhetorical environment assembled by policy-makers in their development of an initiative.

Quite characteristically, the history of that allusion to women in Speech is dispersed across Ottawa and many have claimed a share in its authorship. At the time, it seemed that there was no inevitability about the making of the reference. Indeed, those who were involved in filling the grab-bag argued that its presence was a little arbitrary. The search for origins is accordingly complicated. Officials assert that the Department of the Solicitor General itself tended to lack what they described as the 'political oomph' to get victims included in the Speech, although one of the Department's staff maintained that the reference flowed from a talk he had had in a bus with an official of Status of Women Canada. It appears that there were many such talks and incidents feeding into the Speech. Violence against women was on the 'shopping list' submitted by Health and Welfare Canada. It was mentioned by a number of officials of Status of Women Canada in their discussions with staff of the Privy Council Office. Maureen O'Neil recalled:

Before the Throne Speech was drafted, I sent out a note to the Prime Minister's Office saying that they might be interested knowing that there's never been a mention of women in any Throne Speeches as far back as I could check and here was their big chance.

That chance was improved by a felicitous series of events and policies. After all, the Interdepartmental Committee was sitting, supported by declarations from Liberal and Conservative Governments. Its members had become alert to battering, and they relayed their interest when soundings took place. Violence against women had been described as a federal priority in *Towards Equality for Women* and the succession of statements which followed it. Perhaps the most important of those statements was Linda MacLeod's *Wife-Battering in Canada* which had been published with great approval and much publicity.[32] The book had been isssued by an organization with strong links in Ottawa and palpable authority. It objectified wife-battering. It established the 'magical figure'[33] that one in ten Canadian women were battered, a figure that was to be cited repeatedly in documents and speeches on family violence. It was received with acclaim.[34] Linda MacLeod herself remembered:

> While I was at the Advisory Council, I really had a very strong experience of what an amazing tool publicity is and how incredibly important it was ... [I stated that one in ten women in Canada were battered.] I was amazed and it really raised my level of consciousness to see how people really want something memorable. They latch on to that and suddenly I would see that statistic was being quoted everywhere.

Maureen O'Neil of Status of Women Canada talked of how 'Linda's paper [had] been in the papers all that time and [had] received a lot of comments and without it ... that little pitch would not have been picked out'. *Wife-Battering in Canada* seemed to give great luminosity to a social problem at just the time when the Throne Speech was being drafted.

What was probably as important was the structure of social relations in Ottawa. The Speech from the Throne is drafted by one person, being 'a very centralised document'. The writing of such a document is based upon soundings, reflecting, as an official put it, 'who has whose ear'.

[32] See 'To Love, Honour and Batter', *Liaison*, March 1980, Vol. 6, No. 3. A fairly random selection of allusions to that study includes: *News Release: National Clearinghouse on Family Violence* Health and Welfare Canada, 22 Jan. 1982; *Wife-Battering is Everywoman's Issue*; evidence submitted to the Federal–Provincial Task Force on Justice for Victims by *Justice for Assaulted Women*; D. Wood, 'Women as Victims'; L. Vaughan-Evans *et al.*, 'Women as Victims', debates in the House of Commons on 13 Feb. 1981 and 1 June 1982; and on and on.

[33] For discussions of similar magic figures in the instance of the politics of alcoholism, see C. Wiener, *The Politics of Alcoholism*, p. 195. In the instance of drunken driving, see J. Gusfield, *The Culture of Public Problems*, University of Chicago Press, Chicago, 1981.

[34] See for example, the *Vancouver Sun*, 24 Jan. 1980, the *Globe and Mail*, 24 Jan. 1980.

In 1980 the draftsman of the Speech was the brother of the Minister Responsible for the Status of Women. Commenting upon the process, an official of the Department of the Solicitor General remarked, 'sometimes it's not any more complicated than that'.

Conclusion

The natural history of women, victims, and federal policy lacks a neat beginning, middle, and end. It has not yet ended. It has tended to meander, establishing an array of structures, committees, and changes in law. It has brought about changes in police policy, led to the founding of a National Clearinghouse on Family Violence, and increased funding for transition houses. It has transformed the symbolic maps employed by politicians and policy-makers in Ottawa, giving significance and presence to the raped and battered woman. As the Director of Policy at the Department of the Solicitor General observed, 'concerns with specific victims ... the battered wife, rape victims, were very much because of the feminist movement and they can take total credit for the sensitisation of the criminal justice system ...'. Having constructed a new entity in the world of policy however, feminist organizations and their staff had difficulty in clothing it in its own supportive programmes and services. Their projects seemed sometimes to falter. The Interdepartmental Committee on Family Violence itself became mired. Those organizations lacked the specific agencies, people, charters, and resources to proceed independently. In the words of a policy analyst at the Department of the Solicitor General, 'they're powerless in fact'. Being dependent, they moved to those departments which were empowered to act. Their movement led to a confrontation with radically different schemes of relevance, priorities, and practices.

An attempt to introduce change was read as an encroachment on territories whose frontiers and landscapes had already received ample definition. Within the departments, projects and plans were in the making, beginning to congeal into a future victims initiative. The language that was being deployed talked of 'victims' and 'crime', not 'women' and patriarchy. It was those plans and that language which set a framework for the reception of women. The affinity between proposals for the battered wife and emerging plans for the victim was so great, and the independence of the departments was so well enforced, that efforts to direct policy were resisted. Those efforts were doomed because Status of Women Canada lacked the power and the authority to implement them. Instead, they were transformed into a stage of a joint venture between the two departments that held sway in the Canadian federal criminal justice system. In a sense, the protagonists of women had attempted to employ the Departments of Justice and the Solicitor General, only to be employed in their turn. Their ideas, proposals, and energy were mediated and redeveloped into something quite foreign by powerful Ministries. As a policy analyst of the Department of the Solicitor General reflected:

It was the mandate of the Committee to look at violence against women, not to look at victims. To a large extent it was the departments like Sol. Gen. that were in error. The Committee had been brought together for something and they weren't willing to play the game. ... Health and Welfare already had a large investment in terms of numbers of employees and grants and all these things to child abuse. So it was much handier for them to deal with that. They weren't willing to act in good faith. What they were saying is that we've already got things going on, now we don't want to create extra work of headaches for ourselves, so we'll capitalise on what we've already got going on and redefine it.

The process of confrontation and mediation was complicated by its anchorage in a political context that tended to amplify and extend significance. On occasion, relations were not governed simply by bureaucratic etiquette and organizational piety. On one side, discourse was tinged at the margins with the politics of feminism that read battering as an illustration of patriarchical oppression. Thus officials of Status of Women Canada, some erstwhile members of the Committee, could write:

Women are victimized by individuals who perceive them to be at the 'bottom of the hierarchy' and see the use of force to be a viable means of ensuring the status quo. Women are not only victims of crime, but as well they are victims of an age-old power struggle. Women's victimization belongs in the same category as systemic discrimination and there are a number of reasons why this type of victimization can be viewed as separate from the politics of victims in general. These reasons are: women and men are taught attitudes about women and their role in the society from an early age; women's place in the hierarchical structure of the family, the workplace and society in general is very low; the legal medical and religious institutions persist in tacitly or overtly reinforcing the above two points.[35]

In that interpretative setting, an apparent belittling of the victimization of women, a denial of the distinctiveness of battering, and an attempt to clump women with other victims could be read as an illustration and instance of victimization. The thwarting of Status of Women Canada was open to decoding as another example of the subordination

[35] L. Vaughan-Evans *et al.*, 'Women as Victims', p. 21.

of women at large. The doings of the Committee could then reverberate through the wider politics of an 'age-old power struggle'. They were impregnated with meaning.

On the other side, some representatives of the departments replied by rejecting the trappings and insignia of feminism. Documents were to be criticized for their language and their assumption of a feminist nomenclature. 'I would like it noted that it was not *my* idea to use the word (?) "spokespersons". Yecchhh!' Arguments were inspected for their 'real intentions', significance being overlaid. Appearances were treated as deceptive. Plots were suspected. There was little trust and no validated agreement. When major areas of policy were in the custody of one or two people in a department, that wariness could have quite profound consequences. For a long while, there were but one or two gatekeepers to the realm of victims inside the Department. Their response to the political frame of battering was critical to the admission of women as a separate object of policy.

Yet women were needed. They could not be shed. Indeed, there was sympathy enough to prevent their complete immersion in the Justice for Victims of Crime Initiative. They were needed because criminal justice policy does not receive the attention which Government allots to women. In an area of austerity, when nothing could readily be done for the first time, Cabinet endorsement of policies for women was most valuable. In a number of areas that endorsement fed into the politics and policies of victims. In policing, for instance, the very existence of the Interdepartmental Committee and the Standing Committee, the presence of their mandates, affected the development of policy. As an officer working at the Royal Canadian Mounted Police Crime Prevention Centre remarked:

> It comes back to my shop which gives me the avenue of putting it in as an interrelated issue with the victims initiative. It gives me an avenue to the senior command. And because I've been looking after that area as almost a major responsibility of mine, it lets me build both simultaneously. And it lets the Crime Prevention Centre have a little more say in the way things are going.

Women were needed because there was no other loud voice outside Government. They formed the public and the clients which the nascent victims initiative lacked. Without them there would have been a silence. Reference to that public and use of that Cabinet endorsement established a debt. As Maureen O'Neil of Status of Women Canada argued, 'their victimisation project could ... ride on the back of that Throne Speech commitment by saying this was related. Which is why, in the bureaucratic sense, they owe us something over here.'

Women then became a distinct group within the larger mass of victims. They were not simply merged to lose their gender and their special demands. Their separateness was signified by specific proposals inside the greater whole. It was claimed as a right when discussions took place in the Social Policy Committee, the approval of Status of Women Canada being a precursor to any action. And it was symbolized pictorially in the representations which the Department manufactured to broadcast its intentions. Part of the movement towards a policy was a publicization of the Department's interest in victims. A slide show, later a film, was prepared. And deliberate emphasis was placed on women as victims with peculiar needs. The dramaturgy of victims was quite explicitly intended to include women. In response to an early draft of the slide show's script, one official stated:

> ... I would revamp the section 'Who are the Victims' significantly. ... Your presentation of the facts seems to negate any need for concern with high-risk victims including elderly victims, victims who are native people, victims who are handicapped, battered wives and victims of child abuse. It may be important to mention that even if these groups of victims do not represent the majority of victims, they certainly do merit serious attention because of the severity and trauma of their victimization as a result of their economic and/or physical vulnerability and frequent isolation.

Those high risk victims tend to be people who are most fearful about crime. They were also the target groups distinguished by Government for general policy development. It was an eminently political catalogue, reflecting enforceable claims established by Government. It was a mirror of the Cabinet's own priorities, and it could be cited usefully in any submissions made back to Cabinet. The claims had not been powerful enough to compel a distinct interdepartmental initiative on battering. The politics of battering had to take a different route through the Standing Committee of the House of Commons. Within the bureaucratic world of Ottawa, the claims could only confer some structure and lend some direction to a wider initiative managed by Departments other than Status of Women Canada. Status of Women Canada had to recognize *force majeure*. Its Co-ordinator was to tell the Assistant Deputy Solicitor General, Policy Branch:

> I want to reiterate my support for your initiative in the area of victim assistance. You are, however, aware that my preference would have been to have victims of family violence, especially battered women, singled out for particular attention.[36]

[36] Letter dated 15 June 1981.

X. Priorizing the Options

> The victims area was produced out of discrete strands which got enough coherence and mass to move. It was just the Nth. drop which made the bucket overflow. And it was the opportunity too. (Official, Causes and Prevention)

Introduction

The victims survey, domestic crisis intervention, the Gordon Walker speech of October 1979, the Workshop of March 1980, the report of the delegation to the Sixth United Nations Congress, the aborted Interdepartmental Committee on Family Violence, and the Speech from the Throne were to become some of the principal elements of the foundations of the Justice for Victims of Crime Initiative. They formed a miscellany of facts and processes, created by different people with different objectives, experiences, and schemes of interpretation. The eventual combination of all those elements into one transcending enterprise had not been foreseen or even desired by everyone who had participated in their evolution. It could have been otherwise. Indeed, some people regarded the initiative as a confounding of their own plans and ambitions. Others took it to be a grander venture than any they had contemplated. Most of the time, they could have had little appreciation of how the little histories would grow and coalesce. For instance, it will be recalled that Irvin Waller had resigned in the belief that his efforts had been barren. And others had supervised portions of the process for rather limited periods, retiring before their effects could become evident. In this sense, there was a running uncertainty about the character of the initiative's separate components. There was an even greater uncertainty about the future of those components, about whether they would combine, in what manner and with what form.

It was a while before the victims area was marked off, boundaries were established, a name was given, and connections were made between its facts and activities. When structure did emerge in the early 1980s, victims seemed to attain a kind of tangible presence in the world of those who were involved with them. As they attained a presence, so it became possible to give them further order and solidity. Talk permitted action and action permitted talk.

But it took some time before that state was accomplished. During much of the 1970s victims lacked political form and coherence. They were dispersed with many names under many different authorities. The conferring of order was a lengthy process and it was not uneventful. The definition and classification of victims gave them very particular histories, identities, and visions of the future. It was a matter of some consequence whether battered women were called crime victims or whether child abuse was treated as a criminal offence. Moreover, description plotted out mandates, responsibilities, powers, barriers and opportunities. It was to be an eminently political process. It is not remarkable that people occasionally resisted certain links and championed their own. The fate of the Interdepartmental Committee on Family Violence must be read as the outcome of a battle about the real meaning of wife battering. Again, there had been little enough in common between the Victim-Offender Reconciliation Programs of the Ontario Ministry of Correctional Services and the transition houses which would sever women from the men who oppressed them.[1]

In 1981 Geoffrey Norquay, asked by the Ministry of the Solicitor General to survey the provision of services to Canadian victims, asserted that there were broad descriptive tensions which fragmented the structure of the phenomenon:

> The groups involved in the field still have a long way to go in sorting out what their respective roles are and how they are going to relate to others in the field. And the reason for that is that many of the roles of the groups involved in the field are almost by definition roles that are antagonistic at the worst, or at least fraught with real difficulties such as the relationship between rape crisis—sexual assault movement and Crown Prosecutors, the relationship between rape crisis, transition homes and the police. People are saying, 'let's not go too fast on this. Let's figure out how we might relate to some of these groups. Let us have some time to see if victim interests can be articulated in a fashion that will encompass all groups'. Not that many people are convinced that that's possible.

The materials that were eventually to be amassed into an initiative developed at uneven rates, revealing possibilities at different times and in different ways. That process was complex. So diffuse an activity as crime touches on numerous people and settings, achieving a kaleidoscopic significance. By extension, the victims of crime themselves lack a single identity and fixed political import. They are too varied and unstable to be aggregated without difficulty. They cannot be easily assimilated into

[1] See *Recommendations of the Canadian Advisory Council on the Status of Women: Women and Family Violence*, Canadian Advisory Council on the Status of Women, Ottawa, 1980, p. 4.

one stream of political activity. Links between the proposals that affect them also tended to reflect all that variation and flux. It was not a simple matter to reach agreement about the character and needs of crime victims. Of one committee's deliberations, a policy analyst observed: 'victims became a bit of a buzz word and in some respects ... it lacks cohesion.... Everybody's writing papers all over the Hell's half-acre. A lot of them are contradictory in terms of assumptions and everything else.' In the early days, coherence had sometimes to be imposed or negotiated with effort.

So it was that the little histories were often segregated and private. It took time to bring them together. At first, people involved with child abuse, rape crisis centres, domestic crisis intervention, burglary victims, epidemiology, and transition houses did not always recognize a common purpose, share a joint stock of ideas, or even employ the same language. Thus Norquay argued of the search which he had conducted with Richard Weiler:

> I guess what we found is that in little pockets all over the country, police departments, John Howard Societies, Crown Prosecutors, individually began to become aware of the victims' issue and, in some areas of the provinces, in some areas of the country, they moved very quickly to develop things.... There were little pockets ... all over the country but still not at all a real appreciation that this was part of something larger, and, I think, also very little appreciation of the different pieces among the players or among the individuals involved. Not a lot of understanding about the different roles that other groups could play and have been playing. So, it was really a system that was beginning to develop with very little common awareness.

The sheer passage of time was to become significant in another sense. Some of the acceptability of proposals stems from their familiarity and apparent maturity. Ideas without history lack gravity. The relatively slow development of a coherent interest in victims made it possible for a number of events to accumulate across the country, and their accumulation provided the environment and past which argument required. In a period when the making of policy was beginning to be restricted by financial parsimony, a new federal initiative could not seem to be so very new at all. As Wildavsky observed of the budgetary process in Washington, 'since appropriations for new programs are particularly difficult to obtain, agencies are motivated to claim that what they want to do is just what they have been doing. The funds requested are said to be part of the agency's base, its continuing program, rather than some new way to spend money.'[2] Proposals for a federal initiative cannot be

[2] A. Wildavsky, *The Politics of the Budgetary Process*, pp. 108–9.

presented as if they were an abrupt or inconsistent departure from what had gone before. On the contrary, they must be built on established trends. Accordingly, one of those who drafted the policy proposals on victims reflected:

> We happen to be right now in an era of restraint.... There's been a number of official Government statements that new programmes will not be started, that we will not increase the size of the public service, that foolish spending will not take place. That kind of stuff. In building the argument, that kind of restraint mentality has to be taken into account. So that the general feeling is, in a time of restraint, you don't say you're launching a new initiative. You say you are simply escalating, strengthening, responding in some way to public pressure, regarding something that's already been going on and has a long and solid history.

The manufacture of a long and solid history requires an appropriate logic and suitable materials. Meaning can be imposed on the past, but there must be an adequate past with which to work.

The possibility of naming, amalgamating, and synthesizing all the diverse constituents of the initiative emerged only when understanding had grown and a network of relationships had developed. People were to be transformed by the histories which they had nursed, acquiring commitments, authority, and expertise in the process. They learned about victims and politics during those preliminary years of the late 1970s. And their learning became exposed and accessible when it was unveiled by the social processes that constitute the routine work of the Ministry.

The Workshops and the First Strategic Overview of 1980

I have argued that many claimed that there was no inevitability about the initiative. It was coaxed into life by certain practices inside the Department, and its shape bore their mark. In particular, the central column of Workshops and special meetings devoted to the Strategic Overview gave definition and illumination where none had existed before. Without those meetings, the knowledge and preoccupations of officials would have remained relatively private, locked into their own small spheres of action. It was those meetings that transformed private matters into public property.

The emergence of victims as objects in common ownership had to be prompted. Staff are often too absorbed, busy, and specialized to enquire eagerly into all the minute doings of their colleagues. Such curiosity could be read as impolite and critical, and a number of officials are known to be proprietorial about their patches of territory. The division of labour has established boundaries and areas of independence within which staff are assumed to be competent. It seems to be accepted that people acquire skills and knowledge that place them outside detailed control. That expertise and its autonomy are parts of the professionalism that distinguish members of the Secretariat. One person will dwell on victims, another on crime prevention, and a third on public attitudes. There may be common terrain but there will also be personal stores of theoretical and practical experience which cannot be judged by outsiders. Those who worked on victims need never have shared their competence with others unless some special problem or event invited disclosure. And others may not have interested themselves in that competence. What was required was a novel perspective that could throw the conventional pattern of relations between people, work, and problems into suspense. The Department's meetings sometimes provided just such a perspective, inviting their participants to review what they had done and what they intended to do in the future. They were capable of triggering an awareness of common pursuits.

Those meetings had another function. They constituted the monitoring, evaluating, and ratifying procees of the Ministry. Without them, ideas could never be translated into effective policy proposals. It was during the preparations and deliberations that attended them that victims attained a political substance.

What must be recognized is that the nascent policies on victims were not alone. My focus has obscured all the other copious work of the Ministry. In the years while the initiative was forming, officials were also preoccupied with juvenile justice, cannabis, 'attitudes to criminal justice issues', 'sentence effectiveness', 'community based sentencing alternatives', 'community support', diversion, the social costs of the criminal justice system, white collar crime, crime prevention through environmental design, armed robbery, the role of the private sector and criminal justice, the forecasting of crime, the effectiveness of police patrol work, the effectiveness of criminal investigation, the use of deadly force, police management styles, conditional release from penitentiaries, correctional effectiveness, prison violence, the effects of imprisonment, the determinants of the penitentiary population, the problems of native inmates, the review of the Criminal Code, and the special problems of female prisoners.[3]

[3] 'Criminal Justice—General Issues', Programs Branch Workshop, 8 Dec. 1980.

Victims were but one item on that long catalogue and it was an item in competition with others. The Department is not large. It is not one of the most important in Ottawa. Much of its budget is committed to recurrent expenditure. It can hope only to obtain limited numbers of 'person years' and resources to allot to new ventures. And it would lose authority and credibility if it attempted to advance all or most of its candidates for policy development simultaneously. One of the cardinal functions of the Secretariat is to appraise and select projects for advancement. So important is that ranking process that it has been awarded its own title in Ottawa, 'priorising the issues'. Unless victims were 'priorised', the earlier labours of their advocates would have been largely in vain. Once priorized, they would be adopted and reconstructed by the Policy Branch to become part of the traffic in political negotiations. Quite literally, those meetings and that adoption are policy work.

Punctuating the Ministry's timetable, affording regular opportunities to interpret activity, were the Branch, Secretariat, and Ministry Workshops. In the period before the implementation of the Policy and Expenditure Management System especially, those workshops were the principal arena in which reviews and proposals were discussed, projects were formed, and areas of common knowledge were developed.

In 1976, for instance, it was reported that the Ministry Workshop 'can be viewed as the most important step in the overall Ministry planning and evaluation process. Under the Chairmanship of the Solicitor General, the Senior Executive of the Ministry meets to evaluate the past performance of the Ministry and to plan the direction it should take in the future.' The Deputy Solicitor General, Assistant Deputy Ministers, and heads of agencies would report on the activities which had developed within their areas of responsibility. Some attempt would be made to assess the relative importance of the various issues which confronted the Department. A strategy would be developed. In short, the Ministry Workshops were devoted to a consideration of 'a) what is being done; b) how effective it is; c) what else should be done to resolve the major problems and issues [facing the Ministry] and to obtain the Minister's priorities and direction'.[4]

Branch and Secretariat Workshops, the Research and Statistics Strategy Committee, and other allied bodies also met from time to time to survey the work that had been done in their own spheres. They were to compose a series of interlocking stages which gave development and coherence to activity. Reference would be made backwards and forwards

[4] Letter from Deputy Solicitor General to heads of agencies, 24 May 1978.

between different meetings, knitting the history of the Department into a moving whole. As chronological markers, they allowed people to bestow structure on the progress and character of events. They enforced reflection and imposed a timetable on work. They demanded that people give a public accounting. They juxtaposed processes, letting them form contexts for one another. And, above all, they were regarded as appropriate occasions for the presentation of new candidates for policy.

Work on victims was reported periodically in those meetings. It appeared as part of the Peace and Security Package, and it was recorded from year to year thereafter. In 1976, for instance, it was noted that 'important surveys are also being developed on public attitudes and victimization'. The following year, it was stated 'the main research thrusts will be in the areas of law enforcement/preventive policing, victimization, public attitudes . . .'. And so it went on. Victims were a routine entry on the long lists which the Secretariats composed in its reports to itself.

The very first Strategic Overview of April 1980 was to stem from just such an accounting exercise. It will be recalled that Strategic Overviews were intended to transform emerging policy into precise proposals for submission to the Ministry of State for Social Development and the departments of the Social Envelope. They were supposed to force Ministries to examine themselves and announce what they were planning to do in the year ahead. In actuality, that first Overview was a mock exercise, a rehearsal for the Policy and Expenditure Management System which was to begin the following year.[5] It certainly was not taken to be an authoritative policy document, and its drafting was somewhat tentative and unsure. Irvin Waller described it as a 'trial run', the Ministry of the Solicitor General being one of the few departments in Ottawa to treat it seriously. And a senior Policy official stated:

> At that time, neither the Ministry of State for Social Development nor the departments of the Social Envelope knew very much about the new system. The first Overview was not done on a Ministry basis but on a Secretariat basis. That is to say, there were four 'strategic overviews' for the Ministry. We tried to co-ordinate them but with little success. It was done very much in a hurry and was not treated as a serious priority setting exercise nor did we think it would influence resource allocation in any substantial way. Rather, it was treated as something we had to do to keep the central agencies happy.

The 1980 Overview was composed in a series of little meetings held by the Divisions. Research directors were instructed to prepare short

[5] Indeed, the proclamation establishing the Ministry of State for Social Development was not issued until 19 June 1980. See Privy Council Office; P.C. 1980–1692.

papers 'to match our present policies to those agreed by the Research Strategy Committee and SPAC in February 1979'.[6] Indeed, those preparatory reports were based on the 'Program/Activity Structure' that had already been agreed in 1979, a few new items being added. One such item was battering. In February 1980 it was reported that 'a new area of interest' had emerged since the beginning of 1979: that area was family violence.

The Divisional Overviews were to anchor priorities in the problems and environment of the Canadian criminal justice system, the Ministry's declared policies, and trends in government, 'such as restraint'.[7] Stated Government policies did stamp themselves on the Overviews. Thus crime prevention was reclassified as a contribution to 'cost effectiveness'.

The result of all that stocktaking activity was the compilation of a list of priorities and programmes. Perhaps for the very first time, there was a looking-glass which reflected the extent and diversity of the Department's involvement with victims. It was assembled in the spring of 1980, during the aftermath of the October 1979 Conference of Ministers and the March 1980 Workshop on Services to Victims, at a time when the word 'victims' was beginning to order events and phenomena in Ottawa. In the spring of 1980, too, Irvin Waller was still in a position to give direction to the writing of reports. The sheer number of allusions to victims was impressive. In the Research Division's Overview, for instance, victims appeared as 'victimization studies' within the larger category of *Crime Prevention,* as 'victimization studies' within the category of *Improving Data Base of Criminal Justice System,* and independently as 'Concerns for Victims of Crime', That last category was itself composed of 'victimization studies, evaluation of projects on family violence, evaluation of victim/witness assistance programs, and impact of crime on victims and society'.[8]

All the lesser Overviews were forwarded for merger inside the larger Departmental Overview, the process being co-ordinated by the Policy Branch. The actual final drafting was undertaken by two Policy officials, and it was conducted hurriedly and without great confidence. Those officials came to recognize the importance of work on victims to the Research Division. Its bulk was inescapable. But they could not give exact form and detail to the significance which that work might assume. One of the officials was later to report:

> The Secretariat's planning process in April ... resulted in the identification of a wide range of priority initiatives on which we believed work should be done....

[6] Memo from Director General, Research and Statistics, on *Strategic Overview for Research Strategy Meeting in Early March,* 20 Feb. 1980.

[7] Ibid.

[8] Research Division: An Overview, 12 Mar. 1980.

In submitting our initiatives . . . things became clear . . . a number of . . . initiatives had not been sufficiently developed to allow us to inform MSSD of the likely content and timing of concrete proposals requiring Cabinet decision . . . Victims . . . would be included on that list. . . .[9]

The other official remarked:

Victims were only mentioned as a concern without any indication as to what the Ministry ought to be doing as a result. At that time I personally was at the stage where I was convinced (probably by Irvin) that victims was an area of importance worth considering. What I had not worked out and neither had the Ministry was what we should be doing in that area.

Thus the 1980 Overview gave prominence to the mass of work that the Research Division was doing with victims. But its draftsmen could do little more than transform that mass into a somewhat vague and general statement of interest in the possibility of developing victims into an object of policy. The Overview itself grouped initiatives and proposals into loose regions, and victims were to appear in two of the areas thus mapped. They were introduced once as a strategy for promoting 'Restraint and Cost Effectiveness in the Criminal Justice System', it being argued that assistance to victims might remedy the defects of an ineffective system of law enforcement. Assistance to victims was also described as a means of achieving 'A More Just and Humane Criminal Justice System'. It was suggested that the Department could join with the Ministry of Justice to consider an extension of crime compensation, restitution orders, and training programmes for the police. Special services could be engineered for the elderly, handicapped, children, women, and the victims of family violence.[10] Both proposals clearly melded work in progress with the concerns of the Department of Justice and the declared policy interests of Government: crime and victims had not been defined a priority of the Government, but restraint in expenditure and attention to the elderly, handicapped, women, children, and victims of battering *had* been flagged.

That first Overview was an exercise that received no great answering response from the other departments or from the central agencies. There were no invitations to submit policy proposals on victims. It was not regarded as a major planning document. The Overview's principal audience was to be the Department that had devised it and formed its subject-matter. But it did provide an important chart of the Ministry's work and concerns, pointing to new terrain that was in the making. And

[9] 'Secretariat Workshop', letter of 19 Sept. 1980.

[10] Strategic Overview, Ministry of the Solicitor General: Secretariat, 24 Apr. 1980.

it represented a most fertile source of arguments for later use. After all, the Overview was a report which the Ministry had made to itself about its own vision of future policy. Moreover, it was a report that was admitted to be incomplete, in need of further attention and development. As an unfinished document, it could become a bridging stage in the emerging history of the Department, leading to other phases and greater definition.

On 19 September 1980 one of the two officials who had drafted the April Strategic Overview prepared a paper for a Secretariat Workshop to be held in October: 'it was felt timely for Secretariat officers to get together for a free-wheeling yet focussed set of discussions on the principal issues we face and the approach we ought to take to them'.[11] It was the new Policy and Expenditure Management System that had jolted the Secretariat into assessing itself. Inducing a sense of timeliness was the apprehension that the Ministry's policy environment and future were changing rapidly and fatefully. Revolutionary new structures and timetables were about to be imposed on the Department. Looming ahead was a series of meetings to draft the critical Strategic Overview of 1981; there was an awareness that a number of initiatives and programmes were well advanced, demanding an appraisal that would reveal what 'new directions should be pursued with respect to these general issues'; and there was a conviction that the Secretariat's first essay at an Overview had not been a success. That 1980 Overview had pointed to a range of possible initiatives, but it had been so imprecise that it lacked practical utility. It was certainly ominous that the Ministry had not been able to get any of its proposals included in the final Cabinet workplan, seeming 'to indicate that we have not developed to date a sufficiently concrete set of proposals to put flesh on the bones of such initiatives as victims, criminal justice costs, police accountability ... '. It was to repair those omissions that the Secretariat Workshop had been summoned:

> The principal focus of the workshop is to take those initiatives and develop them in a clear and coordinated way by considering not so much what we *are* doing now—but what we *ought* to be doing to give real meaning to the mandate of the Secretariat ... the aim is to apply our minds to the agenda in [a] spirit of constructive and action-oriented 'brainstorming' in such a way as to emerge from the workshop with a fairly well-developed package of strategies for major new Secretariat initiatives ... A series of papers on 'towards a federal strategy on victims of crime' (for example) could be the goal to aim for.[12]

[11] 'Secretariat Workshop', 19 Sept. 1980.
[12] Ibid.

Victims were one of the eleven topics forwarded for discussion at the Workshop, it being noted that 'various sectors of the Criminal Justice Community ... have been placing increased emphasis on victims of crime'.[13] Introducing the problem and serving as its framework was a paper written by the official who had entered the Secretariat to work on the survey and who had later become the first Chairman of the Interdepartmental Committee on Family Violence. He was the Departmental expert on victims. 'Towards a Victim Justice System for Canada' talked of the 'growing recognition of the need to assist victims', the problems of special groups (the elderly, the poor, and battered wives), the example set by the Law Enforcement Assistance Administration in America, and the diversity of victims services in Canada. Victims assistance programmes were represented as quite consonant with the objectives of the criminal justice system in general and with the objectives of the Ministry in particular. After all, it was argued, criminal justice agencies should devote themselves to justice, and justice embraces the protection of the victim as 'the ultimate client of the CJS'. Victims services were also in accord with other Departmental goals: they would minimize the impact of crime and promote a more humane system of justice; they would increase the 'effectiveness' of the criminal justice system by encouraging public co-operation; they would advance 'community participation' and increase the use of volunteers. The paper alluded to the Secretariat's history of involvement with victims, referring to conferences, 'research & demonstration, policy initiatives re family violence'. It suggested that victims fell within the special territory of the Department: 'because of our work to date and of our mandate and organizational capacity, we are particularly suited for more concerted action, especially re. CJS (police)'. It cited the 'emerging interest of provinces, police (RCMP), ... MRCJ (Walker) ... especially family violence'. It proposed that all these emerging themes could be married in a series of recommendations about the initiation of police-based victim assistance programmes '*but* within a context of the need for more comprehensive programs'. The role of the Secretariat itself would be to urge policy development in Ministerial speeches and in meetings with the provinces and other federal departments; give support to agencies such as the Royal Canadian Mounted Police; and provide a catalyst through experimental projects, conferences, and clearing-houses.

In short, and for the very first time, the Secretariat was offered a vision of victims as a bounded social problem with a distinct and organized

[13] 'Criminal Justice System', undated, unattributed.

history. Further, that social problem was represented as a Departmental responsibility, ownership flowing from the Department's supervision of the Royal Canadian Mounted Police. And a future was bestowed. The official had woven all the little fragments of work on victims into a tenuous unity which could be inspected by outsiders. Victims had become objectified, available for discussion and development. The structure which they received at that time was to remain with them, forming the basic pattern of the problem.

That paper and the discussions that succeeded it were a turning-point. Quite literally, victims were placed on the Ministry's agenda. The official himself recalled:

> If one looks back in twenty years' time and says 'how do you think the victim thing developed here'—if it does develop—'how did it develop?' I think the thing that will stand out will be the Secretariat Workshop ... because that was a five page paper that I prepared with the Policy Branch. What was significant was ... the discussions that went along with it and maybe people who changed their minds from seeing victims as a somewhat non-related activity, not really related to the basic mandate of the Ministry, to be stressed to them that it's not just liberal humanism but it's also dollars and cents and efficiency and policy.

In time, to be sure, that paper and the Workshop would recede in importance, becoming dwarfed by all the happenings that ensued afterwards. They became just two more incidents in a long chain that culminated in the production of Government policy. Indeed, an official who arrived to work on the initiative.rather later tended to endow them with a modest influence: 'by the time I came [the paper] was simply one piece of the puzzle ... although the transition it allowed to transfer expertise from programs to policy branch was probably significant'. Yet 1980 remains the year in which victims acquired a rudimentary order and recognition. In February an inventory of projects had documented the scale of the Ministry's connections with different facets of victims. That scale had been awarded an effective but obscure significance. It was as if something was happening but no one could say quite what it was. It was certainly enough to make victims problematic enough to receive further scrutiny. It gave tham a place on the Ministry's agendas. Moreover, that discovery of the undefined promise of victims came at a time when the Department was beginning to rehearse its replies to the new Policy and Expenditure Management System. There was a call for new initiatives just as victims emerged as an object of interest. It was in that fashion that the Secretariat Workshop was most timely. The Workshop was supposed to give order to all that inarticulate and immanent content. Talk about initiatives coincided with talk about victims, allowing the one to flow into the other and encouraging speculation about an initiative on victims themselves.

Organization itself was entrusted to the official who had written the earlier five-page paper. He shaped the initiative that was to come. Not least significant was the fact that it was he who drafted the *Summary* of the Workshop's Proceedings. The Report recited:

> There was general agreement that increased attention to victims was justified not only for humanitarian reasons (i.e. more equitable justice), but also because better Criminal Justice System Policies and programs to assist victims may increase the cost-effectiveness of C.J.S. Furthermore, as was verified by the Regional Consultants, the provinces and the police community generally recognize this area as a high priority concern and one where federal assistance would be welcomed. Although it was concluded that this was an area where the Secretariat could become more active (especially in the development and promotion of police-based victim assistance policies and programs), it was not possible to decide what the extent of this involvement should be . . . As a result, it was decided that a detailed paper on this issue would be prepared for the Minister for his decision in the coming weeks.[14]

It was at this point that the still plastic and inarticulate problem of victims began to become the concern of the Policy Branch. Research and practical programmes were to undergo metamorphosis into another kind of entity, a policy proposal. The writing of that 'detailed paper' was entrusted to a team drawn from the Research Division, the Consultation Centre, and the Policy Branch. The Research Division representative was the man who had carried victims before the Secretariat, the Department's expert. It was, as he remarked, the first time that Research and Policy were involved in working together to 'make that pitch'. The implication of the Policy Branch was clearly momentous. It was capable of transforming the private institutional concerns of the Department, a few organizations, and a number of agencies into the committed interest of the government of Canada. It might secure considerable sums of money for victims' services. It was likely to give victims a prominence and visibility that had hitherto eluded them. In that process, they passed through a transitional phase which illuminated in miniature some of the otherwise intractable questions which may be raised about the relations between research and policy.

[14] *Secretariat Workshop: Summary*, 6/7 Oct. 1980, p. 3.

The Movement from Research to Policy

Ottawa officials tend to regard policies as phenomena that receive their organization from a particular kind of argument. That argument, in turn, is assembled for presentation in critical stages of a formal process of political selection and endorsement. Policy is void without that argument and the appearances which it manufactures. As a senior policy official observed of the progress of the victims initiative:

> It was basically Irvin who had a sense that this was a burning issue and something ought to be done ... But it wasn't a policy. It was a *concern*: 'victims are getting the short end of the stick, that isn't right, there are problems here'. They were raising an issue. But it wasn't the proper articulation of what that meant and what we ought to do. It occurred *here*. It didn't happen in Programs Branch. And it became a policy of the Ministry because of the work that was done here.

It is in this sense that policy is other than policy until it is given an approved argument. As one who drafted policy papers stated, 'the way Cabinet documents are set up, they have a rigid format. You don't just sort of write one. You have to follow a format.' A Memorandum to Cabinet, for instance, will proceed in orderly fashion from stage to stage, beginning with a statement of objectives, a summary of the decisions required, to an analysis of the problem and a review of the political, social, and economic considerations that bear upon it. As options are charted, so their claimed advantages and disadvantages are listed. The repercussions of the whole upon federal–provincial relations, international obligations, and the like are mapped, the politics of the proposal discussed, and recommendations made. Even in the sphere of crime and criminal justice, that progression of arguments offers little scope for deviation. There is almost no marshalling of evidence from scholarly research. There is no use of footnotes and references. Quotations are not included. On the contrary, a case is made out of a logic of organizational good sense and political obligation. What is paramount is a listing of commitments made, policies declared, and ventures started. Argument is peppered with references to projects, institutions, and processes that Ottawa politicians themselves know and respect. A memorandum thus takes some of its shape from a carefully described landscape of events and phenomena that have acquired an intense local significance.

Research has little place in that kind of argument. It is cosmopolitan and not local. It talks of connections, not of commitments. It tends to a specificity of proposal and finding that is tangential to the general framework of a political argument. It is therefore typically laid aside. What research does appear to accomplish is the accrediting of particular people to speak and write about particular issues. A training in research certifies that one is competent to talk. But there is little interest in the detailed history of the research that has been done to produce and sustain an argument. That is taken on trust. As a policy analyst reflected, 'the actual sort of in-depth research questions just wouldn't come up. They trust that a researcher will know his stuff and that he will be producing credible work, but really nobody cares to have him explain that to them.' In that manner, research work can identify and advance problems. It can put them forward as candidates for translation into policy. Once their candidature has been accepted, however, their research standing will be displaced by the political criteria of constituencies, debts, conflicts, mandates, and demands. Thus one of the policy analysts who began the drafting of the victims proposals was to remark, 'researchers insist on empirical purity and detail but you don't need all that because Cabinet Ministers aren't interested'. At another time, she asserted, 'research ought to be a policy support branch but there's got to be one body for handling all the process'.

There are thus differences in the styles and contents of the discourse which emanates from research and policy officials. As a problem advances into the policy area, it loses its anchorage in documented, minute, and specific studies. It becomes part of a web of politics which is mediated by other concerns. Thus a senior official of the Policy Branch argued of his colleagues in the Programs Branch, 'for some reason, I think it's by dint of their professional formation, all that ever comes out ... is plans for evaluations and studies. Politicians aren't interested in that! ... We talked victims *ad nauseam* until we said, well, here are the specific things that we can be doing.' Part of the transition then becomes the emancipation of a problem from the concrete and the speculative and its reconstruction as a series of precise proposals for action.

As a problem advances, so practical control is relinquished as one group releases and another assumes command over the presentation and direction of argument. There is often a problem in timing and administering the transfer of power. As a senior Policy official argued, 'we always have a little bit of difficulty in sort of passing on the baton'. After all, research preoccupations do not end abruptly when a problem somehow matures into the material for a policy proposal. Problems remain unanswered. The disciplines and methods of evaluation do not become suddenly irrelevant when a paper is prepared for political discussion. Above all, officials tend to form a sense of property in issues. They have given birth to those ideas which others are about to seize as their own. The ideas may well be objects of profound attachment, constituting the materials for a conception of self. Research officials may then retain a lingering proprietorial interest in the phenomena which they have nurtured. It is an interest which is especially pronounced when they have been at the animating core of a problem that was perhaps a matter of indifference to others for some while. There is a propensity for officials to renounce claims more slowly than the pace at which their projects move forward. As a policy analyst remarked of the social circle that centred on victims inside the Programs Branch, 'they couldn't give it up ... they wanted to do it on their own'. Some members of that Branch sought to preserve a stake in 'their' problem, being reluctant to see it deformed by the demands of policy and politics. One observed in 1981, 'let's not get carried away with this as a cult. The fact is that there's only about two needs assessment surveys of victims in Canada. They're poorly done. Very limited information is known about the needs of victims.' He concluded that the initiative had to proceed gingerly and on a sure foundation provided by research.

Victims themselves were a special problem, coming to the Policy Branch from the Programs Branch and representing an instance of 'bottom-up' policy-making. In that even more immediate sense, they were held to be the property of research staff. As a policy analyst argued, 'they seem to have wanted to be in the thick of it right from the start'. The outcome was a brief period in which the relations between abstract processes were enacted in a most concrete fashion by the officials who portrayed them. The ambiguities and opacities of the link between research and policy were illustrated by a time of uncertainty in which observers associated them with an apparent personal contest between senior staff. There was a debate about ownership and control which was depicted as individual rivalry. It was quite widely argued that the personal careers of people were propelled by the initiatives which they steered. Thus one senior official remarked, 'with [an official in the Policy Branch], if you're playing the game of being the key star, you've got consciously or unconsciously to make sure that the high priority issue is one that you're the star of and not someone else. In terms of the Machievellian games, he could compete with [a Programs Branch official] on victims.' More commonly, that contest was described as the jousting of bucks at play. Again, there was some little difficulty about the chairmanship of the Ad Hoc Justice for Victims of Crime Committee, a Committee that was to emerge out of the growing prominence of victims within the Department. The Policy Branch declared its intention to convene and chair the Committee. A senior official in the Programs Branch protested, 'why policy? It is clear at this stage it is a Programs matter.'

These minor tensions in the period of transition underscore one interesting point: research and policy do not exist together as the ideal forms of a Platonic universe. They are created by particular people in particular settings. The movement from one to the other is a social transaction involving losses and gains of independence, power, and authority. It involves claims to territory and possessions as well as debates about the character of practical action. More important, perhaps, it entails the making and unmaking of reputations and personal identities. One who has spent years of a life working on victims, being cited and consulted, will begin to consider that victims are a significant portion of his self. It is not easy to recede.

In 1980 the drafting of that paper by the team of three appointed by the October Workshop reflected some of those liminal problems. It was to go through version after version, circling repeatedly around problems of specificity, scope, and evidence. Instead of appearing on the coming weeks as the Workshop Summary had promised, it was still undergoing revision in March 1981. The policy official on the team maintained that papers should be 'very short, general and simple'. By contrast, she stated that her colleagues sought a meticulous statement which was tantamount to a workplan. Admonitions passed between members of the team. Simple precepts were exchanged. People were told 'this is how you've got to say how the money's going to be spent and how much you need.' It was all 'a doggone hassle'.

The very first attempts at a proposal were slim accounts of the Ministry's involvement with services to victims and descriptions of its possible futures. It was held that a 'victim justice system' could minimize the cost of crime and enhance the efficiency and humanity of the criminal justice system. It could advance in one of three directions: 'continue status quo', 'select and focus on one area of victim services', and 'assume national leadership role in comprehensive victim services'. The first would entail the Secretariat preserving an interest in victims without noise or visible expansion. There would be 'continuing consultations with governmental and non-governmental agencies (federal and provincial) in justice and social service area'; there would be a follow-up to the March 1980 Workshop on Services to Crime Victims; pursuit of the 'family violence initiative', the victimization survey and 'some additional research and demonstration projects'. The second option envisaged an expansion of police-based victim services in response to requests from the Royal Canadian Mounted Police. Such a commitment would be calculated to give the Department a 'high profile in terms of general public visibility'. It would tie 'together the needs of the victim as well as the needs of a criminal justice agency—the police'. The final and most ambitious course would commit the Ministry to the adoption of victims as 'a top priority', giving great prominence to the problem and its management by the Department. 'A national leadership role' would require the Ministry to furnish a coherent policy framework for victims and prepare extensive and intensive consultations and proposals about compensations, legislative reform, and services.

There was evident wariness injected into those first essays at plotting the development of a victim justice system. There was some dissonance of style between the approaches adopted by the representatives of research and policy. After all, the two people had come to the paper with very different aspirations, motives, and stocks of knowledge. The biography of the Programs Branch official had become fused with the social problem of victims. He had actually helped to nurse that problem into existence and he had long since settled any doubts that may once have worried him. By contrast, the past of the policy analyst was not so fused: she had had only a marginal acquaintance with the politics of victims, it had not been entirely happy, and her attachments were correspondingly slight. She had recently been appointed to the dying and rancorous Interdepartmental Committee on Family Violence, but the Committee did not meet during her period of nominal membership. She had had a brief connection with that ambiguous and contested group of victims, abused children. It was a group that straddled the boundaries of National Health and Welfare, provincial ministries, private sector organizations, and the police. Her experience had made her cautious, leading her to observe in a note about a proposed Parliamentary Committee on the sexual abuse of children:

> The subject is complicated and one in which there are overlapping federal and provincial responsibilities. . . . Discussion of intrafamilial violence will necessarily overlap with justice concerns—legislation, policy, administration of justice.

Questions of mandate, responsibility, and territory were to be applied freshly to the newly emergent problem of crime victims. It was written in one of the earliest, undated drafts that co-ordination with 'federal–provincial, governmental and non-governmental agencies . . . could involve friction if we are seen interfering in another's jurisdiction'. More pointedly, another draft observed that officials 'have to be careful of "conflict of interest". Primary focus of the Ministry is on the offender—catching and treating him. Should not devote time, energy, and resources at the expense of the offender and his humane treatment, his rights, etc.' Above all, the Department was 'lacking direction on whether victim services is an issue that this Secretariat should be involved'. One early, obvious, and interesting consequence of incorporating the Policy Branch was the introduction of doubt and a doubter. The representative of Policy Branch began as an unbeliever. She had not been a full participant in any of the little histories and she shared none of their aspirations. Instead, she portrayed the Department's work in its least catholic guise: it was devoted to the police, penitentiaries, parole, and pardons. Victims then became an anomaly. The terrain surrounding the Ministry was described as hazardous and inhospitable, possibly fatal to any projected initiative.

Matters were therefore somewhat indecisive in the autumn of 1980. The Programs Branch had become so generously and diffusely intertwined with the problems of victims that it seemed that a critical mass had been formed. Speculation arose about what might happen. Indeed, one of the tasks of the October Workshop had been to discover meaning in what had been done. In the event, it was declared that victims appeared to be taking form as a social problem but the Ministry's role demanded elucidation. Other demands were being levelled at precisely the same time. The Department was about to ready itself for the 1981 Strategic Overview, a process which forced the Secretariat to announce what areas of policy it intended to develop. Victims seemed to be a prime candidate for promotion, and there were many in the Programs Branch who wished to champion them. But it was undecided what should be done. The transition from research to policy was accompanied by awkwardness, encountering problems of ownership and organization. Complicating everything was the supposition voiced by a strategically situated policy analyst that a victims initiative might become burdened with all the problems that bedevil Canada's inner politics. Doubts were aired about whether the Department was even entitled to enter a region inhabited by crime victims. Those doubts were to be allayed in time, but the progress of the proposals was very slow, lacking confidence, unanimity, and cohesion.

Drafting was performed gingerly and laboriously. Preparations were protracted. Delay and reflection, in their turn, gave time enough for other processes and phenomena to bear upon the sluggish initiative. Drafting occurred when some of the other little histories began to attain a semblance of resolution. Its tardiness allowed them to acquire that show of definition which made them evident and useful. They could gradually be fed into the paper's somewhat torpid flow of argument, changing, speeding, and strengthening it as they were poured in. Tardiness also made possible the growth of that critical play between personal experience, engrossment, activity, and the organization of a social problem that supplies motives and sympathies. The official from the Policy Branch had been involved with the paper from the late summer of 1980 when the October Workshop was first mooted. Indeed, she was sent to the Sixth Annual Meeting of the National Organization for Victim Assistance in Portland, Oregon, instead of attending the Workshop. It was one of the 'best conferences' that she had known. She 'got educated'. The American victims movement thereby began the transformation of yet another key figure in the Canadian initiative, dispelling some doubts and coaxing enthusiasm.

During the six months that the team of three remained together, a number of the little histories passed through decisive crises. First, it became clear that the promised 'family violence initiative' was now unlikely ever to take place. Two of the team were also members of the moribund Interdepartmental Committee and were familiar with its decline. It was becoming ever more spectral, ceasing to present an alternative vehicle for aid to victims, but its mandate remained and had come to the two federal criminal justice Ministries. There could be no talk of the separate initiative on family violence that the earlier drafts had contemplated. Secondly, on 6 November, the reconvened Canadian delegation to the Sixth United Nations Congress recommended that work on victims should become a Government priority. Thirdly, on 22 December, an announcement was made about the funding of the Calgary Victims Service Unit. Fourthly, in January 1981, a new benchmark was fixed when the Department of the Solicitor General agreed to provide some of the money for the Seventh Annual Conference of the National Organization for Victim Assistance which was to meet in October. That Conference was to be employed teleologically, summoning responsive activity from the Ministry throughout the year that preceded it. It was presented as an imminent public manifestation of the Department's interest in victims and the possible platform for the announcement of new policy initiatives. In this manner, facts supplied themselves in abundance, offering themselves as the materials of a policy submission.

Those several months allowed the paper's authors to achieve a greater intimacy with the social circles that centred on victims in North America. Interest, competence, and knowledge grew, reworking perspectives. What had once been described as a marginal and probably inappropriate task began to receive support. And those months accomplished one other matter. As I have argued, a team had been established to concentrate upon one activity. It was bent on identifying and securing materials for a particular argument. Materials began to appear in abundance towards the end of 1980 and at the beginning of 1981. Indeed, members of the team were themselves busy producing them. One had been the midwife of the Calgary Victim Services Unit, the Departmental decision to fund the NOVA Conference, and the assumption of the mandate to respond to the problem of family violence. So it was that the paper's later versions, written in March 1981, were endowed with a solidity and coherence that had formerly been lacking. It could be argued:

> Growing concern expressed by media, community groups, and some provincial government people (Ontario) that the needs of victims are not being addressed in contrast to the resources and concern focused on offenders. Special interest groups have focused on particular victim groups—abused children, sexually-exploited children, battered wives, the elderly, rape victims.... In sum, the efforts of the above groups have highlighted for the public the fact that the dimensions of these problems are far greater than previously known, and the social costs of allowing these injustices to continue are unacceptable. If problems ignored: growing dissatisfaction of public with the operations of the criminal justice system, reduced support and co-operation with, reduced dollars for criminal justice system expenditure as system not seen to be effective.

Elsewhere on the paper a note was made about '6th UN follow-up'. It may be seen that the social problem of victims had acquired a history, an environment, a structure, and an urgency which made it the plausible subject of an initiative. The actual plans for the initiative were not very different from those put forward in October. They hinged on the legislation of victims' rights, the increased funding of programmes, and improved police training. But they had now acquired an air of gravity and political consequence.

There was one other Workshop which gave impetus and support to what was now a rapidly unfolding initiative. In December 1980, as part of its newly-developed planning system, the Programs Branch met to agree upon 'Branch-wide priorities which could then be used in relation to the development of strategies for Program Forecast, Model Projects and Program Teams'.[15]

The Branch had refurbished the process by which it assessed itself and predicted its own future. Instead of the somewhat promiscuous list of the year before, the Workshop attempted to priorize the Branch's options. At an earlier meeting of Branch Managers, held on 27 November, it was proposed that the work of priorizing could pass through two stages: 'sub-program areas' would be identified and then ranked by a range of

[15] Memo from A/Assistant Deputy Minister, Programs Branch, *Programs Branch Workshop*, 2 Dec 1980.

criteria. Amongst the tests to be applied were the relationship of an area to the Minister's concerns, its connections with the mandate and responsibilities of the Department, its 'potential impact', and 'public concerns'. What emerged in December was an impressive accord about ranking. Some forty-eight areas had been distinguished and voted upon. Victims fell into three: family violence, victim assistance, and victimization, the last being amplified as 'evaluation of victimization statistics'. Of the eleven areas described as 'high priority' by the Research Division, two were family violence and victim assistance. Those same two were amongst the nine high priority areas distinguished by the Consultation Centre. And that was not very surprising. After all, there were a number of current projects centring on victims, the Canadian delegation to the United Nations had just reported, the Interdepartmental Committee on Family Violence was still sitting, and a policy paper was under construction. Victims had attained a local prominence. Their high ranking was to be carried forward into the Branch's plans for the 1981 Strategic Overview. It was at that point, perhaps, that victims won the sponsorship which they had hitherto lacked. Until the end of 1980, no one of Assistant Deputy Minister rank or above had publicly championed the policy potential of the victims of crimes. There had been some encouragement, but no vigorous advocacy. The decisions of the Branch's Workshop led the Branch's Assistant Deputy Minister to become a most active patron of victims. His patronage ensured that those decisions would be treated with seriousness: 'when Irvin was plugging victims at the Ministers [Conference of 1979] he hadn't got whatever it was that was necessary to get it going as a major thing; He hadn't got enough oomph behind it.... Victims was given a lot of priority in our Branch Workshop.... Maybe it was then [that victims achieved political stature] because it came forward as a Branch priority with my backing that did in fact turn the tide.' A policy analyst remarked, 'you can get things to the forefront but you need powerful sponsorship to keep things moving'. It was the Workshop that secured that sponsorship.

The 1981 Strategic Overview

Policy Branch was starting to expand, and there were policy analysts free to take on issues other than juveniles. And Irvin went to a lot of meetings. And [the Department's expert on victims] and I talked about it as well, but with still not very much response. And it's not entirely clear to me where the transition appeared, whether it was the weight of so many arguments and it coming up from so many directions, but at some point they got involved. And it was very difficult to know just when they would. Probably ... the thing that really capped it was the Strategic Overview and their involvement in the Ministry planning process. (Official, Programs Branch)

The 1981 Strategic Overview may be described as the formal genesis of the Justice for Victims of Crime Initiative. Before the Overview, victims were an intriguing social problem that had attracted limited funds and some approval from the Ministry. In the main, work on victims had been done in the name of other approved policies, being mediated by concerns and problems that were a little oblique to them. They were the political hangers-on, the Ministry's passengers. After the Overview, it could be declared that victims had been scrutinized and approved by the Government of the day. As the Acting Assistant Deputy Minister, Programs, reflected, 'it shifted quite dramatically just with it going into the Strategic Overview and it being discussed by the Minister and the Minister saying, yes, he thought it was a good idea. And personally, I think that [the Director of Policy] took it on board in that period.' After the Overview, victims ceased to be the politically unsupported interest of officials and became Government policy. The Director of Policy remarked at a meeting of the Regional Consultants some months later, 'victims is not a new issue but what is new is that it has become a ministerial priority'.

1981 was the first year of the new Policy and Expenditure Management System and there was some little confusion about how it was to work. An early memorandum remarked, 'this is a very new process and ... there are many questions which remain unanswered'. The Overview was to pass through a number of drafts as attempts were made to achieve a practical resolution of those questions. In particular, there was to be uncertainty about the permissible scope and length of an Overview written in a policy environment that was beginning to be dominated by talk about austerity. Fluctuations in the scale of the Overview were accompanied by indecision about the number of initiatives that could be proposed. Justice for victims was to appear, disappear, and reappear in sympathy with those movements, being excluded from some versions, only to be included in others.

It was understood that the Strategic Overview was to become the principal prospectus for future planning. It was to bare the Department to the gaze of a Cabinet Committee empowered to reject or amend its proposals: 'the review of this document by the Committee results in confirmation of, or modification to, the department's objectives, general policy direction, and strategies'.[16] It was also understood that the Overview was to be a political document, based upon political arguments and subjected to a political review. It was to be the vehicle through which a Minister would submit his work to the judgement of his colleagues. It was to include any major shift in policy, any expansion or contraction of existing programmes, and any proposal to begin or end substantial projects. Its organization was prescribed precisely.[17] To have consequence, argument was to assume a particular structure, starting with a review of those 'major social and economic trends' that had prompted a responsive move by the Ministry. There was to follow an orderly procession of statements in which the Department surveyed the declared Government policies that affected its work, the relations between those policies and its own opportunities and problems, the constraints by which it proposed to adopt in order to achieve its objectives. The presentation of that kind of paper demanded a familiarity with the discourse of policy. Almost all its constituents had to be interpreted and phrased in a manner that would conform to a local sense of what represented an identifiable and important social trend, a plausible connection between policy and a problem and, indeed, what a significant problem was. The whole had to be organized by the larger political intuition of officials and politicians. Infusing the new System were layers of unstated and probably unstatable assumptions about the character of planning, the political context of government, the links between departments, and the potential character of negotiations in an untried scheme. One Programs Branch official recalled, 'the instructions on the preparation of it were in flux. They kept on changing weekly.'

On 16 December 1980 the Programs Branch forwarded a list of the proposed initiatives which its Workshop had identified. Victims were eighth on the list, a composite of the two 'sub-program areas' of policies dealing with family violence and improved services to crime victims. The Branch's list was lengthy, made up of twelve items, and it was to be combined with other lists from other Branches. It was to be perused by a Policy Branch that was attempting to exercise an untried political faculty. In the very similar case of Whitehall, Heclo and Wildavsky have argued:

> Political administrators learn to assess the climate before determining expenditure strategy. To misjudge the climate may mean to suffer a surprising reverse,

[16] *Guide to the Policy and Expenditure Management System,* Ministry of Supply and Services Canada, Ottawa, 1980, p. 20.

[17] 'Instructions for Preparation of Strategic Overviews', Ministry of State for Social Development, 28 Nov. 1980.

perhaps to be embarrassed, possibly to lose reputation and trustworthiness itself. Yet normally climate can be judged only on an intuitive basis.[18]

The penalties flowing from poor judgement in a novel process moved the Branch to behave with great caution. Policy officials had assumed that Government signals about parsimony were to be obeyed. It was noted that 'Canada's criminal justice system will be affected by the *high inflation and slow economic growth* anticipated in the coming years. . . . The demands for greater *restraint and cost effectiveness* in public expenditures are being directed at elements of the criminal justice system as part of the public sector generally.' Although assistance to victims had once been described as a contribution to cost effectiveness, it was one of a number of schemes that were omitted from the first draft of the Departmental planning document. Instead, that early draft concentrated on six priorities only, dealing with quite crucial commitments in the central areas of police accountability, the federal penitentiary population, juvenile delinquency, parole, reform of the Criminal Code, and internal security. Most of those priorities related to processes that were inescapably in train. The McDonald Inquiry on the Royal Canadian Mounted Police would present ineluctable commitments for instance. All other possibilities were banished. It seemed as if the victims initiative had aborted.

What prevented a miscarriage was an array of representations stemming from inside and outside the Ministry. The first two drafts of February 1981 had made no mention of victims. In the next few weeks, it appeared as if the Programs Branch, the Ministry of State for Social Development, and the Minister himself combined to urge the expansion of the list of priorities and the admission of victims.

The Director of Policy remembered, 'we had victims in real early drafts and dropped it out because we were trying to restrict each area to about four or five and then we put it back in as we went along. . . . I'm sure that there was a lot of insistence by the Programs Branch that it be in.' And the Acting Assistant Deputy Minister, Programs, claimed that it had been his intervention which had induced the Policy Branch to add victims to later drafts. His Branch had recommended victims but that recommendation had been spurned. 'The first draft . . . didn't have victims in as one of the main things. We protested. We must have written back. ———'s memo said "Oy, put it in"' That memorandum of the 19 February complained about the rejection of the catalogue of initiatives submitted by his Branch. Not one initiative had been accepted:

[18] H. Heclo and A. Wildavsky, *The Private Government of Public Money*, p. 29.

I am worried about the way in which we have interpreted instructions over completing the Strategic Overview. I am made more concerned when I read ... that 'the Strategic Overview will be used as the major instrument for policy and expenditure management over the medium term'. None of Program Branch activities and programs appear in the priorities and I am sure that this can only lead to confusion in the future. If the Minister ... gives priority only to those items ... then the work of the Secretariat will be damaged enormously.

The fate of the Programs Branch initiatives then became something of a mirror of the relations between the Branches themselves. The exclusion of victims began to assume larger proportions, symbolizing the exclusion of the entire Branch from a central decision-making process. Victims had attained an emblematic status and a powerful champion. They could not easily be denied.

As important was the correction delivered by the Ministry of State for Social Development. Early versions of the planning document had been submitted for comment, the Ministry being responsible for superintending the whole process and all the Departments of the Social Envelope. On 13 February the Ministry of State for Social Development offered a general endorsement of the draft but observed, 'we note that there is no reference to women as victims of crime as in the speech from the throne'. It may be presumed that such a note was tantamount to a command. It was also encouragement, suggesting that some action on women victims would be supported by the Ministry of State for Social Development. It was a reminder that declared Government policy was being ignored. It was critical, perhaps the most forceful collision yet of the two histories of victims and family violence.

The person who had noticed the Department's failure to include women victims was a policy analyst assigned to the justice area in the Ministry of State. It was her job to know what was happening in her territory, identify trends, and detect omissions. She had once worked in the Ministry of Justice and had served on the Interdepartmental Committee on Family Violence. She was privy to thinking about victims and had contributed to that thinking herself. As a member of the social networks of Ottawa, she was acquainted with people who had attained prominence in the circles that evolved around victims. One of the most prominent was Irvin Waller, now in voluntary exile in the University of Ottawa, and she knew him too. As a policy analyst remarked, 'it was a very interesting alliance. Perhaps the really important thing about giving it to Policy came that way, do you know? Irvin then had an 'in', not to the Programs Branch anymore but to Policy.' It was in that manner that the social structure of the growing initiative folded back on the Ministry which had created it, acting as a constraint on that Department's planning procedures. The social structure included a woman who was to become a vital gate-keeper in the new Policy and Expenditure Management System. She intervened, as it was her duty to do, and victims entered the Strategic Overview of the Solicitor General.

Thirdly, and rather later, the parsimony of the original drafts of the document was questioned both by the Ministry of State for Social Development and by the Solicitor General himself. Its preparation is one of the chief procedures to be superintended personally by the Solicitor General. After all, it frames the policies which he must present and defend in time to come. As one of his Special Assistants reflected about the process, 'that's one point where the Minister has an opportunity to look over what's going to be done and give more directions'. It was to become the understanding of officials that the initially austere list of options was too modest. It failed to give the Ministry a satisfactory presence in the affairs of Government. It was to be expanded. One official recalled:

> He didn't want an abbreviated list but a somewhat larger number. And I think we were all getting some perception that while the central agencies were saying it should be four or five, that was *their* notion, and the fact that it was going to be a document for the Minister, as it was alleged to be, meant that Ministerial level wishes should have something to do with it.

Thus it was that five more priorities were hurriedly and belatedly tacked on to the document. Rough sketches of possible additional initiatives were produced, one provisionally entitled 'developing policies and programs to support a national strategy on assistance to victims of crime'. It was argued that the victim was the forgotten party of the criminal justice system, that interest in the victim married well with Government proposals to assist the elderly, women, and the handicapped, and that the Ministry should seek to increase police-based services and victim assistance projects.

On 10 March the Departmental expert on victims was asked to prepare a detailed statement on victim assistance for the Solicitor General's briefing on the document in three days times: 'unfortunately, we do not have much time to do this—believe it or not, we only have until Friday, March 13th.' What the expert had at hand was the paper on which he had been laboriously collaborating since late September. It was that paper which was adapted for insertion on the Strategic Overview. Under the new title of 'making the criminal justice system more responsive to the needs of crime victims', expanded, rearranged, and redrafted by the

Policy Branch, it absorbed much of the thinking and work that had unfolded since the social problem of victims had first taken form. Its primary objectives were held to be the provision of sensitive and dignified treatment to victims, the reduction of trauma, and the increasing of public confidence in the criminal justice system. It was argued that the victim of crime is the forgotten person in the criminal justice system, most resources being devoted to the offender; that there was a companion neglect of the victim's needs; and that the consequence was 'feelings of alienation, injustice, and disrespect for the legal system'.

The priority was awarded a solid background and history. It was observed that the provinces, and Ontario in particular, had begun to press for a federal–provincial initiative. There had been federal involvement with victims in the realm of family violence, and involvement that had been emphasized in the Government publication *Towards Equality for Women* of 1979 and the last Speech from the Throne. There had been an impressive growth of interest in victim services amongst the police especially. It was reported that the Ministry had built a foundation for the initiative, having promoted work on family violence in London, Ontario, in Restigouche, and elsewhere; embarked on a major survey of Canadian victims; assembled information about services to victims in Canada and the United States; initiated a demonstration project in Calgary; and agreed to contribute to the funding of the Seventh Annual Conference of the National Organization for Victim Assistance. In short, all its scattered projects and contacts were given coherence and purpose by the initiative that was to come. They were a documentation of the extent and persistence of the Department's resolve.

It was proposed that the Department should join with federal and provincial Ministries to develop a concerted comprehensive national strategy on victims. The matter could be raised in June at the Meeting of Ministers Responsible for Criminal Justice and, later at the International Conference on Victim Assistance in October. The proposed strategy itself would include a series of victimization surveys; development of policies and programmes within the Royal Canadian Mounted Police; the promotion of model victim assistance projects; publicity and education about victims' rights; enriched compensation schemes; conferences and workshops; and legislation to guarantee the rights of victims.

It was held that such an initiative would bolster established Government priorities by improving the quality of life; promoting social justice; providing help to the poor, the elderly, natives, the handicapped, and women; advancing community participation; and reducing the costs of criminal justice. Six victimization surveys across Canada would cost

$1,100,000 and five person years for 1981–2 and 1982–3. Increased funding for police-based programmes would cost $750,000 and two person years for each of the years between 1981 and 1984.

The meeting with the Minister was to be held on 28 March. Two days before, one of his officials was lobbied by Irvin Waller's Research Assistant. It will be recalled that Irvin Waller was now outside Government, but his influence was still felt. The official was reminded that the Research Assistant had written to Mr Kaplan before his appointment as Solicitor General had been confirmed: 'I expressed my opinion that he would be named Solicitor General and, more importantly, that I felt that if he was so named, the issue of victim rights should be a priority within his Ministry.' The official was offered some 'pertinent observations' which were designed to 'sensitize him' to the problem of victims. He was told about the fear of crime; about the inequity of the existing provision of private insurance; about the secondary victimization of those who encounter the police and the courts; about the Solicitor General's leadership role and his responsibility for policing matters; that victims are also taxpayers and voters; that victim-assistance work would ease the decanting of the federal penitentiaries; and that American feminism had percolated into Canada: 'What exists as an opportunity for moral leadership for the Solicitor General in this field will soon become the domain of others unless the Minister acts soon.' That letter constituted the only example of conventional lobbying for victims at large during the entire early history of the initiative.

The Minister did act. He approved the transformation of victims into a policy priority:

I think I could say it was an issue that I, as a back bencher, was aware of because there always was a disproportionate attention given to the offender and that was disturbing to our constituents. So I remember always picking up this criticism about the criminal justice system really just helping offenders.... I'd say that was part of it. But it was an initiative that had been floating around before and I guess, as the Solicitor General who had sat on the job a little longer than any of my predecessors, I eventually came around to picking out things that were there, that I felt were worth pushing.

His sole reservation was about the utility of the survey of victims:

My political judgement was that it was wrong to put so much money into the survey part of it in relation to the amount, not that it was a small amount, but in relation to the amount that was being put into pilot projects. But I was met with the argument that, until you had done the survey, you couldn't really justify the pilot projects. I didn't fully agree with that. I thought that we had enough anecdotal information about victims and their situation to be able to design pilot projects without the survey. But I am quite interested in the survey because it ties into an issue that I wanted more work done on anyway, which was the nature of crime in Canada. We don't really know whether the crime rate is going up or going down and you see so many statistics which are interpreted to mean different things. So . . . when I criticized the balance of the proposal, I was met with the argument that I myself had been pressing them to give me accurate statistics on victims.

The Solicitor General's Strategic Overview was considered and approved by the Government in April, and the Department was invited to draft proposals for an initiative. Victims were no longer a mere policy concern. They were the stuff of future political action.

Conclusion

The trial Overview of 1980 and its more demanding successor worked a number of transformations in the diffuse social problem posed by the victims of crime. Before the spring of 1980 the Department had developed a number of contacts with that problem, giving it a rudimentary shape and life as it did so. The same few officials had worked on research and demonstration projects, they had come to form a social circle bent on helping victims, but very little of their activity could take place in the name of a policy on victims. Every significant instance of work had to be referred to a context and mandate that were somewhat tangential to the organizing interests of the circle. In a sense, their programmes had to sail under foreign colours: they were pointed at the regulation of violent crime, wife battering, crime prevention, the collection of social indicators, domestic crisis intervention and the like. Moreover, many of those programmes had not been intended to serve as furtive attempts at a victims initiative. They were supposed to be substantial enterprises in their own right. The final absorption of those programmes into a Justice for Victims of Crime Initiative had not been anticipated or desired by everyone. What gave them a tenuous and sometimes covert unity was their coming together in the work of the Department. The social circle mediated them, awarding them character.

The first Strategic Overview, the October and December Workshops, and what had become the Second Overview repeatedly forced officials to remove themselves from the flow of events and consider what they were doing. Different staff, and Irvin Waller in particular, had had a vision of a victims initiative. Most had not. Some had defined such an initiative as improper. Others had not reflected on the matter at all. The Overviews and Workshops required people to meet, negotiate together, and impose sense on themselves and their world. They gave a communal and coherent appearance to action. Different activities, started at various times and in response to changing priorities, were accordingly scanned for their significance in the future. There was an effort to find new and useful patterns that could be translated into acceptable proposals.

The Strategic Overview process thereby gave coherence and direction to projects. There was a quest for meaning, for novelty, and for structure. Staff were invited to survey the world and rearrange it. Accepting that invitation, they joined the little histories of the initiative and made them one. As a former policy analyst stated:

> The Strategic Overview shouldn't be underrated in the sense that it presented a demand that Ministries come up with potential new initiatives. And that seems to be a logical way of organizing a whole series of different strands in a coherent package which could be understood and prepared again as a small 'p' politically attractive sort of thing which would perhaps appeal to the Minister.

The Strategic Overview process had one other vital effect. It transferred victims to the Policy Branch, giving the social problem new authors and a new set of goals. A scatter of projects which seemed to lack grand design began to acquire a purposiveness. The anchored perspectives of the Programs Branch were replaced by the general structure of argument demanded by the Policy and Expenditure Management System. Victims were subordinated to universal political formulae, refracting wider Government concerns instead of their own special, embedded themes. Thus it was proposed to stress the needs of the elderly, handicapped, women, poor, natives, and children. Some of those groups did undoubtedly suffer the pains and deprivations inflicted by crime. Some also feared crime more acutely than others. But it was a political list which excluded the young males who are the chief victims and agents of criminal violence, homosexual victims and others who lack political stature. Consider its composition. Some of those on the list were there because it was diplomatic to include them, not because much was known about their needs. About natives, for example, one literature review commissioned by the Department observed, 'no objective data are available on the needs of these people as victims of crime'. The same review commented, 'a widely held view of the elderly as victims of crime is that they are relatively vulnerable to injuries due to their physical frailty, and that they suffer greater economic hardship from victimization due to their limited resources and (often) fixed incomes. Results of an American victimization survey . . . however have cast doubt on these assumptions'.[19] By contrast, homosexual men were one of the few groups to protest about their victimization. Like women, they had organized politically and then turned their organizations on the problems of the homosexual as victim. They had proposed 'gay street patrols' to be mustered by the Right to Privacy Committee.[20] There had been disturbances when transvestites were mobbed in Toronto on Hallowe'en.[21] There were reports of a substantial number of homosexuals being murdered in Toronto.[22] Yet, as one senior official remarked, homosexuals were 'nobody's favourite victims'. Moreover, there had been a running conflict in Toronto and elsewhere between the police and homosexuals using bath-houses,[23] and scandals had erupted about paedophiles and the victimization of children.

The list of target victims was not devised by the Programs Branch. It was not based on research. It was modelled on the general template drafted by the Government, on the special interests of allied Departments, and on a sense of what was politically advantageous. As a policy analyst argued, 'in a way it's been defined currently simply by which departments and agencies are taking some interest in it'. It was a pre-eminently political catalogue designed to win political approval.[24]

Yet the reconstitution of the social problem was likely to produce palpable advantages. Remade as an object to be scrutinized by politicians and their advisers, it could begin to assume influence in the world. It might well command resources, money, and effort. Those who were to control its fate were not answerable to an audience of applied social scientists and victimologists, and they were not swayed by academic arguments. Although, as the Solicitor General remarked, 'I don't think you could ever be criticized for being too fair to victims', there were a number of groups who could not be disregarded: women could not be flouted, other departments demanded recognition, and the provinces required deference. Their representatives were able to support, censor,

[19] C. Meredith, *Overview and Annotated Bibliography of the Needs of Crime Victims,* Ministry of the Solicitor General, Ottawa, 1982.

[20] *Toronto Star*, 5 June 1981.

[21] Ibid., 21 Oct. 1980.

[22] Ibid., 22 Sept. 1978.

[23] *Globe and Mail,* 10 Sept. 1982.

[24] For a comparable British instance, see J. Edwards and R. Batley, *The Politics of Positive Discrimination,* pp. 55, 57.

or thwart an initiative. It was important not to affront them. Indeed, since the initiative was thought to be comparatively insubstantial and inexpensive, it would be maldroit to upset the people who would come to judge it. Rather, the initiative was to be tailored to please them, phrased with great care as a political artefact about to be inspected in political settings.

XI. The Cabinet Submission

The acceptance of victims as a Government priority through the Strategic Overview process had transformed the problem of victims into a policy issue in the spring of 1981. A policy issue is understood to be a special entity in Ottawa. It is neither a concern nor a policy but an object in transition. After the spring, victims would no longer be quite so ambiguous and tacit a theme in argument. They could be presented as a proper topic in their own right, being expressly discussed, presented, shaped, and shared in the committees and departments of federal and provincial governments. Instead of receiving their definition and legitimacy from other ratified policies, they could emerge as a framework and authority for events in progress. But victims *were* in transition. They were not yet Government policy in the spring. Much more needed to be done.

Stretching ahead was a chain of critical meetings which would impart further character to the initiative. Indeed, I have argued that proposals are forced to be indeterminate in Canada so that other powerful bodies can be seen to impress their mark upon them. Ambiguity and openness were retained in argument about victims so that they might be resolved by private sector, provincial and federal organizations. Their retention ensured that others would define themselves as properly implicated in the process of policy formation. It would not necessarily be the content but the *fact* of contribution that assumed political significance. Whatever certainties the staff of the Department of the Solicitor General may have possessed, they had to be suspended as part of a show of deference to others. If victims were to succeed as the subject of a policy initiative, they would need general patronage from the powerful institutions which controlled their fate. Federal initiative required an extension of proprietorship. It would not do to appear overly dictatorial, endangering the fragile structure of the constitution.

At the Minister's briefing on the planning document, it had been observed that the Department might contemplate playing a co-ordinating role in the national provision of services to victims. But it was also observed that such a role would result in jurisdictional problems involving the Department of Justice. Some form of joint action would be necessary but the problem of a leadership role and the diffusion of decision-making and Ministerial responsibility which often occurs in these areas could result. Similarly, it was noted that women's groups were unhappy about battered and raped women being lost within a large and anonymous population of victims. They might consequently be reluctant partners in any overall strategy unless their special needs received explicit recognition. The future movement of a victims policy would quite evidently be affected by the diplomatic hazards that lay ahead. In particular, attention had to be given to the preparation of appearances, the issues being designed to advertise concern for the interests of others. In the words of Heclo and Wildavsky, it is best 'to create a nexus of interest so that cooperation flows from a sense of mutual advantage'.[1] It is the manufacture of those appearances and that nexus that is the special aptitude and work of the Policy Branch. It is that Branch's duty to turn proposals into bundles of significant gestures incorporating responses to the likely reactions of groups and individuals who might judge them. Even the authors of the proposals were chosen to signal reassurance to important groups.

Thus one important gesture, accomplished at this time, was the appointment of Linda MacLeod to the Department. A former official of National Health and Welfare, a member of Working Group Three, once a research worker at the Advisory Council on the Status of Women, and author of *Wife-Battering in Canada*, Linda MacLeod embodied the determination of the Department of the Solicitor General to remember the special status of women in any forthcoming initiative. She took up her position on 1 April, being asked immediately to collaborate on the writing of a policy paper on victims for a meeting of the Joint Justice Committee on 16 April. As the Co-ordinator of Status of Women Canada observed, 'if she weren't there, I would have less hope of this being useful to women'.

Another gesture, and one that had become routine since 1975, centred on a visible turning towards the Department of Justice. On 17 March the Deputy Solicitor General wrote to the Deputy Minister of Justice to propose that 'the subject of assistance to victims with particular reference to family violence including wife battering' be placed on the agenda of the Joint Justice Committee meeting of 16 April in preparation for the May meeting of Deputy Ministers Responsible for Criminal Justice. On 2 April the Assistant Deputy Minister in charge of policy wrote to the Director of Policy and Planning in the Ministry of Justice. He forwarded a copy of the Solicitor General's Strategic Overview, stating 'although time constraints made it impossible to properly coordinate the overviews

[1] H. Heclo and A. Wildavsky, *The Private Government of Public Money*, p. xv.

of the two Ministries I suggest we review them at the next meeting of Joint Justice. In one sense, the two overviews taken together will determine the work of the federal government in the criminal justice system, in the mid-term.' That process of co-ordination flowed from the joint planning procedures adopted since the difficulties of the Peace and Security Package. It also reflected the novel problems that flowed from the new Policy and Expenditure Management System. It was an effort to inject some coherence into planning.

The Department of Justice had not actually referred to victims in its own planning document. And, apart from its involvement with criminal injuries compensation schemes and proposed changes to the law on rape, it had evinced little ambition to respond to the social problem of victims. As one of its own policy analysts remarked:

> I've got really no sense that the vision of the Department of Justice went beyond the compensation funding issue. There were some elements working on that and they were largely concerned with the administration of the compensation agreements which at some point were going to have to be renegotiated. Some of the people working on that saw serious problems and shortcomings with the current schemes. But it struck me that they had no constituency higher up at all.

And a senior policy official within the Department of the Solicitor General observed that his Ministry had received little response when it initially approached the Department of Justice: 'I think they were genuinely not interested and, secondly, they've never liked the victimisation surveys over there. There it was. We were doing it on our own. We went to Joint Justice [eventually] because you know, at that point, the Deputy Minister said, "well, where are we? Where's Justice?"' The resort to the Department of Justice was not then prompted by any goal but that set by the inner politics of the Canadian federal government. The Department of Justice may have manifested no great interest in the problems of victims, but it was the senior Ministry and it could not be disregarded. Unilateral action might be resisted. Obeisances had to be made, requiring formal consultations in the special committee designed to patrol the internal frontiers of the Canadian criminal justice system. The initiative could not remain private.

It will be recalled that other bodies had dispatched victims to that meeting of the Joint Justice Committee. A number of the maturing little histories were about to converge, leading to an 'over-determination' of the agenda. Victims had been channelled by the Strategic Overview, the report of the Canadian delegation to the Sixth United Nations Congress, and some of the members of the collapsing Interdepartmental Committee on Family Violence. There was something of a clamour. Demands coincided on that occasion, giving an impression of scale and urgency.

As preparations for the meeting of 16 April started, so the progress of the victims initiative began to receive a standardized form, being scheduled for one timetabled occasion after another in sequence. Just before 16 April Godparents were appointed to represent the Department which had acquired a stake in victims: the Ministries of the Solicitor General, Justice, Health and Welfare Canada, and Status of Women Canada. And the initiative was given two new pilots, the older pilots of the Programs Branch being dropped. One was Linda MacLeod. She remembered:

> I came in . . . on one day and it was either the next day or the day after that we had a meeting with Justice and Sol Gen and [the Director of Policy] was there and Jack was there and I was there and ———, ——— and a bunch of people like that, not Programs people, just Policy people. And they said, well, Linda will write this paper, and it was only latterly decided because of my [lack of preparation] that Jack would also be involved. . . . At the beginning, we were to have almost like first go of the paper production. The way the meeting started was that [the Director of Policy] brought me along as the person who was going to write the paper and then he also suggested that Jack should do it because it was going to be a joint thing.

The representative of the Department of Justice was an assurance and possible mediator, having worked in both the departments which regulated the federal system of criminal justice. It had been he who had served as the Chief Staff Officer of the Canadian delegation to the United Nations Congress. He was one of the few officials in the Department of Justice who had developed a competence and interest in victims, and his prominence was emphasized by his previous experience as an official of the Solicitor General. He had prepared the report of the Canadian delegation, having raised the importance of the neglect of victims. He had convened the October 1980 Secretariat Workshop, remarking in its preparatory papers that victims might profit from policy development. He was part of the process that had developed inside the Department of the Solicitor General, and he exported that process when he changed position. According to one of his colleagues in the Ministry of Justice, that official had begun to loom large when victims became an object of discussions with the Department of the Solicitor General. His salience is a nice illustration of the dialectical movements that unite officials, ideas in motion, timetables, and the policy processes of Ottawa. As one of those who had helped to give birth to the very conception of victims as a social problem, he was later to be awarded significance as that problem began to influence the world around itself. He and Linda MacLeod had contributed to the political emergence of victims, only to be given work and stature by their own creation. In yet another movement of the dialectic, they were now entrusted with a further transformation of the proposals.

The translation of the policy issue of victims into a bundle of significant gestures was an eminently political process. It made the issue accessible to the intervention of others, allowing those who intervened to become possessive and responsible for what happened. It was supposed to defuse opposition and enlist support in Cabinet, in the provinces, in departments and in the agencies. Its presentation was a matter for the strategists of the Policy Branch, and it was their entrance that was identified by the senior officials of that Branch as the formal beginning of the politics of victims. As the Director of Policy stated:

If you look at the paper that was prepared by Linda and Jack you'll see that it goes a long ways towards saying here are the problems and here are some of the things that we should be looking at. Raising the issue to that level is important. ... It's very attractive to politicians in some respects, but I think that it needs that kind of definition and it needs specific things. ... Irvin was very much responsible for identifying that as an issue, no question, but I think probably I provided sufficient definition as to what could be done and knew how to write the Cabinet document and get it into the proper channel. It's a question of knowing how Government works at that point, and knowing you cannot go to Cabinet and saying we need money to do something without being very specific about time frame, process and output as to what that is.

Victims and their problems ceased to be an immediate response to the arguments that had poured out of research, demonstration projects, and the other work of the Programs Branch. They were transmuted into the material of practical politics. Such a metempsychosis did not commend itself uniformly to all those who had been the early guardians of the initiative. Just as there had been a lingering reluctance to surrender victims to the Policy Branch in the first instance, so some of those guardians maintained their opposition to the newly proclaimed diffusion of ownership and control. People who had protected victims during years of indifference found it difficult to share them with others when their concern was taken seriously and redefined as a policy issue. One of those who had been centrally involved, the Department's expert on victimization research, argued:

It will be difficult for Joint Justice to decide on the overall federal strategy on victims. ... In my opinion, each department should be allowed to develop its own priorities and strategies in this area, but within the *ultimate* need for a concerted and comprehensive federal initiative. In particular, the Solicitor General's Department had gone through a long process of developing its victim initiatives so that these also relate directly to its priorities in policing, crime prevention, and community involvement with CJS. These initiatives can be pursued without being tied to an all-encompassing federal strategy involving complex issues such as CAP [Canada Assistance Plan] or victim compensation funding agreements.[2]

But that protest was solitary and late. By 6 April the first outline of the paper for the Joint Justice Committee had already been drafted.

Much of the construction of the policy paper was sketched in that early meeting of 2 April, and it is interesting to observe how the process was accomplished. The policy officials from the Departments of Justice and the Solicitor General scanned the history of the initiative as they knew it, gave it the structure and appearances that politics required, and wove the whole into a coherent argument. The paper that emerged was an embodiment of very general principles of political persuasion:

I had no idea of this issue at all. ... They talked the paper at that meeting. I mean, they said, 'obviously we would emphasize this, this and this. Obviously, we would want to make reference to this'. And so I would make notes like 'look up speech of this'. And when it was decided that it would be done in two days, it was, right. The first draft would be done in two days and it would be circulated and finalised in a week. ... So it wasn't like a research thing where we sat down and did this. I mean, we sat in a room and we pulled out what we could. We 'phoned up someone and said 'get us this quote'. I mean we didn't read at all for it.

Part of that process was devoted to an emphaisis on the uninterrupted continuity of the politics of victims, its anchorage in a network of commitments and obligations, its rootedness in a solid environment, its sheer familiarity. A victims initiative was not a new venture to be appraised anew but little more than a simple and obvious extension of all that had gone before. It was no more than the next step, not a jarring break with things known and approved. Everything that had been done became a kind of rhetorical furniture for the new document:

[The paper prepared by the team of three] was given to me and of course I took some phrases out of it. ... I read it. ... [Similarities between that paper and the paper written for the Joint Justice Committee reflect] the history, how you write things. You look at everything that's been said. You get the Throne Speech and the stuff that the Ontario guy said. You get all that and put it in front of you and you crib phrases because otherwise no-one will recognise it. What you try

[2] Memo of 9 Apr. 1981.

to do when you create a policy document is try to let people see themselves in it, and see their history in it, because if it's totally new they'll be scared about it. ... You don't come in as a new person to an area ... and just sort of start from scratch and create something totally out of the blue because it'll be threatening. No matter how brilliant it is, no-one will accept it. What you have to do is massage and regurgitate, you know, and put it into some kind of coherent package.

The paper talked of the shifting foci of government and public attention, the political drift towards the victim, and the history of federal involvement with victims. Being part of a joint venture, it made reference to the work done by the Department of Justice in the area of compensation agreements for victims of violent crime, legal changes in the status of rape, and a number of research projects. There were other allusions to the activities of Health and Welfare Canada and the Secretary of State Women's Program. There was a recital of the historical antecedents and political lineage of the proposals, argument pointing to the speech made by Gordon Walker, the findings of the Canadian delegation to the Sixth United Nations Congress, and public demands from women. The example of American industriousness was given. The Strategic Overview exercise itself became a source of authority, it being asserted that the Priorities and Planning Committee of Cabinet would base its list of Government priorities upon the Overviews that were then under scrutiny. Typically, an instrument had become a constraint, moving action onwards.

It may be seen that by early April there was an approved, almost objective story attached to the social problem of victims. By that time, the story had a plot, characters, and style. It had begun to acquire an autonomous life that confronted its own authors. The objectivity and conventionality of the social problem stemmed, in part, from the social composition of the initiative's circle. People had been replaced, and the newcomers could treat what their predecessors had done as a series of facts that was independent of their wills. After all, they had not written the paper ordered by the Secretariat Workshop: it had come as part of the paraphernalia of an impending initiative. Moreover, the emerging story proved to be really quite serviceable. It had worked in the past, proving acceptable to the Policy Branch of the Ministry of State for Social Development, and, quite probably, to the Committee of the Social Envelope. There seemed no good reason to change it radically. As one of the authors of the policy paper written for the Joint Justice Committee argued, 'it's the fruit of word processing ... there were a number of people involved in supervising or approving the contents of various papers that were put forward, who were extremely sensitive to the way in which things were phrased ... and when we happened upon a formulation of words that appeared to get some support, we stuck very close to it.'

The draft outline borrowed two options from the report of the Canadian delegation to the United Nations Congress and added one of its own. The first possibility reviewed was a retention of the status quo, affirming the Government's interest in victims and emphasizing new activities to contend with wife-battering. The second possibility envisaged the Government assuming 'a major national leadership role' by developing new initiatives and instituting a new 'process and mechanism to implement this priority at all levels of government'. And the third acknowledged the principal responsibility of the provinces for victim services, offering federal aid as a support to provincial work. There had, indeed, been some trepidation about the possible provincial response to a federal initiative on victims. Despite the interest shown by Ontario, there was evidence that other provinces, and Quebec in particular, would repel a federal strategy. As one of the authors of the draft outline argued, 'the central agencies, by which I mean the Federal–Provincial Relations Office, Ministry of State for Social Development and Privy Council Office, read this as an extremely sensitive area and we had to tread very, very carefully'.

The draft was circulated and two replies were received. From without, Status of Women Canada told the authors that there might be greater emphasis given to the pressures which had emanated from women and from rape crisis centres and the transition houses. It was pointed out that women had been declared a 'priority client group' by Government and that battered women had been mentioned in the Speech from the Throne. It was also suggested that the paper should include some distinctions which would, 'in fact, priorize our victims and bluntly show where our first emphasis should be, i.e. victims of violence are more 'victims' than those of break and enter'. Within a day, a new draft had been prepared which laid a greater stress on women, the federal government's commitments to women, and the part played by women's organizations. Thus, for the first time, there was a reference to the National Plan of Action. There was a new paragraph attending to the work of women's organizations which had 'independently responded to the needs of victims of rape and family violence by setting up a network of rape crisis centers and transition houses ... and have actively lobbied for changes in legislation, in the delivery of criminal justice and social services ... '.[3]

[3] *Victim Justice—Options for a Federal Approach*, 10 Apr. 1981.

Following representations from the Department's own expert on victimization research, the sole source of an internal response, 'the active federal priority initiative' was expanded to allude to police-based services, a national resources centre, and a number of rather specific projects and ventures. By 15 April, two weeks from Linda MacLeod's appointment, a final draft was distributed to the initiative's Godparents.

The Joint Justice Committee meeting of 16 April approved the paper and forwarded it on to the meeting of Deputy Ministers Responsible for Criminal Justice, a meeting which took place on 6 and 7 May. That meeting, in its turn, gave birth to 'an informal working group', chaired by the Department of the Solicitor General, which was entrusted with the preparation of yet another issues paper for review at another meeting of the Deputy Ministers to be held at the end of June. The June meeting would examine whatever proposals might be made and decide whether to forward them for later discussion by the Ministers. The informal working group contained representatives from Ontario, British Columbia, Alberta, and Saskatchewan. It was another illustration of the propensity to arrange processes so that major organization after major organization could be seen to imprint its stamp upon an emerging national policy and claim it as its property. There could be no neglect of the provinces. It was to be in their domain that much of the initiative would be played out, and they possessed a simple power of veto.

It may be seen that the initiative had moved on. Having received a sanction from the federal departments, it was displayed before the provinces. The preservation of provincial sensibilities thus became the dominant concern at the end of April and the beginning of May 1981. In a process akin to the fairies' blessing of the Sleeping Beauty, the pilots approached each body with some nervousness, hoping to receive a benevolent reply. An anguished provincial government could always condemn the initiative to sleep or some other unpleasant fate. A federal policy analyst recalled that officials had 'reacted almost hysterically to the immediate question of jurisdiction in Quebec'. And other intelligence impressed upon policy-makers how very prudent it would be to protect provincial sensibilities.

One instance of such intelligence was presented to federal officials at the very time that the new paper was being written for the Deputy Ministers. Linda MacLeod had been sent with two officials from the Department of Justice to the meetings held during 'Victims' Week' in Washington in late April. The Canadian federal government's adoption of victims was about to coincide with the American federal government's movement away from victims. In particular, the work of the Law Enforcement Assistance Administration was in imminent decline. The American Victim Assistance Initiative had been a 'sunset programme' designed to be assessed in 1981. Its review was conducted just as the Canadians stirred themselves for action. Hence it came about that the Canadian delegation observed the Americans observing themselves during the waning of a victims initiative. The Canadians were to conclude that American disunity was pregnant with warnings for Ottawa. They argued that there had been no orderly evaluation of what had been done in assistance programmes. There had been no efficient strategy for delegating projects to local and state organizations. They reported that they had encountered a radical uncertainty about the future of services to victims in the United States.

It was recommended that the Canadian government should heed American experience by implementing 'evaluation which collects standardized hard data', a sensible co-ordination of services, and a means of ensuring that the 'special needs of particular groups of victims [are] not overlooked or subsumed'. It was claimed that any federal programme would necessarily depend on 'community and grass-roots input' but that such an input could not be secured merely by direct funding: 'a significant Federal role is desirable and feasible ... but great sensitivity must be demonstrated not only to provincial activity and jurisdiction in the area, but also to the interests and programs of private and volunteer groups.' In short, it would be best if the federal government designed its initiative to preserve the independence and vitality of provincial and private bodies.

During the time that the federal officials were searching for a provincial blessing, it was Ontario again that offered its support. The earlier speech of Gordon Walker had been politically invaluable, being cited repeatedly afterwards. In 1981 Ontario acted once more. The Deputy Provincial Secretary of Justice wrote to the Deputy Minister of Justice for Canada: 'I believe not only that the "victim" item most certainly should be on the Ministers' meeting agenda but that a very worthwhile presentation could be developed and I wish to assure you that the Secretariat here will be most willing to do all we can to ensure that this is the case.' At a moment when federal ideas were being cautiously paraded before the provinces, that gesture was welcome and timely.

The Letter from the Ministry of State for Social Development

The initiative might have continued to advance for some little while, being presented to a succession of significant figures for endorsement, discussion, negotiation, and modification. Just as the wolf cubs were supposed to have been brought before the Pack Meeting at the Council Rock, so victims were displayed for recognition, acceptance, and ownership. The provinces would have to approve. Deputy Ministers would have to commend the new issues paper. The Ministers would be consulted. There was a stately progression planned.

What transformed that progression, turning it into a brisk trot, was the second major intervention from the Ministry of State for Social Development. The Minister of State had been charged with advising on 'the allocation of financial, personnel and other resources to federal programs that provide support to the welfare of the individual and social development in Canada'.[4] As Chairman of the Social Envelope Committee, he presided over the distribution and expenditure of some twenty-six billion dollars in 1981,[5] dollars to be spent on health services, unemployment benefits, the federal police and penitentiaries, the federal courts, and the like. Such a colossal sum tends to defy absolutely precise control. It is never entirely possible to forecast and regulate the use of every portion of the budget. Indeed, there has to be provision for the unanticipated. In turn, there is always a chance that there will be overspending or underspending at the margins, creating awkward surpluses or deficits, problems of accounting, and financial anomalies. And so it came to pass. By the end of the financial period, a sum of money had not been spent.

The budget had been parcelled out into different items. Part was set aside for 'cost over-runs' which could not be minutely estimated. As I have argued, it could be expected that there would be unexpected contingencies and allowance had to be made for unplanned expenditures on criminal justice, education, health and employment. Part was to be spent on new programmes. Part was to be spent on old, continuing programmes that came up for periodic assessment and financial review. Some of those programmes were cut in 1981, and the result was that a 'policy reserve' of some three hundred million dollars was left.

The policy reserve is a sum devoted specifically to the funding of new proposals. It was available for use, but it was not being used heavily: the Ministry of State had received only a modest number of applications for funds. According to the Ministry's financial officials, it was not imperative to spend those hundreds of millions of dollars in 1981–2: lapsed funds

[4] Proclamation of the Ministry of State for Social Development, Privy Council Office, 19 June 1980.

[5] The Minister of State for Social Development, speaking in the House of Commons, 16 June 1980.

could be carried forward to the next accounting year. Further, although there was a new talk of austerity in Canada, the Ministry of State for Social Development was not beginning to restrict expenditure in earnest in the early spring of 1981. That was still to come. What did tax the Ministry was the problem of how best the new and untried Policy and Expenditure Management System could be animated. It was the very first year of that System's operation, and it seemed to the Ministry's officials that the departments of the federal government had not yet learned how to orchestrate and implement their planning cycle. Too few applications and proposals were forthcoming. The departments required 'jollying', and there were many attempts to prod them into action.

It seems that some of the departments themselves had formed a different interpretation of the significance of the policy reserve and the cajoling that was associated with it. The cuts in programmes were thought to be severe, ominous, and visible. The new principle of austerity appeared to be so transparent that planners and policy-makers were daunted. According to a senior official in the Policy Branch of the Ministry of the Solicitor General, 'they scared the daylights out of everybody and, basically, no-one was coming forward for new money. ... As a consequence, this three hundred million dollars was not being depleted very quickly.' It was understood that the Ministry of State for Social development had to discover uses for that money lest it face a budgetary cut itself in the following year:

> What they said was, 'well, we want to spend that money but we don't want to spend it in a way that's going to jeopardise us for the next policy reserve'. They sent out the word, and it was, unless you really can understand Bureaucratese, you didn't know what the hell they were talking about, but the word came down that 'if you've got one-shot dollar items, one or two years, three years, of a non-repetitive nature which matched priorities, please come and we'll talk to you'.

With very little warning, and in the midst of a stately progression, an opportunity was presented for a rather special kind of initiative. A new shape and timetable were offered for the federal work on the victims of crime.

There had been an intelligible timetable before the intervention from the Ministry of State for Social Development. Plans were in train to shepherd papers and arguments through meetings until a climax was reached in the Conference of Ministers Responsible for Criminal Justice in the autumn. Thereafter, there would be preparations for the submission of proposals to Cabinet. The actual shape of the initiative was a little less certain. Indeed, there was indeterminacy by design, allowing room for change to be negotiated by significant others in the meetings to come. The absence of detail and structure reflected the manner in which the initiative had been assembled so far: it was a pragmatic, piecemeal, political construction which incorporated diverse interests, histories, and circumstances rather than one coherent plan. All that shapelessness also mirrored the lack of time devoted to a consideration of contents. It now seemed as if the matter would be resolved by the insistence that the initiative should be presented as modest, short-term, and 'one-shot'.

The Deputy Minister of State for Social Development was to send out a number of letters coaxing the departments to make proposals. On 14 May 1981 he sent such a letter to the Deputy Solicitor General. The Deputy Solicitor General was told that the Ministry of State had perused the discussion paper which had been presented to the meeting of the Joint Justice Committee on 16 April. He was also told that the Ministry's policy analysts had inspected the Strategic Overviews and workplans of the departments of the Social Envelope. It transpired that there was some accord about the need to enlarge and improve services for the victims of crime. Those victims tended to coincide with the groups who had been awarded priority in the social development field. Their sufferings were frequently neglected in the hunt for the offender and the subsequent imposition of punishment on those found guilty of crime. The criminal justice system had failed in its response to the physical injuries, financial losses, trauma, and stress of victims. It was now proper and timely to consider establishing a comprehensive programme of assistance to victims. The Deputy Solicitor General was accordingly invited to prepare a memorandum to Cabinet before the next 'banking day' at the end of June. Banking days occur when proposals which have already been agreed in principle are assessed solely in terms of their financial standing. There could be no money for victims until Cabinet had approved their case, and it would be prudent to secure that approval before the end of the financial year.

The pace and activity of the progression underwent a radical acceleration. One of the initiative's pilots recalled:

> We got word from MSSD sort of informally . . . that it would be unlikely that we would get any funds for an initiative such as this in the Fall because there were going to be all sorts of stringent cutbacks and definite dictums like 'thou shalt not spend'. Plus there were already so many people on the Fall agenda to ask for money that we were strongly encouraged to get our act on the road and get it submitted in the late Spring, simply because there are these funny things called Banking Days in which pools of money are decided upon. There were not

a lot of submissions for this Summer Banking Day. And that's the pure reason why it got speeded up. In fact, it was very awkward because it was very difficult to sort of second guess what was going to happen with the federal–provincial thing. . . .

It was in this manner that victims came to be one of the initiatives that were escorted to the Summer Banking Day by the Ministry of State for Social Development. They were to be at the centre of an initiative which was indefinite enough to permit adaptation for the Ministry's purposes. They were timely, coming to the fore just when the calendar of another major organization had created a demand for them. They met the criteria advanced by the Ministry and Government. Indeed, they had been reconstructed by the Solicitor General's policy analysts to satisfy those very criteria. And they fed into the plans that had been developed informally by the social circles and networks of Ottawa.

In a sense, the focus adopted by the policy analysts in the Ministry of State for Social Development represented a great looping of ideas and influence. The processes and structures of the little histories had begun to fold back upon the Department of the Solicitor General as external and coercive forces. In particular, feminism, the women's movement, and an interest in the possibility of a general initiative for victims had become the property of a number of people in the central agencies and departments of the federal government, returning as demands on those who had given them birth. I have already described how a gatekeeper, a criminal justice expert, had suggested that victimized women be inserted in the Solicitor General's Strategic Overview. It was that self-same gatekeeper who mooted the acceleration of the victims initiative and proposed that it should be translated into a memorandum to the Government by June. It was she who had been a member of the Interdepartmental Committee on Family Violence and had once worked in the Department of Justice. She had learned from members of the social circle based in the Department of the Solicitor General about 'the good things that were being done'.

The policy issue of victims was so novel that few people working inside the Ministry of State for Social Development could have known much about it. Indeed, a senior policy analyst of the Ministry of State argued that the Department of the Solicitor General tended 'not to figure' in the deliberations of the Ministry. The Department is a minor organization in Ottawa, its work being dwarfed by the money and effort expended on such matters as employment and housing. The Ministry of Justice tended to attain something of a presence because of its labours on the review of the Criminal Code. But the Department of the Solicitor General was relatively inaudible and invisible inside the Social Envelope. It may be surmised that the victims initiative itself was even pettier, too insignificant to announce itself unaided. a proposal for under two million dollars could not have loomed large in a budget of twenty-six billion. Victims needed an agent and a guardian, and the gatekeeper provided just such a service. As the eyes of the Ministry of State, she had recognized victims as a possible candidate for advancement. It had been her duty to inspect the planning documents which touched on criminal justice, she had noted the omission of women from the Solicitor General's draft, 'and she had read about the proposed victims initiative in the amended version. It was her briefing to her Deputy Minister that had formulated some of the Ministry of State's perspectives on the dawning problems of victims. And she, in her turn, had been advised by Irvin Waller. Waller recalled:

> The Deputy Minister probably said that we've got to be proactive in some way and ... at the bottom of the line had to think up something to do and it ended up by being crime victims. The initiative came from her. I spent a lot of time briefing her on the thing, both on the proposal that went up to the Deputy Minister to say that this was something they should do and on all the various things that happened. That helped it.

It was in this fashion, too, that the original moral entrepreneur continued to exert an oblique and distant influence. The man who had left the federal government because of frustration was able to affect events from without. Indeed, as a Programs Branch official commented, 'this is what he said he would try to do when he left'. The outcome was that events jerked forward with great suddenness, A member of the Consultation Centre stated:

> We were advised that there was money available that had to be spent. ... This submission had to be done quickly and that's why, once the momentum was gained, it was like 'oh, we had to do this by tomorrow morning'. And that went on for quite a period of time.

It was at this stage that the evolution of a victims policy was complicated by its bifurcation. One stream of activity focused upon the development of victims as a social problem in the joint possession of federal and provincial governments. It was a stream that had flowed out of the early May meeting of Deputy Ministers Responsible for Criminal Justice. The four provincial Deputy Ministers who had displayed interest had been invited to name representatives to participate in a body that came to be called the Federal–Provincial Working Group on Victim

Assistance. Quite characteristically, that group was charged with writing an issues paper for the June meeting of Deputy Ministers and for possible consideration by Ministers in September. The actual drafting of the paper was to be undertaken by Linda MacLeod and her colleague from the Department of Justice for eventual review at the first meeting of the Working Group on 28 May. A career was plotted for that paper, projecting it forward into the summer when the Deputy Ministers met and then into the autumn when the Ministers themselves convened. It would prepare a foundation for the Federal–Provincial Task Force on Justice for Victims, a Task Force that was eventually to report in June 1983. At each phase of the development of that stream, provincial sensibilities and sentiments would be sounded. At each stage, it would come to incorporate those sensibilities, passing through a dialectical sequence of discussion, objectification, review, and synthesis. Its terminus was to be endorsement by the eleven governments of Canada.

At the same time, victims had become the materials of a different stream, regulated by different people, addressed to different significant others. The Ministry of State for Social Development had released all that activity, establishing a climax in what had now become the banking day in July. Together with the Department of Justice, the Ministry of the Solicitor General was to supply policy proposals urging a modest, non-recurring, and inexpensive initiative that would be funded out of the policy reserve of the Ministry of State for Social Development. That initiative required its own very careful assembly within a separate field of interests, figures, and obstacles described by the politics of the federal government. It would undoubtedly defer to the provinces and the private sector. In an uneasy federal state, that deference was a cardinal concern of the federal government. But the memorandum's prime audience was to be the array of Federal departments and agencies which clustered around and were defined by the formation of social policy. A victims initiative charted a landscape of involved organizations. It was to be submitted to National Health and Welfare, the Ministry of State for Social Development, Treasury Board, the Department of Finance, and Status of Women Canada. Above all, it was to be paraded through meetings of the Joint Justice Committee in order to integrate the work of the two sponsoring departments.

The policy proposal was also written and navigated by Linda MacLeod and her colleague from the Department of Justice. Two papers by the same authors on the same theme were about to be convoyed simultaneously through distinct chains of committees. It was as if identical twins had been separated and housed with different families, uncertain about how much they knew about each other but visited repeatedly by attentive parents. Indeed, the twins could not meet until they had come of age. The Government would defer the announcement of its decision until the full Conference of Federal-Provincial Ministers Responsible for Criminal Justice, a Conference that was to be delayed until December 1981. There was some subtle play of 'awareness contexts', significant people in the different chains forming surmises about how much they knew about each other, how much the others knew about their surmises, and so on in an indefinite regress.[6]

The Memorandum to Cabinet

At the beginning of May it was quite evident that a coincidence of timetables and processes had unexpectedly made the environment most propitious for victims. Indeed, the Director of Policy tended to view the world around him as a series of changing opportunities for action. It was his job to be knowledgeable and attentive enough to respond when the right possibilities presented themselves. It had been suggested as early as 1972 that the senior staff of the Policy Branch were to determine opportunities and identify specific alternatives for the intervention of the Ministry in specific areas of national policy concern. The Director said himself:

> There's an infinite number of good things you can do in criminal justice but the way ... I look at it is that there're sort of policy windows, they're always going by and there're some things you can throw through the window and there're other things that you can't. And then, once the window's gone by, it doesn't matter if you've got the [right policy] that you could've put through the window. It's now gone.

One such window was now unambiguously in front of the Director. He wrote to Linda MacLeod on 8 May, 'I think we have got a real opportunity here and we need to really get on top of this one in the next couple of months.'

The Issues Paper, engendered by the Canadian Delegation to the United Nations and the Secretariat Workshop, transformed in a march of drafts through the Strategic Overview, the Joint Justice Committee and the meeting of Deputy Ministers Responsible for Criminal Justice, was about to be born again as the Draft Cabinet Discussion Paper. The written presence of the policy issue of victims had acquired a reasonably lengthy history and a conventional appearance. The draft Discussion

[6] See B. Glaser and A. Strauss, *Awareness of Dying*, Aldine, Chicago, 1964.

Paper may have contained greater detail, a more authoritative style, and considerable embellishment, but it was still the recognizable descendant of the first essays that had been written some nine months before.

The very first draft was completed by 11 May. It drew into itself the observations and argument put to the Deputy Solicitor General by the Deputy Ministry of State for Social Development. It narrated how there had been a growth of public and Government awareness of the imbalance between the concern awarded to the offender and that offered to the victim. It talked of the multiple injuries of crime: physical, financial, practical, and emotional. It talked of secondary victimization by the criminal justice system. It reflected that those who suffer from crime are the emotionally and physically vulnerable: the poor, the elderly, and victims of sexual and family violence. In short, the introduction was a synthesis of the Department's stock preface and the Ministry of State's portrayal of victims, a portrayal which emanated from the descriptive imperatives of the Priorities and Planning Committee and the mediated work of the Department of the Solicitor General itself, the Interdepartmental Committee on Family Violence, and the victims movement. It was a necessary and politically sagacious introduction, holding up a mirror to those who would judge it. It had been tried in practice and virtually dictated by a central agency. If the memorandum was to succeed, there could be little indecision about how the character of victims and victimization should be drawn. I have argued that the initiative became the property of others as it moved. By the middle of May the mark of the Ministry of State for Social Development was quite visible.

The draft proceeded to recite the long history of federal involvement in the area of victims, a history punctuated by the Speech from the Throne, the Government's commitment to the victims of family violence and to children, the National Plan of Action, the report of the Canadian Delegation to the United Nations Congress, and the approved Strategic Overview. The burden of that history was the emergence of a pronounced concern with the problems of crime victims in general and with the victims of family violence in particular. The draft concluded with a catalogue of federal achievements: the demonstration and research projects aimed at the victims of family violence, projects which stressed the role of the police; the cost-sharing agreements with the provinces on the funding of compensation programmes; the long-promised initiative on battered wives; the financial support of transition houses and rape crisis centres; and amendments to the Criminal Code. It was at that point that the first draft ended, a preamble to a much longer document yet to be written. It was described as 'hastily got together' by its author. The draft was submitted to others inside the Department of the Solicitor General and rewritten by 16 May.

Consultations with members of the Programs Branch indicated that the most profitable way of spending the policy reserve funds might be to advance police-based services and conduct the national victimization survey which had already been the subject of elaborate pre-tests. It was put that 'we lack solid information on victims', and that much money and time had already been devoted to the pilot surveys: 'we have the experience and know-how to mount in a reasonably short period of time a very sophisticated victimization survey on a national level'.[7] There could be a similar exploitation of the work done in Calgary, Edmonton, and elsewhere. In this quite pragmatic manner, the structure of the initiative began to take shape, reflecting the readiness of certain phases of the Department's activity, the competences which staff had already developed, and the possibilities described by a short-term, non-recurring, and modest initiative. The practical exigencies of the Department of the Solicitor General and the Social Affairs Envelope had given a framework to proposals. Timeliness, expediency, and opportunity gave salience to special features of what could be done, emphasizing the survey and police-based victim service units.

Once again, the two pilots of the initiative performed the little movement of genuflection, submitting the new version to the Godparents and future proprietors of the issue. It was as if each phase of the process demanded its own round of obeisances. Everyone was to receive a courtesy in the hope of a blessing. Just as the English parishes sometimes confirm their frontiers by 'beating the bounds', so the departments and agencies of the federal government were allowed to trace a symbolic line around their territories, authorities, and powers.

What is of some little interest is the manner in which significant others were identified in that process. The world of Ottawa is stratified politically and functionally, laying out a map of those who must and should be acknowledged. The evolving structure of an initiative will project into the future the character of the landscape through which it must pass. There are people and institutions whose activities will probably be affected by a new area of policy, and they require consultation. Each phrasing of an initiative will entail a slightly different route and a different procession of involved figures, and each phrasing must thereby accommodate a different set of solutions to the negotiations which it will

[7] Memo from Director, Criminal Justice Policy, 2 June 1981.

generate. In terms of consequence, and describing the most prominent path of action and response, the federal departments and agencies stretched ahead of the draft that was being prepared. It was for them that appearances were being so busily organized.

Lesser groups tended to feel forgotten. For instance, left behind and rendered politically insignificant for a while were some of the Divisions of the Programs Branch. By June 1981 the Branch had done much of its job in that preliminary phase: it was no longer navigating the initiative and its title to property in victims was being temporarily reduced. There was to be further involvement as research staff and the members of the Consultation Centre came to guide funds, programmes, and demonstration projects after the Government's decision. But in May and June 1981 the baton had passed and there was a practical denial of the importance of some of the Branch's divisions. The occasionally abstract relations between research and policy were once more given flesh by the Resentment expressed at the partial political displacement of the Branch. Thus, on 17 June an official of the Planning and Liaison Division wrote to the Acting Assistant Deputy Minister, Programs Branch:

> I want to register our concern in not having been consulted until this week on ... the submissions ... concerning Victims Services' initiatives. As I understand it, other components of the Programs Branch were involved last month in a sort of 'think' session to consider resource implications for the Programs Branch. These implications, however, did not include those relating to the Planning and Liaison Division. At the last minute, the Division did pull together information relating to dissemination for Linda MacLeod, and I have since spent a number of hours with her developing a public information section of the Cabinet document.... I do not feel the task has been given the attention it warranted. Perhaps more to the point is the fact that it is very difficult to tune in effectively to an issue when you are coming to it cold, as we did not have the benefit of working on it for the past month.

Other bodies were consulted somewhat earlier. The ritual of viewing and talks has its precedence. First was the Department of Justice and the meeting of the Joint Justice Committee. On 2 June the Director, Criminal Justice Policy, reminded the Deputy Solicitor General that 'time is of the essence and it is very important that we get this initiative into the Social Envelope Committee in the very near future'. Accordingly, he proposed that the Department of Justice should be informed at that day's meeting of the Joint Justice Committee that draft proposals would be presented to it within a few days for discussion on 11 June. In his turn, the Deputy Solicitor General wrote to the Deputy Minister of Justice about the formulation of a response to the Deputy Minister of State for

Social Development: if there are 'aspects of victims assistance which could be enhanced by an infusion of short term resources and which would be consistent with the development of broader policy in this area, we have been invited to put something before the committee'. He mooted the idea of making a joint submission, an idea which could also be discussed on 11 June.

The draft paper was distributed in Ottawa in readiness for that meeting. Health and Welfare Canada reported that it was proceeding with its own response to the needs of its client victims, children, and the victims of 'intrafamily violence'. It was about to establish a Clearinghouse on Family Violence.[8] It approved the plans and arguments of the draft paper, but it expressed no desire to join the Departments of Justice and the Solicitor General in making a submission. Status of Women Canada also extended a broad welcome to the proposals. The Ministry of State for Social Development echoed the Solicitor General's own reservations about the utility of the survey. Its gatekeeping policy analyst was reported to have stated that 'the arguments for the victimization survey are not convincing and there is no persuasive detail given the cost of the survey on the advantages of this data collection vehicle over other forms of information gathering'.[9] One of the initiative's pilots had pencilled in the marginal comment, 'we've always been concerned about this', and the Director of Policy himself wrote to the Assistant Deputy Minister, Programs:

> I'm back with the same problem. The data on the Victimization survey *costs* and *results* is too thin and won't make it through the process. We've taken the process as far as we can and it is now up to Research to provide the 'detailed' costing and the *rationale* needed to support this survey, if we can't get it this week, then we should withdraw the submission.

Reticence about the survey illuminates some of the transitional problems of research and policy. It will be remembered that the survey had first entered the work of the Ministry in the context of improving information about the effects of crime prevention campaigns. It had evolved, but its evolution had touched rather tangentially on the bald and immediate problems of victims. Indeed, in some ways, the information generated by victimization surveys tends to depress the political urgency of the social problems of victims. Reports tend to suggest that the experience of crime is typically fleeting and mild, lacking the intensity of a trauma which demanded an institutional response. Further, there could

[8] The Clearinghouse was actually formally declared open on 22 Jan. 1982.
[9] Memo from Linda MacLeod to Director, Criminal Justice Policy, 9 June 1981.

well be a disparity between the portraits of victims delivered by surveys and those furnished by the political imperatives of the policy processes of Ottawa. A policy analyst surmised in 1982:

I think it's going to destroy some myths that women are highly victimised and that elderly are highly victimised, that children are highly victimised. Which is a danger for those who are trying to promote them. People may say, 'hey, 80% of victims are young, male, between twenty and twenty four. Many of them know their attackers. It's the males living in the lower class spectrum. So I don't know if that's going to help.

Further, in 1981 it seemed to some that surveys were rather remote, secluded in the recesses of research and speculation, irrelevant to the immediate provision of succour. In the dramatization of assistance, the victimization survey appeared somewhat unhelpful and impractical. The Solicitor General himself had expressed anxiety about the 'political balance' of the proposals. And all the talk of austerity had begun to give prominence to projects that were patently useful. Those that were merely interesting or informative had started to lose lustre. As one of the pilots stated:

There's a general negativity towards research of any sort [within Government] these days, and that's a main part of the restraint thing. You can couch things like that in different terms. That's partly also why evaluation has become an important buzz word because *research* is now a dirty word. Evaluation is a positive word because it smacks of research that looks at efficiency and effectiveness and discipline. It isn't sort of airy-fairy and looking for concepts and that sort of thing.

It was not therefore feasible to advance the survey simply as a potential source of interesting information. Ironically, what had served as the Trojan Horse of a victims initiative was now considered a political handicap, a Greek gift. In the early drafts, surveys had been lauded as a basis of data about the nature, magnitude, and costs of problems faced by the victims of crime. It was held that those data would be radically superior to the figures made available by police forces, allowing a better direction of crime prevention effort. Little more was stated. In later drafts it had to be stressed by the literal and metaphorical underlining of argument that surveys would be essential to any initiative, being the sole fount of statistics about the effectiveness of crime prevention, the extent of unreported crime, the risks of victimization, and consumer responses to the criminal justice system. It was implied that the survey was indispensable to any intelligently controlled programme of work. But the survey remained politically vulnerable and it was to suffer a little when decisions were finally made. It was not accepted as attractive by the political groupings which posed very direct questions about the immediate benefits of action.

The new, amended discussion paper recited the standard history of victims and the federal government. Unlike its predecessors, it was no longer exercised by the problem of whether to move to a major national leadership role' on victims. That role had been thrust upon the Departments of Justice and the Solicitor General. What was at issue was the form that an initiative could take. In response to some of the apparent frailties of the survey, the Department of the Solicitor General severed the provision of services to victims from the proposal to conduct a survey. It offered three options: the first concentrated on the stimulation of services, the second combined stimulation with a relatively cheap national urban victimization survey, and the third married stimulation with a more expensive comprehensive national survey of victims. It was evident that, like the lizard's tail, all or part of the survey could be amputated, leaving a surviving body behind.

In June 1981 the Ministry of State for Social Development submitted its own proposals to Government on the Social Policy priorities. It had received reports about how extensively the Departments of the Solicitor General and Justice were involved in furthering the interests of the victims of crime. The Ministry of the Solicitor General proposed to devote a little over a million dollars to that end in 1981–2 and a similar sum in 1982–3. Those sums were classified as 'small expenditures' and, indeed, in the context of the projected expenditure of thirteen hundred million dollars on new initiatives in 1984–5, less than two million dollars *was* small. Overall, the work envisaged for victims was dwarfed financially and politically by the issues of the management of unemployment, inflation, and energy. As a marginal venture, it was almost certainly heeded but not subjected to intense scrutiny. In turn, the Government endorsed victims as an issue. They now required a planned future which could be discussed further.

On 11 June the Joint Justice Committee decided that there should be an interdepartmental discussion paper on victim justice to be tabled for deliberation by the Ministry of State for Social Development on 18 June and discussed a week later. As Linda MacLeod observed, 'the push is now very obviously on'. Yet another timetable had to be plotted, moving the initiative through the Ministry of State for Social Development towards a formal submission to Cabinet that was planned for early July. Yet another draft was to be written. Staff were offered three days in which 'to provide additional information, deletions or editorial comments'.

What remained to perturb the pilots were the twin problems of the survey and the provinces. People were asked to consider whether 'enough information [is] now provided on the advantages and disadvantages of each option and particularly on the usefulness of the victimization survey'. One of the policy analysts who had performed some of the early work on the proposals after the Secretariat Workshop had commented, 'there're no votes in surveys', and it was evident that her fear lingered on throughout the drafting process. Simultaneously, the possible effects of upset provincial sensibilities tended to haunt the pilots. Those effects were to become especially worrying and ominous when on 23 June the Meeting of Deputy Ministers Responsible for Criminal Justice disclosed considerable provincial trepidation about federal intentions. Some of the Deputy Ministers announced that victims were quite palpably their concern, that the federal government was acting improperly, and that Ottawa would do best to pass money directly to the provinces and refrain from interfering.

The victims initiative should have been discussed by the Ministry of State for Social Development on 2 July, but it was removed from a busy agenda and deferred until the following week. At that meeting of 9 July, the Department was led to expect support from National Health and Welfare, Status of Women Canada, and Central Mortgage and Housing. It received a general approbation from the Ministry of State itself. The discussion paper's third option was supported. But after that officials of the Ministry of State also injected some doubts, questioning the nature of the burden which might be laid upon provincial governments, enquiring whether focused supplementary studies might not reduce the expense of a national survey, and asking whether the new Justice Statistics Centre might not be the body best eqippped to conduct the survey.

The appearance and presentation of the initiative then required one final revision. It was to be the Department's new position that the burden upon the provinces would be slight because all projects would be brief and 'stimulative' rather than lengthy, designed to save money rather than consume it. Further, it was to be argued that sub-samples could well concentrate upon specific populations of victims but it was necessary to associate them with a larger survey that would unearth the small groups in the first instance. It was also to be claimed that the Justice Statistics Centre was not yet able to undertake the task of mounting a survey.

In its final form, the discussion paper paid greater deference to provincial sensibilities. It was stressed that novel projects would not be transformed into onerous provincial obligations. And it was proposed to postpone the announcement of increased federal involvement until federal and provincial Ministers were all assembled at their projected conference in November. It would have been indelicate to disclose a new federal initiative in that area before any other audience. Indeed, the planned announcement of the initiative at the NOVA Conference in October would not now take place. As an official of the Planning and Liaison Division reflected, 'great efforts were expended in *not* announcing things at NOVA'. It was decided that all projects that came to life before November should not be represented as parts of a comprehensive national initiative. And there would be no formal submission of the Discussion Paper prepared for the Ministry of State for Social Development, that paper being a public document that would have upset a difficult calendar. In fact, as I have indicated, the intervention from the Ministry of State for Social Development had induced a premature birth and the initiative had to incorporate the warps which had been introduced into the timetable and logic of the policy-making process. As one of its authors remarked, it had originally been envisaged that the Department would wait until the Federal–Provincial Working Group:

> Got a little bit along the road and until the provinces let us know what they really thought. So it would have been much easier to write and much more rational because then you could have said, 'according to this, it has been decided that this is really what the provinces want and this is approximately what they would like funded'.

The final draft was also more robust in its advocacy of a national survey. After all, Health and Welfare Canada had stated that 'carefully developed surveys could provide useful information as to the varying needs of victims within different milieux, urban, rural, and/or minority communities'. Status of Women Canada had expressed interest in the documentation of violence to women. And, distilling their arguments, the Ministry of State for Social Development had itself come to approve what it had once questioned. Arguments were now marshalled behind the third and most ambitious option, rewritten to recommend the stimulation of services for victims, a national survey of victims and detailed follow-up studies of special groups of victims. It was understood that those groups would be people exposed to violent crime and women.

In that final guise, the discussion paper told a story that took its coherence from a single theme and a simple logic. It was a creative accomplishment. One of its authors argued:

> We had to just sit down for hours on end saying things like, 'it's so nebulous, how can we make it sound like it's something?' And I've forgotten a lot of that

now, and I've come to believe the phrases myself and repeated them so often that they sound okay. They've gone through enough talking about that it sounds like a reality but all that was a creation. Here we are with [options] that have no substance at all. What can we do about it? So it was interesting and you should look back on it that way.

Stories are the standard form which people employ to give order to what might otherwise be an unintelligible chronicle of events. They give a frame, a definition, a logic, and a progression to processes. They animate actors, actions, and scenes. They are a 'systematic means of storing, bringing up to date, rearranging, comparing, testing, and interpreting available information about social behavior'.[10] Their structure becomes a way of giving objectivity to understanding.[11] Indeed, plot and argument can become synonyms for one another, plot being a dramatization of connections traced by analysis. As Surmelian observed:

> Causal plotting—requires wisdom, and at its best it is a philosophical exercise of a high order. One has to reason it out, supply the inner connections and the correct answers. The action is inevitable by the inner logic of the events, or at least highly plausible.[12]

And so it was with the discussion paper. The story of the emergent victims initiative had a central character, a policy awaiting birth. It was given a pedigree and a biography in a series of scenes composed of dense masses of specific facts. It borrowed some of its concreteness from those facts, becoming more substantial in the process. It was given unity by a structured natural history: demands from inside and outside Ottawa, from the United States, the provinces, and women had built upon one another to produce a social movement that was beginning to be reflected in the programmes and commitments of the federal government. Indeed, important voices in the government were amplifying that movement. The programmes and the movement were about to feed upon each other in ever more energetic fashion, producing a clamour that had to be answered. The needs of victims had been quite improperly neglected in the past, but they were now acquiring a form, substance, and political presence. In particular, the very groups which the government itself had

[10] W. Bennett and M. Feldman, *Reconstructing Reality in the Courtroom*, Tavistock, London, 1981, p. 5.

[11] See T. Sullivan, *Writing*, National Extension College, Cambridge, 1979, p. 5.

[12] L. Surmelian, *Techniques of Fiction Writing*, Anchor Books, New York, 1969, p. 100.

preferred were victims of crime, unable to help themselves and deserving of aid. They were multiply victimized, hurt by the very criminal justice system that was supposed to help them. Their plight and the role of Government would be made luminous in October when the National Organization for Victim Assistance convened to discuss victims and services in Canada and the United States. It would be a coercive setting which could be put to good use if an announcement were made to foreshadow a more definite statement from the November meeting of Ministers Responsible for Criminal Justice. It should be on that stage in November that the initiative should make its official appearance into the world.

Government Approval

Justice for Victims of Crime was considered by Cabinet in July.[13] The Solicitor General was satisfied that it had been well received in large measure because of the earlier consultations. However, as a political matter, less money was made available than had been expected. The survey was the chief problem.

The decision was made to approve the initiative but to refer the matter of funding back to the Ministry of State for Social Development. It was later determined that the allocation to the Department of the Solicitor General should be cut simply by removing funds after the decimal point: the Department had requested over one million dollars for each of the two years from 1981–3. The sums were actually reduced to one million dollars precisely for both years, but the disclosure and logic of that decision eluded Department officials for some while. In fact, although many other departments had had their budgets depleted in exactly the same fashion, the Ministry of State for Social Development claiming that it was a routine measure, the Solicitor General's officials were anxious and baffled. A Government decision had been given, yet there was uncertainty about how much money and how many person years were to be allocated to the Department in support of the initiative. In the midst of that uncertainty, there was doubt about the very viability of the survey, now awarded only a meagre sum.

[13] See *Solicitor General Annual Report* 1981–1982, Ministry of Supply and Services Canada, 1983.

Conclusion

Between April and July 1981 there was a transitional period in which the social problem of victims passed from the status of a concern, became a policy issue, and then flowered into a government policy. In its passage, it was forced to deck itself in an ever-growing set of political trappings. Paraded around Ottawa and in the provinces, offered to one significant group after another, it was presented as an object in which others might care to interest themselves. The formulation of a national policy implicated a host of organizations which policed their own terrain. If they were to adopt that policy as their own, admitting it into their preserves, it would be necessary to present it as an entity in which they could acquire property. Even if there was no desire to implement change, the very obeisance to authority was an important means of forestalling difficulties. The political transformation of a social problem revolved round elaborate rituals of respect. At every stage, the problem was proferred. At every stage, it was visibly altered to carry the brand of important organizations. And there were many such stages, reflecting the multiplicity and complexity of Government organizations in a country with two Ministries regulating the federal system of criminal justice, ten provincial governments, and a host of bordering departments and institutions. The phenomena of victims were to be very practical political constructions, artfully contrived to be as attractive to as many major bodies as possible. As one of the initiative's pilots observed, 'we sort of coddled the process along all the way, making sure that all the different bureaucratic levels supported us. . . . In a way it's been defined currently simply by which departments and agencies are taking some interest in it.'

The final product was given structure and logic by the great mass of historical antecedents and obligations which had accumulated since 1974, embellished by the particular demands of involved organizations, and affected by the special circumstances of the lapsed funds of the social policy reserve. It was rather distant from the claims and arguments that had been made at the beginning of the march of committees. But those arguments would not have attained sufficient legitimacy in a political arena. Research officials were somewhat alienated from politics and politicians, and their alienation was mirrored in their discourse. As papers moved away from them through the linked stages of the ratification process, so politics superseded the logic of research. In the end, what had taken years to develop took a short while to approve. An official in one of the central agencies reflected, 'it's a very small initiative, you know'.

XII. Out of the Shadows

The offender. The police.
The legal fraternity. The witness.
The victim.
Some are bathed in the limelight
of public attention . . .
Some stand unnoticed in the shadows.

Introduction

Victims stood unnoticed in the shadows of more than one political theatre in 1981. They were about to be presented publicly but they had to wait for their time and their audience. There could be no foregoing of the proper ritual. Just as the birth of the heir to a kingdom was attended by the more powerful barons of the medieval state, so the birth of victims had to be witnessed if it was to be acknowledged politically. Problems of legitimacy and etiquette were paramount. There could be no formal announcement of the initiative until the Ministers responsible for criminal justice had met in conference and, once announced, the initiative would require the most fastidious management.

Before the summer, the social problem had been under the tutelage of only a few people, a social circle, who had acquired a working knowledge of one another. The problem had been developed in only a small number of sites and under constant surveillance. It had been endowed with a conventional history, a certain structure, and a probable future. It had been escorted from one setting to another in a regulated sequence. It had been reasonably controlled. Even so, victims had displayed emergent properties and there had been abundant surprises in their making. Control had never been complete. The early history of the initiative had been composed of a series of encounters between things familiar and things unfamiliar. There had been repeated collisions with alien developments and, with every collision, contexts, contents, directions, and mandates had shifted. There had been even more galvanic transformations in the very centre of the federal government: Peace and Security and the new Policy and Expenditure Management System had upset plans, distorted timetables, and accelerated projects in a manner that could never have been anticipated. Over time, too, the initiative had become substantial enough for portions of its social structure to bend back and affect its progress in unpredictable ways. The structure had started to become a little attenuated at the margins, its members beginning to lose full knowledge of each other's doings. Parts had passed beyond the boundaries of the Department of the Solicitor General, shielded from view and no longer quite explicable.

All those accidents in the early phases were slight compared with what might come after the initiative had been ushered officially into the world. Victims would then become a public spectacle, observed by many groups who might well take a stance towards them. The universe of relations and institutions touching upon victims was about to be enlarged immeasurably. There could be no certainty about which groups would be made visible by the newly prominent policy, how many they would be, where they would emerge, what configurations they would form, how their appearances would be staggered over time, and precisely what demands they would make. Before the summer of 1981, a crude map of involved agencies and people could be drawn, plotting a route and a character for proposals. There could be some limited rehearsal of the political negotiations that might come, some preparation of the outward show of the initiative. After the summer, no sure map existed. Such are the dialectics of policy-making that it could be expected that the initiative would actually create many of the groupings that lay ahead in its path. It could further be expected that those selfsame groupings would attempt to change the initiative, acting as the constraints, promoters, and guides of its future growth. A continually transformed and moving initiative would be preceded by its own bow wave of change in the organizations about it. No policy-maker could ever unravel the transformational logic of that pattern of development. There would always be something to disconcert the planner as new institutions were born and old institutions were reconstructed.

The federal government could not simply command the compliance of the organizations it would encounter. Policy-making was not supposed to subdue or avoid obstacles, it was to court them, showing a conspicuous deference. The fate of victims would be determined by the responses which they received as they left Ottawa and travelled into the provinces, municipalities, and communities of Canada. A brief, non-recurring, and modestly financed initiative would perish unless it was embraced by people working in institutions outside the government of Canada. It had to be sponsored actively by new bodies who were prepared to give their own labour, money, and protection to victims. It had to be sponsored quickly. After all, federal funding would lapse after a mere two years. The initiative would wither if maladroit administration failed to implant it securely in the provinces and the private sector. Those who contemplated what should be done in the wake of the sudden opportunity of the summer were correspondingly prudent. They could turn their gaze on the United States and see before them the ominous example of just such a withering of the Law Enforcement Assistance Administration's Victim Assistance Initiative. Between 1974 and 1981 the American federal government had allotted some twenty-three million dollars annually to projects providing services to the victims and witnesses of crime. The initiative was a 'sunset programme' to be reviewed in 1981. In September Linda MacLeod, one of the two new pilots of the Canadian initiative, was sent to a conference held in Rensselearville, New York, where the co-ordinators of the Law Enforcement Assistance Administration met with the managers of victims projects to discuss the future of the American initiative. She returned with the conclusion that 'direct federal funding to grass-roots groups had not proved successful':

> Despite the implicit assumption that following a period of strong federal support in this area, programs could then be supported by state and local concerns, no comprehensive rationale was developed, and no co-ordinated evaluation system instituted to expedite this responsibility shift, either before the government initiated its program in 1973, or subsequently. As a result, the expected transition and the future of victim/witness initiatives in the U.S. are now extremely uncertain.[1]

Linda MacLeod made the repeated recommendation that the Canadian initiative should profit from the example set by the American Victim Assistance Initiative. She argued that any new projects should be grafted on to local bodies from the very start:

> Community and grass-roots input is essential in the planning and implementation of any victim/witness program to maximise the utility and credibility of the programs;... great sensitivity must be demonstrated not only to provincial activity and jurisdiction in the area, but also the interests and programs of private and volunteer groups;... workers at the grass-roots level, and private agencies must be involved at the planning stage and throughout the implementation of any project to increase cross-fertilization and support through information exchange and co-operation.[2]

[1] L. MacLeod, 'L.E.A.A. Meeting to Evaluate Funding of Victim Oriented Services', 10 Sept. 1981.

[2] Ibid.

There were other influences about to bear on the emerging policy. Not only would new institutions be created or discovered, but it was probable that they would frequently be under the dominion of others who were more or less independent of the social circle that had fathered the federal initiative. Those others could be described as the local barons of the criminal justice system and they had experienced their own little histories, struggles, reverses, and successes. A judge running a Victim–Witness Assistance Program in his or her court or a Police Chief administering a Victim Service Unit need not have shared in the genesis of the initiative nor be overly impressed by the particular arguments that sustained it. To them, the past of the initiative would tend to be foreign, opaque, and possibly without interest. They would not necessarily have known of the moral enterprise of Irvin Waller or the travails of the Interdepartmental Committee on Family Violence. All that would be occluded. They would not appreciate how the initiative had arisen as a very specific response to the special problems of a cluster of federal institutions. They would not have been privy to that cluster's perspectives, rhetoric, or preoccupations. They would not have learned of the little compromises and assumptions that had grown out of the natural history of the initiative. In short, it could not be presumed that they shared a universe of ideas about victims, the character of the services which victims required, or the ends to which an initiative should be put. A novel, numerous, and possibly wary cast of actors would have to learn the beginnings of co-operation. They would have to be schooled, and all within the space of a few months.

Simultaneously, of course, the original social circle of the federal initiative would have to change. Before the summer, it had determined much of what it had to know and how it would become affected by that knowledge. Now the world would answer back and it would be impolitic to disregard that reply. Members of the circle were about to encounter strange ideas and practices. As the initiative proceeded to travel out into Canada, it would envelop themes that had never been heeded before. It would become fused with the interests of very diverse groups scattered across the face of the country. Thus, for example, federal officials would discover that the staff of the Corrections Branch of the Ministry of the Attorney General of British Columbia had awarded great importance to the work of the Law Reform Commission of Canada. It would become known that the members of that Ministry believed that the Commission had done much to bring about the resurgence in the politics of victims. Federal officials would read the Ministry's report which argued that 'the change of attitude in Canada which sees a switch of focus to the victim is best demonstrated by the Law Reform Commission of Canada espousing the goal of restitution ...'.[3] In that discovery, the Law Reform Commission of Canada inevitably acquired something of a prominence and a position that it had hitherto been denied. It started to exert a modest influence on the two federal departments. Those who had contributed to the espousing of the goal of restitution would begin to be seen in the company of officials from the two federal departments.

The victims initiative would absorb more than one alien history as it moved across the nation. Each history would then become a stage of the initiative, just as the initiative entered the history, and the two would fold into each other and give meaning to each other. The work of the Attorney General of British Columbia and the Law Reform Commission of Canada would be newly affected by the Departments of the Solicitor General and Justice, and the federal departments would become entangled in the British Columbian history of restitution and reparation. The staffs of all institutions would eventually be found attending a National Symposium on Reparative Sanctions held in Vancouver at the end of May and the beginning of June 1982. They would hear the Acting Assistant Deputy Solicitor General of Canada and the Director of Research of the Ministry of the Attorney General of British Columbia. John Hogarth, who had written about mediation for the Law Reform Commission of Canada, would be invited to a Policy Roundtable in the company of the Solicitor General's Director of Policy, the Assistant Deputy Attorney General of British Columbia, and the Director of Policy Planning from the Ministry of Justice, Canada. In such conferences, many little histories would flow into one another. In more than one site, people had to enquire how it was that a concern for victims was thought to have arisen.

In the months after July, a rudimentary social organization had to be built in order to conduct the new policy through all that difficult terrain. Its structure was to bear the marks of a number of dilemmas that flowed out of the special character of a brief, inexpensive initiative that had been forced before its time. The eighteen months of the initiative represented a much shorter period than that normally awarded to federal projects: schemes would have to be inaugurated which could never yield much inside the Government timetable; and policies would have to be drafted before needs assessment and demonstration projects had been evaluated. As a member of the Causes and Prevention Division reflected, 'it's hard to evaluate anything. How can we evaluate a programme that's only

[3] 'Restore: Corrections Program to Assist the Victims of Crime', Corrections Branch, Ministry of Attorney General, British Columbia, January 1982, p. 5.

started six months ago? So we can't do it. So the evaluation part is going to be very difficult.' The second phase of the initiative was dominated by something of a sense of rush and of things failing to synchronize properly.

Delays were most vexing, yet nothing could be done publicly until after the Meeting of Federal-Provincial Ministers Responsible for Criminal Justice. The first dilemma was thus that it was imperative to make a start but that no such start could be managed as if it were a beginning: 'despite the low profile we are forced to assume, we must launch projects almost immediately if we are to fulfill the terms of the [Government] decision.'[4]

Problems of timing were to complicate all that happened next. Things had to be done rapidly and sometimes in rather perverse order. Different sequences fell out of gear with one another from time to time. Events that had been planned to assume one meaning sometimes had to acquire another. The timetable that had flowed out of the Ministry of the Solicitor General and the Joint Justice Committee had been caught up and swept along by the greater stream of the Policy and Expenditure Management System. And there was a confusion of other timetables as well. Victims had been injected into the working calendars of a number of organizations, and they were moving at different speeds, with different pasts and with different destinations. They had become even more conspicuously multivocal without a central bureaucratic navigator. The little happenings and occasions scheduled for them were in danger of becoming jumbled, interfering with the significance that a carefully arranged history was supposed to give to its parts. For example, the conference designed to dramatize the Government's response to victims was now about to precede the Meeting of Ministers Responsible for Criminal Justice. Members of the American and Canadian victims movement about to gather in Toronto for the NOVA Conference in October could not be told of the Government's new resolve. They had been brought together, in part, to present a show of the demand which the initiative could satisfy. What had been staged as the teleologically compelling moment of the initiative, the convention that would force policy-makers to act, could now give little more than a hint that something might be in the offing.

Money, too, was short. Without additional funding, the million dollars of the initiative could not build much of an edifice. The initiative was supposed to be 'stimulative' but it could not be allowed to stimulate such

[4] First Meeting of the Interdepartmental Committee on Justice for Victims of Crime, 23 Sept. 1981.

a flood of requests and proposals that the provinces and municipalities became apprehensive. After all, there was a very real likelihood that the federal government would cease to provide financial support after eighteen months. There was a risk that the initiative would be regarded as yet another piece of federal faddishness. Thus the second dilemma was that the new social organization was required to advertise the importance of victims' needs and sketch opportunities for their relief, yet refrain from exciting an excessive demand for services from the provinces and the private sector. Expectations were to be raised but not 'unrealistically'. In particular, the initiative had to abstain from taking action that the provinces might regard as meddlesome. As the Director of Policy Planning argued at a meeting held on 23 July 1981, 'we don't want to do the obtrusive things that would upset the provinces'. A fine compromise had to be reached between responding to a 'growing public concern' and so inflating that concern that it attained troublesome proportions. A tactful and modest prominence was to be sought, a combination of the unassuming and the self-publicizing. And out of that second dilemma, a third was to appear. If the initiative was not to be presented too flamboyantly, it might well fail to attract that interest which would indicate what was needed. As the minutes of the first meeting of the Interdepartmental Committee on Justice for Victims of Crime reported:

> That although one central activity should be to raise the consciousness of the general public and of service providers regarding the needs of victims of crime, expectations should not be falsely inflated before services are in place or at least emerging to meet the needs of victims. On the other hand it was noted that until consciousness was raised, it is unlikely that we will be able to identify needs.

In turn, a nice question would revolve around the problem of whether the raising of consciousness produced or merely illuminated the needs and identities of victims. It was possible that the probing and publicity accompanying the initiative would generate some of the phenomena of victimization, an instance of the observer effect giving structure to the world. Thus one who was to undertake research on victims' needs reflected:

> The thing that worries me about asking people what they need is that it's self-fulfilling. You know. At one point we considered asking an open-ended question: 'what is required, what is it you need?' Well, people don't have any idea of what's possible. 'What do you need?' 'I don't know'. The word doesn't have any meaning to them. So what we've done is compose a hopefully sort of comprehensive reasonable list of what's possible and then ask whether this would have been of any use to them. Now, again, by virtue of the fact that we've tried to make it reasonable, it's easy to say 'yes'. You know: 'would you have liked

more information on your case?' 'Sure, why not?' So you're kind of driving the positive response just by the way you're asking the question.

The Seventh Annual Conference of the National Organization for Victim Assistance

The Justice for Victims of Crime Initiative may be read as a succession of efforts to propagate ideas and stimulate activity without engendering conflict. Quite prominent was its first anticipatory stage, the gathering together of people who might become implicated in its fate. The Seventh Annual Conference of the National Organization for Victim Assistance was to be held in Toronto in the middle of October 1981, and it was then that the principal groupings of the Canadian and American victims movements would meet in the one place and for the very first time. A party of officials would leave Ottawa to see the inhabitants of the world they were about to reshape. They would reveal a little of what was stirring in the capital. It was to be an entirely appropriate beginning, an iconic representation or tableau of what was in train. It seemed as if the array of policies that had just come together in the initiative was to be mirrored in the physical meeting of those whom it touched, the one group giving meaning to the other. And it was an interestingly indeterminate beginning: there was never any certainty about the future of the initiative, about the connections and structures that might appear in the Conference, or about the interplay between the Conference and the initiative. In a sense, the unfolding character of the Conference would disclose something of the fate of the initiative itself.

It will be remembered that the National Organization for Victim Assistance was the somewhat evangelical confederation of American groups that had fired central members of the animating social circles of Ottawa, Toronto, and beyond. Those who ventured south to the United States for instruction and example were often guided towards the meetings of the National Organization for Victim Assistance. In the summer of 1980, for instance, an official of the Ontario Community Programs Support Services Branch had written to a colleague in the Provincial Secretariat for Justice: 'I am advised by the paralegals [I met in Colorado] and by other contact persons I met at the National Symposium on Pre-Trial Services that the [forthcoming 1980 NOVA Conference] is the one that will yield more information, resource materials, ideas, etc.' In the same manner, one of the team charged with writing the policy paper after the Secretariat Workshop was sent to that selfsame conference in Portland, Oregon, and believed it to be 'one of the best conferences ... I got educated'. Canadians were often moved by what they saw of

NOVA. Some looked upon its Chairperson, Marlene Young, as charismatic. They met and talked at the NOVA Conferences, speculating about what might be attempted in Canada. They joined the National Organization for Victim Assistance. Irvin Waller had done so. In 1980 he had become a member of the NOVA Advisory Board.

The proposal to take NOVA to Canada flowed out of the core of the Solicitor General's animating social circle. In the summer of 1980 Irvin Waller and members of that circle met with NOVA in Washington. It had been the original intention of the NOVA Board to convene in Florida in 1981 but the State of Florida had refused to endorse the Equal Rights Amendment. That refusal rendered the State ineligible as a site. Besides, as the Publicity Officer of NOVA reflected, 'Irvin had been persuasive'. The man entrusted with the promotion of research on victims, the one-time Chairman of the Interdepartmental Committee on Family Violence, the member of the team of three, recalled:

> I was in Washington and met with NOVA people, okay, and with Irvin Waller also, and we talked about the whole possibility of having the next conference in Toronto. I came back and [the Canadian Council on Social Development] who was doing that project for me—[*Services to Victims and Witnesses of Crime in Canada*] had a meeting with me and Irvin Waller and we said 'look, we would like to pursue having NOVA. It'll be very good timing if we're successful to have this victims conference at this time and at that point'.

One of his colleagues remarked:

> ——, —— and —— started negotiations, but it wasn't just them ... it was Irvin because he got himself on their Board ... they were all mucking around somehow to merge our interests with NOVA's Conference, and to get them to Canada and that we would mastermind it so that the Conference would get held here and the issues that concerned us would get dealt with.

The arranging of the 1981 Conference was to be a solid instance of the Ministry of the Solicitor General enacting its own environment. The animating circle held that it would not do for the federal government to appear too *dirigiste* in the delicate matter of victims: 'I didn't want us to approach NOVA and us to be like the 1980 Workshop, the Solicitor General's conference on victims. So I said to CCSD, "I want CCSD to approach NOVA formally".' Accordingly, the social circle held meetings with the Canadian Council on Social Development in the summer of 1980. The Council, in its turn, wrote on 23 September to the Chairperson of NOVA, proposing that the next year's conference be held in Canada. Irvin Waller was to act as intermediary: he 'will be attending your conference next week and will be pleased to answer any questions you may have respecting the content of our proposal'. It would not do for the federal government to neglect provincial sensibilities: 'I told CCSD to write a joint letter to us and Ontario because I know Ontario is interested but Ontario may back down and see us being too pushy right after our 1980 Workshop.... So have the initiative come from CCSD joint to both Ontario and to us and ... tell Ontario that you've had some preliminary discussion and it looks like we're interested.' On 13 January 1981 the Council returned with a request to the Ontario Provincial Secretariat for Justice and to the official of the Solicitor General who had been entrusted with research on victims, a request that the two Ministries should fund and host the NOVA Conference in October. The objectives of the Conference would be fourfold: the exchange of knowledge between those involved with victims in Canada and America; 'to give added stimulus to emerging Canadian interest in the development of victim/witness services'; 'to provide the opportunity for Canadians involved in this emerging field to become knowledgeable of each others programs and experiences'; and 'to explore the possibility of developing a Canadian counterpart to the National Organization on Victim Assistance in the United States'.[5] The provision of funding was approved by the Research Projects Committee in January 1981, the official responsible for research on victims having:

> briefed the Committee on the importance of this Conference and how timely the issues of Victim Assistance was in Canada at this time. He explained how this Conference would afford an opportunity for Canadians to draw from the American experience in this area of victim assistance policies and programs.[6]

In effect, the members of the animating social circle were about to embark on a special venture, a venture that would be coloured by the prolonged discussions, the intimacy, the ambition, and the heightened understanding of a small group that was determined to alter policy. Knowledge and sentiments about the conference were consequently stratified. It was clear to everyone in the ministry that the meeting was intended to educate, consolidate, and stimulate a world. That had been argued in writing and before committees. But members of the inner circle had added an excitement and an urgency that tended to elude officials on the margins for some while. Their excitement was generated by an appreciation that plans and hopes long nursed were about to be disclosed; by the prospect of playing host to a charismatic organization that had been a source of continuing inspiration; by the idea of staging a major

[5] Letter dated 30 Sept. 1980.
[6] Minutes of meeting held on 28 Jan. 1981.

drama; by the apprehension that people and events once obscure were about to become luminous; and by desire for something of a moral and political wakening in Canada. Outsiders were not always privy to those emotions. One commented:

> For me, that conference was not important or it was always important but it didn't take on the emotional overlay [until quite late]. [The man responsible for research on victims] had always attributed a lot but that is his personal style. I mean, people hoped ... [The man responsible for research] had always hoped it would go like this. I don't know if anyone else did.

The venture of the animators was dialectical and complicated. Mindful that the initiative would have but a short life and that the world of Canadian victims lacked order, they attempted to produce an external event that would stand apart from the circle and influence not only themselves but also that incoherent world of the victim. A member stated, 'I don't want a federal thing. I want it national and, if *I* do it, it'll be federal. Irrespective of what I say, they'll see it as the Solicitor General being pushy again.' The Conference was intended to leave a visible mark. It was understood to be a turning-point, an irreversible transition. I have argued that the meetings of victimology and the victims movement are distinguished by their rites of solidarity and their use in the making of history. The Toronto Conference would announce that a section of the Canadian political system had been transformed. It would summon anticipatory activity before it came. After it had come, it would be represented as a public and indelible phase in the evolution of Canadian criminal justice policy. Things seen and commitments given would govern choice in the future. In particular, it was thought for a while that the Conference would serve as a platform for the formal declaration of the Justice for Victims of Crime Initiative. It was envisaged that the Meeting of Ministers Responsible for Criminal Justice would take place in October. The International Conference on Victim Assistance, Scheduled for 14–17 October, could then reveal federal and provincial plans to the world. The Solicitor General himself would speak at the opening of the Conference. So would Gordon Walker, Ontario Provincial Secretary for Justice. Their very participation was a major portent. So was the funding which their Ministries had supplied. Together, they would give a political future to the social problem of victims.

The Conference would be an exercise in the building of a social world. Meeting together, Canadians could translate a nascent victims movement into its own audience, the movement becoming both subject and object. People working in victims' services would be able to survey one another and themselves and understand that they were parts of a larger enterprise. The Conference would *objectify* the politics of victims. And such objectification was thought to be necessary. As one of the Conference's organizers reflected in a meeting held in August, two months before the Conference, 'in this country, many people who're involved in victim services don't think of themselves involved in victim services. That has meant we've had to spend hours describing what we're talking about.' One of his fellow organizers said 'in Canada, people don't know much yet. It's too new.' And a third said, 'I'm beginning to wonder whether there is such a thing as a criminal justice system. The thing seems to be much looser with different actors with different interests and conflicts.' One end of the Conference, then, became the giving of a corporate identity to a disorderly mass, a mass that appeared to lack character and the capacity to move on its own. People would be invited as 'Canadians involved in victim assistance'. They would gaze upon others and learn about their accomplishments. They would hear Canadians talking about work in Canada and Americans about work in America. They would become their own spectacle. They would be shown a slide show prepared by the Ministry of the Solicitor General and the Film Board of Canada, a show in which the unevenness of aid to victims would be deplored and remedial action would be urged. They would be given a leaflet echoing the arguments of the show. The leaflet would be published in the name of the Solicitor General of Canada, and it would announce:

> few ... services can be called truly nation-wide. A group operating in one part of the country might have no counterpart in another. And often the services that exist in the city are rarely found in the countryside. [Citizen groups should] Join an agency or start one. Form coalitions with other agencies. Study local victim–witness needs.[7]

It would be argued that assistance to victims was a sensible foundation for organizations and campaigns. In its turn, the Conference might begin to give a special definition to victims, act as the midwife to the birth of a new Canadian movement, and do so before the group whose very attendance would make the birth possible, a group that was supposed to be both the parent and the child of the movement.

More was to be expected of that movement than its mere birth, although a birth would be valuable enough in the making of future policy. A newly created politics of victims would have to attain inde-

[7] 'Victims: A View from the Shadows', Solicitor General of Canada, Ottawa, 1981.

pendence and permanence. It would have to survive the passing of the federal initiative and the redeployment of federal officials. It should spur politicans and their staff. Like God breathing life into Adam, members of the circle sought to give vitality and freedom to their own offspring. Unless they succeeded in doing so, they would remain alone in the criminal justice system: 'we don't have lobbies here. The Government funds everything. We're trying to stir the private sector.' A stirred private sector would be able to turn on the animating circle and give it a justification for acting. Thus Irvin Waller remarked before October:

> We hope to achieve public pressure. We hope the Conference will get a lot of public attention, newspaper coverage on crime victims, television, radio coverage. The public will begin to think about crime victims as a matter of some interest. They will therefore be generally supportive of any government initiatives to help crime victims. You'll generally get a sort of social interest in crime victims that will help push Government, encourage agencies you want to get involved, and generally be part of something which will reinforce those people who already want to do something about it.

The federal government could not direct the private sector to act. Instead, the stirred private sector had to be given what was tantamount to a virgin birth. And a dilemma arose as a result. It was unlikely that a victims movement could form in time without the coaxing of Government, yet any coaxing would subvert attempts to create a movement and it would certainly erode the movement's independence. It was said by one organizer at a preparatory meeting, 'the best way of killing the idea is to have a general organization and instruct all the voluntary organizations like transition houses to subscribe'. A dictatorial style had to be averted.

One answer was for the impetus to pass to bodies in the private sector. The animating circle had expanded temporarily to embrace bodies outside Government and it was those bodies which now acted. The Canadian Council on Social Development and the Canadian Association for the Prevention of Crime became the joint promoters of much that ensued. It was in their name that people were invited to the Conference. It was they who mooted the idea of a new movement for victims in Canada, a Canadian Organization for Victim Assistance or some such entity. The Canadian Council on Social Development was to publish *Rights and Services for Crime Victims* on the very eve of the Conference.[8] Its accompanying communiqué asserted that the pamphlet would 'be one

[8] *Rights and Services for Crime Victims*, Canadian Council on Social Development, Ottawa, 1981.

of several documents discussed at a Canada–United States conference to be held ... in Toronto'. Based in part on 'the contribution of Irvin Waller', *Rights and Services for Crime Victims* urged the public to 'pressure legislators and private agencies to deal effectively with victim needs' and voluntary agencies to 'organize a national association for victims'. The Canadian Council on Social Development advocated the recognition of the rights of crime victims in its journal *Perception*.[9] In time, it would combine with the Canadian Association for the Prevention of Crime to chair a meeting at the Conference, a meeting called to review the possibility of a national association akin to NOVA.

A dictatorial stance could also be avoided by importing inspiration from abroad. Irvin Waller, the animator in exile, the member of the NOVA Advisory Board, the organizer of the 1981 Conference, described NOVA as inspiring:

> I know what we want to accomplish. Really organize it to give a huge shot in the arm to try and better meet the needs of crime victims in Canada. We hope to achieve the shot in the arm because the Americans working in the crime victims field are inspiring.... We're hoping that bringing the event to Canada and rubbing shoulders with Canadians is going to inspire them, give them the feeling that they can do something.

Drama, urgency, and a model were about to be presented to Canada. It was to be argued that 'the enthusiasm of a new organization working on a long overlooked problem would provide a tremendous added stimulus to the awakening Canadian concern and programs in this area.... the impetus from a conference held with NOVA could help crystallize the formation of a Canadian movement concerned with crime victims.'[10] The bringing of NOVA to Canada would 'build towards the momentum we hope to generate in the Fall'.[11]

Some 100 Americans came to Toronto. Marlene Young was there with the Board of NOVA. She was to tell the Conference, 'we hope Canadians learn from our mistakes.... We have to deal with our own survival because if we don't survive, then our victims don't survive.'[12] Some 200 Canadians came.[13] It may be seen that officials from provincial

[9] G. Norquay and R. Weiler, 'Crime Victims' Rights Proposed', *Perception*, Spring–Summer 1981.

[10] 'National Organization on Victim Assistance (NOVA) Conference for Toronto in October 1981', 22 Sept. 1980.

[11] Memo from the Director, Policy Branch, 26 June 1981.

[12] Quoted in R. Doyon, 'The Victim in Focus', *Liaison*, Vol. 7, No. 10, November 1981, p. 16.

[13] The figures in Table 4 are based upon a list of registrants compiled on 8 Oct. The actual number attending the Conference was rather larger.

and federal government loomed large, and that the Government of Ontario and the federal Departments of Justice and the Solicitor General were especially prominent. In some measure, the 1981 Conference was an encounter between a source of inspiration, the policy-makers who had been inspired, and the population who might inherit and enact a policy that was in the making.

The very beginning of the Conference was symbolically fitting. On the evening of 14 October the two political Godfathers of the initiative spoke at a meeting chaired by the father of the initiative, Irvin Waller. Waller turned to one of the Godparents, Gordon Walker, and called him 'the political name associated with the victim movement in Canada'. Gordon Walker turned to Irvin Waller and said, 'Irvin, I'd like to compliment you as the spark plug of this conference and this movement.' He proceeded to state:

... I think we have reached the stage where there's no need for more study of victim needs. You know what those needs are.... What we need is action.... As a politician, I am committed to help bringing about ... change. Two years ago I introduced the concept of victim rights at a Federal/Provincial Conference of Justice Ministers. I was heartened by the reaction of my colleagues from other provinces, as well as the federal Government. I am pleased that my colleague, the present Solicitor General of Canada, has also become a keen advocate of victim rights. The simple fact is that it will take political support to transform the total justice system into a more compassionate process that acknowledges, rather than ignores, the needs of victims. I think that in Canada we now have the political will to provide that support at the federal and provincial levels.[14]

Irvin Waller turned to the Solicitor General of Canada and said 'I'm sorry we haven't heard more about concrete initiatives from the federal Government. I hope we hear more.' And, for his part, the Solicitor General talked about 'Justice for Victims'. What might have been a public proclamation of an initiative was instead a more modest 'foreshadowing' of what was to come. Yet it would be unambiguous enough to the informed listener:

'I expect this conference and its aftermath to lead to many significant, innovative approaches to improving how we deal with and treat victims in the Canadian criminal justice system ... There is a role for the national government to play in improving assistance to victims and ensuring that Canadians generally address this area as a legitimate matter of public policy. In fact, we have taken a number

[14] Remarks by the Honourable Gord Walker, QC, Provincial Secretary for Justice and Minister of Consumer and Commercial Relations, to the Conference on Victim Assistance, Canada and the United States, 14 Oct. 1981.

Table 4: *Canadian Participants in the 1981 NOVA Conference*

Government of Canada		
Ministry of the Solicitor General	7	
Ministry of Justice	5	
Health and Welfare Canada	4	
Status of Women Canada	3	
Privy Council Office	1	
Lew Reform Commission of Canada	1	
	21	(12.7%)
Government of Ontario		
Ministry of the Attorney General	2	
Ministry of Correctional Services	21	
Ministry of Community Services	1	
Provincial Secretariat for Justice	7	
Ombudsman	1	
	32	(19.3%)
Other Provincial Governments		
Alberta	4	
British Columbia	1	
Manitoba	1	
New Brunswick	1	
Nova Scotia	1	
Prince Edward Island	1	
Quebec	2	
	11	(6.6%)
Agencies and Kindred Organizations		
Police	7	
Probation and Social Services	4	
Native Counsellors	2	
Crown Attorneys	10	
Criminal Injuries Compensation Boards	4	
	27	(16.3%)
The Private Sector		
Transition Houses	8	
Rape Crisis Centres	6	
Child Abuse Agencies	2	
Elizabeth Fry Society	2	
John Howard Society	11	
Salvation Army	3	
	32	(19.3%)
Universities and Colleges	12	(7.2%)
Victim–Offender and Victim–Witness Projects	8	
Other	23	
	166	

of steps both at the federal and the provincial level which reflect our commitment to the issue. . . . I am sure that we all will want to expand and improve available victim services. . . . Encouraging a truly national effort of this sort is one of my priorities as Solicitor General of Canada. However, to be successful, anything we undertake must be done in concert and with the full co-operation of the provinces. Officials of my Ministry and the Department of Justice have already begun an informal process of consultation with their provincial counterparts. Early next month I will be raising my concerns for victims of crime with my provincial counterparts and I will be underlining the commitment of the national government in achieving these objectives. I am confident that in the relatively near future we may be able to make some formal commitments about the improvement and expansion of victim services all across Canada.[15]

Irvin Waller then pressed the Solicitor General: 'is there going to be any federal action on the criminal code and a bill of rights for victims?' and he was told, 'Gordon and I had quite a different scenario for this Conference. It was meant to follow a Federal–Provincial Meeting that was postponed. I had every intention of being much more concrete about initiatives but I must consult my provincial colleagues first.' The jumbling of timetables and the problems of disclosure were there revealed. The Conference had effectively signalled the imminent transformation of portions of the Canadian criminal justice system. Its work as a benchmark had been done. One ambition had been achieved. But the Conference's work as the midwife of a Canadian victims movement was to be done less effectively.

The Canadian Council on Social Development had called for 'a national association for victims' before the Conference. The Solicitor General himself had said in that selfsame speech on the eve of the Conference:

Your efforts to develop state-wide co-ordinating networks to support non-government programs and to develop joint intergovernmental initiatives would be of special interest to Canadian criminal justice policy officials at all levels. The concept of a national victim information and advocacy group, such as the NOVA organization, is also an intriguing concept for us to consider in Canada.

Yet it was to be the Canadian Council on Social Development and the Canadian Association for the Prevention of Crime that would bring matters deliberately to a climax on the first full day of the Conference and at a meeting directed solely at Canadians. The prospect of founding

[15] Notes for a Speech by the Honourable Bob Kaplan, PC, MP, Solicitor General of Canada at the Conference on the National Organization Victim Assistance, Toronto, Ontario: 'Justice for Victims of Crime', 14 Oct. 1981.

a Canadian equivalent to NOVA was addressed but it was aired gingerly and without great expectations. After all, there had been only one earlier occasion when Canadians had been invited to meet as people participating in the provision of help to victims. That occasion, the National Workshop on Services to Crime Victims, had not been entirely auspicious. There had been difficulty in persuading people that they shared a common identity and similar purposes. Women's groups, in particular, had voiced their trepidation about the idea of an overarching organization for victims. The *Report of the Proceedings* had asserted that women questioned 'the development of generalized services for victims within existing networks, charging that this could lessen the attention given to the needs of specific types of victims, including battered wives'.[16] The author of that *Report*, Richard Weiler, was later to become involved in the preparation of *Services to Victims and Witnesses of Crime in Canada*. He had become a consultant attached to the Canadian Council on Social Development. It was he who was later to preside over the meeting of 15 October and make the formal proposal that a Canadian Organization for Victim Assistance be considered.

Weiler's collaborator in the organization of the Conference, co-author of *Services to Victims and Witnesses of Crime in Canada*, Director of Programs of the Canadian Council on Social Development, fellow advocate of a national association for victims, was Geoffrey Norquay. In the wake of the National Workshop of March 1980, and as part of the work devoted to the drafting of *Services to Victims and Witnesses of Crime in Canada*, Norquay had canvassed Canadian institutions about their dealings with victims. He had concluded that 'the groups involved in the field still have a long way to go in sorting out what their respective roles are and how they are going to relate to others in the field. And the reason for that is that many of the roles of the groups involved ... are almost by definition roles that are antagonistic ... or at least fraught with real difficulties.' He had no substantial expectance that all those diverse, contradictory, and ill-ordered groups would willingly band themselves together in one united organization. Not all called themselves by the name of support to victims. Some were hostile to the very category of *victims* and to the demand for a victims' movement. Women's groups envisaged that they would be swallowed whole by an emergent Canadian Organization for Victim Assistance. The second of the two proposers associated with the Canadian Council on Social Development was also hesitant.

[16] *National Workshop on Services to Crime Victims*, p. 23.

Officials in and about the animating social circle amplified their reticence. One stated, 'it's insane to think there'll be an organization within a year.' Others could recall the reproofs and warnings that had been administered by people in the private sector. It was to be the opinion of most members of the circle that any advance had to be the subject of careful planning and discreet presentation. Weiler stated at a preparatory meeting, 'the response here is "Haven't we got enough organizations now? Shouldn't we use what we've got? Do we need new organizations?" You have to do a lot of explaining.' And Norquay replied, 'we simply have to deal with people where they are. If some think there are problems, you have to deal with that.'

On 15 October Richard Weiler spoke at a meeting of the private sector called by the Canadian Council on Social Development and the Canadian Association for the Prevention of Crime. He offered a presentation on 'Victim Services: "Where to From Here?"' It was organized around a paper that was markedly open and tentative. It was described as the fruit of the 'expectations of sponsoring organization', the 'direct interest of many contacted during course of the CCSD study [*Services to Victims and Witnesses of Crime in Canada*] and the preparation of the conference', and 'awareness/interest in the American approach'.[17] It was offered to the private sector by the private sector in an attempt to excite discussion about 'the desired future Canadian direction regarding services to victims of crime'. Many institutions approached by the Canadian Council on Social Development were said to have voiced 'an interest in developing a distinctively Canadian capability directed to facilitating interest in and supporting efforts of services organizations' and that 'most wished that some non-governmental mechanism be charged with provision of much of the responsibility'. But it was also reported that there was no accord about the character of the public and audiences awaiting the arrival of such a mechanism. And 'there was considerable caution expressed regarding the possible creation of a new national organization.' Members of Canadian organizations held that there were enough non-governmental national organizations in Canada already, and that those organizations which did exist could well absorb the new tasks that were beginning to emerge around the provision of services to victims. Weiler remarked upon the hesitation of the Canadians: 'the majority contacted were in support of a further discussion process prior to decision regarding a formal organization/structure to deal with victims.'

[17] 'Victim Services: "Where to From Here?",' The Canadian Council on Social Development and the Canadian Association for the Prevention of Crime, 15 Oct. 1981, p. 1.

If a new organization *were* to appear, it could adopt one of a number of forms, being based on the consumers of services, on the providers of services, or on some national advisory council. It could arise from 'the utilization of and/or redesign of components of the existing non-governmental national based organizational network', introducing a coalition allied to government or a coalition outside government. It could lead to the reform of an existing body or the birth of one that was utterly novel.

The future history of the private sector would turn on predictions made about the intentions of government, on the 'fear of assimilation', and 'the need for preservation of a distinctive identity'. Weiler talked of 'the concern that a national mechanism not be "used" by government' and of the requirement that a national initiative should remain sensitive to the sensibilities of provincial and local groups. He concluded by proposing the founding of a national information clearing-house on victims and the conducting of 'a detailed consultation' on 'possible organizational developments required in better meeting the needs of victims'. It was unwise to become excessively entangled with government at this stage: 'we're not at present quite clear how much and what kind of government interest there is.... We could get caught up in a new trippy cause that would just go away again.' There was to be no brute recommendation about the formation of a Canadian Organization for Victim Assistance. It was Weiler's judgement that such a recommendation was not timely.

The private sector replied and its reply was rather guarded. In the brief discussion that followed, the fragmentation and divisions of the politics of victims were laid bare in an enactment of Weiler's fears. The components and strains of the history of the initiative were all there in microcosm. The private sector presented itself as a tenuously united and unevenly evolving collection of segments and regions that lacked full knowledge of one another, a corporate identity or a common purpose. First to speak was a representative of the John Howard Society of Alberta who claimed that a national clearing-house supported by government funds might force the private sector to dispense government propaganda. A representative of the Salvation Army Correctional Services claimed that he had not been aware of any consultation with the Salvation Army at the national or local level: 'because we're so new in the victim organization but I would welcome a clearing-house which does not lock us in but gives us a chance to dialogue and explore.' Representatives of women claimed that a national organization would inflict losses on women. Debra Lewis of Clarke and Lewis and Battered Women Support Services said:

I've quite a lot of concerns about this kind of proposal as someone who's worked with women. People are prepared to talk about almost any other kind of abuse but not wife battering. How much would we lose in a general victims movement when trade-offs are going to be made? I may sound paranoid but if an organization's not focused expressly on women and their concerns the people who lose are women.... How should resources be used in victim work? Women need all the resources they can get. Whatever resources are available should go to women so that they don't get lost in the shuffle.

There was applause. And another woman said:

Women are not new to victim assistance. So why all of a sudden is it a new issue? This is a fogging of the issue. The majority of victims of violent crime are women. So why is it a new issue?

Geoffrey Norquay answered her: 'we've never got together before—police, Salvation Army etc. It's a relatively new issue.' Got together in one assembly, the private sector and the agencies dramatized the political and organizational difficulties that confronted the initiative, its animators, and its attendant moral entrepreneurs. They were combined in the one room and they surveyed one another. The policy-makers, in particular, witnessed what occurred and felt constrained not to speak: there was acrimony and there was dissent but the intervention of an official would only exacerbate discord. An official from Ontario reflected, 'this is not an appropriate forum to speak', and a federal colleague concurred 'as government people we should not be too involved'. The result was frustration and anxiety. An animator declared: 'we asked them to raise COVA as an issue.... Can you imagine the conference headlines? "The Government proposes a victim organization". My worry is nothing will happen or something stupid will happen.' Yet perhaps the greatest dismay was shown by Irvin Waller. Beholding the failure of the Canadian victims movement to coalesce at its most opportune and critical moment, he pleaded with those in the room:

I find a national clearing-house rather a disappointing outcome from a conference like this. The Government could organize its own clearing-house.... I'm very aware of what's gone on in the battered wives and sexual assault [area] but it's been a very hard, up-hill battle. Many agencies are institutionalised but there are forty or sixty or eighty sexual assault centres [and] as I understand it, they have difficulty with stable and secure funding. They have difficulty in getting professional staff. There are quite a number of other victims who do not have agencies to service them, who have similar (not identical) needs, and I guess people should consider the possible formation of a group in Canada which would lobby and push Government. We've been lucky to get money....

Transition homes and centres are short-lived. Will grants go on? I'm not sure that a victim group would either, but there is a communality of interest to get funds from Government. Many of the people who came to crime victims with a feminist position found they had to enlarge their work as they went on. We should engage in advocacy or a special interest group. We live in an age where budgets are coming back. There's not going to be any new money. We're going to have to fight against other needs. We'll have to bring these things to public attention.

The meeting had been scheduled outside the timetable of the Conference proper and it ended abruptly when that timetable resumed its course. It was put that the discussion should be postponed for a day and people trooped out. Officials and animators were left behind in an emptying room, forced to reflect on what had happened. Debate had been short, intense, and volatile, affording officials little time to take stock or make plans. They had participated in a series of quiet exchanges amongst themselves, producing a running commentary and a communal sense of what was unfolding in front of them. They had been obliged to play the part of spectators as the private sector refused to unite. In the immediate aftermath of that refusal, there was something of a post-mortem, a search for causes and solutions. One feminist official explained the failure by the inept sexual politics of the presentation: 'what did you expect? There were three men up on the platform, not one woman. You could have had one.' A member of the Canadian Council on Social Development replied, 'we couldn't get one'. The more general consensus was that talk about a Canadian Organization for Victim Assistance had come before its time, that the private sector was not ready. One of the quiet animators said, 'it's premature. We've run into a barrier of perception about what a victims movement might look like.' A member of the Canadian Council on Social Development stated, 'we discovered that there was a feeling that this was premature'. Geoffrey Norquay turned to Irvin Waller. 'I'm very sympathetic to what you said but there are many reasons why we wrote what we did.' Later, it was said, 'you must not cry "to the barricades". You'll ruin it. There must be no hard speeches at all. Don't push it.'

In a sense, it became evident that the portion of the social world centred on the politics of victims had drifted free of its environment. The animating circle had evolved independently and unobserved, and there was an ensuing cultural and cognitive lag. Animators had acquired a certain cosmopolitanism and sophistication in matters touching on victims. They had passed through processes of learning and conversion, emerging with a new sense of form and order. They had confronted problems and subdued them. They had seen what had happened in the United States. Above all, they had seen what was moving inside the provincial and federal government of Canada, and they were aware that government required an appropriate milieu to proceed. Much of that was strange to the private sector. The women's movement and voluntary organizations had never been immersed in that history. Indeed, they were not even conscious that such a history had elapsed at all. Their knowledge of victims was mediated by the vivid detail of their own struggles, reverses, and conquests. Thus it was that the politics of patriarchy transcended the minute requirements of an unannounced initiative.

What seemed to remain for the animators was a return to Weiler's proposal about a consultation to be conducted at some time in the future. A provincial official put it that the 'saleability' of a consultation would be enhanced if it were suggested that 'there may be a task force and that regional conferences would be useful to that'. And a federal colleague responded, 'it could be called *timely*'. (Will you make a note of that, *timely*, Paul?)' What also remained was an urgent need to gain intelligence about the response and mood of the private sector, to explore what that mood portended, and to plan repairs. Later that night the Canadian Council on Social Development met with representatives of the women's organizations: it was reported that there was a feeling that the representatives 'had been taken by surprise. Women's groups want to be involved but they want further discussion and consultation.' It was also reported that the women's groups feared being taken over, that they were mistrustful of ideas emanating from Ottawa, and that they were not themselves united. They wanted time.

In the months before the Conference, people gathering in preparatory meetings had had to work without a clear understanding of how many Canadians would want to be invited to Toronto, how they could be identified, and what they would do. It had not been possible to bestow a collective personality on the Canadians who were involved in the provision of services to victims. Indeed, it had been that lack of a personality that had encouraged the animators to promote the Conference. It was that lack of a personality that had been dramatized at the first meeting on 15 October when the Canadians had come together to discuss their fate as Canadians. It had become evident that many groups were foreign to one another. The intentions of Government and established organizations were unfamiliar. The basic vocabulary of the victims movement was somewhat alien. People had come with a sense of strangeness, not knowing what was afoot and how they should respond. The meeting had revealed in a graphic fashion how very lumpy and parochial was the distribution of knowledge and sentiments about the politics of victims.

The first task of the meeting of the second day was to return to the beginning, to retreat to a point where animators and the private sector were at one with each other. A working accord had to be achieved, dispelling the lag that had emerged. As a senior official murmured to the man responsible for research on victims at the Ministry, 'we must try to avoid the appearance of a schism. It's very early yet.' It was agreed that some of the work of the first meeting had been premature, based on misleading assumptions about what was known and shared. A new start had to be made, providing an elementary lexicon of terms, introducing central organizations, and repairing the damage wrought by a precocious move.

The meeting of 16 October was chaired by the Canadian Association for the Prevention of Crime. It was addressed first by Geoffrey Norquay of the Canadian Council on Social Development and, as part of the cautious return to new beginnings, there was an explanation of just what the Council was: 'a number of people have suggested that not everyone knew what CCSD is, a national organization devoted to research and advocacy . . .' Norquay proceeded to recapitulate what had been said by Weiler on the day before, displaying a marked tentativeness in the use of words and the making of proposals. He bowed repeatedly before the fact of the stratification of knowledge and the indexicality of language. He tried to ward off those animators who might try too eagerly to impart vitality to the sleeping Canadian victims movement. He could not presume that there was a world taken-for-granted:

> Weiler's work with thirty agencies suggested that there was a clear demand for a national clearing-house on victim services. Some people don't like that term so we can call it an information service. Second, should there be a national organization focused on victim issues? I use that term guardedly because there is no agreement about what that should be. So the second part of our proposals is that there should be a consultation process to find out what that organization should be. These two proposals should be kept separate. Some of the organizations here have been in business for a very long time; others have been going for a shorter time; some have just started. . . . Those who want an activist advocate organization must realise that it will take time before things can be resolved. . . . Form follows function. Let's find out whether there are needs that an organization can serve and whether there should be an organization. Is there consensus about the need for a consultation centre? Should such a centre be housed with CCSD? Is there consensus on the need for a consultation process to flesh out the need for a centre?

A dilemma of the disorderly array of bodies serving victims was that there was wariness about a national organization, that it was only through a consultation process that the matter of an organization could be reviewed, and that it would require an organization to arrange and fund the consultation process. The very mounting of talks demanded management. Norquay put it to those assembled that they could turn to the Steering Committee that had organized the Conference itself, a Committee that had drawn on the Canadian Council on Social Development, the Canadian Association for the Prevention of Crime, the Government of Ontario, the Ministry of the Solicitor General, Irvin Waller and two others. It was they who had had experience of drawing boundaries around an embryo victims movement, bringing people to the one place where a social world might begin to form. Norquay was met with the politics of the Canadian private sector.

A woman from Vancouver said:

I have one statement. As a person from the West, I have one objection. It seems like an Ontario group, very much Eastern.

A feminist official of the federal government said:

It may be emotional but I don't feel that the organization comes from the whole group. We need have discussion from the floor before we vote.

A Regional Consultant said:

I come from a region where our backs are put up about centralisation too. We need further consultation in the area of services to victims, but, with the information we know now, I would say that there should not be a national organization devoted to victim services.

A feminist official from Health and Welfare Canada said:

A national initiative may slight certain groups of victims. Women and children always come last and there's a great deal of concern about their being slighted.

A woman from a rape crisis centre said:

I can't make a decision until I bring all the information back to the women in my group.

And Debra Lewis said:

To take a vote would be really disrespectful to the groups working on battering. They need to know more before they can take a decision.

An official from the Ontario Provincial Secretariat said:

The group gathered here is not appropriate to vote. I am an information-gathering representative from a government department. If I voted, I would commit people from voluntary agencies. Whatever I might want, I don't think I ought to vote.

The paradoxes and difficulties of the movement's struggle for life were all recorded there. There was to be other talk, but the themes were consistent enough. A gathering of people from disparate groups could not pledge themselves or others to immediate action. They were not empowered to make decisions. They were mistrustful of anyone else who offered to act in their name. They were mistrustful of anyone who wished to discover how a representative body might be furnished.

A Regional Consultant stated, 'there should be a national referendum', and a member of the John Howard Society announced, 'if we must build, we must build soundly from the bottom up'. But there was no conductor of referendums and no builder of organizations. Richard Weiler asked, 'if we do move ahead, how do we do it? Our difficulty is, where to next? Who takes responsibility? Should it be representative of nongovernment organizations?' The Chairman asked, 'who's got the ball now?' Answering him, a senior official of the Ministry of the Solicitor General muttered *sotto voce*, 'not me'. And the Chairman repeated, 'if the ball's not in this room, where is it?' A woman echoed him plaintively, 'where will the balls go?' And the talk about a national organization expired. It was not the business of central or provincial government to propose itself as the guardian of a victims movement speaking for the private sector. Thus it was that the Seventh Annual Conference of the National Organization for Victim Assistance failed to give birth to a Canadian Organization for Victim Assistance.

There *was* to be some support for a clearing-house. Objections were raised by the private sector, a member of a rape crisis centre arguing, for instance, 'what makes me really nervous is that the federal and provincial governments are involved'. But many declared their need for information. A representative of the Salvation Army talked of 'how we've started a victim–witness assistance programme . . . and we urgently required help about how to do it'. Similarly, a member of the Elizabeth Fry Society said, 'we've been setting up a programme and the problems are formidable. We've written all over Canada and the States. It takes too much time and the real work we should do should be with young girls.' In reply to the Chairman's request for organizational and financial support for a clearing-house, the man responsible for research on victims volunteered the aid of the Ministry of the Solicitor General. He was supported by Acting Assistant Deputy Solicitor General of Canada.

Months later, on 29 June 1982, the Victim Working Group of the Ministry of the Solicitor General was to agree to the funding of a Victims Clearing House. The thing was done.

The following day, at a final meeting, Irvin Waller took stock of what had been accomplished:

When I wanted to invite NOVA, I thought they were a fantastic group of people who have a great sense of fun. The aim was to bring a group who were very committed and involved in the victims' issue. I have certainly seen discussions between unlike people but there is a great communality about the need to fight the vicious state which sets up the game of cops, courts and corrections. I think it's worth the anguish. We've heard new arguments and met new people. We've also learned an enthusiasm. The follow-up to the Canadian meetings: people are going to go away, I'm not sure whether they'll feel part of a specific Canadian movement, but they'll have got to know some others in the victim movement. There may be a conference in a year's time ... The network will be an important form of clearing-house. The access to NOVA is an important sort of clearing-house. The fact that I think there should be an important sort of lobby group, that hasn't happened and I never expected it would. The fact that such a lobbying group has not yet started is not the end of the world. It'll be a long slow process. But I have a gut feeling that it'd be a good idea.

Irvin Waller retired from the Conference a little saddened by the inability of the Canadian victims movement to coagulate. Long after, he continued to foster the idea of an active lobby championing the victim of crime. He was to turn to an organization led by Don Sullivan. Victims of Violence was founded in February 1982 in Ajax, Ontario, by the parents and families of murdered young people:

We have decided to devote the rest of our lives to doing whatever we can to spare others the grief and pain that we have all suffered. We will do whatever we can, legally, to achieve this goal. We have stood up in public and bared our anguish in order to try and make the general public understand that violence can happen to anyone unless they act to prevent it. Thus we have formed a lobby group and a self help group. We are combatting the many groups that place the welfare of convicted felons ahead of the welfare of society.[18]

Don Sullivan had approached Irvin Waller in January 1983 about an article[19] that 'prominently mentions you'.[20] The article recited how Irvin Waller had resigned from the Ministry 'because I did not feel governments were concerned enough about programs to prevent crime or

[18] Brief to Task Force on Public Violence Against Women and Children, 23 Nov. 1982.
[19] *The Packet*, 4 Dec. 1982.
[20] Letter to Irvin Waller, 25 Jan. 1983.

programs that would help victims of crime recover from the experience'. Sullivan told Waller of the murder of his daughter by a man released from penitentiary, of the horror and isolation experienced by his family, and of how a reporter covering the murderer's trial had informed him about another set of parents undergoing an identical ordeal: 'I contacted the ——— and right away we both had someone to talk to who understood our feelings, words and most importantly our silences. We realized that maybe we could help other parents because if we were going through this sort of anguish then obviously other parents were.' Their first unadvertised meeting attracted the families of thirty victims and the organization grew.

Waller replied to Sullivan and a correspondence ensued. He wrote: 'I have seen the advantages of a national organization to represent the interests of victims in Canada for some time. In fact, I have had a lot of pressure put on me to form one. I have always declined, because it is not something that I personally want to do and because I felt that it should be led by somebody other than a professor . . . However, if one gets going, I hope to get involved. I have a number of ideas of how to start one.'[21] Waller and Sullivan were to meet in Washington at a National Forum sponsored by NOVA. Waller was to feed Sullivan and Victims of Violence into the networks which he had known and cultivated. He recognized in Sullivan the passion and the animation that had failed to appear in Toronto in 1981. Victims of Violence had emerged late and outside the major structures and networks of victim assistance in Canada: 'we have been groping in the dark trying to find someone to help us.'[22] It was an organization with fire. It had welled up from the 'nightmarish happenings that families of murdered children go through'.[23] It encouraged 'emotional outbursts'.[24] It was the direct voice of those hurt by crime, showing little of the caution and suspiciousness of the private sector that had congregated on 15 and 16 October 1981, a private sector that 'could not agree on the next step'.[25]

The officials of the Ministry of the Solicitor General retired with a miscellany of reactions. Their responses were mediated by the part which they had played in the animating work of the initiative, by their expectations, and by what they had seen of a large and diverse meeting. Most were tired. Some were elated, some had undergone a kind of

[21] Letter from Irvin Waller, 7 Apr. 1983.

[22] Letter from Don Sullivan, 5 Mar. 1983.

[23] D. Sullivan, 'Speech to be delivered on May 9th., 1983, in Peace River Alta at the Workshop and Seminar of the Alberta Association of Registered Nurses Assistants.'

[24] Ibid.

[25] R. Doyon, 'The Victim in Focus', p. 19.

catharsis, and some were confused. The hitherto diffuse and inchoate problem of victims had become a public spectacle, objectified in time and space, arrayed as a series of organizations and people. It was now possible to visualize quite concretely who composed the victims movement in Canada, how they formed a body, and how they moved as a mass. The sheer numbers of people gave gravity and solidity to what had once been largely the subject of talk and speculation. But the numbers still possessed no coherence and firm outlines. It was not entirely evident what it would do. There were splits. What *was* evident was that the victims movement lacked consensus and that it would be imprudent to dictate its future, and that had been surmised from the beginning. A senior official was to reflect afterwards:

> The conference participants were an interesting group, covering all parts of the political spectrum from far left to far right—victims issues seem to appeal to everyone. . . . The meetings themselves were chaotic. . . . The result was that nothing was agreed to. . . . It was quite clear that . . . at this stage, this Department should not encourage the setting up of a Canadian national organization with either moral or financial backing.

The social problem of victims had become objectified at the NOVA Conference. It had passed into the public domain. And it was affected by the very management of the process by which it became an object. As it moved, so different people busied themselves in its fate. It was to become increasingly unclear precisely who owned and controlled the politics of victims. Initially, invitations had been issued in the name of two private sector organizations and with the sponsorship of two government departments. That phase of invitation had enlarged the political patronage of Canadian victims. It was known that governments could not promote their own lobbies, and the work of advocacy had been pursued by a body outside the formal limits of the State. But it seemed that no one wanted to assume responsibility for a national organization for victims. Rights to ownership simply lapsed. In the main, the arguments of 15 and 16 October had turned on the illegitimacy of various claims to leadership and all claims had been found wanting. The extra-governmental politics of victims were without a head. And, throughout, could be detected the hand of Irvin Waller. He had chaired the very first meeting and he had chaired the last. An official of the Planning and Liaison Division mused 'it's a Waller affair'. As a Waller affair, it did not move exactly in the direction that Waller had desired. What thus emerged as an outcome were the beginning of devolution without a local response. A member of a rape crisis centre observed at the meeting of

16 October, 'the budget for the conference ends with the conference. Who's going to pay and who's it going to go back to?' There was no answer.

The Meeting of Ministers Responsible for Criminal Justice

The Justice for Victims of Crime Initiative was driven by a great teleology: it could take form only in the Meeting of Ministers Responsible for Criminal Justice, and it was towards that Meeting that much had to be directed. No national policy for Canada could emerge without the sanction of the provinces. Nothing could be disclosed until the provinces had approved. Only after the Meeting might the initiative be allowed to come into its own.

It will be recalled that the development of the initiative had forked in the summer of 1981. One segment had been detached by the Ministry of State for Social Development and propelled through a succession of federal committees on its way to Cabinet in July. As it moved, that segment began to refract the sensibilities and concerns of the federal departments, becoming politically coded. The other segment had been entrusted by a June Meeting of Deputy Ministers Responsible for Criminal Justice to an *ad hoc* federal–provincial working group with the instruction that a paper should be prepared for possible inclusion in the agenda of the autumn conference of Ministers Responsible for Criminal Justice. That paper was to embody the responses of the provinces, becoming a kind of significant gesture which would anticipate how provincial governments might reply to a new politics of victims. It too would be coded, an answer to the political sensitivities of a particular world. The very composition of the working group was part of that gesture or code, incorporating as it did representatives from the governments of Canada, Ontario, British Columbia, Alberta, and Saskatchewan.

From the first, there had been apprehension that the victims of crime might become enmeshed in a welter of political and jurisdictional difficulties. An official of the Policy Branch had warned in one of the initiative's earliest policy papers that work with 'federal–provincial, governmental and non-governmental agencies ... could involve friction if we are seen interfering in another's jurisdiction', and similar warnings had been sounded at intervals thereafter. The June Meetings of Deputy Ministers itself had been cautious about the possible effect of a federal incursion into what was believed to be provincial terrain, it having been argued by some that aid to victims was not a federal matter at all and by others that any federal activity must be anchored in consultations with the provinces. There had been the insistence of a provincial Attorney General that projects devoted to victims should be placed under the control of Crown prosecutors. The Meeting had told the *ad hoc* federal–provincial working group that it should define clearly what belonged to the provinces and what to the government of Canada. Later, as it began to draft its paper for the Meeting of Ministers, the working group was reminded by a provincial Deputy Attorney General that 'many justice agencies have already done a great deal in this field, and that proposals to do more entail the provision of new funds, or extremely difficult decisions about shifting existing priorities and resources, or both'. Later still, it was alerted publicly to provincial wariness by the communiqué of the Conference of the Provincial Council of Attorneys General and Ministers of Justice, a communiqué which announced on 2 October 1981:

> The Ministers noted the recent interest of the Federal Government in this area [of assistance to victims and witnesses] and agreed that, although the responsibilities for these services were provincial, discussions would continue with the Federal Government. As these matters are further discussed, the Ministers wish to ensure that the federal proposals are consistent with provincial programmes and priorities, recognizing that the needs and priorities vary within the various provinces.

Clear signals were there emitted that some powerful provincial figures claimed victims as their own, offering the government of Canada a role only under licence. Other figures had already conveyed their anxiety about funding, about the federal government beginning an expensive enterprise which the provinces would have to finish, and about interference with the work of the courts. If arguments about a national policy were to prosper, they would have to be built to contend with what had been said. Accordingly, at their meeting on 19 October, federal and provincial Deputy Ministers approved the submission of a report to the next conference of Ministers, but they echoed concerns about 'the risk of escalating public expectations unduly'. Austerity was growing in the provinces, and there was trepidation about ambitious new ventures. It was thought sensible to concentrate on the establishment of a federal–provincial task force to review victim issues, and the task force itself would be responsible solely for gathering information, sensitizing the public, and making recommendations. Earlier proposals about acting as the catalyst of local and national initiatives and about co-ordinating initiatives were discarded. It would not do to essay too much. Further, the Solicitor General of Canada was advised by his officials that it would be prudent to stress the primacy of the provinces in matters affecting victims: anything attempted by the government of Canada would be consistent with what the provinces themselves were doing.

Lawyers and Attorneys General were busy in the late summer and autumn of 1981 with the changes in the constitution which might follow upon the repeal of the British North America Act. The Meeting of Ministers Responsible for Criminal Justice was postponed more than once, confounding some plans and upsetting some timetables. When it came, from 7 to 9 December, it was intended that the conference would consider the federal–provincial report on Justice for Victims of Crime and hear Bob Kaplan, Solicitor General of Canada, and Gordon Walker, Provincial Secretary for Justice. The report resonated some of the structure of argument that had first taken shape in the policy proposals of six months before. It talked of the increase in crime in Canada and the alienation of the victim: it referred to the swelling of public demand for action, a demand voiced especially by women; it reviewed measures taken by federal and provincial governments to respond to that demand, one measure being the NOVA Conference of October; and it surveyed future possibilities of redress. Mindful of the complexities of jurisdiction between the provinces and the federal government, and alert to the difficulties posed by fiscal restraints, it concluded that public pressure was likely to grow, a pressure that might be met without enormous expense. Its proposals were that Ministers should make a clear public statement recognizing the needs of victims, encourage the development of information and projects for victims, and, finally, found a task force which could report back with recommendations for further action.

The Solicitor General spoke of the one million victims who are created in Canada every year, 'victims who suffer loss, injury and emotional distress which can cause significant trauma, financial and physical problems for themselves and their families. And the hardships these victims suffer don't always end with the results of the crime itself.' He spoke of the growing interest that the problem of victims had attracted in Canada, citing the Conference that had just been held in Canada. He talked of the need to produce a co-ordinated effort which 'recognizes the primary responsibility of the provinces for the delivery of criminal justice and social services, the important traditional role of private agencies in this area, and the need for federal involvement and support'. To promote that effort, and 'in this spirit of cooperation', the Solicitor General announced the Justice for Victims of Crime Initiative:

> The federal government within its jurisdiction, hopes to play a catalytic role to support the growing concern of provincial government and advocacy groups for

> more effective justice for victims of crime. Towards this aim, my department and Mr Chrétien's department have allocated over the next year and a half approximately $1,000,000 in short-term resources in addition to the resources we have already committed ... to stimulate and support improved assistance for victims of crimes in Canada.

The million dollars would be devoted to the stimulation of 'immediate but short-term services for victims', the Department of Justice assuming responsibility for Court and Crown based services and the Department of the Solicitor General for work attached to police forces and community based programmes. All that would be done with the understanding that:

> we are very aware of the danger of raising public expectations unduly by stimulating services in this area, and the related danger to the provinces of being left to absorb long-term expenses for services initiated by the federal government.

Much could be accomplished by making better use of existing resources and services. Nothing would be attempted without 'very thorough consultation with the provinces involved'.

Long-term action would require proper deliberation and planning and the Solicitor General endorsed the idea of a federal-provincial task force 'in order that these longer-term plans, and complex issues can receive the attention they deserve'. Gordon Walker succeeded Bob Kaplan, and he too urged the greater succour of victims, proposing in particular an amendment to the Criminal Code enabling a fine surcharge to be levied on all convicts to support victims' compensation programmes.

The Solicitor General, the Minister of Justice, and the Provincial Secretary for Justice were successful. The Ministers present agreed 'to intensify their present efforts by taking steps to stimulate and improve information and support services'. They 'requested their officials to come forward within one year with specific proposals for further action which both levels of government can take to more effectively assist victims of crime'. Thus was christened publicly the Justice for Victims of Crime Initiative. The Federal–Provincial Task Force on Justice for Victims was born. The Director of Policy reported, 'I think we can be very pleased with the outcome of the recent Conference as it relates to Victims Assistance. We now have Ministerial support for a heightened and co-operative initiative in this area.' Victims had come out of the shadows.

The Briefing Sessions

One of the principal tasks of the Justice for Victims of Crime Initiative was to stimulate and foster the provision of services to victims. It was to be a catalyst. After December it was possible to pour the initiative out into the world, distributing it across the face of Canada. Only by taking ideas out into the provinces could the initiative become known. Federal officials were to traverse the country talking about what the government of Canada, the provinces, and the private sector had done. The agenda of the very first meeting of the new Interdepartmental Committee on Justice for Victims announced in September 1981 that issues of process were important: the government was committed to devising something of a marketing project as well as launching specific services. Officials were to promote services for victims, discussing exemplary projects, injecting coherence into work already started, exploring opportunities for new work, seeking local sponsors for victims, and attempting generally to devolve and sustain what would otherwise be an ephemeral scheme. Their briefing sessions were to mediate and transport the initiative from place to place. They were built in part on a memory of how an earlier, poorly advertised diversion initiative had been spurned by some of the provinces. They were built on the example set by the United States. The Justice for Victims of Crime Initiative was planned at a time when American programmes were in visible decline, and their demise was instructive, demonstrating that the spending of money alone was no guarantee of the success of policy. Support for victims had to be grafted on to local organizations. In September 1981 Linda MacLeod returned from consultations in America with the report that 'regional conferences are invaluable in promoting networking. The conferences should have at least three aims: a) to sensitize the police, b) to involve the business community, c) to facilitate networking among local practitioners.'[26] Without such conferences, there was a risk that a federal initiative would remain tied to the capital, adopted by no one, dying as the life which it had been given by the central government expired.

The form and content of the briefing sessions were affected by the sometimes confusing imperatives that had grown out of the history of the initiative itself. As it evolved, so the initiative began to acquire a distinct logic of argument and strategy. It had become quite clear that the initiative was to be a short-term venture, modestly financed, which could not prosper without local patronage. It was designed to stimulate but not to over-excite the public, to respect provincial and private preserves, and to avoid every semblance of dictation. It would not do for the briefing sessions themselves to turn directly towards the public at large because that might prompt the excessive reaction feared by the provinces.

[26] 'LEAA Meeting to Evaluate Funding of Victim Oriented Services: Implications for Canadian Initiatives of American Experience', 10 Sept. 1981.

It would be improper for the federal government to be seen advertising victims' services when these were paid and administered by the provinces. The sessions would be addressed instead at local 'specialized groups' which might choose to broadcast information to the public later. People would be told 'it's you in your local areas who will be responsible for acting and organizing follow-up meetings in your communities'.[27] The information that would be conveyed was a little uncertain on occasion. One aim of the initiative was actually to discover precisely what *could* be learned about victims and projects in Canada. At the beginning, the survey had not been done and projects were incomplete: 'it was felt that, at the present time, we weren't exactly sure of what kind of information we wanted to give out. And that, in fact, much of the present information comes to us from the United States.'

The sessions were to be scattered across Canada, following the lines of one of the structures prepared by the Royal Canadian Mounted Police. As a geographically dispersed agency reporting to the Minister, an agency extending into every province and territory, the Royal Canadian Mounted Police could offer intelligence, connections, and communications. At the heart of an RCMP structure that touched on the victims initiative was a Staff Sergeant working in the Crime Prevention Centre in Ottawa, an officer who had worked as an animator for years. It was he who helped to mobilize a network and arrange meetings:

> That became the process.... You've got to remember at the working level we've got people there that interact the same way as I interact with the people downtown. We can talk with our counterparts in the Provinces and for example our Co-ordinator makes personal contact with Crown Attorneys, senior members will contact Deputy Ministers to suggest a meeting is being arranged and extend personal invitations. Much of the networking is informal while there is formal communications between the senior administrators of the Force occurring at the same time. Personal contacts with members who have worked together and later work in other parts of the country is important. Senior NCOs in charge of the hundreds of Detachments are the backbone of the organization and are receptive to suggestions for change when they have someone explain all the issues and the reasons for the change. The networks are subtle and complex ... and if a person knows how to use them, if the person knows how to use them, if the person knows what the mechanisms are and how to use them, you can be so much more effective.

It was those mechanisms and that network which were to be deployed. The RCMP had become systematically and comprehensively involved

[27] 'Hey, What About Me?', *Liaison*, April 1983, Vol. 9, No. 4, p. 23.

with the initiative after the declaration in December. Experimental projects were planned for its various detachments and, as the official responsible for research on victims reported:

A few of the COs said 'yes, we're interested. We'd like to meet with people from the R.C.M.P. Headquarters and with people from the Secretariat, from Research, Consultation, etc.' Once these responses from the COs were starting to come back, there was also the need for the working committee to not just have a briefing to talk with the R.C.M.P. but to combine those meetings with provincial representatives, and that's what was done. So, in most of those, it was the R.C.M.P. connexion but those meetings were married with a broader meeting with provincial representatives.

Each of the briefing sessions occurred at an RCMP Divisional Headquarters and each was conducted by the animating Staff Sergeant accompanied by some combination of a member of the Victim Working Group, the local Regional Consultant, and an official from the federal Department of Justice. A journey akin to a Royal Progress was planned for the initiative: in late January 1982 there was to be a visit to 'K' Division in Edmonton; on 9 and 10 February to 'B' Division in St John's, Newfoundland; thence to 'F' Division in Regina on 15, and 17 February; to 'D' Division in Winnipeg on 17 and 18 February; to 'G' Division in Yellowknife on 22 and 23 February; to Whitehorse on 24, 25, and 26; to 'L' Division in Charlottetown, Prince Edward Island, on 1 and 2 March; to 'H' Division in Halifax, Nova Scotia, on 3 March; to 'J' Division in Fredericton on 4 March; and back to Ottawa on the 5th.[28] The initiative had exploded and, like Odysseus' crew opening the bag of Aeolus, officials found themselves tossed around Canada. The Staff Sergeant reflected, 'I'm just mind-boggled all the time. I just don't have the time to think the issues through as much as I should.'

At each of the briefing sessions, there would be assembled representatives of provincial and federal government, the police and the private sector. At one meeting in Newfoundland, for example, were present the Assistant Deputy Attorney General a Provincial Court Judge; a Crown Prosecutor; three senior RCMP officers stationed in Newfoundland; the Deputy Chief and another officer of the Royal Newfoundland Constabulary; the Staff Sergeant from the Crime Prevention Centre of RCMP Headquarters in Ottawa; and an official from the Research Division of the Ministry of the Solicitor General of Canada. At that and at other meetings, a recital would be given of the context,

[28] That itinerary was not followed precisely but it does point to the scale and pace of the briefing sessions.

ambitions, accomplishments, and prospects of the initiative, a statement of what had been done and what might yet be done. It was a recital composed of new arguments joined with familiar phrases plucked from other speeches and other occasions. The rhetoric and presentation of the initiative had achieved their own conventional forms. Thus the recital began as the Solicitor General had begun in December. It resonated the script of the slide show from the NOVA Conference. It echoed the many pamphlets, documents, and lectures that were starting to punctuate the initiative:

> Concern with the problems and needs of victims of crime is an issue whose time has come. Each year in Canada, there are over one million crimes involving violence or loss of property. Over one million crimes create over one million victims, . . . victims who suffer loss, injury and emotional distress which can cause significant trauma, financial and physical problems for themselves and also for their families. And the hardships these victims suffer don't always end with the results of the crime itself. Victims of crime also have real complaints about the lack of protection from crime which led to their victimization . . .[29]

Those being briefed would then be told of the growth of a response to the problems of victims, how assistance was being given, and how public confidence in the criminal justice system was being improved. They would be told about federal, provincial, and private enterprise in the area. In New Brunswick, for example, they would be told about work in British Columbia; the Winnipeg Victim–Witness Assistance Program; a scheme run by the Salvation Army and police in Ottawa; the Fredericton Victim–Witness Needs Survey; the Restigouche Family Crisis Intervention Project; provincial criminal injuries compensation programmes and the work of the transition houses. In particular, people attending briefing sessions would be informed about how 'the Ministry and the Department of Justice in July 1981, made a joint submission to Cabinet, approved on July 23rd, to undertake a short term, coordinated initiative, with resources in addition to those already committed to victim assistance'. The aims of the initiative were to assess the needs of victims and the gaps in the services which they received, to improve services, and to disseminate information and launch 'policy related research projects'. Briefing sessions and workshops designed to 'sensitize individuals, community, and criminal justice personnel' were in train. What remained

[29] Format used by Justice and MSG Representatives during Visits with Provincial Representatives and Local RCMP Officials on the Subject of Victims of Crime: Notes for Briefing Sessions: Assistance to Victims of Crime, Ministry of Solicitor General and Department of Justice, January 1982.

was the need to enhance co-ordination and to develop an effort 'which recognizes the primary responsibility of the provinces for the delivery of criminal justice and social services, the important traditional role of private agencies in this area, and the need for federal involvement and support'. To that end, the Ministry of Justice and the Department of the Solicitor General had begun to build a social structure that would bear the initiative onwards.

XIII. A Short Summary and Some Conclusions

A number of themes have wandered through my argument, appearing and disappearing with the flow of problems and processes. It would be useful to retrieve those which are more prominent and place them together in one final chapter. Such a list should not be confused with a formal model or theory of policy-making at large. After all, it will be remembered that I have concentrated on but one instance of work in one Ministry. Yet there may be a few similarities between the history of the Justice for Victims of Crime initiative and other episodes of policy-making elsewhere. At the very least, the unique and distinctive features of social problems seem to submit to a standard discipline and a general timetable before they become accepted as policy issues. They are required to lose their special properties after a while. Moreover, a number of officials displayed a certain universality of style. Not all had received their training in the government of Canada alone. One had pursued an earlier career in the Home Office in London. Others had been in provincial government, in official agencies, and other departments. Their work on the initiative sometimes betrayed a little of that wider experience, making it familiar and intelligible to outsiders. Indeed, when I discussed some of the arguments of this book with English civil servants, they claimed that they recognized themselves and their problems in what I had written.

The Justice for Victims of Crime Initiative may be portrayed as the confluence of a number of little histories that were on the move in Canada and the United States in the 1970s and 1980s. Each of those little histories represented a field of action for a group of people. Each developed in some isolation from the others. Few were intended to culminate in a federal government initiative for the victims of crime. What brought them together was the conjunction of three sets of social arrangements which stimulated and defined action. One was the general catalyst supplied by the American victims movement, a movement that had developed early and in response to the prompting of the Law Enforcement Assistance Administration. At a number of critical points, that movement fired, articulated, and illuminated the social problem of victims, presenting it as a spectacle and model for interested Canadians. Not all Canadian enterprise was grounded in American example, but much was organized and fused by the rape crisis movement, schemes for battered women, victim–witness assistance programmes, victim–offender reconciliation projects, and the like. Officials from Albertan police departments, the Onatrio Ministry of Correctional Services, the Department of the Solicitor General and the Department of Justice explored what happened in the south and they severally adopted some parts of what they had seen. They secured motives, precedents, and plans from America. Diffusely woven together, those groups began to feed old American and newer Canadian themes to one another, changing and synthesizing ideas in long skein of activity. To be sure, some of those ideas were independently Canadian, but it seemed that it required the borrowed organization of the National Organization for Victim Assistance, the Law Enforcement Assistance Administration, and the Department of Justice to galvanize what was in train.

The second lens and spur was offered by Irvin Waller, a moral entrepreneur in a classical guise, who was inspired by the victims movement and imported it into the core of the Secretariat of the Ministry of the Solicitor General. Waller's early work had given him a presence in the emerging circles of victimology and the victims movement. There followed a courtship, a conversion, and the dedication of Waller's career to the victims of crime. Waller constructed social networks, disseminated ideas, and seized lines of action as they developed, forcing them together. His influence was transparent in many passages. It was his effort that welded cause to effect, introducing a pattern to the history of victims. He brought victims into the federal government and he became their walking champion. For those very reasons, perhaps, he was unable to conduct them to their goal himself. As a man entrusted with the management of research, personifying a social problem, known as Mr Victims, he tended to bar some of the onward movement of victims away from himself and the Programs Branch and into those parts of the Ministry that revolved around the making of policy.

The third lens was the little world of political animators that had grown in and around the problems of victims. Appearing first at the time of the Peace and Security Package, they were charged with the surveying of victims and the evaluation of crime prevention campaigns. So charged, they became exposed to the concerns and accomplishments of victimology, they became attached to its networks, and they acquired some of its preoccupations as their own. In particular, they attained something of an existential stake in victims, devoting a portion of their lives to them, and founding their professional identities upon what became of them. They became a source and an audience of attempts to foster a politics of victims in Canada.

The path taken by that world was shaped by the territory allotted the Ministry and by stirrings in the environment that surrounded it. There was an emphasis on police-based programmes, The Royal Canadian Mounted Police being the peripatetic mandate of the Solicitor General. There was an emphasis on violence against women, such violence having become politically laden, producing a public voice demanding a response from the criminal justice system. There was an emphasis on work done in the provinces, provincial government having suzerainty over much of the Canadian criminal justice system.

Over time, and in a fashion that might have been anticipated but never planned, a somewhat haphazard accumulation of projects, programmes, and political statements began to emerge about the area of victims. Civil service activity being constrained by policies that have been approved by government, little could be done baldly in the name of work for the victims of crime. Rather, efforts were scattered under different titles, budgets, and authorities. What gave form and urgency to that pile of accomplishments, lending it a political immediacy, was the new planning process imposed on the departments of the federal government in 1981. Required to project their work into the future, casting around for nascent policies that might be cultivated, staff looked upon the social problem of victims as most timely. Its timeliness was enhanced by the response of monitoring officials in the Ministry of State for Social Development. Little by little, the world of the political animators had expanded to embrace people in a number of departments and agencies. It was one such person, lodged in the Ministry of State, who replied to the first plans of the Ministry of the Solicitor General and urged the inclusion of proposals for victims. Later, its Strategic Overview having been approved, the Ministry of the Solicitor General was invited to submit plans for a modest, short-term initiative intended to stimulate and inform the development of services for victims. How victims were defined and grouped, how services evolved, and how arguments were phrased and paraded bore the mark of the groups which inspected proposals and controlled their progress through the numerous committees of the Canadian government. What had been achieved was the introduction of new inflections in the criminal justice system, the beginnings of a lattice-work of programmes, and a trail of actions and reactions without a predictable future.

The substantive history of the Justice for Victims of Crime Initiative can be made to deliver an array of more formal arguments. First, and quite obviously, policy-making required the intervention of a body of officials who sought energetically to work some change in their domain.

It is certain that, without a direct command, nothing would have stirred inside the Ministry unless people had been prepared to act themselves. It required an attentive group to amplify political and economic movements in the wider world. Without diligent nursing, the campaigns of the victims movement would have had no echo in the government and the social problem of victims would have withered. The attendants had to support the problem during the early period of indifference, they had to compete with other problems, and they had to experience some isolation. They were at risk of being identified as assertive and, on occasion, as self-aggrandizing. It was something of a paradox that some but not all the animators appeared to advance their project with methods that tended sometimes to stunt its growth.

Once a beginning had been made, the evolving policy started to describe a web of tasks, roles, and relations. New staff were appointed and old staff were assigned to work in a relatively novel region. About policy-making there emerged patterns of work that changed the structure of the office and the organization of the Department. In turn, those who worked in that new area and within that shifting structure discovered that they themselves changed in sympathy with their environment. They acquired stocks of knowledge, perspectives, and experiences. They achieved a new sense of what was possible. More especially, they acquired motives, ambitions, and selves that were interlaced with the work in hand. They were addressed, and they addressed themselves, as people with a special stake in a problem. Their careers, reputations, and, indeed, lives, came to be implicated in the fate of victims. A sense of territory and property developed, imposing claims to authorship and control that directed the movement of proposals and the manner in which they were treated. In a fashion, a stance towards a proposal also became something of a gesture towards its creator. Boundaries arose to strengthen the topography engendered by the division of labour. What was done within them could not always be done by outsiders, and the occasional outcome was a lag between the schemes of relevance of those who were attached to the social problem of victims and those where were not.

In time, that sense of possession came to be threatened as more staff were appointed to the business of supervising policy proposals and as the structures of policy-making attained a kind of autonomy. What had once been open and negotiable became ever more objective and anonymous, receding into the past as the unalterable contexts of action. Event led to event in a way that was apparently inexorable. Policy-makers found themselves attending to phenomena that had their own life, identity, compelling logic. Indeed, as those phenomena became known to outsiders, as others displayed interest in them, so they became a form of public property that was detached from its original authors. The business of producing policy appears to turn on the manufacture of proposals that must be ceded to others. Ideas will not thrive if they remain under the dominion of a small set of patrons. Strangely, control must be relinquished if management is to succeed.

Of particular importance is the way in which policy-making is staggered over time. It is constituted by the timetables of organizations and governments, timetables which set out a teleology and a structure for politics. No policy will prosper until it has been ratified by the proper sequence of proper bodies. It will take its form from its passage through committees. As it nears each committee, it will be attired in the arguments that are supposed to win approval. It will be precise enough to respond to the demands that may be levelled by significant groups. It will be imprecise enough to permit those groups to make their own visible impression on policy, an impression that advertises that they have been consulted and paid deference. In this sense, arguments are a moving refraction of political networks, the encoded anticipation of what an audience will want to see, a series of genuflections before power.

Policies seem to acquire a special identity as they move in time. Projected back and forth in the imagination of their guardian officials, offered a succession of temporal markers by committee meetings and planning deadlines, it is as if they pass from conception to birth to death in a great cycle. They will achieve a more or less predictable life-span that will summon a responsive pattern of official activity. There will be *rites de passage* that confirm their coming of age. Actions will be framed to complement their life-history. The idea of *timeliness* will attain local prominence, emphasizing the theme of the temporal scheduling of things. To be sure, not every policy passes smoothly through a life-cycle. Some proposals are stillborn, others die in their youth. Others still undergo an unexpected rejuvenation, being rediscovered and resuscitated. Yet the organic analogy does play a part, allowing officials to affix a future and a meaning to the schemes they nurture.

Part of that process of attaining identity revolves around the manufacture of a kind of carapace which lends solidity and form to policy proposals. Arguments cannot be presented simply as an extrusion of reputable research and the inner logic of the next move, although they should be that as well. They must achieve a very special version of political gravity, a gravity that stems from an interplay with significant demands and audiences. At a certain point, policy-makers will have to furnish evidence of the political necessity of what they propose. Policies must seem to be centrally implicated in major movements of public opinion and the popular will. Officials will be under some compulsion to illuminate those features of their environment which serve to corroborate their arguments. In effect, they will develop an unusually alert sensitivity to the signs that might lend meaning to a current project. They will look for the external constituencies that give objectivity to otherwise domestic schemes. A legitimate constituency voicing supportive sentiments at an appropriate time will then become magnified in the field of vision which an emerging policy prepares about itself. The constituency, the sentiments, and the time may all be recognized as situational accomplishments which reflect the special sensibilities of a group which is exploring its terrain with particular purposes. Processes the phenomena tend to acquire an added lustre and importance in the scheme of relevance established by those sensibilities, sometimes gaining a significance that surprises those who have been made thus prominent.

After a while, as policy-making becomes purposive, as it begins to take on pilots, as it is fitted into the timetables of government, so the work of building a carapace will advance beyond developing an acuity of response to propitious features of the environment. It will start to contribute to the cultivation of those features, enacting them in Weick's phrase. Officials live for much of their time in a kind of phenomenological marcher territory that uncertainly separates subjectivity and objectivity. Theirs is a dialectical world in which accomplishments rapidly attain the standing of independent precedents, facts, and constraints. They devote themselves to producing those items which will move their projects forward. The arguments they advance and the things they do are intended to appeal to the special audiences who will inspect them: it is the response of those audiences which will ratify and objectify any proposal. By extension, the world of the policy-maker has its own colloquial logic of presentation and persuasion: themes will attain a sort of parochial authority that is quite emphatically local. Effort will be expended in generating events and achievements that may be recognized by significant monitors as compelling reasons for action. A successful policy-maker will spin around himself or herself webs of causality that propel activity forward. Conferences will be arranged, speeches written, commitments given, which will then be reported as justifications for action. Officials will move backwards and forwards in a continuous and busy dialectic that gives reasons for what they do. In a very real sense, those reasons are a looking-glass held up before those who will judge what has been done. They will mirror current priorities and emphases disclosed by Party, Cabinet, and Government. They will, following constitutional practice, bear the impress of current political contexts, being designed as a reply to decisions already approved.

Every policy proposal will betray its birth in a time and place. Every proposal will be designed to appeal to those who are wooed as its potential custodians. It will be made to resemble their features. The result will be substantial enough. There will be a palpable decline in the policy-maker's freedom. Not only will policies attain a definite shape and pedigree that set much of their future course. They will also become the property and concern of those who have their own ambitions and visions of the future. What is one's policy's enacted environment is another's substance. In all their encounters with other groups, in all their attempts to emancipate a policy from a small group of local authors locked in one Department, events may become deflected in ways that were unanticipated and perhaps even undesired by those who first sponsored them. They may be given a very alien appearance indeed. Meetings designed to push a process in one direction can lead to a quite contrary outcome. The pathos of policy-making is thus that success often demands a kind of failure, a loss of control, and a shift of purpose. Policies become anonymous, foreign structures that stand apart from their parents and defy them.

At each stage, then, there may be a palpable reluctance to relinquish command over an emerging policy even though retention of control enfeebles work. The transfer of policies from phase to phase almost invariably entails some reconstruction, leaving lines of development incomplete and questions unanswered. Very often the focused expertise of one who has been with a policy for some time will be appreciably greater than that of those who are to take over, and there may be some trepidation about bequeathing work to the relatively inept. Very often, too the self of the policy-maker will have become anchored in his or her work, and a surrender of control will be a belittling of selfhood. The tempo of development can then be uneven, slowing down at the liminal point between stages where the old order is undone and a new order is supplied. Simultaneously, of course, pressure is likely to be at its greatest at that liminal point. It is frequently the unexpected opportunity that moves a policy on, and such an opportunity tends to be accompanied by strains to accelerate activity.

Every new piece of policy-making is a wave of revelation and change. It creates and discloses new facts and possibilities of social organization. People will discover themselves doing new things in rather different ways, transforming the institutional setting within which work is done. In this fashion, a supplementary dialectic tends to be launched by the policy process: tasks change their environment only to be changed in reply.

Policy-making thereby releases ripples of disturbance which progressively redefine what an institution is, what it can achieve, and what it is entitled to do. All subsequent work will be affected by that work of redefinition, linking episodes in a complicated and changing chain.

No official or politician is capable of foreseeing the internal workings of all those processes. At best, he or she can make the appropriate moves at the right time, and trust that events will march forward in a desirable manner. An occurrence in the future may always wreck, transform, or accelerate what is in train. Matters that now seem auspicious can always founder. Little beginnings can prosper. It is the task of the official to be aware of the patterning of things, the manner in which phenomena cohere together not only now but from some as yet unimaginable vantage point in time to come. There will be a continuing effort to set in place the materials of a possibly useful pattern, even though its exact political content and context can never be predicted with precision. In turn, some time will be allotted to endowing events with just that measure of ambiguity which could be useful in future. There will be a tendency to deposit markers that can be revisited later and exploited in the preparation of an argument. There will be a recognition that the titles, names, and purposes of work are fluid, not always quite what they seem.

And, within that world of the policy process, people come and go with fluctuating enthusiasms, producing a great diversity and turbulence of emotion. It takes initiative to create the beginnings of policy, and investment of character. At the very core of any piece of action will usually be found those officials who have staked something of their identity and reputation. Materials that define a policy become the materials for defining a self. Officials may take the career of a policy very personally, their own occupationally grounded selves evolving in sympathy with its fortunes. About them are other officials whose work never involves sustained commitment to one policy or whose biography has not been entangled with the particular policy that is on the move. In the environment of the one policy, those officials may begin to seem detached and disinterested, people whose commitments are rather diffuse. The public self of such an official will not be so readily affected by the fate of the policy. They will play the part of occasional participants and frequent spectators, commenting on what others have done in any particular area. In this manner, policies engender about themselves an uneven landscape of sentiments and ties. Activity will be experienced very differently in the various regions that are thus described.

The animating official at the core will monitor what is done to his or her achievements, very frequently being credited with no part in their creation. There is always a risk that ideas will be disfigured when they are presented to others, yet it would be improper and impolitic to intercede on their behalf. Policy-makers are often reduced to becoming an audience as their offspring are dismembered in conference, committee, and debate. There is an ensuing strain between releasing a proposal so that it may thrive and protecting it inside one's own territory. The fate of policies hinges on their reception, and it is bedevilled by the twin perils of possessiveness and indifference.

As policies move out into the world, there must be a forcible renunciation of claims and affections, a moving on to other things which may be greeted as not so very different after all. Policies spread as they become more anonymous and less distinct, claimed by many owners and possessed of their own local forms. They tend to become fused with other initiatives elsewhere, and it will be only the most fastidious examination that will permit their separation after a while. Indeed, they may well have begun to work most effectively when they can no longer be prised away from the world which they have entered.

All this argument has had one principal thrust. It is that the business of making policy seems to be governed by its own grammar. It is considerably more complicated than the result of intrusive outside forces. Ministries and governments work in an environment of politics, conflicts, and crises. But that environment is mediated by a series of lenses, and those lenses are moulded by a busy world manufactured in some measure by its inhabitants. What is an instance of conflict or crisis, what it signifies and how it is managed must be referred to that inner logic of the policy process, a logic which is more than a simple extension of processes elsewhere.

Index

Ad Hoc Federal–Provincial Working Group, 370
Ad Hoc Justice for Victims of Crime Committee, 295
Advisory Council on the Status of Women, and violence against women, 214, 215; and Consultation on Wife Battering, 218; *Report*, 242; and attempts to mobilize transition houses, 227
Allmand, W., 50, 121; and capital punishment, 125; and speech to American Bar Association, 130
Amir, M. and Amir, D., 82
'Animators', 48
Antilla, I., 76
Auditor General of Canada, 144

Banking days, and the preparation of the initiative, 325
Basford, R., and Peace and Security, 132
Battered Women Support Service, 218
Battering, in America, 85; in Canada, 172, 217; and feminism, 218
Becker, C., 73, 92
Becker, H., 104
Bégin, M., 232
Bellagio, and the International Study Institute on Victimology, 102; and the conversion of Irvin Waller, 103
Berger, P., 8, 100
Bergson, H., 44
Bibliographies, role of, 68
Bittner, E., 37, 148, 156
Blackmore, J., 84
Blackstone, W., and the definition of crime, 187
Blain, C., 217
Brampton Victim–Witness Assistance Program, 178; and the San Mateo Victim–Witness Program, 185
Briefing sessions, and the Justice for Victims of Crime Initiative, 373 *passim*; dilemmas and organization, 375; and Royal Canadian Mounted Police, 376
British North America Act, 3–4; its repeal and delays in the initiative, 372
Brooklyn Victim–Witness Assistance Project, 88; and proposals in Canada, 98

Calgary Police Service, and victim service unit, 153; and Workshop on Services to Crime Victims, 196
Calgary Status of Women Action Committee Conference, 220
Campbell, G. and Szablowski, G., 249
Canadian Association for the Prevention of Crime, and 1981 NOVA Conference, 353; and attempt to form COVA, 364
Canadian Council on Social Development, and 1981 NOVA Conference, 349, 353; and *Rights and Services for Crime Victims*, 353; and Canadian Organization for Victim Assistance, 357 *passim*; and women's organizations at 1981 NOVA Conference, 363
Canadian Organization for Victim Assistance, stillborn, 353, 359 *passim*; and second attempt at formation, 364
Capital punishment, and the Ministry of the Solicitor General, 124; development in Canada, 125; proposals for abolition, 127; and police opposition to abolition, 128; and protests about proposed abolition, 129
Causality, the allocation of, 66; problem of, 67
Chrétien, J., 216
Clark, L., 78; as a campaigner, 233; and National Action Committee, 233
Clark, L. and Lewis, D., 77, 212; and *Rape: The Price of Coercive Sexuality*, 233
Cleaver, E., 86
Committee on Social Development, 40; and consideration of 1981 Strategic Overview, 309
Community Programs Division, of the Ministry of Correctional Services, 178
Community service, and VORP, 179
Conference of the Provincial Council of Attorneys-General and Ministers of Justice, and wariness and initiative, 371

Conferences, and their role in policy-making, 69; and the victim's movement, 102; as turning-points, 102; the 1980 NOVA Conference, 102
Consultation Centre, described, 29; and Regional Consultants, 30; and development of police victim service units, 154
Consultation on Wife Battering, 218
Crime prevention, and victimization surveys, 136; and victims and the police, 149
Criminal Injuries Compensation, and the lack of impact on the Ministry of the Solicitor General, 70; the Solicitor General's attempt to introduce reforms, 121
'Criminal justice community', 150
Cronin, R. and Bourque, B., 88

Daniels, A., 171, 176, 178, 179; and Workshop on Services to Crime Victims, 197
Decade for Women, and the National Plan of Action, 225, 242
'Decarceration', in Ontario, 176
Demonstration projects, defined, 30
Dewey, J., 234
Domestic crisis intervention, and the police, 156; and Family Consultant Service, 159; and Restigouche Family Crisis Intervention Project, 160; and the women's movement, 161
Doob, A., 83
Douglas, M., 221
Downes, D., 72
Dramaturgy, and the politics of feminism, 235
Durkheim, E., 100
Dussich, J., 74, 103

Edelman, M., 16
Edmonton Police, and victim service unit, 152, 200
Elizabeth Fry Societies, 22; and Workshop on Services to Crime Victims, 198
'Enacted environment', and policy-making, 272; and 1981 NOVA Conference, 349
Erikson, K., 124
Errington, G., 255 *passim*, 260, 265; and *Research on Wife Battering*, 262
Ettorre, B., 224

Family Consultant Services, 159; and transformation into response to family violence, 162
Family violence, in Canada, 157; its emergence as an issue, 241; and feminism, 242; and diversity of interpretations, 243; and working party of the National Plan for the Status of Women, 244; and Standing Committee of Health, Welfare and Social Affairs, 268; and the 1980 Strategic Overview, 287
Fattah, E., 102
Federal–Provincial Conferences of Ministers, 17; and initiative, 1, 170; and Gordon Walker's 1979 speech, 188; and Interdepartmental Committee on Family Violence, 267; as target of policy-making, 324; and problems of disclosure, 329, 337; and anticipation of announcement of initiative, 339, 341; and the launch of the initiative, 370 *passim*; and Solicitor General's speech, 372
Federal–Provincial relations, and the initiative, 11, 168, 320, 371; and the Ministry of the Solicitor General, 11; and stagecraft, 16; and Regional Consultants, 30; and relations between lawyers, 168; and the construction of political argument, 170; and the delegation to the United Nations Congress, 203; and the memorandum to Cabinet, 336
Federal–Provincial Task Force on Justice for Victims of Crime, 94; and Federal–Provincial Working Group on Victim Assistance, 328; proposed, 371, 373
Federal–Provincial Working Group on Victim Assistance, and bifurcation of policy-making for victims, 327; *Report*, 372
Feldman, M., 52
Feminism, and the Justice for Victims of Crime Initiative, 62; and victimology, 78; and the definition of victims, 82, 220; and domestic crisis intervention and the police, 156; and victims, 212; and violence against women, 212, 222; and battering, 218; and victim-precipitation, 219; as a political resource, 234
Feminist Karate Union, 90
Flynn, E., 74

Garcia, I., 85
Gusfield, J., 79, 275n
Gwyn, S., 22

Hammurabi, and the origins of the Justice for Victims of Crime Initiative, 68

Heclo, H. and Wildavsky, A., 16, 38, 51, 58, 97, 303, 314
Holmes, L., 238
Holmes, R., 148, 196; and Restigouche Family Crisis Interveners Project, 160
Howie, J., 268
Hughes, E., 3

Interdepartmental Committee on Family Violence, 240, 241 *passim*; and women's organizations, 236; and competing definitions of family violence, 243, 251, 258; and *Towards Equality for Women*, 248; membership, 249; and Status of Women Canada, 250, 252; its striking, 251; and strains, 252; initial recommendations, 253; and National Consultation on Women Battering, 254; and change of Government, 254; and the discussion paper, 255; and change of Chair, 261; and *Some Considerations and Suggestions for Work . . .*, 261; and criticism by officials of the Department of the Solicitor General, 263; and the legitimacy of professional expertise, 264; and effective withdrawal of officials from the Department of the Solicitor General, 266; and Federal–Provincial Conference of Ministers Responsible for Criminal Justice, 267; its demise and aftermath, 267; and Joint Justice Committee, 270; and the 1980 Speech from the Throne, 275
Interdepartmental Committee on Justice for Victims of Crime, 347
International Year of Women, 225

Jaffe, P., and Family Consultant Service, 159, 164
John Howard Society, 22; of Saskatchewan, 69
Joint Justice Committee, founding, 6; and Strategic Overviews, 43; and follow-up to United Nations Congress, 207; and Interdepartmental Committee on Family Violence, 270; and first discussions of a victim's initiative, 314; and drafting of policy paper on victims, 318
Justice, Department of, founding, 4; and the politics of rape, 215; and involvement in the Justice for Victims of Crime Initiative, 313, 314; and absence of interest in policies for victims, 315
Justice for Victims Initiative, and reasons for its analysis, xii; announced, 1, 372; and violence to women, 46; and careers, 47; as property, 48, 317, 332, 382; and the organization of knowledge, 49; and legitimation, 53; and Peace and Security, 53; and the problem of origins, 59; and diversity of conceptions, 59; and personal authority, 61; and manning, 61; and the division of labour, 62, 382; and community programmes in Ontario, 62; and the creation of origins, 68; and the provinces, 168; and the National Action Committee on the Status of Women, 235; and the importance of women, 278; and the politics of history, 283; and the acquisition of pilots, 316; and the growth of objectivity, 319; and problem of provincial reaction, 320, 371; and support from Ontario, 322; and the intervention of the Ministry of State for Social Development, 322; and the policy reserve, 323; and the June banking day, 325; and the memorandum to Cabinet, 328; and problems of disclosure, 337; approved by Cabinet, 339; and uncertainty after disclosure, 342; and negotiation of politics of victims, 345; and distorted timetables, 346; and organizational dilemmas, 346; and the proposal of a Federal–Provincial Task Force, 371, 373; and the briefing sessions, 373; and its eventual character, 374; and Law Enforcement Assistance Administration, 379
Justice Statistics Centre, and the Canadian Victims Survey, 336

Kaplan, R., 308; and the Cabinet Submission, 339; and speech to 1981 NOVA Conference, 355–7; at 1981 Federal–Provincial Conference of Ministers Responsible for Criminal Justice, 372
Keegan, J., 60
Kitchener–Waterloo Victim–Offender Reconciliation Project, 200

Lalonde, M., 216, 232
Law Enforcement Assistance Administration, and the American Victims Movement, 84; and Victim–Witness Assistance Programs, 86; and the Crime Victim Initiative, 88; and Victim Assistance Initiative, 89; and National Organization for Victim Assistance, 93; and the Ministry of the Solicitor General, 98; at Workshop on Services to Crime Victims,

Law Enforcement Assistance Administration—*contd.* 196; and Justice for Victims of Crime Initiative, 379
Law Reform Commission, 345
Lawrence, A., 18, 191
Leger, G., 68
Levens, B. and Dutton, D., 157
Lewis, D., 218; as a campaigner, 234; at 1981 NOVA Conference, 360, 366
London Police, and Family Consultant Services, 159, 200

McHugh, P., 44
MacLeod, L., 148, 157, 172, 196, 245; and recommendations about battering, 98; and *Wife-Battering in Canada*, 214, 226, 227; and Status of Women Canada, 239; and the working party on family violence, 244; and Standing Committee on Health, Welfare, and Social Affairs, 268; and appointment to the Ministry of the Solicitor General, 271; and the 1980 Speech from the Throne, 275; and appointment as a significant gesture, 314; and drafting of policy paper for Joint Justice Committee, 318; and Federal–Provincial Working Group on Victim Assistance, 328; and memorandum to Cabinet, 328; and Victim Assistance Initiative, 343, and the briefing sessions, 374
Mannheim, K., 34
Manning, P., 9
Marchand, P., 86
Marsland, D., 56
Matza, D., 67, 157
Mead, G., 53
Meetings, and the structure of decisions, 285
Memorandum to Cabinet, 328, 329 *passim*; and drafting, 329; the second draft, 335; and structure of final draft, 337; and objectification, 338; as a form of story, 338; approved, 339
Mendelsohn, B., 72, 74, 104
Mennonites, and Victim–Offender Reconciliation, 177
Methods, employed in *A View from the Shadows*, xiii
Mills, C. Wright, 69
Ministry of State for Social Development, xiv, 40; and the 1980 Speech from the Throne, 274, 305; and 1981 Strategic Overview, 305; and submission to Cabinet, 322; and the policy reserve, 323; and the influence of Irvin Waller, 327; and the phrasing of the draft memorandum to Cabinet, 330, 335; and initiative, 381
Ministry of the Solicitor General, and 'turf wars', 3; establishment, 4; and the provinces, 9; and the funding of projects, 13, 23; and criticisms of faddishness, 13, 65; and lobbies, 18; and Cabinet, 18; as a 'fire-fighter', 18; and the domestication of offices, 58; and the victims movement, 94; and victim service units, 153; and Family Consultant Services, 159; and Restigouche Family Crisis Intervention Project, 160; and Gordon Walker's speech to the Federal–Provincial Conference of Ministers, 190; and the Workshop on Services to Victims, 193; and Status of Women Canada, 239; and the 1980 Speech from the Throne, 274; and the 1981 NOVA Conference, 349; and foundation of victim's clearinghouse, 366; and reaction to 1981 NOVA Conference, 368
Moynihan, D., 79

National Action Committee on the Status of Women, 215; and victims, 221, 231; its role and origins, 228 *passim*; and Government, 229, 235; and violence against women, 230; and publications, 230; and conference resolutions on violence, 230; and lobbying, 232; and Lorenne Clark, 233; and the Justice for Victims of Crime Initiative, 235; and Status of Women Canada, 235
National Association of Women and the Law, 215, 217
National Associations Active in Criminal Justice, 23
National Clearinghouse on Family Violence, 276, 333
National Consultation on Women Battering, and Interdepartmental Committee on Family Violence, 254; approved by Joint Federal and Provincial Councils on the Status of Women, 255
National Consultative Network, 203
National Health and Welfare, and participation in the initiative, 55, 333; and interpretations of family violence, 243; and Status of Women Canada, 244; and working party on family violence, 244;

Report, 245; and Interdepartmental Committee on Family Violence, 259
National Information Clearinghouse on Victims, proposed at 1981 NOVA Conference, 360, 366; established as Victims Clearing House, 367
National Organization for Victim Assistance, and the history of the Justice for Victims of Crime Initiative, 69; and its foundation, 92; membership and objectives, 93; and Law Enforcement Assistance Administration, 93; and Conference, 1980, 102, 299; the 1979 Conference and Irvin Waller, 109; and Irvin Waller as a member of the Advisory Committee, 113; and 1981 Conference, 227, 299, 337, 348 *passim*; and teleological role of 1981 Conference, 339, 346; and 1981 Conference arranged by Irvin Waller, 349; and role of the Ministry of the Solicitor General, 349; and joint sponsorship by Ontario and Ministry of the Solicitor General, 349; and joint sponsorship by Ontario and Ministry of the Solicitor General, 350; and objectification of Canadian politics, 352; and Canadian Organization for Victim Assistance, 353; as a source of inspiration, 354; attendance at 1981 Conference, 355–7; and opening speeches at 1981 Conference, 355; and final speech by Irvin Waller at 1981 Conference, 367; 1981 Conference and reactions of Ministry of Solicitor General, 368
ity for Women, 246
National Victims Week, 90, 321
Networking, and Irvin Waller, 112; and Workshop on Services to Crime Victims, 197
Nixon, M., 217
Norquay, G., 80, 358; and work for *Services to Victims and Witnesses of Crime in Canada*, 281; and Canadian Organization for Victim Assistance, 358, 361; and second attempt to form COVA, 364
Norquay, G. and Weiler, R., 155, 172; and commissioning of *Services to Victims and Witnesses of Crime in Canada*, 200

O'Neil, M., 236, 239, 242, 246, 250, 267, 271, 278; and the 1980 Speech from the Throne, 274
Ontario, and the Justice for Victims of Crime Initiative, 62, 174, 322; and Ottawa, 174; and the Ministry of Correctional Services, 175; and the wariness of the Ministry of the Attorney General, 175; and 'decarceration', 176; and Victim–Offender Reconciliation Projects, 177; and the politics of victim–witness programmes, 180; and coalition of rape crisis centres, 226; and joint sponsorship of 1981 NOVA Conference, 350
Osanka, F., 91
Ottawa, as a little society, 51, 201
Ottawa Rape Crisis Centre, 226

Paltiel, F., 245
Parents of Murdered Children, 90
Peace and Security Package, and relations between departments, 5; and research, 29; and the structure of the Justice for Victims of Crime Initiative, 53; drafted, 132; and the assembling of proposals, 132
Pima County Victim/Witness Program, 88; and recommendations about battering in Canada, 98; and Workshop on Services to Crime Victims, 196
Pines, A., 91
Pitt, D. and Smith, B., 24
Pizzey, E., and victim-blaming, 77
Police, and opposition to the abolition of capital punishment, 128; and the development of programmes for victims, 145; and effects on policy-making for victims, 146, 164; and crime and victims, 149; and the pretesting of the victimization survey, 151; and Victim Service Units, 152; and preventive policing and victims, 155; and evidence of growth of interest in victims, 155; and domestic crisis intervention, 157; and London Family Consultant Service, 159; and Restigouche Family Crisis Intervention Project, 160
Policing, and the provinces, 10
Policy and Expenditure Management System, described, 40; and opportunities for reflection, 44; and structure of decision-making in Department of Solicitor General, 285; and initial uncertainties, 302; and problems of implementation, 324
Policy Branch, described, 30; and relations with Programs Branch, 31; and initial involvement with victims, 292; assumption of control over victims, 310
Policy issue, defined, 313

Policy-making, defined, 30, 293; as a sequence of acts, 39; and timetables, 45, 384; and social structure, 47; and motives, 47; and uncertainty, 52; and multivocality, 53; and conceptions of the past, 53, 319; and vagueness, 56, 313; and conceptions of time, 64; and women, 210; and the 'enacted environment', 272; and workshops, 283; and structure of argument, 293, 318; and the place of research, 293; and the reconstruction of research, 294; and the political reconstruction of victims, 311, 317; and the significant gesture, 314, 332; and the growth of objectivity, 319; as courtship, 342; and the rhetorical carapace, 384
Policy reserve, and the Justice for Victims of Crime Initiative, 323
President's Crime Commission, 97
Pressure groups, and women, 210; and attempts to form Canadian Organization for Victim Assistance, 359
Prince, M., 34
'Priorising', as an activity, 285; and victims at the 1980 Programs Branch Workshop, 300; and sponsorship by Assistant Deputy Minister, 301
Priorities and Planning Committee, and Strategic Overview, 42; and definition of victims, 279
Private sector, and the Ministry, 17; and Canadian Organization for Victim Assistance, 360
Programs Branch, described, 28; and policy development, 29; and research, 29; and the Consultation Centre, 29; and relations with Policy Branch, 31; and property in victims, 295; and Workshop of 1980, 300
Pross, A., 22
Provinces, and anticipated opposition to a victims initiative, 143; and services for victims, 170
Punch, M., 60

Quebec, and the victims initiative, 15, 168, 320, 321
Quinney, R., 84

Rape, and the American victim's movement, 84; and politics in Canada, 214, 217; and the Ministry of the Solicitor General, 214; and Bill C-52, 215; and the lobbying of the Department of Justice, 215; and Bill C-127, 216; and interest in family violence, 245
Rape crisis centres, in America, 85; in Canada, 172, 214, 225; and political mobilization, 226
Regional Consultants, described, 30
Reiss, A. and Bordua, D., 187
Research, and conceptions of time, 63; and continuity of effort, 63; and Irvin Waller, 110; and work on victims in the Ministry, 111; and policy-making, 119; and the transition from research to policy, 292; in policy-making, 293; and evaluation, 334
Restigouche Family Crisis Intervention Project, 160, 165, 200; transformation over time, 162
Reverse record checks, 151
Right to Privacy Committee, 311
Rights and Services for Crime Victims, 354
Rosenberg, H., 87
Royal Canadian Mounted Police, and provinces, 4, 10; functions, 10, 144; and the Ministry of the Solicitor General, 10; and 'turf rights', 143; and mandates for programmes for victims, 146; and the briefing sessions, 375; and organization of initiative, 381
Royal Commission on the Status of Women, 228; and Status of Women Canada, 236

Sacramento Victim/Witness Program, 88
Schafer, S., 68
Seale, B., 86
Seattle Rape Relief, 225
Secretariat, role described, 25; the staff, 33; and liberalism, 34; and style, 36, 96; and character of work, 39; and the open-planned office, 57; and evangelism, 97; and workshops, 283; and autonomy of individual officials, 284; and 1980 Workshop, 289; 1980 Secretariat *Workshop Summary*, 292
Services to Victims and Witnesses of Crime in Canada, 200; and 1981 NOVA Conference, 358
Skogan, W., 166
Smith, D., 224
Smith, G., 119
Solicitor General, and change of office, 16; and knowledge about the Justice for Victims of Crime Initiative, 62; and capital punishment, 124; and 1981 Strategic

Overview, 308; and 1981 NOVA Conference, 351
Solomon, P., 18
Speech from the Throne, 161, 272 *passim*; and the Department of the Solicitor General, 273; and *Putting People First*, 274; and political significance, 274; its drafting, 274; and *Wife-Battering in Canada*, 275; and draft policy paper for Joint Justice Committee, 320
'Spousal immunity', and the law, 215
Standing Committee on Health, Welfare and Social Affairs, and family violence, 268; *Report*, 269
'Stars', 48
Status of Women Canada, and the Justice for Victims of Crime Initiative, 46, 279; founding, 236; and the United Nations Decade for Women, 237; powers, 238; and social networks, 239; and Government departments, 244; and assumption of Chair of Interdepartmental Committee on Family Violence, 261; and lack of power, 276; and redrafting of policy paper for Joint Justice Committee, 320
Stein, J., 88
Strategic Overview, 20; and Policy and Expenditure Management System, 41; and Priorities and Planning Committee, 42; and the provinces, 169; the 1980 Overview, 286; and family violence, 287; as an incomplete document, 289; and the 1980 Secretariat Workshop, 280; the 1981 Strategic Overview, 301; and structure of argument, 303; and Ministry of State for Social Development, 305; and Bob Kaplan, 308; and meeting of Committee on Social Development, 309; and transition to Policy Branch, 310
Strauss, A., 8, 99
Sullivan, D., and Victims of Violence, 367; and Irvin Waller, 367
Surmelian, L., 338

Talk, and organization, 8; and the character of the Justice for Victims of Crime Initiative, 66
Time, organized conceptions of, 63
Timetables, and teleology, 45, 384
Towards Equality for Women, 246; and domestic crisis intervention, 161; and recommendation about a study of violence against women, 248
Transition houses, 218; growth in Canada, 226; and political mobilization, 227

United Nations Congress on the Prevention of Crime, 201; and selection of Canadian delegation, 203; and preparatory consultations, 204; and agenda, 204; and preparatory discussions of victims, 205; and Irvin Waller's draft declaration for the 7th Congress, 205; and deliberations at 6th Congress, 205; and the retrospective discovery of victims, 205; and the Joint Justice Committee, 207
United Nations World Plan of Action for Women, and Canada, 242

Vaillancourt, R., and controversy about capital punishment, 126
Vance, J., 256
Van Maanen, J., 2, 47
Viano, E., 102, 103, 104
Victim Assistance Initiative, and Justice for Victims of Crime Initiative, 322, 343
Victim blaming, 77
Victim–Offender Reconciliation Programs, in Ontario, 177
Victim precipitation, and victimology, 76; and Canadian feminism, 219
Victimology, 71 *passim*; origins, 72; and marginality, 72; its agenda, 73; and politics, 74; and contradiction, 75; as a flawed plausibility structure, 100; and the corrobbori, 100
Victims, as a disparate group, 81, 173, 211, 281; and emergence as a policy issue in the Ministry, 139, 173, 192, 199, 283 *passim*; in the provinces, 171; as a possible anomaly in the criminal justice system, 297; and political definition, 310; as property, 317
Victim Services, and 1981 NOVA Conference, 359
Victims Services Directory, 172
Victim service units, and City of Edmonton Police, 152; and the Ministry of the Solicitor General, 153; and American victim–witness programmes, 154
Victims movement, 79; its absence in Canada, 80; in America, 83; and the politics of rape, 84; and the emergence of a superstructure, 91; and the Ministry of the Solicitor General, 94; and fears of vigilantism, 96; and conferences, 102; as a source of inspiration, 103; and appointment of staff, 141

Victims of Violence, 79; foundation, 367; and Irvin Waller, 367
Victim surveys, 97, 122; and the Peace and Security Package, 134, 380; and crime prevention, 135; and evolution of goals, 137; and pretesting in Alberta, 151; and 1981 Strategic Overview, 309; and draft memorandum to Cabinet, 331, 333, 336
Victim–Witness Assistance Programs, 86; and economy, 180
Violence, as a policy issue, 123, 211
Violence against women, 211; as a political issue, 222; and the National Action Committee on the Status of Women, 230
Visiting Scholars Program, xii
Von Hentig, H., 72

Walker, G., 179, and speech at Federal–Provincial Conference of Ministers, 17, 170, 188; as Minister of Correctional Services, 178; his political career, 180; and prison over-crowding, 181; and 'workfare', 183; and schemes for victims, 183; and the 1981 NOVA Conference, 351, 355
Waller, I., 93, 102, 197; and John Howard Society, 22; and resignation from Ministry, 37, 61, 117, 281; and crime surveys, 98; and dissemination of American work, 98; and the importation of the American victims movement, 99; and the 1980 NOVA Conference, 103; and the Bellagio Study Institute, 103; as moral entrepreneur, 104, 380; and *Burglary: The Victim and the Public*, 106, 116; and the 1979 NOVA Conference, 109; and networking, 112; and the Peace and Security Package, 134; speech at NOVA Conference, 1981, 170; and Allan Lawrence's reply to Gordon Walker, 191; and draft declaration for 7th United Nations Congress, 205; and 1981 Strategic Overview, 305; and the lobbying of Bob Kaplan, 308; and influence over Ministry of State for Social Development, 327; and the organization of the 1981 NOVA Conference, 349, 353 *passim*, 369; and Canadian Organization for Victim Assistance, 361, 367; and Victims of Violence, 367
Weick, K., 206, 208, 228
Weiler, R., 198, 282; and Canadian Organization for Victim Assistance, 358; and *Victim Services*, 359
West, G. and Snider, S., 174
Wiener, C., 94, 105, 143
Wife-Battering in Canada, 214; and Standing Committee on Health, Welfare, and Social Affairs, 268; and the 1980 Speech from the Throne, 275
Wildavsky, A., 20, 166, 282
Wilson, B., 100
Women, and the politics of victims, 210 *passim*; as a pressure group, 210; and victims, 210; and the social construction of political demand, 234, 278; and the dramaturgy of politics, 235; and censure of Government, 236; and Cabinet priorities, 278; and meeting about Canadian Organization for Victim Assistance, 363
Wood, D., 220
Working Party 3, and the National Plan of Action, 244; *Report*, 246
Workshop on Services to Crime Victims, 193, 202; and political argument, 198; *Report*, 358
Workshops, and decision-making in the Ministry, 283; the 1980 Secretariat Workshop, 289; and 1980 Programs Branch Workshop, 300
World Society of Victimology, prospectus, 73

Yantzi, M., 177
Young, M., 84, 95, 96, 349; at 1981 NOVA Conference, 354
Young, M. and Willmott, P., 58
Yukon Women's Transition Home, 218